Urban economic theory

Urban economic theory

Land use and city size

MASAHISA FUJITA
University of Pennsylvania

The right of the University of Cambridge to print and sell all manner of books was granted by Henry VIII in 1534. The University has printed and published continuously since 1584.

CAMBRIDGE UNIVERSITY PRESS
Cambridge
New York New Rochelle Melbourne Sydney

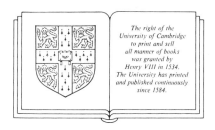

Published by the Press Syndicate of the University of Cambridge
The Pitt Building, Trumpington Street, Cambridge CB2 1RP
32 East 57th Street, New York, NY 10022, USA
10 Stamford Road, Oakleigh, Melbourne 3166, Australia

First published 1989

Printed in Canada

Library of Congress Cataloging-in-Publication Data

Fujita, Masahisa.

Urban economic theory: land use and city size/Masahisa Fujita.

p. cm.

Bibliography: p.

ISBN 0-521-34662-2

1. Land use, Urban. 2. City planning. 3. Urban economics.
4. Cities and towns – Growth. 5. Housing – Location – Planning.
I. Title.
HD111.F85 1989 88-18867
330.9173′2 – dc19 CIP

British Library Cataloguing in Publication Data

Fujita, Masahisa

Urban economic theory: land use and city size

1. Urban regions. Land use. Economic aspects
I. Title
333.77

ISBN 0-521-34662-2

For
Beethoven
Symphony No. 2

Contents

Preface

This book presents the basic theory of urban land use and city size in a unified framework. The residential location behavior of households is analyzed in a microeconomic framework, and the equilibrium and optimal patterns of residential land use are examined. In addition, the corresponding equilibrium and optimal city sizes are studied in a variety of contexts. Extensions of the theory to a general equilibrium framework (i.e., simultaneous determination of location of both households and firms) and to a dynamic framework will be considered in a planned second book.

The present book is an outgrowth of a series of lectures given to graduate students at the University of Pennsylvania over the past several years. Throughout the text, mathematical analyses are accompanied by intuitive explanations and diagrams. Hence, although this book is written primarily for graduate students (in the fields of urban economics, location theory, urban geography, and urban planning), any reader who has reasonable patience with mathematical notation will be able to follow the main body of the book.

My central purpose is to develop the existing theory of urban land use and city size in a manner that is accessible to students. To do so, I have attempted to unify the main results of the theory in terms of the *bid rent function approach*. The origin of this approach is quite old. Indeed, von Thünen (1826) created his original model of agricultural land use, which stands as a cornerstone of land use theory, using this approach. But, surprisingly, the approach is closely related to the *duality approach* of modern microeconomics. Consequently, by employing it, one can develop modern land use theory in a manner that is not only more intuitive but also more rigorous than traditional methods.

In connection with this work, my indebtedness to others is very great. First of all, I am enormously indebted to Tony E. Smith for his continuous encouragement and help. I am also grateful to Walter Isard, Ronald E. Miller, and Jacques-François Thisse for their valuable suggestions and encouragement. In addition, ongoing discussions with Larry Bissett, Tatsuhiko Kawashima, and Kunio Kudo have been invaluable. I am also beholden to Noboru Sakashita and Hiroyuki Yamada, who helped to develop my initial interest in urban economics.

I acknowledge a special debt of gratitude to Richard Arnott and Yoshitsugu Kanemoto, who read an earlier version and offered many valuable comments. I also greatly benefited from their work in developing the framework of the book. In addition, Takeo Ihara, Yoshio Itaba, Masuo Kashiwadani, Hisayoshi Morisugi, Yasoi Yasuda, and Komei Sasaki read a part of an earlier version and offered valuable suggestions and comments. I am also enormously appreciative of my former students at the University of Pennsylvania. In particular, I acknowledge the contributions of Hesham Abdel-Rahman, Takahiro Akita, Asao Ando, Yasushi Asami, Hiroyuki Koide, Hideaki Ogawa, Akihiko Tani, and Chung-Hsin Yang through their work related to some of the topics covered in this book. I am also grateful to the former editorial director of Cambridge University Press, Colin Day, for his continuous encouragement.

I am very grateful to Laura Huntoon, Tatsuaki Kuroda, Shin Kun Peng, Mary Nevader, Elizabeth Titus, and Robert Walker for their excellent work in editing this book and to Yasushi Asami and Mitsuru Ota for their beautiful drafting of the figures. I thank Kathy Kane for her skill and patience in typing the manuscript. This book is based on a part of my research supported by NSF Grants SOC 78-12888, SES 80-14527, and SES 85-028886 over the past decade, which are gratefully acknowledged.

I acknowledge my deepest appreciation to my former adviser at Kyoto University, Kozo Amano, for his help and moral support throughout the study. I further express my warmest thanks to Caroline Isard, Judy Smith, Donald and Suzzane Rudalevige, and Snitt and Teddy Snyder for their encouragement and hospitality during the stay of my family in the United States. Finally, I am grateful to my wife, Yuko, whose unfailing encouragement and patience enabled me to complete this book.

CHAPTER 1

Introduction

1.1 Nature of the book

The history of cities is almost as old as that of civilization. Cities have been centers of wealth and power, innovation and decadence, dreams and frustrations. During the past several decades, many countries have experienced rapid urbanization. As a consequence, a large proportion of the world's population now resides in cities. Yet cities are among the most complex human creations, and in many ways the least understood. This became dramatically clear with the eruption of urban problems throughout the world starting in the late 1950s. Since that time, a great number of scientists in various fields have endeavored to develop a better understanding of cities. With respect to economics in particular, these urban problems have triggered the birth of a new field, namely *urban economics*.

Modern urban land use theory, which forms the core of urban economics, is essentially a revival of von Thünen's theory (1826) of agricultural land use. Despite its monumental contribution to scientific thought, von Thünen's theory languished for more than a century without attracting the widespread attention of economists.[1] During that time, cities grew extensively and eventually outpaced the traditional concepts of urban design. The resulting rise in urban problems since the late 1950s has manifested an urgent need for a comprehensive theory of modern urban systems and, in particular, has helped to refocus the attention of location theorists and economists on the seminal work of von Thünen. Following the pioneering work of Isard (1956), Beckmann (1957), and Wingo (1961), Alonso (1964) succeeded in generalizing von Thünen's central concept of *bid rent curves* to an urban context. Since that time, urban economic theory has advanced rapidly, inspiring a great deal of theoretical and empirical work. Prominent among the efforts in this area are the works of Muth (1969), Mills (1972a), Henderson (1977), Kanemoto (1980), and Miyao (1981), to name a few.[2] The central purpose of this book, together with the planned second book, is to present in a unified manner the state of the art of the economic theory of urban land use and city size, including both positive and normative aspects of the theory.

In most Western societies, land is allocated among alternative uses mainly by means of private markets, with more or less public regulations. In such societies, the current spatial structure of a city is thus the outcome of billions of individual actions taken in the past. Hence, one might suspect that the outcome of such unregulated individual actions would be near chaos. However, the history of science suggests to the contrary that the larger the number of individual actors in a system, the stronger are the regularities it will exhibit. Indeed, many studies have revealed that strong regularities exist in the spatial structure of different urban areas. The task of *positive theory* is to provide explanations for these regularities and to suggest testable hypotheses for further investigation. We will not, however, be content with the mere confirmation of regularities. The existence of regularities does not necessarily imply that the given spatial structure of a city is a desirable one. Hence, we shall also be interested in *normative theory* for identifying the efficient spatial structure and size of cities, and for suggesting means of achieving them. This viewpoint was eloquently expressed by Lösch (1954, p. 4): "No! The real duty of the economist is not to explain our sorry reality, but to improve it. The question of the best location is far more dignified than the determination of the actual one."

The theory of urban land use and city size is an especially appealing topic of study because much of traditional economic theory cannot be readily applied. Although traditional economic theory aptly describes competitive markets typical of most Western societies, it is essentially designed to deal with spaceless problems. Hence, many of the basic assumptions of this theory are no longer appropriate for spatial problems such as land use. First, one generally finds empirically that households, as well as many firms and government agencies, choose one and only one location. As will be explained in the next section, this implies, in the terminology of traditional economic theory, that there is a strong *nonconvexity* in consumers' preferences and production technologies. Second, since the essence of cities is the presence of many people and firms in close quarters, *externalities* are a common feature. Public services, noise, pollution, and traffic congestion all involve externalities. Moreover, the necessity of nonprice interactions such as information exchange through face-to-face communication is one of the major reasons that people and firms locate in a city. Third, the existence of distance among cities implies that the producers of local goods (both public and private goods) can enjoy a monopolistic situation. The same is true for producers of neighborhood services within each city. Hence, *oligopolistic* or *monopolistic competition* is a common feature of urban markets. Finally, buildings and other urban infrastructures are among the most durable of all human products, and this limits the usefulness of classical static theory. Because many spatial phenomena such as urban sprawl and renewal can be treated in a satisfactory way only within a *dynamic* framework, we must eventually combine urban land use theory with capital theory. Clearly, the city is fertile ground for economic study.

1.2 Bid rent function approach

This book aims not only to summarize the main results of existing theory, but also to present them in a unified manner. For this purpose, we adopt the *bid rent function approach*, which was introduced into an agricultural land use model by von Thünen (1826) and later extended to an urban context by Alonso (1964). This approach is essentially the same as the *indirect utility function approach*, which was introduced into an urban land use model by Solow (1973). Hence, it is also closely related to the *duality approach* of modern microeconomics.

The main focus of urban economic theory is, of course, land. But in economic terms, land is a complex object endowed with dual characteristics. First, land is a *commodity* in the usual economic sense. But, second, unlike other commodities, land is completely immobile. Hence, each piece of land is associated with a unique *location* in geographical space. These dual characteristics of land induce strong nonconvexity in consumers' preferences (as in production technologies). In particular, each household generally chooses to reside at one and only one location. This implies that the preferences of each household exhibit strong nonconvexity. To understand this, let us consider land consumption at two possible locations. If the consumption of all other goods is fixed, then Figure 1.1 describes the consumption space for a household, where s_1 and s_2 represent the consumption of land at location 1 and location 2, respectively. Hence, if at each given land price ratio R_1/R_2 the household never consumes land at both locations, this implies that its indifference curves must exhibit some concavity, as in Figure 1.1.[3]

In order to avoid the mathematical difficulties associated with this nonconvexity in preferences, we shall follow traditional location theory by adopting two convenient assumptions.[4] First, it is assumed *a priori* that each household chooses one and only one location. Hence, the consumption space for each household can be defined separately at each location in terms of the consumption of land at that location together with the consumption of all other goods. Second, the number of households

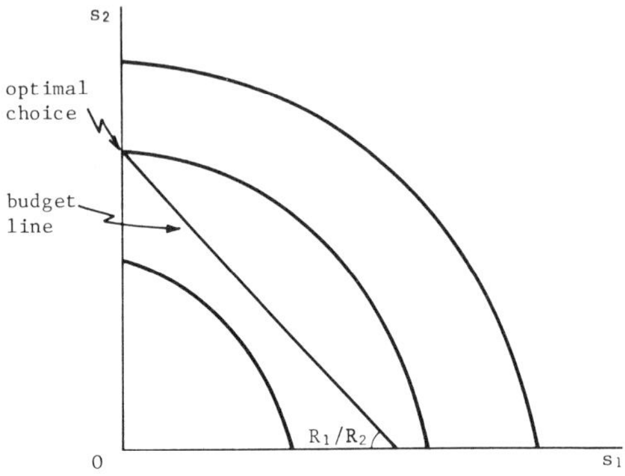

Figure 1.1. Concave indifference curves and the choice of a single location.

of each type is assumed to be so large that their distribution throughout the city can safely be represented in terms of a density function.[5] These two assumptions enable us to employ the bid rent function approach in determining the equilibrium location of each household as well as the equilibrium and optimal land use patterns of the city. A bid rent function essentially describes a particular household's ability to pay for land (at each location) under each fixed utility level. This function can be considered to be a transformation that maps indifference curves in consumption space into corresponding indifference curves in urban space (with dimensions of location and land rent), that is, *bid rent curves*. Given these indifference curves defined in urban space, one can graphically analyze the locational choice of the household. Moreover, since bid rent curves are defined in terms of monetary bid per unit of land, they are comparable among different land users. We will therefore be able to analyze competition for land among different agents, again graphically in urban space. Mathematically, it turns out that the bid rent function is the inverse of the indirect utility function (also of the expenditure function). Therefore, one can also use the powerful tools associated with these functions in modern microeconomics. Hence, not surprisingly, with this approach one can develop modern land use theory not only more rigorously but also more simply than with traditional methods.

1.3 Scope and plan of the book

The scope of this book is limited to the *static* theory of *residential* land use and city size. Namely, in the context of the standard monocentric city model, we examine the *stationary* (or *long-run*) equilibrium and optimal patterns of residential land use under a given set of time-invariant data.[6] The extensions of the theory to a general equilibrium framework (i.e., simultaneous determination of location of both households and firms) and to a dynamic framework will be considered in the planned second book referred to in the Preface.

In particular, this static approach assumes that both the land price P (i.e., asset price of land) and land rent R per unit of land at each location are *constant* over time. Hence, provided that land can be used for urban purposes without additional cost, it follows that land price is always related to land rent by the simple identity,

$$P = \int_0^\infty e^{-\gamma\tau} R \, d\tau = \frac{R}{\gamma}, \tag{1.1}$$

where γ is the time discount rate (or interest rate), which is assumed to be common for all market participants. Hence, in this book we focus only on the equilibrium pattern of land rent R.

The main body of the book consists of two parts. Part I develops the basic theory of residential land use and city size within the context of a monocentric city in the absence of externalities. This part consists of four chapters, which can be briefly summarized as follows.

In Chapter 2, a simple, *basic model* of residential choice is introduced. The *bid rent function* and (bid-max) *lot size function* are defined. The relationship between these functions and the relevant concepts of standard microeconomics (i.e., indirect utility functions, expenditure functions, and Marshallian and Hicksian demand functions) is explained. By using the concept of *bid rent curves*, we examine how the equilibrium location of the household is determined in the city. We also examine the relative locations of households having different bid rent functions. In the second half of Chapter 2, we extend the basic model by introducing the time cost of commuting as well as differences in family structure. We also introduce the Muth model of housing industry.

In Chapter 3, we assume that all households in the city are identical. Under this condition, we first examine the *equilibrium structure* of residential land as determined through a competitive land market. Depending on the specification of migration possibilities and the form of landownership, we consider the following four market models: (a) the closed-city model under absentee landownership, (b) the closed-city model under public landownership, (c) the open-city model under absentee landownership, and (d) the open-city model under public landownership. For each case, the existence and uniqueness of equilibrium are explained by means of a constructive graphical method based on the concept of *boundary rent curves*. We then consider the case of the closed-city model under absentee landownership and, by using the same boundary rent curve approach, study graphically the *comparative statics* of equilibrium spatial structure in terms of population, transport cost, income, agricultural rent, and land taxation and zoning.

Next, we study the *optimal allocation* of residential land and households within the city, and examine the relationship between the optimal land use and equilibrium land use patterns. The optimal land use problem is formulated in terms of the *Herbert–Stevens model (HS model)*. We show that by appropriately changing the two parameters (target utility level and population) of the HS model, we can obtain the equilibrium solution for each of the four market models by solving some HS model. From this, we can conclude that in the present context, land use equilibria are always efficient. Finally, we return to the Muth model of housing industry and examine changes in land use intensity in the city.

In Chapter 4, we extend the analyses of Chapter 3 to the case of a city with multiple household types. We focus mainly on the closed-city model under absentee landownership.

Having examined the spatial structure of cities in the previous three chapters, we turn our attention in Chapter 5 from spatial structure to *urban aggregates*. That is, within the same context of monocentric cities, we examine the relations among urban macrovariables such as the population, total income, total land rent, and total transport cost for a given city. The concepts of *population supply functions* and *population cost functions* are introduced. We also discuss the *causes of city formation* and examine the *equilibrium and optimal city size* in various contexts. This chapter thus provides a connection between urban land use theory and city-system theory.

In Part II, we extend the basic theory of Part I by introducing various kinds of externalities. This development involves three separate chapters, which can be summarized as follows.

In Chapter 6, we introduce local public goods and examine how to achieve the efficient provision of these goods among cities or within a city. We consider four kinds of local public goods: *pure city goods*, *congestible city goods*, *neighborhood goods*, and *superneighborhood goods*.

In Chapter 7, we focus on the *negative externalities* that arise as consequences of interactions among households themselves. In particular, we consider three types of such externalities: *crowding externalities*, *racial externalities*, and *traffic congestion* associated with commuting. In the presence of each type of externality, we examine the *first-best policies* and various *second-best policies* for enhancing the efficiency of land markets.

Finally, in Chapter 8, we examine the roles of *external economies* and *product variety* in city formation. In particular, we develop the *external economy model* and the *monopolistic competition model* of urban agglomeration and examine the relationship between the two models. We show that the urban aggregates derived from the two models have the same structural relationship. Thus, from the viewpoint of descriptive analyses of urban aggregates, the monopolistic competition model can be considered to be a specific example of the external economy model. However, from the viewpoint of normative analyses, the two models lead to substantially different results. Thus, in empirical implementations of these models, it is essential to identify which model more closely represents the actual city economy.

Three appendixes follow the main text. In Appendix A, we review some of the basic mathematical concepts and results from consumer theory that have been used in the text. Appendix B is an extension of Chapter 5. In this appendix, we show that under a set of reasonable assumptions on transport cost function and land distribution, a simple general relationship holds between the total transport cost and total differential rent of a city. Appendix C provides proofs for some of the results in the text.

Finally, the logical structure of this book is summarized in the following diagram:

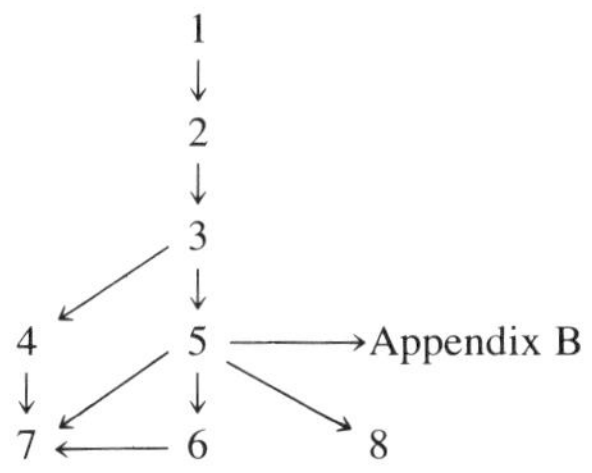

Notes

1. For an excellent appraisal of von Thünen's achievements from the viewpoint of modern economic theory, see Samuelson (1983), who states that "Thünen belongs to the Pantheon with Leon Walras, John Stuart Mill, and Adam Smith" (p. 1482).
2. For an early history of the development of urban economic theory, see, e.g., Alonso (1964, Ch. 1). For recent developments in urban economic theory, see the survey articles by Richardson (1977a), Anas and Dendrinos (1976), Wheaton (1979), Fujita (1986a), Wildasin (1986b), and Miyao and Kanemoto (1987) and the survey articles in Mills (1987).
3. Recall that in the traditional literature of general equilibrium analysis (e.g., Debreu 1959; Arrow and Hahn 1971), economists have treated land as just

another commodity by attaching a locational index to it. A drawback of this approach is that one can no longer assume that preferences of consumers (and technologies of firms) are convex in the entire consumption space (as illustrated in Figure 1.1). This drawback was pointed out, for example, by Malinvaud (1972, p. 22) and Hildenbrand (1974, pp. 83–4).

4. Recall that in a finite economy, nonconvexity of preferences will cause possible nonexistence of competitive equilibria.
5. For a mathematical justification of this *density approach* (or *continuous population approach*), see Asami, Fujita, and Smith (1987) and Papageorgiou and Pines (1987). In essence, we regard this density model as a mathematical device for approximating the solutions of appropriately defined discrete population models, when the number of individuals is sufficiently large. Berliant (1984, 1985a, b), Berliant and Dunz (1987), and Berliant and ten Raa (1987) have proposed an alternative approach, called the *discrete population approach*, in which each consumer is assumed to occupy a subset of two-dimensional Euclidean space. Although the latter approach is theoretically more satisfactory, it involves enormous mathematical complexity. We will compare the two approaches in our planned second book.
6. Pedagogically, of course, it is preferable to study static theory before introducing complications due to time. Moreover, when a city is growing relatively slowly, static theory can effectively describe the equilibrium spatial configuration of the city at each point in time.

PART I

Basic theory

CHAPTER 2

Locational choice of the household

2.1 Introduction

Any household that moves to a city and has to choose a residence is faced with a complex set of decisions. We can view this situation as a trade-off problem, in which there are three basic factors: accessibility, space, and environmental amenities.

Accessibility includes both pecuniary and time costs associated with getting to and from work, visiting relatives and friends, shopping, and other such activities. The space factor consists of the need for some land as well as the size and quality of the house itself. Finally, environmental amenities include natural features such as hills and scenic views as well as neighborhood characteristics ranging from quality of schools and safety to racial composition.

In making a residential choice a household must weigh all three factors appropriately, yet also meet budget and time constraints. For example, a location with good accessibility usually commands a high price for space. So the household may have to sacrifice space for accessibility. Accessible locations, however, are typically lacking in environmental quality. Thus, the household also confronts a choice between accessibility and environment.

Even though in actual practice all three factors are important for making a residential choice, when constructing theory it is difficult to treat all factors at once. Following the time-honored wisdom of theory building, we shall begin by studying a pure case and expand the framework later on. Part I examines the trade-off between accessibility and space in residential choice. Part II introduces environmental factors.

2.2 Basic model of residential choice

The development of our understanding of residential land use begins with the basic model, which focuses on the trade-off between accessibility and space. The model rests on a set of assumptions about the spatial character of the urban area:

1. The city is monocentric; that is, it has a single prespecified center of fixed size called the central business district (CBD). All job opportunities are located in the CBD.
2. There is a dense, radial transport system. It is free of congestion. Furthermore, the only travel is that of workers commuting between residences and work places. (Travel within the CBD is ignored.)
3. The land is a featureless plain. All land parcels are identical and ready for residential use. No local public goods or bads are in evidence, nor are there any neighborhood externalities.

In this context, the only spatial characteristic of each location in the city that matters to households is the distance from the CBD. Thus, the urban space can be treated as if it were one-dimensional.

Consider a household that seeks a residence in the city. As is typical in the economic analysis of consumer behavior, we assume that the household will maximize its utility subject to a budget constraint.[1] We specify the utility function $U(z, s)$, where z represents the amount of *composite consumer good,* which includes all consumer goods except land, and s the consumption of land, or the *lot size* of the house.[2] The composite consumer good is chosen as the numeraire, so its price is unity. The household earns a fixed income Y per unit time, which is spent on the composite good, land, and transportation. If the household is located at distance r from the CBD, the budget constraint is given by $z + R(r)s = Y - T(r)$, where $R(r)$ is the rent per unit of land at r, $T(r)$ is the transport cost at r, and hence $Y - T(r)$ is the *net income* at r. So we can express the residential choice of the household as

$$\max_{r,z,s} U(z, s), \qquad \text{subject to} \quad z + R(r)s = Y - T(r), \tag{2.1}$$

where $r \geq 0$, $z > 0$, $s > 0$. This is called the *basic model* of residential choice.

By definition the choice of r is restricted to the range $r \geq 0$. It is reasonable to assume that the subsistence of the household needs some positive amounts of both z and s. That is, both goods are *essential*. Therefore, we require the utility function $U(z, s)$ to be defined only for positive z and s. This is equivalent to saying that indifference curves in the consumption space do not cut axes. Considering this, we introduce the following set of assumptions:[3]

Assumption 2.1 (well-behaved utility function). The utility function is continuous and increasing at all $z > 0$ and $s > 0$; all

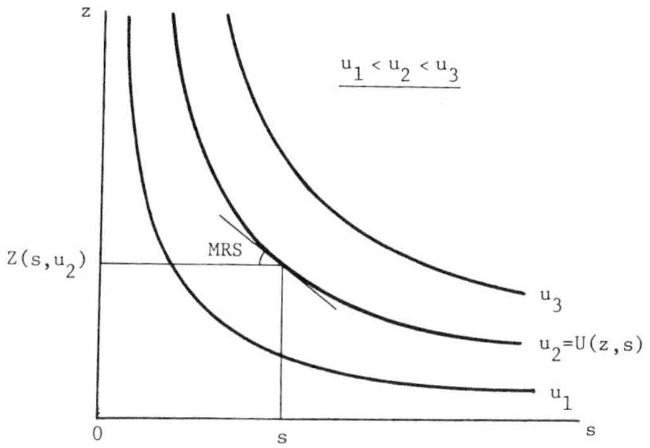

Figure 2.1. The consumption space and indifference curves.

indifference curves are strictly convex and smooth, and do not cut axes.

Assumption 2.2 (increasing transport cost). Transport cost $T(r)$ is continuous and increasing at all $r \geq 0$, where $0 \leq T(0) < Y$ and $T(\infty) = \infty$.

These assumptions are always taken to hold in the subsequent analysis. On the basis of Assumption 2.1, indifference curves in the consumption space can be depicted as in Figure 2.1. Recall that an indifference curve is the locus of all consumption bundles from which the household derives the same utility level. The indifference curve with utility level u can be expressed in implicit form as $u = U(z, s)$. Or solving $u = U(z, s)$ for z, the *equation of the indifference curve* with utility level u can be stated as

$$z = Z(s, u). \tag{2.2}$$

By definition, $Z(s, u)$ represents the amount of composite good that is necessary to achieve utility level u when the lot size of the house is s (see Figure 2.1).

Throughout our study, differential calculus will often be used to make the analysis simple. Whenever differential calculi are involved, we are also implicitly assuming that utility function $U(z, s)$ is twice continuously differentiable in z and s (i.e., all its second-order partial derivates exist and are continuous), and transport cost function $T(r)$ is continuously differentiable in r. Then in terms of differential calculus, the fact that utility function is increasing in z and s (Assumption 2.1) means[4]

$$\frac{\partial U(z, s)}{\partial z} > 0, \qquad \frac{\partial U(z, s)}{\partial s} > 0. \tag{2.3}$$

That is, the *marginal utility* of each good is positive. Note that this condition can be equivalently expressed as

$$\frac{\partial Z(s, u)}{\partial u} > 0, \qquad \frac{\partial Z(s, u)}{\partial s} < 0. \tag{2.4}$$

The term $-\partial Z(s, u)/\partial s$ is called the *marginal rate of substitution* (MRS) between z and s (Figure 2.1). Then the strict convexity of each indifference curve means that the MRS is diminishing in s:

$$-\frac{\partial^2 Z(s, u)}{\partial s^2} < 0. \tag{2.5}$$

Likewise, the fact that the transport cost function is increasing in r means

$$T'(r) > 0, \tag{2.6}$$

where $T'(r) \equiv dT(r)/dr$.

By directly solving the optimization problem implied by the basic model (2.1), we could ascertain the household's residential decision in a straightforward manner. But there is another approach, conceptually much richer, that leads to a desirable elaboration of theory. This approach, which mimics the von Thünen model of agricultural land use, requires the introduction of a concept called bid rent.

2.3 Bid rent function of the household

Bid rent is a conceptual device that describes a particular household's ability to pay for land under a fixed utility level. It is not to be confused with the market rent structure of the city, which arises from the interaction of many households. We define bid rent as follows:

Definition 2.1. The bid rent $\Psi(r, u)$ is the maximum rent per unit of land that the household can pay for residing at distance r while enjoying a fixed utility level u.

In the context of the basic model (2.1), bid rent can be mathematically expressed as

$$\Psi(r, u) = \max_{z,s} \left\{ \frac{Y - T(r) - z}{s} \;\middle|\; U(z, s) = u \right\}. \tag{2.7}$$

That is, for the household residing at distance r and selecting consumption bundle (z, s), $Y - T(r) - z$ is the money available for rent, or land payment, and $(Y - T(r) - z)/s$ represents the rent per unit of land at r.

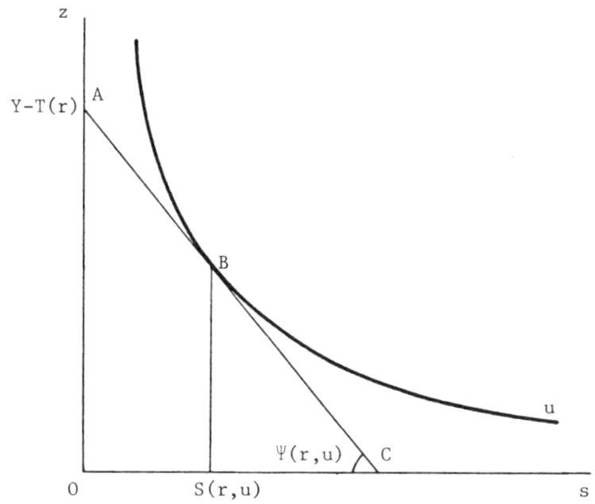

Figure 2.2. Bid rent $\Psi(r, u)$ and bid-max lot size $S(r, u)$.

According to Definition 2.1, therefore, bid rent $\Psi(r, u)$ is obtained when $(Y - T(r) - z)/s$ is maximized by the appropriate choice of a consumption bundle (z, s) subject to the utility constraint $U(z, s) = u$. Alternatively, in the maximization problem of (2.7), we may first solve the utility constraint $U(z, s) = u$ for z and obtain the equation of an indifference curve as (2.2). Then the bid rent function can be redefined as

$$\Psi(r, u) = \max_{s} \frac{Y - T(r) - Z(s, u)}{s}, \tag{2.8}$$

which is an unconstrained maximization problem.[5] When we solve the maximization problem of (2.7) or (2.8), we obtain the optimal lot size $S(r, u)$, which is called the *bid-max lot size*.[6]

Graphically, as depicted in Figure 2.2, *bid rent $\Psi(r, u)$ is given by the slope of the budget line at distance r that is just tangent to indifference curve u.*[7] To see this, let us generally denote the land rent at r by parameter R. Then the household's budget constraint at r can be generally expressed as $z + Rs = Y - T(r)$, or

$$z = (Y - T(r)) - Rs. \tag{2.9}$$

In Figure 2.2, under each value of land rent R, equation (2.9) defines a straight line that originates from point A and has the (absolute) slope R. If land rent R is greater than the slope of line AC, the budget line is entirely below the indifference curve u. This implies that in order to achieve the required utility level u, the household cannot pay land rent as high as R. Conversely, if land rent R is smaller than the slope of line AC, the budget line intersects indifference curve u. This implies that even under a slightly higher land rent, the household can achieve utility level u. Thus, we can conclude that bid rent $\Psi(r, u)$, that is, the highest land rent at r under which the household can achieve utility level u, is given by the slope of budget line AC. The tangency point B determines bid-max lot size $S(r, u)$. This graphical approach is useful to cement the definitions not only here, but also in our subsequent analysis. Next, notice that in the maximization problem of (2.8), function $(Y - T(r) - Z(s, u))/s$ is maximized in s at the point where the marginal change of the function with respect to s is zero. This leads to the next relation:[8]

$$-\frac{\partial Z(s, u)}{\partial s} = \frac{Y - T(r) - Z(s, u)}{s}. \tag{2.10}$$

Solving this equation for s, we obtain the bid-max lot size $S(r, u)$.[9] Or, since at the optimal choice of s the right side of (2.10) equals $\Psi(r, u)$, condition (2.10) can be restated as

$$-\frac{\partial Z(s, u)}{\partial s} = \Psi(r, u). \tag{2.11}$$

In terms of Figure 2.2, this means that at the tangency point B, the slope $-\partial Z(s, u)/\partial s$ ($\equiv$ MRS) of indifference curve u equals the slope $\Psi(r, u)$ of budget line AC.

Example 2.1. Suppose that the utility function in model (2.1) is given by the following *log-linear function:*

$$U(z, s) = \alpha \log z + \beta \log s, \tag{2.12}$$

where $\alpha > 0$, $\beta > 0$, and $\alpha + \beta = 1$. It is not difficult to confirm that this utility function satisfies all the conditions of Assumption 2.1. The equation of the indifference curve is given as $Z(s, u) = s^{-\beta/\alpha} e^{u/\alpha}$. Solving the maximization problem of (2.8) by using condition (2.10), we have[10]

$$\Psi(r, u) = \alpha^{\alpha/\beta} \beta (Y - T(r))^{1/\beta} e^{-u/\beta}, \tag{2.13}$$

$$S(r, u) = \beta(Y - T(r))/\Psi(r, u) = \alpha^{-\alpha/\beta}(Y - T(r))^{-\alpha/\beta} e^{u/\beta}. \tag{2.14}$$

Now that we have introduced bid rent $\Psi(r, u)$ and bid-max lot size $S(r, u)$, which are concepts unique to land use theory,[11] it is helpful to relate them to familiar microeconomic notions. In this way, we will then be able to take advantage of the well-established tools of traditional economic analysis. To this end, let us return to Figure 2.2. This figure can be interpreted in several revealing ways.

To begin with, consider the following *utility-maximization problem* under land rent R and net income I:

$$\max_{z,s} U(z, s), \qquad \text{subject to} \quad z + Rs = I. \tag{2.15}$$

When we solve this problem, we obtain the optimal lot size,

$$\hat{s}(R, I), \tag{2.16}$$

as a function of R and I, which is called the *Marshallian (ordinary) demand function* for land. The maximum value of this problem is represented as

$$V(R, I) = \max_{z,s} \{U(z, s) | z + Rs = I\}, \tag{2.17}$$

which is called the *indirect utility function*. This gives the maximum utility attainable from net income I under land rent R. If we set $R = \Psi(r, u)$ and $I = Y - T(r)$, problem (2.15) becomes

$$\max_{z,s} U(z, s), \qquad \text{subject to} \quad z + \Psi(r, u)s = Y - T(r). \tag{2.18}$$

Now, we can interpret Figure 2.2 as indifference curve u being tangent to budget line AC from above at point B. Since the equation of line AC is $z + \Psi(r, u)s = Y - T(r)$, this means exactly that point B is the solution of problem (2.18), and u is its maximum value. Hence, setting $R = \Psi(r, u)$ and $I = Y - T(r)$ in (2.16) and (2.17), it must hold identically that

$$S(r, u) \equiv \hat{s}(\Psi(r, u), Y - T(r)), \tag{2.19}$$

$$u \equiv V(\Psi(r, u), Y - T(r)). \tag{2.20}$$

In other words, the maximum utility under land rent $\Psi(r, u)$ and net income $Y - T(r)$ equals u, and the bid-max lot size at utility u equals the Marshallian demand for land under land rent $\Psi(r, u)$.

Next, consider the following *expenditure-minimization problem* under land rent R and utility level u:

$$\min_{z,s} z + Rs, \qquad \text{subject to} \quad U(z, s) = u. \tag{2.21}$$

When we solve this problem, we obtain the optimal lot size,

$$\tilde{s}(R, u), \tag{2.22}$$

as a function of R and u, which is called the *Hicksian (compensated) demand function* for land. The minimum value of this problem is denoted by $E(R, u)$, that is,

Table 2.1. *Bid rent and related functions*

	Alonso	Solow	Marshall	Hicks
Bid rent	$\Psi(r, u)$	$\psi(I, u)$	—	—
Lot size (land)	$S(r, u)$	$s(I, u)$	$\hat{s}(R, I)$	$\tilde{s}(R, u)$
Indirect utility	—	—	$V(R, I)$	—
Expenditure	—	—	—	$E(R, u)$

$$E(R, u) = \min_{z,s}\{z + Rs \mid U(z, s) = u\}, \tag{2.23}$$

which is called the *expenditure function*. If we set $R = \Psi(r, u)$, problem (2.21) becomes

$$\min_{z,s} z + \Psi(r, u)s, \qquad \text{subject to} \quad U(z, s) = u. \tag{2.24}$$

Now, this time we can interpret Figure 2.2 as budget line AC being tangent to indifference curve u from below at B. Since the equation of line AC is $Y - T(r) = z + \Psi(r, u)s$, this means exactly that point B is the solution of problem (2.24), and $Y - T(r)$ is its minimum value.[12] Hence, setting $R = \Psi(r, u)$ in (2.22) and (2.23), it must hold identically that

$$S(r, u) \equiv \tilde{s}(\Psi(r, u), u), \tag{2.25}$$

$$Y - T(r) \equiv E(\Psi(r, u), u). \tag{2.26}$$

In other words, the minimum expenditure needed to reach utility u at land rent $\Psi(r, u)$ is $Y - T(r)$, and the bid-max lot size at utility u is identical to the Hicksian demand for land at utility u under land rent $\Psi(r, u)$.

Since the characteristics of indirect utility functions, expenditure functions, and Marshallian and Hicksian demands are all well known, identities (2.19), (2.20), (2.25), and (2.26) provide us with powerful tools that will be useful in the sequel.[13] Table 2.1 summarizes various functions introduced. [Functions $\psi(I, u)$ and $s(I, u)$ are to be introduced in Section 3.2.]

Next, we examine important properties of bid rent and bid-max lot size functions. Consider first how bid rent and bid-max lot size change with r. To this end, let the utility level be fixed at u, and take two distances such that $r_1 < r_2$. Then since $T(r_1) < T(r_2)$, we have $Y - T(r_1) > Y - T(r_2)$. Recall that bid rent $\Psi(r, u)$ at distance r is given by the slope of the budget line at r, which is just tangent to indifference curve u. Then from Figure 2.3 it is easily grasped that $\Psi(r_1, u) > \Psi(r_2, u)$ and $S(r_1, u) < S(r_2, u)$. That is, bid rent decreases in r and bid-max lot size increases

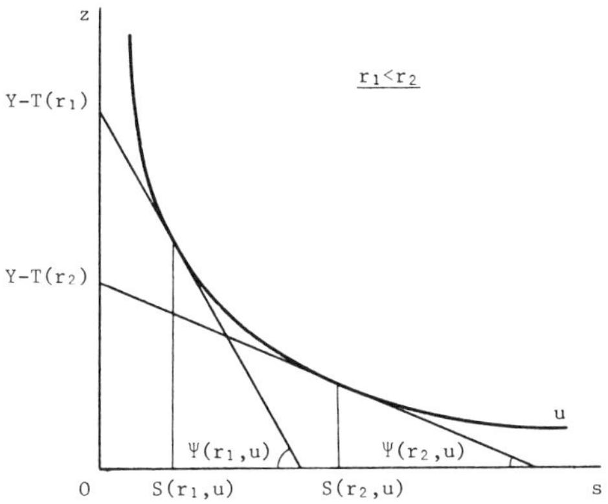

Figure 2.3. Changes in $\Psi(r, u)$ and $S(r, u)$ with an increase in r.

in r. These properties make intuitive sense. Given a reduction in net income, a household can retain its prior utility level only if the rental price of land is also reduced, enabling the household to substitute land for the composite good (the price of which is fixed at unity).

The rate of change of bid rent with respect to r can be calculated through an application of the *envelope theorem* to equation (2.8) as follows:[14]

$$\frac{\partial \Psi(r, u)}{\partial r} = -\frac{T'(r)}{S(r, u)} < 0. \tag{2.27}$$

Observe from equation (2.8) that an increase in r produces two effects on $\Psi(r, u)$. One is the *direct effect* that occurs through an increase in transport costs. A unit increase in commuting distance increases transport cost by the increment $T'(r)$, which in turn reduces the net income by the same amount; thus, the land payment ability per unit of land (i.e., the bid rent) decreases $T'(r)/S(r, u)$. The other effect is induced via changes in the optimal consumption bundle $(Z(S(r, u), u), S(r, u))$ as r increases. However, the envelope theorem indicates that this *induced effect* is negligible when changes in r are small. We are left then with only the direct effect shown above.

Combining the result of (2.27) and the identity $S(r, u) = \tilde{s}(\Psi(r, u), u)$, we can calculate the rate of change of bid-max lot size with respect to r as

$$\frac{\partial S(r, u)}{\partial r} = \frac{\partial \tilde{s}}{\partial R}\frac{\partial \Psi(r, u)}{\partial r} = -\frac{\partial \tilde{s}}{\partial R}\frac{T'(r)}{S(r, u)} > 0, \tag{2.28}$$

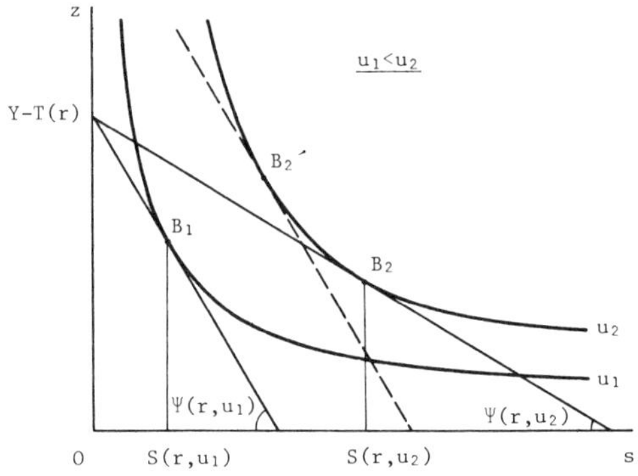

Figure 2.4. Changes in $\Psi(r, u)$ and $S(r, u)$ with respect to u.

which is positive, since its own price effect on Hicksian demand $\tilde{s}$ is always negative (see Appendix A.3).

Next, let us investigate how bid rent and bid-max lot size change with utility level. Let distance r be fixed, and choose two utility levels such that $u_1 < u_2$. Then since indifference curve u_2 lies above curve u_1, it is easy to see from Figure 2.4 that $\Psi(r, u_1) > \Psi(r, u_2)$. This conclusion also makes intuitive sense in that a household can attain higher utility with fixed net income only if land rent is reduced. The impact of a utility change on the bid-max lot size is more complex. According to Figure 2.4, an increasing utility level causes an increase in the bid-max lot size. This result, however, cannot always hold true without some additional assumptions. The following assumption represents a sufficient condition for ensuring such a result:

> ***Assumption 2.3 (normality of land).*** The income effect on the Marshallian demand for land is positive.

To explain the meaning of this assumption, it is convenient to consider the movement in Figure 2.4 from point B_1 [the original consumption bundle under the land rent $\Psi(r, u_1)$] to point B_2 [the new consumption bundle under a lower land rent $\Psi(r, u_2)$] as the sum of the movement from B_1 to B_2' and that from B_2' to B_2. Here B_2' represents the consumption bundle that will be achieved when the land rent is fixed at $\Psi(r, u_1)$ and the income increases from $Y - T(r)$ to the one associated with the dashed budget line. The normality of land means that the movement from B_1 to B_2' (i.e., the *income effect*) causes an increase in land consumption. Then since the movement from B_2' to B_2 [i.e., the *substitution effect* associated with a reduction in land rent from $\Psi(r, u_1)$ to $\Psi(r, u_2)$ while the utility level is held constant at u_2] always causes an increase in land consumption, we necessarily have that $S(r, u_1) < S(r, u_2)$. Since the normality of land is empirically supported, we assume that Assumption 2.3 also always holds in the subsequent analysis. Notice that the normality of land means graphically that at each fixed s, slopes of indifference curves (in absolute value) become greater as u increases. Notice also that the log-linear utility function of Example 2.1 satisfies this assumption.

We can calculate the rate of change in bid rent with respect to u by applying the envelope theorem to equation (2.8) as follows,

$$\frac{\partial \Psi(r, u)}{\partial u} = -\frac{1}{S(r, u)} \frac{\partial Z(s, u)}{\partial u} < 0, \tag{2.29}$$

which is negative since $\partial Z/\partial u > 0$ from (2.4). So recalling identity $S(r, u) \equiv \hat{s}(\Psi(r, u), Y - T(r))$, we have

$$\frac{\partial S(r, u)}{\partial u} = \frac{\partial \hat{s}}{\partial R} \frac{\partial \Psi(r, u)}{\partial u} > 0. \tag{2.30}$$

The positivity is obtained since $\partial \Psi/\partial u < 0$ and since the normality of land implies that its own price effect $\partial \hat{s}/\partial R$ on Marshallian demand $\hat{s}$ is negative (see Appendix A.3).

Finally, the continuity of transport cost function and the assumption of a well-behaved utility function imply that both the bid rent and bid-max lot size functions are continuous in r and u. Therefore, summarizing the discussion above, we can conclude as follows:

Property 2.1

(i) Bid rent $\Psi(r, u)$ is continuous and decreasing in both r and u (decreasing until Ψ becomes zero).

(ii) Bid-max lot size $S(r, u)$ is continuous and increasing in both r and u (increasing until S becomes infinite).

From (i) the general shape of bid rent curves can be depicted as in Figure 2.5; from (ii) above, the general shape of *(bid-max) lot size curves* can be depicted as in Figure 2.6. Each bid rent curve (lot size curve) is downward- (upward-) sloped. With an increase in utility level, bid rent curves (lot size curves) shift downward (upward). Each lot size curve approaches infinity at the distance where the corresponding bid rent curve intersects the r axis.[15]

Bid rent curves need not always be convex as depicted in Figure 2.5. But they are if we assume that the transport cost function is linear or

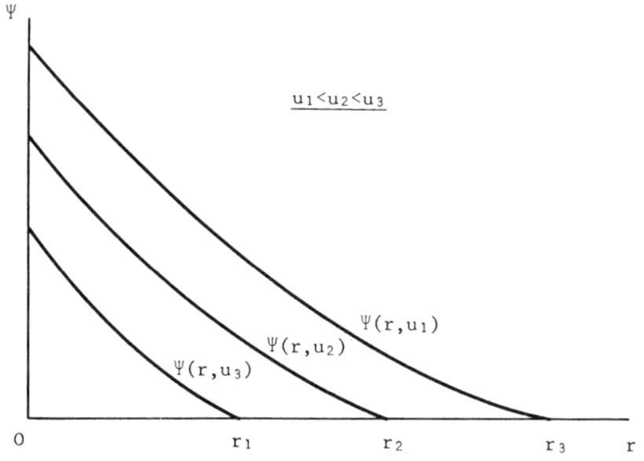

Figure 2.5. General shapes of bid rent curves.

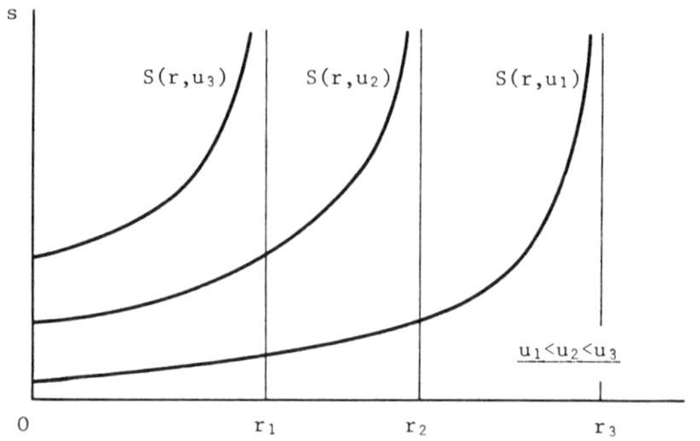

Figure 2.6. General shapes of lot size curves.

concave in distance r so that $T''(r) \equiv d^2T(r)/dr^2 \leq 0$. From (2.27),

$$\frac{\partial^2 \Psi(r, u)}{\partial r^2} = -\frac{T''(r)}{S(r, u)} + \frac{T'(r)}{S(r, u)^2} \frac{\partial S(r, u)}{\partial r}. \tag{2.31}$$

$T'(r) > 0$ by assumption, and $\partial S(r, u)/\partial r > 0$ from (2.28). Hence, if $T''(r) \leq 0$, then $\partial^2 \Psi(r, u)/\partial r^2 > 0$, which means that bid rent curves are strictly convex. A linear or concave transport cost function is one in which the marginal transport cost is nonincreasing; this is the most commonly observed case.

Property 2.2. If the transport cost function is linear or concave in distance, then bid rent curves are strictly convex.

Next, recall the following well-known characteristics of the indirect utility function (see Appendix A.3):

Property 2.3

(i) $V(R, I)$ is continuous at all $R > 0$ and $I > 0$.
(ii) $V(R, I)$ is decreasing in R and increasing in I.

Under the differentiability assumption of utility function, (ii) means

$$\frac{\partial V(R, I)}{\partial R} < 0, \qquad \frac{\partial V(R, I)}{\partial I} > 0. \tag{2.32}$$

If $R(r) = \Psi(r, u)$, then, of course, $V(R(r), Y - T(r)) = V(\Psi(r, u), Y - T(r))$. Since V is decreasing in R, we can also conclude that $V(R(r), Y - T(r))$ is greater (smaller) than $V(\Psi(r, u), Y - T(r))$ as $R(r)$ is smaller (greater) than $\Psi(r, u)$:

Property 2.4. At each r,

$$V(R(r), Y - T(r)) \gtreqless V(\Psi(r, u), Y - T(r)) \quad \text{as} \quad R(r) \lesseqgtr \Psi(r, u).$$

This property also turns out to be very useful in the subsequent analysis.

In closing this section, we make the observation that bid rent curves are indifference curves defined in urban space (consisting of the dimensions of distance and rent). Identity (2.20) implies that if the actual land rent curve $R(r)$ of the city coincided everywhere with a bid rent curve $\Psi(r, u)$, the household could obtain the same maximum utility u at every location by appropriately choosing its consumption bundle. Thus, the household would be indifferent between alternative locations. Since for each indifference curve in Figure 2.1 there exists a bid rent curve in Figure 2.5, the bid rent function can be thought of as a transformation that maps the indifference curves in commodity space into corresponding curves in urban space. With these indifference curves defined in urban space, we will be able to analyze graphically the locational choice of the household. Moreover, since bid rent curves are stated as a pecuniary bid per unit of land, they are comparable among different land users. We will therefore be able to analyze competition for land among different agents, again graphically in urban space.

2.4 Equilibrium location of the household

We are now ready to examine how the equilibrium location of the household is determined under a given land rent configuration of the city.[16]

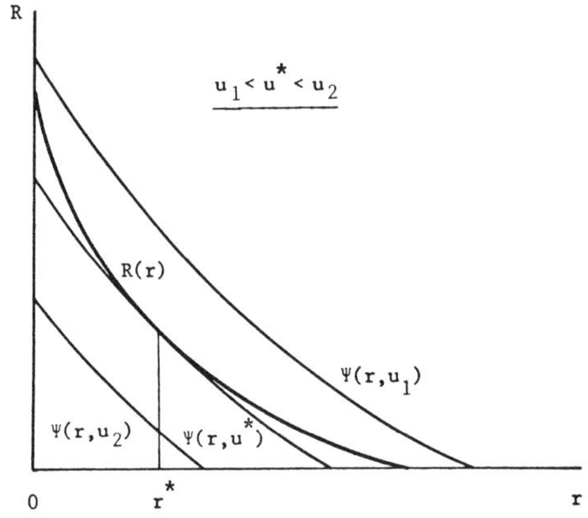

Figure 2.7. Determination of the equilibrium location.

The market land rent curve is given by $R(r)$, and the household takes it as an exogenous factor. The residential choice behavior of the household is represented by the basic model of (2.1).

We can approach the equilibrium location problem graphically, as shown in Figure 2.7. Here a set of bid rent curves is superimposed on the market rent curve $R(r)$. By inspection, it is evident from the figure that the equilibrium location of the household is distance r^* at which a bid rent curve $\Psi(r, u^*)$ is tangent to the market rent curve $R(r)$ from below. That is, when the household decides to locate somewhere in the city, it is obliged to pay the market land rent. At the same time, the household will maximize its utility. Since the utility of bid rent curves increases toward the origin, the highest utility will be achieved at a location at which a bid rent curve is tangent to the market rent curve from below. This result can be stated informally as the following rule:

> ***Rule 2.1'.*** The equilibrium location of the household is that location at which a bid rent curve is tangent to the market rent curve from below.[17]

This rule can be restated in terms of the indirect utility function of (2.17). Let us call the maximum utility that the household can achieve in the city the *equilibrium utility of the household,* denoted by u^*. Recall that given the market rent curve $R(r)$, $V(R(r), Y - T(r))$ gives the maximum utility attainable for the household at each location r. Hence, u^* is the equilibrium utility of the household, and r^* is an optimal location if and only if

$$u^* = V(R(r^*), Y - T(r^*)) \tag{2.33}$$

and

$$u^* \geq V(R(r), Y - T(r)) \qquad \text{for all} \quad r. \tag{2.34}$$

From Property 2.4, these conditions can be restated as

$$R(r^*) = \Psi(r^*, u^*)$$

and

$$R(r) \geq \Psi(r, u^*) \qquad \text{for all} \quad r.$$

Therefore, Rule 2.1′ can be formally restated as follows:

> ***Rule 2.1 (individual location equilibrium).*** Given the market rent curve $R(r)$, u^* is the equilibrium utility of the household, and r^* is an optimal location if and only if
>
> $$R(r^*) = \Psi(r^*, u^*) \qquad \text{and} \qquad R(r) \geq \Psi(r, u^*) \qquad \text{for all} \quad r. \tag{2.35}$$

Note that this rule is valid under any shape of curves $R(r)$ and $\Psi(r, u)$. At this point, we designate the bid rent curve $\Psi(r, u^*)$ that corresponds to the equilibrium utility u^* as the *equilibrium bid rent curve*.

Given that curves $R(r)$ and $\Psi(r, u^*)$ are smooth at r^*, the fact that two curves are tangent at r^* implies

$$\frac{\partial \Psi(r^*, u^*)}{\partial r} = R'(r^*), \tag{2.36}$$

where $R'(r) \equiv dR(r)/dr$. Thus, recalling equation (2.27), we have

$$T'(r^*) = -R'(r^*)S(r^*, u^*). \tag{2.37}$$

This result, called *Muth's condition,* asserts that at the equilibrium location the marginal transport cost $T'(r^*)$ equals the marginal land cost saving, $-R'(r^*)S(r, u^*)$. If this were not the case, the household could achieve greater utility by moving [closer to the CBD if $T'(r^*) > -R'(r^*)S(r^*, u)$; farther from the CBD if $T'(r^*) < -R'(r^*)S(r^*, u)$].

The *equilibrium lot size* at optimal location r^* is, by definition, the Marshallian demand for land, $\hat{s}(R(r^*), Y - T(r^*))$. From (2.35) and identity (2.19), this in turn equals the bid-max lot size $S(r^*, u^*)$:

$$\hat{s}(R(r^*), Y - T(r^*)) = S(r^*, u^*). \tag{2.38}$$

Example 2.2. In the context of the log-linear utility function of Example 2.1, let us suppose further that

$$R(r) = Ae^{-br}, \qquad T(r) = ar,$$

where A, a, and b are all positive constants. Then recalling (2.13) and (2.14), and using conditions (2.35) and (2.37), we can obtain the equilibrium location (i.e., optimal location) r^* of the household as follows:

$$r^* = \frac{Y}{a} - \frac{1}{b\beta},$$

provided that it is positive; otherwise, $r^* = 0$.

Thus far we have examined only the locational decision of a single household. We can now extend the analysis and ask what land use pattern will arise given many different households having different bid rent functions.

Suppose there are two households, i and j, having bid rent functions $\Psi_i(r, u)$ and $\Psi_j(r, u)$, respectively.[18] A general rule for ordering equilibrium locations of different households with respect to the distance from the CBD is as follows:

> ***Rule 2.2.*** If the equilibrium bid rent curve $\Psi_i(r, u_i^*)$ of household i and the equilibrium bid rent curve $\Psi_j(r, u_j^*)$ of household j intersect only once and if $\Psi_i(r, u_i^*)$ is steeper than $\Psi_j(r, u_j^*)$ at the intersection, then the equilibrium location of household i is closer to the CBD than that of household j.

In short, *a steeper equilibrium bid rent curve corresponds to an equilibrium location closer to the CBD*. This result is depicted in Figure 2.8. Note that neither household's equilibrium bid rent curve can dominate the other's over the whole urban space. If this were so, Rule 2.1, which states that each equilibrium bid rent curve must be tangent to $R(r)$ from below, would be violated. But if one curve cannot entirely dominate the other, then both curves must intersect at least once. In Figure 2.8, this occurs at distance x. Since the curve for household i is represented here as the steeper one, the equilibrium bid rent curve of household i dominates that of household j to the left of x. The reverse is true to the right of x. Hence, the equilibrium location r_i^* (r_j^*) of household i (j) must be to the left (right) of x.[19]

In order to apply the rule just stated, we must know beforehand which equilibrium bid rent curve is steeper at the intersection. In general, this information is difficult to obtain *a priori*. Matters can be greatly simplified, however, if we are able to determine the *relative steepness of bid rent functions*. Relative steepness we define as follows:

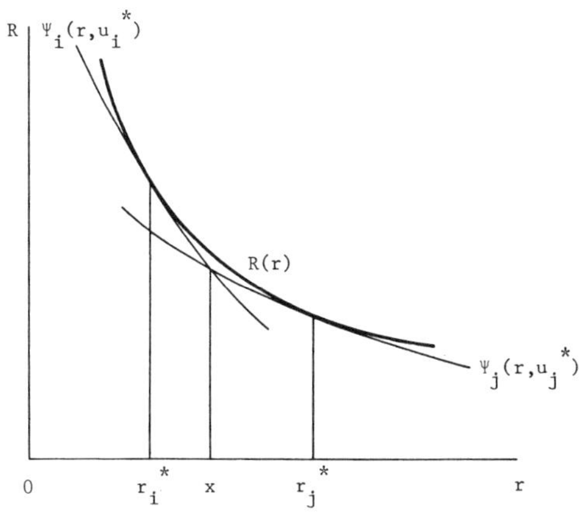

Figure 2.8. Ordering of equilibrium locations.

Definition 2.2. Suppose that bid rent functions Ψ_i and Ψ_j are continuous in r. Then we say that Ψ_i is *steeper* than Ψ_j if and only if the following condition is satisfied: Whenever $\Psi_i(x, u_i) = \Psi_j(x, u_j) > 0$ for some (x, u_i, u_j), then

$$\Psi_i(r, u_i) > \Psi_j(r, u_j) \qquad \text{for all } 0 \leq r < x$$

and

$$\Psi_i(r, u_i) < \Psi_j(r, u_j) \qquad \text{for all } r \text{ such that } r > x \text{ and } \Psi_i(r, u_i) > 0.$$

In other words, Ψ_i is steeper than Ψ_j if and only if the following condition is met: Whenever a pair of bid rent curves $\Psi_i(r, u_i)$ and $\Psi_j(r, u_j)$ intersects at a distance x, the former dominates the latter to the left of x and the latter dominates the former to the right of x. The important point is that this condition must be satisfied by every pair of bid rent curves. When bid rent curves are nonincreasing, Definition 2.2 can be restated in a simpler way as follows:

Definition 2.2′. Suppose that bid rent functions Ψ_i and Ψ_j are nonincreasing and differentiable in r. Then Ψ_i is steeper than Ψ_j if the following condition is met:[20] Whenever $\Psi_i(x, u_i) = \Psi_j(x, u_j) > 0$, then

$$-\frac{\partial \Psi_i(r, u_i)}{\partial r} > -\frac{\partial \Psi_j(r, u_j)}{\partial r} \qquad \text{at} \quad r = x.$$

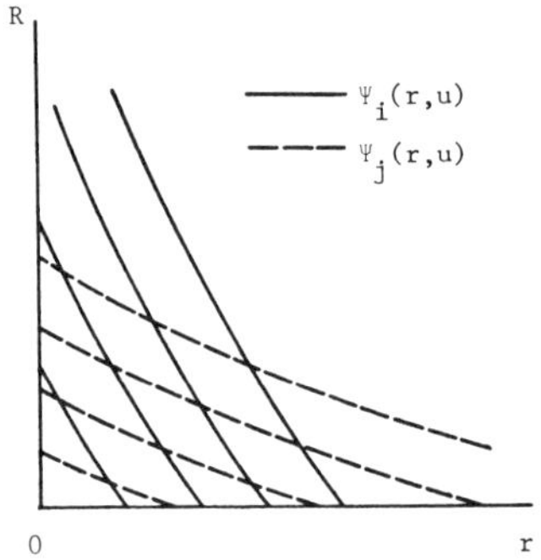

Figure 2.9. Relative steepness of bid rent functions.

That is, Ψ_i is steeper than Ψ_j if at the intersection of each pair of bid rent curves, apiece for households i and j, the former is always steeper than the latter (Figure 2.9).

It is obvious that if Ψ_i is steeper than Ψ_j, *no pair of bid rent curves intersects more than once (before reaching the r axis)*. This means, in particular, that the equilibrium bid rent curve $\Psi_i(r, u_i^*)$ and the equilibrium bid rent curve $\Psi_j(r, u_j^*)$ intersect only once. Moreover, by definition, curve $\Psi_i(r, u_i^*)$ is steeper than curve $\Psi_j(r, u_j^*)$ at the intersection. Therefore, from Rule 2.2, we can state the following:

> ***Rule 2.3.*** If the bid rent function of household i is steeper than that of household j, the equilibrium location of household i is closer to the CBD than that of household j.

The applicability of this rule is limited in that we may not always be able to ascertain the relative steepness of bid rent functions among households. Nevertheless, we will see that it is very useful in comparative static analysis, where the effects of difference in model parameter values are examined. In fact, when a definite conclusion can be obtained from a comparative static analysis of household location, the relative steepness of bid rent functions (determined by parameter values) can almost always be ascertained. An important example is the effect of income level on household location.[21]

In the context of basic model (2.1), let us arbitrarily specify two income levels such that $Y_1 < Y_2$. It is assumed that both households possess the same utility function and face the same transport cost function. Denote by $\Psi_i(r, u)$ and $S_i(r, u)$ the bid rent and bid-max lot size functions of the household with income Y_i ($i = 1, 2$). Let us arbitrarily take a pair of bid rent curves $\Psi_1(r, u_1)$ and $\Psi_2(r, u_2)$, and suppose that they intersect at some distance x: $\Psi_1(x, u_1) = \Psi_2(x, u_2) \equiv \bar{R}$. Recall identity (2.19). Since $Y_1 - T(x) < Y_2 - T(x)$, from the normality of land,

$$S_1(x, u_1) = \hat{s}(\bar{R}, Y_1 - T(x)) < \hat{s}(\bar{R}, Y_2 - T(x)) = S_2(x, u_2).$$

Thus, from (2.27),

$$-\frac{\partial \Psi_1(x, u_1)}{\partial r} = \frac{T'(r)}{S_1(x, u_1)} > \frac{T'(r)}{S_2(x, u_2)} = -\frac{\partial \Psi_2(x, u_2)}{\partial r}.$$

Since we have arbitrarily chosen two bid rent curves, this result means that function Ψ_1 is steeper than Ψ_2. Thus, from Rule 2.3, we can conclude as follows:

> ***Proposition 2.1.*** Households with higher incomes locate farther from the CBD than households with lower incomes, other aspects being equal.

This result has often been used to explain the residential pattern observed in the United States.[22]

In closing this section, note that Proposition 2.1 was obtained through an examination of the way the steepness of a bid rent function changes with income. The same approach of examining the change in steepness of a bid rent function with respect to a parameter will often be used in the subsequent analysis. For this reason, it is helpful to introduce a mathematical operation that is useful for examining the change in relative steepness. Consider a general bid rent function $\Psi(r, u \mid \theta)$ with parameter θ. In order to examine how the relative steepness of function Ψ changes in θ, we arbitrarily choose a bid rent curve $\Psi(\cdot, u \mid \theta)$, and take a point $(r, \Psi(r, u \mid \theta))$ on that curve. Then *by keeping the value of* $\Psi(r, u \mid \theta)$ *constant,* we examine how the slope of that bid rent curve changes at r when parameter θ is changed (Figure 2.10). That is, we perform the following calculation:

$$-\frac{\partial \Psi_r(r, u \mid \theta)}{\partial \theta}\bigg|_{\Psi(r,u|\theta)=\text{const}}, \tag{2.39}$$

where $\Psi_r(r, u \mid \theta) \equiv \partial \Psi(r, u \mid \theta)/\partial r$. Operation (2.39) is often simply expressed as

$$-\frac{\partial \Psi_r}{\partial \theta}\bigg|_{d\Psi=0} \tag{2.40}$$

Then recalling Definition 2.2′, we can immediately conclude as follows:

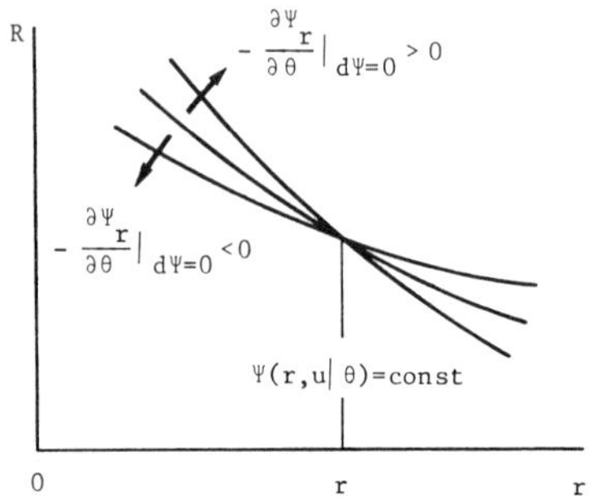

Figure 2.10. Change in the relative steepness of bid rent function $\Psi(r, u \mid \theta)$.

Rule 2.4. If $-(\partial\Psi_r/\partial\theta)\,|_{d\Psi=0}$ is positive (negative) at every point such that $\Psi(r, u \mid \theta) > 0$, then Ψ becomes steeper (less steep) as θ increases.

This rule is explained in Figure 2.10. As an illustration, let us derive Proposition 2.1 by applying this rule. In order to emphasize that Y is the parameter of interest, let us denote the bid rent and lot size functions obtained from (2.8) by $\Psi(r, u \mid Y)$ and $S(r, u \mid Y)$, respectively. Then from identity (2.19),

$$S(r, u \mid Y) = \hat{s}(\Psi(r, u \mid Y), Y - T(r)). \tag{2.41}$$

And from (2.27), $\Psi_r(r, u \mid Y) = -T'(r)/S(r, u \mid Y) = -T'(r)/\hat{s}(\Psi(r, u \mid Y), Y - T(r))$. Therefore, since $I = Y - T(r)$ at distance r,

$$\begin{aligned} -\frac{\partial\Psi_r}{\partial Y}\bigg|_{d\Psi=0} &= \frac{\partial[T'(r)/\hat{s}(\Psi(r, u \mid Y), Y - T(r))]}{\partial Y}\bigg|_{\Psi(r,u|Y)=\text{const}} \\ &= -\frac{T'(r)}{\hat{s}^2}\frac{\partial\hat{s}}{\partial I}\frac{\partial(Y - T(r))}{\partial Y} \\ &= -\frac{T'(r)}{\hat{s}^2}\frac{\partial\hat{s}}{\partial I} < 0, \end{aligned}$$

which is negative because $\partial\hat{s}/\partial I > 0$ from the normality of land. Since this result holds at any point such that $\Psi(r, u \mid Y) > 0$, from Rule 2.4 we can conclude that the bid rent function $\Psi(r, u \mid Y)$ becomes less steep as income increases. Therefore, Proposition 2.1 follows from Rule 2.3.

2.5 Extended models

Having mastered the basic model (2.1), it is appropriate to incorporate some of the important factors that we have previously neglected. In the first subsection, we introduce time cost in commuting and examine how the household's location is affected by wage income and nonwage income. In the second subsection, we examine the locational implications of family structure. In the third subsection, we study the so-called *Muth model,* in which the housing service is produced by the housing industry.

2.5.1 Time-extended model

Although we have not explicitly considered the time cost of commuting, in practice time cost is as important as pecuniary cost. In order to examine the effects of pecuniary cost and time cost on residential choice, we assume that the household will maximize its utility subject to a budget constraint and a time constraint. The utility function is specified as $U(z, s, t_l)$, where z and s are the same as before, and t_l represents the leisure time. Suppose the household chooses distance r from the CBD. Then the total available time $\bar{t}$ is spent on the leisure time t_l, the working time t_w, and the commuting time br, where b is a constant representing the commuting time per distance. Thus, the time constraint of the household is given as $t_l + t_w + br = \bar{t}$. The income of the household is the sum of nonwage income Y_N and wage income Wt_w, where W represents the wage rate. This total income is spent on composite good z, land rent $R(r)s$, and transport cost ar, where a is a constant representing the pecuniary commuting cost per distance. Hence, the budget constraint of the household is given as $z + R(r)s + ar = Y_N + Wt_w$. We assume that the household can freely choose its leisure time and working time. Then the residential choice of the household can be expressed as

$$\max_{r,z,s,t_l,t_w} U(z, s, t_l),$$

$$\text{subject to} \quad z + R(r)s + ar = Y_N + Wt_w \quad \text{and} \quad t_l + t_w + br = \bar{t}, \tag{2.42}$$

which is called the *time-extended model* of residential choice.

From the time constraint, $t_w = \bar{t} - t_l - br$. Substituting this into the budget constraint, the above model can be restated as[23]

$$\max_{r,z,s,t_l} U(z, s, t_l), \qquad \text{subject to} \quad z + R(r)s + Wt_l = I(r), \tag{2.43}$$

where $I(r) \equiv Y_N + I_w(r) - ar$, and $I_w(r) \equiv W(\bar{t} - br)$. This formulation suggests that the household makes the following transaction: It sells all available time (net of commuting, $\bar{t} - br$) to employers at the wage rate W; it then purchases back its leisure time t_l at the same unit price of time, W. Thus, wage rate W also serves as the *unit price of leisure time*. We may call $I_w(r)$ and $I(r)$ the *potential wage income* and the *potential net income* at distance r, respectively. At this point, it is also convenient to define

$$T(r) = ar + Wbr, \tag{2.44}$$

which represents the total commuting costs at distance r.

We assume that with obvious modifications Assumptions 2.1–2.3 hold for this time-extended model.[24] Then recalling Definition 2.1, the bid rent function for this model is stated as

$$\Psi(r, u) = \max_{z,s,t_l} \left\{ \frac{I(r) - z - Wt_l}{s} \;\middle|\; U(z, s, t_l) = u \right\}. \tag{2.45}$$

From this, the bid-max consumption bundle $(z(r, u), S(r, u), t_l(r, u))$ can be derived in a manner essentially identical to that in the case of the basic model. First, solving the utility constraint $U(z, s, t_l) = u$ for z, we obtain the equation of the indifference surface as $z = Z(s, t_l, u)$. Substituting this into (2.45), we obtain the unconstrained version of the bid rent function:

$$\Psi(r, u) = \max_{s,t_l} \frac{I(r) - Z(s, t_l, u) - Wt_l}{s}. \tag{2.46}$$

The first-order conditions for the optimal choice of (s, t_l) are

$$-\frac{\partial Z}{\partial s} = \Psi(r, u), \qquad -\frac{\partial Z}{\partial t_l} = W, \tag{2.47}$$

which express the familiar marginality conditions asserting that at the optimal choice of consumption bundle, the marginal rate of substitution between each pair of goods equals the corresponding price ratio (recall that the price of z equals 1).

Example 2.3. Suppose that the utility function in model (2.45) is given by the following log-linear function:

$$U(z, s, t_l) = \alpha \log z + \beta \log s + \gamma \log t_l, \tag{2.48}$$

where $\alpha > 0$, $\beta > 0$, $\gamma > 0$, and $\alpha + \beta + \gamma = 1$. Then $Z(s, u, t_l) = s^{-\beta/\alpha} t_l^{-\gamma/\alpha} e^{u/\alpha}$, and using (2.47) we obtain

$$\Psi(r, u) = \alpha^{\alpha/\beta}\beta(\gamma/W)^{\gamma/\beta}I(r)^{1/\beta}e^{-u/\beta}, \tag{2.49}$$

$$z(r, u) = \alpha I(r), \qquad t_1(r, u) = \gamma I(r)/W, \tag{2.50}$$

$$S(r, u) = \beta I(r)/\Psi(r, u) = \alpha^{-\alpha/\beta}(\gamma/W)^{-\gamma/\beta}I(r)^{-(\alpha+\gamma)/\beta}e^{u/\beta}. \tag{2.51}$$

As with the basic model, a number of useful identities can be obtained. In particular, the two most important are described below. Let us generally represent the unit price of leisure time by P_1.[25] We define the Marshallian demand $\hat{s}(R, P_1, I)$ for land from the solution of the following utility-maximization problem:

$$\max_{z,s,t_1} U(z, s, t_1), \qquad \text{subject to} \quad z + Rs + P_1t_1 = I. \tag{2.52}$$

Then it holds identically that[26]

$$S(r, u) \equiv \hat{s}(\Psi(r, u), W, I(r)). \tag{2.53}$$

That is, the bid-max demand for land under utility u is just the Marshallian demand under land rent $\Psi(r, u)$ and leisure price W. Similarly, if we define the Hicksian demand $\tilde{s}(R, P_1, u)$ for land from the solution of the next expenditure minimization problem,

$$\min_{z,s,t_1} z + Rs + P_1t_1, \qquad \text{subject to} \quad U(z, s, t_1) = u, \tag{2.54}$$

then it holds identically that

$$S(r, u) \equiv \tilde{s}(\Psi(r, u), W, u). \tag{2.55}$$

That is, the bid-max demand for land at utility u is identical to the compensated demand at utility u under land rent $\Psi(r, u)$ and leisure price W.

With these identities just stated, we can use the same techniques as before to confirm that Properties 2.1 and 2.2 of bid rent curves also pertain to the time-extended model.[27] In addition, Rule 2.1′ (or Rule 2.1) can similarly be used to determine the equilibrium location. The marginal change in bid rent with respect to distance is, as before,

$$\Psi_r \equiv \frac{\partial\Psi(r, u)}{\partial r} = -\frac{T'(r)}{S(r, u)}, \tag{2.56}$$

where

$$T'(r) = a + Wb. \tag{2.57}$$

We are now ready to examine the effects of nonwage income and wage income on the household's location. First, the effect of nonwage income Y_N is essentially the same as that of income Y in the basic model. Substituting identity (2.53) into (2.56), $\Psi_r = -T'(r)/\hat{s}(\Psi(r, u), W, I(r))$. Applying the method developed at the end of Section 2.4, we have

$$-\left.\frac{\partial \Psi_r}{\partial Y_{\mathrm{N}}}\right|_{d\Psi=0} = \left.\frac{\partial[T'(r)/\hat{s}(\Psi(r, u), W, I(r))]}{\partial Y_{\mathrm{N}}}\right|_{\Psi(r,u)=\text{const}}$$

$$= -\frac{T'(r)}{\hat{s}^2}\frac{\partial \hat{s}}{\partial I}\frac{\partial I(r)}{\partial Y_N}$$

$$= -\frac{a + Wb}{\hat{s}^2}\frac{\partial \hat{s}}{\partial I} < 0,$$

which is negative, since income effect $\partial \hat{s}/\partial I$ is positive from the normality of land. From Rule 2.4, this means that bid rent function Ψ becomes less steep as Y_N increases. Therefore, from Rule 2.3, we can conclude as follows:

> ***Proposition 2.1'.*** Households with higher nonwage incomes locate farther from the CBD than households with lower nonwage incomes, other aspects being equal.

With Propositions 2.1 and 2.1', we can conclude that as long as the transport cost is independent of income level, the affluent live farther from the CBD than the less affluent.

The next logical question is, How does wage income influence the locational choice of the household? Since wage rate affects both the transport cost function and the demand for land, the overall effect is not simple. In order to examine the effect of the wage rate on the steepness of the bid rent function, from (2.56) we calculate

$$-\left.\frac{\partial \Psi_r}{\partial W}\right|_{d\Psi=0} = \left(\frac{1}{S}\frac{\partial T'}{\partial W} - \frac{T'}{S^2}\frac{\partial S}{\partial W}\right)_{d\Psi=0}$$

$$= \frac{T'}{SW}\left(\frac{\partial T'}{\partial W}\frac{W}{T'} - \frac{\partial S}{\partial W}\frac{W}{S}\right)_{d\Psi=0},$$

where $S = S(r, u)$ and $T' = T'(r)$. Therefore,

$$-\left.\frac{\partial \Psi_r}{\partial W}\right|_{d\Psi=0} \gtreqless 0 \quad \text{as} \quad \underbrace{\left.\frac{\partial T'}{\partial W}\frac{W}{T'}\right|_{d\Psi=0}}_{\substack{\text{wage elasticity}\\ \text{of marginal}\\ \text{transport cost}}} \gtreqless \underbrace{\left.\frac{\partial S}{\partial W}\frac{W}{S}\right|_{d\Psi=0}}_{\substack{\text{wage elasticity}\\ \text{of lot size}}}. \tag{2.58}$$

The issue, then, reduces to a question of elasticities.[28] Since $T'(r) = a + Wb$,

$$\left.\frac{\partial T'}{\partial W}\frac{W}{T'}\right|_{d\Psi=0} = \frac{\partial T'}{\partial W}\frac{W}{T'} = \left(1 + \frac{a}{bW}\right)^{-1}. \tag{2.59}$$

A simple calculation yields[29]

$$\left.\frac{\partial S}{\partial W}\frac{W}{S}\right|_{d\Psi=0} = \eta\frac{I_w(r)}{I(r)} + \varepsilon, \tag{2.60}$$

where

$$\eta = \frac{\partial \hat{s}}{\partial I}\frac{I(r)}{\hat{s}}, \qquad \varepsilon = \frac{\partial \hat{s}}{\partial P_l}\frac{P_l}{\hat{s}}. \tag{2.61}$$

By definition, η represents the *potential-net-income elasticity of lot size* and ε the *cross-elasticity of lot size to the price of leisure time*.[30] Since land is a normal good, η is always positive. We assume that these elasticities are constant in the relevant range of analysis.[31] Substituting (2.59) and (2.60) into (2.58), we obtain the following:

Property 2.5. In the context of the time-extended model.

$$-\left.\frac{\partial \Psi_r}{\partial W}\right|_{d\Psi=0} \gtreqless 0 \quad \text{as} \quad f(r, W) \equiv \left(1 + \frac{a}{bW}\right)^{-1} - \left(\eta\frac{I_w(r)}{I(r)} + \varepsilon\right) \gtreqless 0, \tag{2.62}$$

where $I(r) = Y_N + I_w(r) - ar$ and $I_w(r) = W(\bar{t} - br)$, and a and bW are, respectively, the marginal pecuniary cost and the marginal time cost of commuting.

Since the elasticity difference $f(r, W)$ is generally a function of r and W, it is difficult to obtain general conclusions about the effects of wage changes on the steepness of the bid rent function. But let us consider the special case in which households are pure-wage earners (i.e., $Y_N = 0$) and pecuniary transport costs are negligible relative to time costs (i.e., $a = 0$).[32] Under these conditions,

$$f(r, W) = 1 - (\eta + \varepsilon).$$

Hence, with Property 2.5 and recalling Rules 2.3 and 2.4, we can state the following proposition:

Proposition 2.2. Given that households consist of pure-wage earners whose pecuniary transport costs are zero (i.e., $Y_N = 0$, $a = 0$), then[33]

(i) if $\eta + \varepsilon > 1$, the equilibrium location of the household moves out from the CBD with increasing wage rates;
(ii) if $\eta + \varepsilon < 1$, the equilibrium location of the household moves in toward the CBD with increasing wage rates;
(iii) if $\eta + \varepsilon = 1$, wage rates do not affect location.

In Japan, for example, pecuniary commuting costs are often paid by employers ($a = 0$). Hence, Proposition 2.2(ii) can be used to explain the general tendency in most large Japanese cities for wealthy households to live closer to the CBD than less affluent households (provided that condition $\eta + \varepsilon < 1$ holds, which is the most common case). In the United States, however, pecuniary commuting costs are not negligible,[34] and the Proposition 2.2 is inapplicable.

When pecuniary commuting costs are not negligible, we can reconsider relation (2.62) in light of the pure-wage earners ($Y_N = 0$), for whom the following holds:

$$\frac{I_w(r)}{I(r)} = \left(1 - \frac{ar}{W(\bar{t} - br)}\right)^{-1}.$$

This ratio is 1 at $r = 0$, and it increases as r increases. Hence, if $\eta + \varepsilon \geq 1$, then $f(r, W) < 0$ for all r, and we can conclude from (2.62) that

$$\text{if} \quad \eta + \varepsilon \geq 1, \qquad \text{then} \quad -\left.\frac{\partial \Psi_r}{\partial W}\right|_{d\Psi=0} < 0,$$

which implies that high-wage earners reside farther from the CBD than low-wage earners.[35]

If $\eta + \varepsilon < 1$, function $f(r, W)$ can assume both positive and negative values. For this case, observe that in a realistic range of parameters r, a, b, and W, the elasticity of ratio $I_w(r)/I(r)$ in W is very small relative to the comparable elasticity of a/bW; note also that $I_w(0)/I(0) = 1$, and the rate of increase of ratio $I_w(r)/I(r)$ in r is very small.[36] Hence, we can safely state that

$$f(r, W) \doteqdot f(W) \equiv \left(1 + \frac{a}{bW}\right)^{-1} - (\eta + \varepsilon). \tag{2.63}$$

Assuming $0 < \eta + \varepsilon < 1$, the behavior of function $f(W)$ is depicted in Figure 2.11a. The wage elasticity of marginal transport cost $(1 + a/bW)^{-1}$ is increasing from 0 to 1, while the wage elasticity of lot size

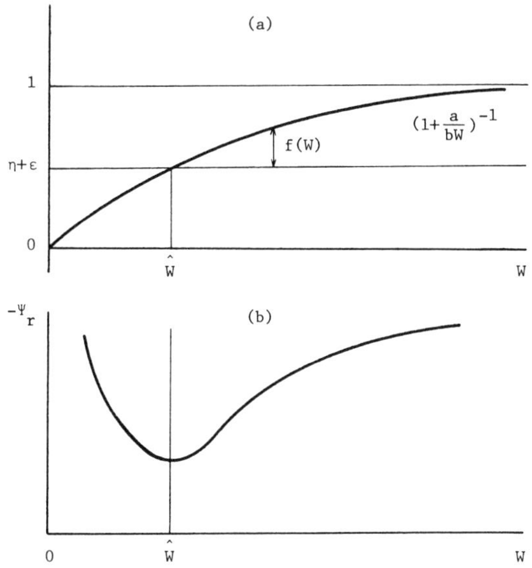

Figure 2.11. Effects of wage rate on the slope of the bid rent function ($\eta + \varepsilon < 1$).

stays constant at $\eta + \varepsilon$. Hence, the difference $f(W)$ is first negative for $W < \hat{W}$, then positive for $W > \hat{W}$, where

$$\hat{W} = \frac{a}{b} \frac{\eta + \varepsilon}{1 - (\eta + \varepsilon)}. \tag{2.64}$$

Thus, from Property 2.5, with changing wage rate, the slope of the bid rent curve ($-\Psi_r$) at each rent-location point varies as depicted in Figure 2.11b. It follows from Rules 2.3 and 2.4 that the equilibrium location of the household moves out from the CBD as the wage rate increases to $\hat{W}$, after which it moves in toward the CBD while the wage rate continues to increase.[37] This makes intuitive sense as follows. For low-income households, pecuniary transport costs are crucial, as are wages lost in time spent for commuting. For these reasons, low-income households tend to locate near the CBD. As incomes rise, such costs are less important, so households locate farther from the CBD. At some high wage rate, however, the opportunity cost of time spent for commuting becomes very significant. Households with such high wage rates tend to shift their locations back toward the city center. In short, we can conclude the following:

Proposition 2.3. Given that households consist of pure-wage earners whose pecuniary transport costs are positive (i.e., $Y_N = 0$, $a > 0$), then

(i) if $\eta + \varepsilon \geq 1$, the equilibrium location of the household moves farther from the CBD with increasing wage rates;
(ii) if $0 < \eta + \varepsilon < 1$, increases in the wage rate first move the equilibrium location away from the CBD; but beyond the wage rate $\hat{W}$, which is given by (2.64), additional increases retract the household location again.

When the substance of Proposition 2.3(ii) holds, both those who earn very low wages and those who earn very high wages tend to reside near the city center; middle-wage earners gravitate toward the suburbs. This is consistent with what has been observed in large cities in the United States.[38] The behavior of the curve in Figure 2.11b is also consistent with the estimate of slopes of bid rent curves in San Francisco by Wheaton (1977).

In closing this subsection, we note that Proposition 2.3 yields an important policy implication. Regardless of the wage elasticity of lot size ($\eta + \varepsilon$), low-income households will always prefer central locations. Thus, the demolition of low-quality housing in city centers does not induce a more even distribution of income classes throughout the entire city. It merely displaces a certain group, which will continue to seek a central location.[39]

2.5.2 *Family-structure model*

We now extend the model of Section 2.5.1 in order to encompass the effects of family structure on the locational decision. Following Beckmann (1973), we assume that the family structure of a household is characterized by two parameters: d, the number of dependent members, and n, the number of working members in the household. The utility function of the household is now generalized as $U(z, s, t_l; d, n)$, d and n being parameters. Thus, model (2.42) becomes

$$\max_{r,z,s,t_l,t_w} U(z, s, t_l; d, n),$$

$$\text{subject to} \quad z + R(r)s + nar = Y_N + nWt_W \quad \text{and} \quad t_l + t_w + br = \bar{t}, \tag{2.65}$$

which is called the *family-structure model* of residential choice. The second constraint represents the time constraint for *each* working member. Here all working members of the household are assumed to have the same leisure time t_l, working time t_w, and commuting time br. The first constraint represents the *family* budget. Each working member of the household is also assumed to have the same pecuniary transport cost ar, as well as the same wage rate W. Composite good z and land s are consumed in aggregate by all household members.

As in Section 2.5.1 we can rewrite the family-structure model as follows:

$$\max_{r,z,s,t_1} U(z, s, t_1; d, n),$$

$$\text{subject to} \qquad z + R(r)s + nWt_1 = I(r, n), \tag{2.66}$$

where $I(r, n) = Y_N + nW(\bar{t} - br) - nar$. Thus, the bid rent function is now given by

$$\Psi(r, u) = \max_{s,t_1} \frac{I(r, n) - Z(s, t_1, u; d, n) - nWt_1}{s}, \tag{2.67}$$

where $Z(s, t_1, u; d, n)$ is the solution of $U(z, s, t_1; d, n) = u$ for z.

As an example, let us consider the case of the next log-linear utility function,

$$U(z, s, t_1; d, n) = h\alpha \log (z/h^{\lambda}) + h\beta \log (s/h^{\mu}) + n\gamma \log t_1 + d\delta \log \bar{t}, \tag{2.68}$$

where each of α, β, γ, δ, λ, and μ is a positive constant, and $h = d + n$ represents the family size.[40] For example, $\lambda = \mu = 1$ means that all family members equally share z and s. In practice, μ will be less than unity (reflecting the public-good nature of z and s for the household members). By direct calculation, the bid rent function and the bid-max consumption can be obtained as follows:

$$\Psi(r, u) = A\left(\frac{h\alpha}{B}\right)^{\alpha/\beta}\left(\frac{h\beta}{B}\right)\left(\frac{n\gamma}{B}\frac{1}{nW}\right)^{n\gamma/h\beta} I(r, n)^{B/h\beta} e^{-u/h\beta},$$

$$z(r, u) = \frac{h\alpha}{B} I(r, n), \qquad S(r, u) = \frac{h\beta}{B}\frac{I(r, n)}{\Psi(r, u)},$$

$$t_1(r, u) = \frac{n\gamma}{B}\frac{I(r, n)}{nW},$$

where $A = \{h^{h\alpha\lambda + h\beta\mu}(\bar{t})^{-d\delta}\}^{-1/(h\beta)}$ and $B = h\alpha + h\beta + n\gamma$. A simple calculation yields

$$-\frac{\partial \Psi}{\partial r} = \frac{\alpha + \beta + (n/h)\gamma}{\beta} \frac{a + bW}{(Y_N/n) + W(\bar{t} - br) - ar} \Psi(r, u). \tag{2.69}$$

Then since $h = d + n$,

$$-\left.\frac{\partial \Psi_r}{\partial d}\right|_{d\Psi=0} = -\frac{n\gamma}{\beta h^2}\,\frac{a + bW}{(Y_N/n) + W(\bar{t} - br) - ar}\,\Psi(r, u) < 0,$$

which means that *the bid rent function becomes less steep with an increasing number of dependents*. Increasing d augments the weight on lot size in the utility function relative to the weight on leisure time of working members. This in turn increases the demand for lot size, and therefore the bid rent function becomes less steep. Next, we can see from (2.69) that *in the case of pure-wage earners* ($Y_N = 0$), *the bid rent function becomes steeper with an increasing n/h, the commuter–family size ratio*. Similarly, we can see from (2.69) that *in the case of pure-wage earners with no dependents* ($d = 0$, *and hence* $n/h = 1$), *the steepness of the bid rent function is independent of family size (= the number of commuters)*. Therefore, recalling Rule 2.3, we can conclude as follows:

> ***Proposition 2.4.*** In the context of the family-structure model with a log-linear utility function, we have that
>
> (i) the more dependents a household has, the farther is its equilibrium location from the CBD;
> (ii) given that households consist of pure-wage earners, locations can be ranked by the households' commuter–family size ratio n/h; the smaller the ratio, the farther is the location from the CBD;
> (iii) given that households consist of pure-wage earners with no dependents, locations are independent of family size (i.e., the number of commuters).

These conclusions, first obtained by Beckmann (1973), are consistent with many casual observations from U.S. cities. Although these conclusions result from a log-linear utility function, it is not difficult to obtain similar conclusions from the original model of (2.65).

2.5.3 *Muth model of housing industry*

In the basic model of (2.1), it is implicitly assumed that each household manages the construction of its house by itself. There is, however, another class of models, originated by Muth (1969), in which households are assumed to consume an aggregate commodity called the *housing service*. That is, each household behaves as

$$\max_{r,z,q} U(z, q), \qquad \text{subject to} \quad z + R_H(r)q = Y - T(r), \tag{2.70}$$

where $R_H(r)$ is the unit price of housing service q at location r, and z represents the amount of composite consumer good excluding housing service. In turn, the housing industry produces the housing service with production function $F(L, K)$ from land L and capital (or nonland input) K. That is, each profit-maximizing firm of the housing industry behaves as

$$\max_{L,K} R_{\mathrm{H}}(r)F(L, K) - R(r)L - K, \qquad \text{at each} \quad r, \tag{2.71}$$

where $R(r)$ is the land rent at r, and the price of capital, which is assumed to be a fixed constant independent of location, is normalized to unity.

When combined, (2.70) and (2.71) can be called the Muth model of the housing industry. There are two different ways to treat this model. One is to reformulate it as a version of the basic model. Let q be the amount of housing service consumption by a household, and define

$$s \equiv \frac{q}{F(L, K)} L, \qquad k \equiv \frac{q}{F(L, K)} K. \tag{2.72}$$

Then, s and k represent, respectively, the land input and capital input per household. Let us assume, as in Muth (1969), that the housing production function F has constant returns to scale. Then a simple calculation yields[41]

$$q = F(s, k), \tag{2.73}$$

which represents the housing production function in terms of inputs and output per household. Again, since F has constant returns to scale, in equilibrium the housing industry gets zero profit at each location: $R_{\mathrm{H}}(r)F(L, K) - R(r)L - K = 0$. Hence,

$$\begin{aligned} R_{\mathrm{H}}(r) &= R(r)L/F(L, K) + K/F(L, K) \\ &= R(r)s/q + k/q. \end{aligned} \tag{2.74}$$

Substituting (2.73) and (2.74) into (2.70), the Muth model is equivalent to the following *reduced-form model,* in which each household chooses land and capital inputs by itself:

$$\max_{r,z,s,k} U(z, F(s, k)), \qquad \text{subject to} \quad z + k + R(r)s = Y - T(r). \tag{2.75}$$

Except for the addition of a new choice variable k, this is essentially the same as the basic model.[42]

Another way is to keep the context of the Muth model, which is more appropriate for the study of apartment-type houses. Let us define the *bid housing rent function* $\Psi_{\mathrm{H}}(r, u)$ as

$$\Psi_H(r, u) = \max_q \frac{Y - T(r) - Z(q, u)}{q}, \tag{2.76}$$

where $Z(q, u)$ is the solution of $u = U(z, q)$ for z. Note that except for notational differences, this is the same as (2.8). Therefore, if we replace $R(r)$ and $\Psi(r, u)$, respectively, with $R_H(r)$ and $\Psi_H(r, u)$, then all the results of the previous sections hold true for the Muth model. Specifically, let us assume that Assumptions 2.1–2.3 hold when s is replaced with q. Then, Propositions 2.1–2.4 can also be derived from the Muth model.[43] In this sense, they represent very robust conclusions. We will continue discussion of the Muth model in Section 3.7.

2.6 Conclusion

In this chapter, we have examined the residential choice of the household as determined by the trade-off between space for living and accessibility to work. We began with the basic model, in which only pecuniary transport costs were explicitly considered. Then we introduced the time cost of commuting, family structure, and housing consumption.

Our models produced results which suggest that a particular land use pattern will prevail in the monocentric city. Suppose the pecuniary transport costs are not negligible and the wage elasticity of lot size is less than unity. Then according to Propositions 2.1, 2.3, and 2.4, the following land use pattern will prevail. Wage-poor and wage-rich households with few dependents (such as singles and working couples with few children) will tend to reside close to the city center. Beyond them and out toward the suburbs, middle-income households with large families and few commuters will be found. Farther away, asset-rich households with larger families and few commuters will locate. This pattern is consistent with what has been observed of large cities in the United States.

Recall that all the propositions of this chapter have been obtained by the same, simple method of analysis. That is, we examined how the steepness of the bid rent function changed with the change in parameter values. If the bid rent function becomes steeper with an increasing parameter value, the households with greater parameter values will locate closer to the city center than will those with smaller parameter values and vice versa. Note that our analysis made no assumptions about the shape of the market rent curve or about the behavior of landowners except to assume that households are price takers who see the market land rent curve as an exogenous factor. Therefore, these conclusions about the land use pattern hold irrespective of the shape of the market land rent curve and the behavior of landowners.

However, if we want more detailed information about the equilibrium land use pattern, such as population density and the shape of the market rent curve, we must, of course, specify the behavior of landowners too. We will do this in the next chapter.

Bibliographical notes

The theory of household location presented in this chapter is derived in large part from the pioneering work of Alonso, Beckmann, and Muth. The basic model of Section 2.2 is a simplification of Alonso's model (1964, Ch. 2). In the original Alonso model, utility function includes another variable, the distance to the CBD, which is supposed to represent the disutility of commuting. However, with the Alonso model it is hard to obtain any general result on the location of the household. Therefore, in order to obtain clear-cut results, most subsequent works adopted the simpler framework of the basic model.

The bid rent function approach described in this chapter was first established by Alonso (1964). This is, of course, a generalization of the agricultural bid rent theory of von Thünen (1826). This approach is essentially the same as the indirect utility function approach introduced into an urban land use model by Solow (1973). Many urban economists, notably Schweizer, Varaiya, and Hartwick (1976) and Kanemoto (1980), further developed this bid rent/indirect utility function approach. The concept of relative steepness of bid rent functions was introduced by Fujita (1985).

The time-extended model of Section 2.5.1 is an extension of similar models by Beckmann (1974), Henderson (1977), and Hochman and Ofek (1977), which consider only the time cost of commuting, neglecting the pecuniary cost. Our discussion of this extended model is based on Fujita (1986a). A similar model was independently studied by DeSalvo (1985). Proposition 2.2 is essentially the same as Corollary 3 of Hochman and Ofek (1977). We can also consider the time-extended model as a simplified version of Yamada (1972). In Yamada's work, other factors such as the disutility of working time and commuting time and environmental external effects are also considered. Note that here the household can freely choose the length of working time. For the case in which maximum working length is considered, see Moses (1962) and Yamada (1972).

The family-structure model of Section 2.5.2 is an extension of Beckmann (1973). In Beckmann's model, the pecuniary transport cost is assumed to be zero and the working time is fixed. The housing industry model of Section 2.5.3 was, of course, introduced by Muth (1969). In Muth's study, transport cost is implicitly assumed to be a function of income level. In our model, wage income and nonwage income are treated separately, and hence pecuniary transport costs are assumed to be independent of income.

In this chapter, in order to explain the general pattern of household location observed in the United States, we have focused mainly on the time-extended model. LeRoy and Sonstelie (1983) present an alternative model that introduces multiple transport modes.

Notes

1. For an introduction to the consumer theory relevant to the following discussion, the reader is referred, e.g., to J. M. Henderson and R. E. Quandt (1980) and Varian (1984). See also Appendix A.3 for a summary of important results from consumer theory.
2. This utility function is simple, yet general enough to serve our present purpose of focusing on lot size and household density changes in the city. The function that appears in the text was derived as follows: First assume that the original utility function of the household is given by $U(z_1, \ldots, z_n, s)$, where each z_i $(i = 1, 2, \ldots, n)$ represents the amount of consumer good i (other than land), and s the lot size. Some of the z_i's represent nonland inputs for housing. Assuming that the price of each consumer good i does not vary within the city; we represent it by p_i, $i = 1, 2, \ldots, n$ (this assumption is appropriate because compared with land rent, the prices of other goods are relatively constant within a city). Under each fixed combination of (z, s), define

$$U(z, s) = \max\left\{ U(z_1, \ldots, z_n, s) \,\middle|\, \sum_1^n p_i z_i = z \right\},$$

   where z represents the total expenditure for all consumer goods other than land. This derived utility function is the one in the text (refer to the Aggregation theorem of Hicks 1946, pp. 312–13). For alternative specifications of the utility function, see Section 2.5.
3. For some of the mathematical terminology used in the following discussion (e.g., strictly convex and smooth curves), see Appendix A.1.
4. Strictly speaking, the fact that the utility function is increasing in z and s implies that condition (2.3) holds *almost everywhere*. That is, it cannot rule out the possibility that $\partial U/\partial z$ or $\partial U/\partial s$ becomes zero on a set of points with measure zero. However, this minor difference does not affect our results in any essential way, and hence we neglect it in the following discussion. The same note applies to conditions (2.5) and (2.6).
5. Formally, we have a constraint $s > 0$. However, since any indifference curve does not cut axes, whenever it exists, the optimal s for the maximization problem of (2.8) is positive (Figure 2.2). Hence, we can neglect the positivity constraint on s. Note also that given s, it may not be possible to solve

the equation $u = U(z, s)$ for z. In this case, we define $Z(s, u) = \infty$. Then in the maximization problem of (2.8), such s will never be chosen as the optimal lot size.

6. Since each indifference curve is strictly convex, if it exists, the bid-max lot size is unique (Figure 2.2). We introduce the following convention: When there is no solution to the maximization problem of (2.8), we define $\Psi(r, u) = 0$ and $S(r, u) = \infty$. Note also that when we solve the maximization problem of (2.7) or (2.8), we also obtain the *bid-max composite good consumption* $z(r, u) \equiv Z(S(r, u), u)$. However, since we will never use function $z(r, u)$ in the subsequent analysis, we omit its discussion.
7. More precisely, if we denote the angle ACO by θ, then $\Psi(r, u) = \tan\theta$. But for simplicity, we use this graphical expression throughout the book.
8. In detail, we have

$$\frac{\partial}{\partial s}\left(\frac{Y - T(r) - Z(s, u)}{s}\right) = -\frac{1}{s}\frac{\partial Z(s, u)}{\partial s} - \frac{Y - T(r) - Z(s, u)}{s^2} = 0,$$

which leads to (2.10).

9. Using (2.10),

$$\frac{\partial^2}{\partial s^2}\left(\frac{Y - T(r) - Z(s, u)}{s}\right) = -\frac{1}{s}\frac{\partial^2 Z(s, u)}{\partial s^2} < 0$$

from (2.5). This implies that function $(Y - T(r) - Z(s, u))/s$ is strictly concave in s, and hence the first-order condition (2.10) gives the necessary and sufficient condition for optimal s.

10. For the actual calculation, see Appendix C.1.
11. More generally, the concept of bid rent is useful in any market where buyers choose one good (or at most a few) from a family of highly substitutable goods. Examples are automobiles and housing.
12. Note that under each value of E, the equation $E = z + \Psi(r, u)s$ represents an expenditure line (i.e., budget line), which is parallel to line AC in Figure 2.2. This expenditure line shifts upward with increasing E. Hence, $Y - T(r) = z + \Psi(r, u)s$ gives the lowest expenditure line under which utility level u is attainable.
13. See Appendix A.3 for a summary of important characteristics of demand functions and related functions.
14. For the envelope theorem, see Appendix A.2.
15. In Figure 2.5, bid rent curves are depicted as intercepting the r axis at different points. This is not always true, however. For example, in the case of a log-linear utility function (Example 2.1), we see that all bid rent curves intercept the r axis at distance $\bar{r}$ defined as $Y - T(\bar{r}) = 0$. A shared interception point occurs *if land is completely substitutable for the composite good;* that is, if the utility function from which the bid rent curves are derived is imbued with the feature that for every u, indifference curve $Z(s, u)$ approaches the s axis as $s \rightarrow \infty$. However, this minor difference in the shape

of bid rent curves does not cause any important difference in the subsequent analysis.

16. The terms *equilibrium location* and *optimal location* are often used interchangeably. Note that *optimal* simply means the best for the household, and it does not imply any social value judgment.
17. This statement is intuitively appealing, but not very precise. Since the optimal location of the household may not be unique, it is more accurate to call the equilibrium location an optimal location. Also, tangency must be interpreted broadly so as to include the possibility of a corner solution. Finally, if more than one bid rent curve is tangent to $R(r)$, we must choose the lowest among the curves.
18. We may assume that the residential choice behavior of household i is described as

$$\max_{r,z,s} U_i(z, s), \qquad \text{subject to} \quad z + R(r)s = Y_i - T_i(r)$$

and that of household j as

$$\max_{r,z,s} U_j(z, s), \qquad \text{subject to} \quad z + R(r)s = Y_j - T_j(r),$$

where U_i, Y_i, T_i are, respectively, utility function, income, and transport cost function of household i, and U_j, Y_j, T_j are those of j. Then we can derive the bid rent function $\Psi_i(r, u)$ of household i and $\Psi_j(r, u)$ of household j as explained in Section 2.3. However, the following rules (including Rule 2.1) are valid regardless of the specifications of residential choice behaviors from which bid rent functions have been derived. Hence, we simply assume that these bid rent functions have been derived from some residential choice models.

19. An exception may occur when $R(r)$ is kinked at x. In this case both households may possibly reside at x. But for any shape of market rent curve, it never happens that the household i with steeper equilibrium bid rent curve resides to the right of household j.
20. In order for one to say "if and only if," the following condition must be changed as follows: Whenever $\Psi_i(x, u_i) = \Psi_j(x, u_j)$, then $-\partial\Psi_i(r, u_i)/\partial r > -\partial\Psi_j(r, u_j)/\partial r$ at $r = x$, or $\partial\Psi_i(r, u_i)/\partial r = \partial\Psi_j(r, u_i)/\partial r$ and $\partial^2\Psi_i(r, u_i)/\partial r^2 < \partial^2\Psi_j(r, u_j)/\partial r^2$ at $r = x$.
21. For other examples, see Sections 2.5.1 and 2.5.2.
22. This result depends critically on the assumptions that all households have the same utility function and that transport costs are independent of income. A completely reversed spatial pattern can be observed in many European, Latin American, and Asian cities. In the United States as well, luxury apartments and townhouses are often found near the urban center. See Alonso (1964, Ch. 6), Muth (1969), and Wheaton (1977) for empirical studies of household location. These observations suggest that factors other than income, such as the time cost of commuting, family structure, externalities,

and dynamic factors, also affect residential choices and spatial patterns. These factors will be introduced one by one in the rest of the book.

23. In the following, we assume that t_w is always positive at the optimal choice (i.e., the household is not living retired); and hence we neglect the non-negativity constraint on t_w.
24. Specifically, Assumption 2.1 is changed as follows: The utility function is continuous and increasing at all $z > 0$, $s > 0$, and $t_l > 0$; and all indifference surfaces are strictly convex and smooth, and do not cut axes. Assumption 2.2 is simply changed as $a > 0$, $b > 0$. Assumption 2.3 remains as it is. Finally, it is assumed that the utility function is twice continuously differentiable, having no singular point.
25. The price of leisure time means the opportunity cost of leisure time. In our model, of course, it happens to be $P_l = W$. Here, we treat the price of leisure time as a parameter represented by P_l.
26. This can easily be seen because the two conditions of (2.47) also represent the optimality conditions for the problem (2.52) with $R = \Psi(r, u)$, $P_l = W$, and $I = I(r)$. Similar arguments apply to identity (2.55).
27. Since the transport cost function $T(r) = ar + Wbr$ is linear, Property 2.2 also holds trivially.
28. $(\partial T'/\partial W)(W/T') = (\partial T'/T')/(\partial W/W)$, which represents the percent change in marginal transport cost with respect to the percent increase in wage rate. Similarly, $(\partial S/\partial W)(W/S) = (\partial S/S)/(\partial W/W)$, which represents the percent change in lot size with respect to the percent increase in wage rate.
29. From (2.53), $S(r, u) = \hat{s}(\Psi(r, u), W, I(r))$, and $P_l = W$ by definition. Hence,

$$\left.\frac{\partial S}{\partial W}\frac{W}{S}\right|_{d\Psi=0} = \left(\frac{\partial \hat{s}}{\partial I}\frac{\partial I(r)}{\partial W} + \frac{\partial \hat{s}}{\partial P_l}\frac{\partial P_l}{\partial W}\right)\frac{W}{\hat{s}} = \left(\frac{\partial \hat{s}}{\partial I}(\bar{t} - br) + \frac{\partial \hat{s}}{\partial P_l}\right)\frac{W}{\hat{s}}$$

$$= \frac{\partial \hat{s}}{\partial I}\frac{I_w(r)}{\hat{s}} + \frac{\partial \hat{s}}{\partial P_l}\frac{W}{\hat{s}} = \left(\frac{\partial \hat{s}}{\partial I}\frac{I(r)}{\hat{s}}\right)\frac{I_w(r)}{I(r)} + \frac{\partial \hat{s}}{\partial P_l}\frac{P_l}{\hat{s}}.$$

30. What we can observe in the market is not η, but the *realized-net-income elasticity of lot size* defined as

$$\eta_R = \frac{\partial \hat{s}}{\partial I_R(r)}\frac{I_R(r)}{\hat{s}},$$

where $I_R(r)$ is the realized net income at location r given as $I_R(r) = I(r) - Wt_l(r, u)$. The relation between η and η_R can be obtained as follows: Let $\hat{t}_l(R, P_l, I)$ be the ordinary demand for leisure time, which is obtained from the solution of the utility-maximization problem of (2.52). Then it immediately follows that $t_l(r, u) = \hat{t}_l(\Psi(r, u), W, I(r))$, and hence $I_R(r) = I(r) - W\hat{t}_l(\Psi(r, u), W, I(r))$. So

$$\frac{\partial \hat{s}}{\partial I} = \frac{\partial \hat{s}}{\partial I_R}\frac{\partial I_R}{\partial I} = \frac{\partial \hat{s}}{\partial I_R}\left(1 - W\frac{\partial \hat{t}_l}{\partial I}\right).$$

Hence,

$$\eta = \frac{\partial \hat{s}}{\partial I}\frac{I(r)}{\hat{s}} = \frac{\partial \hat{s}}{\partial I_{\mathrm{R}}}\left(1 - W\frac{\partial \hat{t}_1}{\hat{s}}\right)\frac{I(r)}{\hat{s}}$$

$$= \frac{\partial \hat{s}}{\partial I_{\mathrm{R}}}\frac{I_{\mathrm{R}}(r)}{\hat{s}}\left(1 - W\frac{\partial \hat{t}_1}{\partial I}\right)\frac{I(r)}{I_{\mathrm{R}}(r)} = \eta_{\mathrm{R}}\left(1 - W\frac{\partial \hat{t}_1}{\partial I}\right)\left(1 + W\frac{\hat{t}_1}{I_{\mathrm{R}}(r)}\right).$$

That is,

$$\eta = \eta_{\mathrm{R}}\left(1 - W\frac{\partial \hat{t}_1}{\partial I}\right)\left(1 + W\frac{\hat{t}_1}{I_{\mathrm{R}}(r)}\right).$$

31. When this assumption does not hold, we must read Propositions 2.2 and 2.3 with care. For this point, see note 33.
32. This simplifying assumption is often adopted in urban economics (e.g., Beckmann 1974; Henderson 1977; Hochman and Ofek 1977).
33. When η and ε are not constant, we must read, e.g., (i) as follows: "(i) if $\eta + \varepsilon > 1$ *in the relevant range of the analysis,* the equilibrium location of. . . ." The same note applies to Proposition 2.3.
34. E.g., Altmann and DeSalvo (1981) estimate that for the period 1960–75, the value of the ratio a/bW for an urban household with average income was equal to 0.9. Mills (1972a, p. 85) uses a value of $a/bW = 0.6$. It is reasonable to assume that this ratio is even greater now since the oil price increases in 1973.
35. An example is the case of the log-linear utility function (Example 2.3), for which $\eta = 1$ and $\varepsilon = 0$. In fact, from (2.49), $-\Psi_r = I'(r)\Psi(r, u)/\beta I(r) = T'(r)\Psi(r, u)/\beta I(r) = (a + Wb)\Psi(r, u)/\beta I(r)$. So assuming $Y_{\mathrm{N}} = 0$,

$$-\frac{\partial \Psi_r}{\partial W}\bigg|_{d\Psi=0} = -\frac{a\bar{t}\Psi(r, u)}{\beta I(r)^2} < 0.$$

36. The elasticity of a/bW in W is -1, while the elasticity of $I_{\mathrm{w}}(r)/I(r)$ in W is $-x(W)/(1 - x(W))$, where $x(W) = ar/W(t - br)$. If we use parameter values from Altmann and DeSalvo (1981), we have $b = 1$ (round trip)/35 miles/hour $= 1/17.5$ (miles/hours), and $a = 1$ (round trip) $\times$ 4.61 (cents/mile $\cdot$ car) $= 0.0922$ (dollars/mile $\cdot$ car). Let us set $\bar{t}$ equal to 24 hours and r equal to 50 miles, which is more than the radius of the largest city today. Then the elasticity of $I_{\mathrm{w}}(r)/I(r)$ in W is $0.22/(W - 0.22)$, which is close to zero under any reasonable value of wage rate (dollars/hour) in the United States. Similarly, $I_{\mathrm{w}}(0)/I(0) - I_{\mathrm{w}}(50)/I(50) \doteqdot 1 - 1/(1 - 4.6/21W)$, which is also near zero for U.S. wage rates.
37. If we use parameter values from Altmann and DeSalvo (1981) once again, then $\hat{W} = (a/b)(\eta + \varepsilon)/(1 - (\eta + \varepsilon)) = \$1.61(\eta + \varepsilon)/(1 - (\eta + \varepsilon))$, and $\eta_{\mathrm{R}} = 0.875$. The last equation in note 30 suggests that η will be close to η_{R}. Hence, if we assume that $\eta = \eta_{\mathrm{R}} = 0.875$ and $\varepsilon = 0$, we have $\hat{W} = \$11.27$/hour. So the annual wage income $= \$11.27 \times 40$ hours/week $\times$

50 weeks = \$22,540/year · worker. If we adjust this number by average number of workers per household and by nonwage incomes, we obtain a considerably higher value than mean urban household income, which was \$12,577 in 1970.

38. Recent studies in the United States indicate that the wage elasticity of lot size, $\eta + \varepsilon$, may be considerably less than unity. Sample values from the literature for the realized-gross-income elasticity of housing are 0.75 cited by Muth (1971), 0.5 cited by Carliner (1973), and 0.75 cited by Polinsky (1977). Wheaton (1977) estimates the realized-gross-income elasticity of land to be 0.25. Since the value of ε will be close to zero, these numbers suggest that $\eta + \varepsilon$ may be considerably less than unity.
39. This is the point emphasized by Muth (1969).
40. When (2.66) and (2.68) are combined, the model represents an extension of Beckmann (1973) in which pecuniary commuting cost has been added.
41. From the first equation of (2.72), $q = F(L, K)s/L = F(s, Ks/L)$ (from the assumption of constant returns to scale) $= F(s, (kF(L, K)/q)(s/L))$ [from the second equation of (2.72)] $= F(s, (F(L, K)/Lq)(ks)) = F(s, (1/s)(ks))$ $= F(s, k)$.
42. Mathematically, this reduced model can be considered to be a special case of the basic model. That is, let us put $c = z + k$, and define $U(c, s) = \max_{z,k}\{U(z, F(s, k)) \mid z + k = c\}$. Then (2.75) is equivalent to the following: $\max_{r,c,s} U(c, s)$, subject to $c + R(r)s = Y - T(r)$. If we further replace c with z, we have the basic model.
43. In order to derive Propositions 2.2–2.4 from the Muth model, we must, of course, replace (2.70) with (2.42) or (2.65), in which s and $R(r)$ are replaced by q and $R_H(r)$, respectively.

CHAPTER 3

Equilibrium land use and optimal land use: single household type

3.1 Introduction

We have already examined how an individual household chooses a location in the city. Every household will take the market rent curve as given and seek the most desirable location, without concern for others. The next question that naturally arises concerns the overall balance of demand and supply for land, taking account of all the households' and landowners' decisions. Specifically, is consistency among decisions assured? What land use patterns are generated in the context of an urban land market?

These questions lead to two concepts: equilibrium and optimal land use. The concept of *competitive equilibrium* land use refers to the situation in which the decisions of all individuals made under a given land rent curve are mutually consistent; in particular, equality between demand and supply for land is achieved everywhere. However, the fact that an urban land market is in equilibrium does not necessarily imply that the resulting spatial structure is desirable. Therefore, it is also important to define *optimal allocations* of land within a monocentric framework and to study the relationships between equilibrium and optimal land use.

This chapter begins to explore these two concepts. It deals with a simple case in which all households are assumed to be identical. It also introduces the *boundary rent curve,* which will be a useful tool in much of the subsequent analysis. The chapter begins by introducing an alternative expression of bid rent functions that is more convenient for the purposes of this chapter. Then we examine equilibrium land use in four different situations, described according to whether the city is open or closed and whether land is owned by absentee landlords or by a city government. After establishing the existence and uniqueness of competitive equilibrium, we consider optimal land allocations, in the framework of the Herbert–Stevens model. Here we also introduce the *compensated equilibrium*. We show that mathematical conditions for the optimal allocation coincide with market conditions for compensated equilibrium, and also establish the existence and uniqueness of optimal allocation. Next, we examine the relationship between the competitive equilibrium and optimal land use, and show that (a) competitive equilibria are always efficient (*first welfare theorem*), and (b) any efficient allocation can be achieved through the competitive market by the choice of appropriate income taxes or subsidies (*second welfare theorem*). We then analyze the effect on equilibrium land use of changes in exogenous parameters such as agricultural rent, population, transport costs, household income, land tax, and zoning. Finally, we return to the Muth model of the housing industry and examine the change in land use intensity, or the height of building, in the city.

3.2 A preliminary analysis: alternative expressions of bid rent functions

Equation (2.7) defines the bid rent as a function of distance r and utility level u. When income Y is fixed, this is a convenient expression. However, in the study of equilibrium land use and optimal land use, the income of each household may change because of taxes and subsidies. Hence, it is more convenient to express the bid rent and lot size as functions of the net income and utility level.

To this end, let us recall the basic model (2.1) of residential choice, and return to Figure 2.2. This figure suggests that the basic determinants of bid rent $\Psi(r, u)$ are the net income $Y - T(r)$ and utility level u; the distance r affects the bid rent only indirectly, through the change in the net income. Considering this fact, it is theoretically convenient to introduce a function $\psi(I, u)$ that defines the bid rent as a function of net income I and utility level u. This can be achieved by replacing $Y - T(r)$ with I in (2.7) or (2.8), and we have

$$\psi(I, u) = \max_{z,s} \left\{ \frac{I - z}{s} \,\middle|\, U(z, s) = u \right\}, \tag{3.1}$$

or

$$\psi(I, u) = \max_{s} \frac{I - Z(s, u)}{s}. \tag{3.2}$$

Solving either (3.1) or (3.2), we obtain the bid-max lot size $s(I, u)$ as a function of net income I and utility level u.[1] When the distinction is necessary, we call $\Psi(r, u)$ and $S(r, u)$ the *Alonso* bid rent and bid-max lot size functions and $\psi(I, u)$ and $s(I, u)$ the *Solow* functions (see Table 2.1).

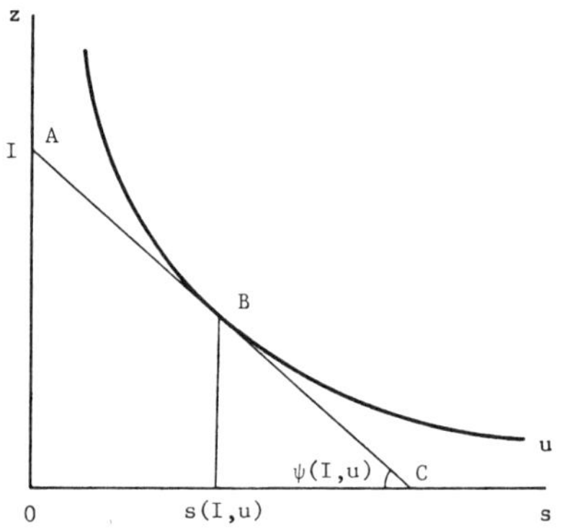

Figure 3.1. Bid rent $\psi(I, u)$ and bid-max lot size $s(I, u)$.

Graphically, as depicted in Figure 3.1, bid rent $\psi(I, u)$ is given by the slope of the budget line under net income I, which is just tangent to indifference curve u. Notice that when $I = Y - T(r)$, the budget line ABC of Figure 3.1 coincides with that of Figure 2.2. Hence, comparing the two figures, it is apparent that

$$\Psi(r, u) \equiv \psi(Y - T(r), u), \tag{3.3}$$

$$S(r, u) \equiv s(Y - T(r), u). \tag{3.4}$$

That is, the Alonso bid rent at distance r equals the Solow bid rent under the net income $Y - T(r)$, and the Alonso bid-max lot size at distance r equals the Solow bid-max lot size under the net income $Y - T(r)$.

Next, by setting $Y - T(r) = I$, from (2.19), (2.25), (3.3), and (3.4), we can obtain the following identities:

$$s(I, u) \equiv \hat{s}(\psi(I, u), I) \equiv \tilde{s}(\psi(I, u), u). \tag{3.5}$$

Similarly, by setting $Y - T(r) = I$, from (2.20), (2.26), and (3.3), we obtain the following identities:

$$u \equiv V(\psi(I, u), I), \tag{3.6}$$

$$I \equiv E(\psi(I, u), u). \tag{3.7}$$

Equation (3.6) implies that the Solow bid rent ψ is the inverse function of the indirect utility function with respect to land rent R. From (3.7), ψ is also the inverse function of the expenditure function with respect to R.

As with Property 2.1, under Assumptions 2.1 and 2.3 we can readily obtain the following characteristics of Solow functions:

Property 3.1

(i) Bid rent $\psi(I, u)$ is continuously increasing in I and continuously decreasing in u (until ψ becomes zero).

(ii) Bid-max lot size $s(I, u)$ is continuously decreasing in I and continuously increasing in u (until s becomes infinite).

That is, applying the envelope theorem to (3.2) and using (2.4), we have

$$\frac{\partial \psi}{\partial I} = \frac{1}{s} > 0, \qquad \frac{\partial \psi}{\partial u} = -\frac{1}{s}\frac{\partial Z}{\partial u} < 0.$$

Therefore, using identity (3.5) we have[2]

$$\frac{\partial s}{\partial I} = \frac{\partial \tilde{s}}{\partial R}\frac{\partial \psi}{\partial I} < 0, \qquad \frac{\partial s}{\partial u} = \frac{\partial \hat{s}}{\partial R}\frac{\partial \psi}{\partial u} > 0.$$

Note also that Properties 2.1, 2.2, and 2.4 and Rule 2.1 hold true when functions $\Psi(r, u)$ and $S(r, u)$ are replaced by $\psi(Y - T(r), u)$ and $s(Y - T(r), u)$. Hence, we freely use these results in the context of the new notation.

Because of identities (3.3) and (3.4), it is a matter of convenience whether we use Alonso functions Ψ and S or Solow functions ψ and s. In Sections 3.3–3.5, since their objective is the comparison of different models, it turns out that Solow functions are more convenient. In Sections 3.6 and 3.7, however, we use Alonso functions for brevity of notation.

3.3 Equilibrium land use

Equilibrium land use describes a state of the urban system that shows no propensity to change. Essential to the nature of equilibrium land use is the *competitive land market.* When land markets are competitive, in the economic sense of the word, all participants, households and landowners alike, have *perfect information* about land rents throughout the city. Furthermore, no participant or select group of participants is able to exercise monopolistic power; this means that *everyone takes land rents in the city as given*. Under these idealized conditions, an equilibrium land use describes a situation in which the land market clears everywhere and in which no household or land owner is motivated to annul prior decisions. Since the environment of the city is assumed to remain the same through time, such an equilibrium can continue forever and may therefore be thought of as a *stationary-state equilibrium*.

In the literature, it is traditional to classify market models as *closed-city models* and *open-city models*. In the closed-city model, the population of the city is exogenous. In the open-city model, households are assumed to be able to move costlessly across the city boundary; hence, the utility of residents equals that of the rest of the economy, which is exogenously fixed, while the population of the city is determined endogenously. Although the emphasis here will be on the closed-city model because it is more fundamental from a theoretical point of view, both will be developed.

The closed-city model is a useful conceptual device for analyzing urban land use in large cities or "average cities" of developed countries. The open-city model, however, better describes urban conditions in developing countries that have surplus labor in rural areas. In the latter case, rural life often establishes the base utility level of the economy.

In both models, we must also specify the form of landownership. Two popular specifications are the *absentee ownership model,* in which land is owned by absentee landlords, and the *public ownership model,* in which the revenue from land is equally shared among city residents. This section will examine the four cases in turn. As noted before, we assume that all households in the economy are identical. We denote by $L(r)$ the *land distribution* in the city [i.e., the amount of land available for housing between distance r and $r + dr$ equals $L(r)dr$]. We make the following assumption:

> ***Assumption 3.1.*** $L(r)$ is continuous for all $r \geq 0$ and positive at each $r > 0$.

Whenever differential calculi are involved, we also assume that $L(r)$ is continuously differentiable in r. In addition, we also assume that land not occupied by households is used for agriculture, yielding a constant rent R_A. In terms of the von Thünen model, R_A represents the *agricultural bid rent.*[3]

Case 1 is the *closed-city model under absentee landownership (CCA model).* There are N identical households in the city. We assume that households behave according to the basic model of (2.1) and that the household income Y is given exogenously. Assumptions 2.1–2.3 are also taken to hold here. Then the bid rent function $\psi(Y - T(r), u)$ and bid-max lot size function $s(Y - T(r), u)$ can be derived as explained before; and these functions hold those characteristics summarized in Properties 2.1, 2.2, and 2.4.

In order to describe the conditions for equilibrium land use, the first observation is as follows: Since all households are assumed to be the same, *in equilibrium all households must achieve the same maximum utility level independent of location.* If this were not so, some household could increase its utility level by imitating the residential choice of an identical household with a higher utility. Thus, an incentive to make a new decision would exist, and hence such a situation could not be an equilibrium.

We call the common maximum utility achieved in equilibrium the *equilibrium utility* and denote it by u^*. Let $R(r)$ be the market rent curve prevailing in equilibrium. Then in terms of the indirect utility function defined in the previous chapter, u^* and $R(r)$ have the following relationship:

$$u^* = \max_r V(R(r), Y - T(r)). \tag{3.8}$$

That is, the equilibrium utility u^* is the maximum utility attainable in the city under the market rent curve $R(r)$. Next, let $n(r)$ be the *household distribution* in equilibrium [i.e., the number of households between distance r and $r + dr$ equals $n(r)\,dr$].[4] Suppose $n(r) > 0$ at some r. This implies that some households actually choose distance r as their optimal location. Then the condition of individual location equilibrium (Rule 2.1) requires the following relations to hold between market rent curve $R(r)$ and equilibrium bid rent curve $\psi(Y - T(r), u^*)$:

$$R(r) = \psi(Y - T(r), u^*) \quad \text{if} \quad n(r) > 0, \tag{3.9}$$

$$R(r) \geq \psi(Y - T(r), u^*) \quad \text{for all} \quad r. \tag{3.10}$$

From identity (3.6), $u^* = V(\psi(Y - T(r), u^*), Y - T(r))$. Thus, condition (3.9) ensures that equilibrium utility u^* is realized when $R(r)$ equals $\psi(Y - T(r), u^*)$. From Property 2.4, $R(r) \geq \psi(Y - T(r), u^*)$ means $V(R(r), Y - T(r)) \leq V(\psi(Y - T(r), u^*), Y - T(r)) = u^*$. Hence, condition (3.10) ensures that under the market rent curve $R(r)$, households can nowhere achieve a higher utility than u^*. Similarly, equilibrium in agricultural activity requires that

$$R(r) = R_A \quad \text{in the agricultural area}, \tag{3.11}$$

$$R(r) \geq R_A \quad \text{for all} \quad r. \tag{3.12}$$

Condition (3.11) ensures that agricultural activity gets zero profit (i.e., normal profit) at r. And condition (3.12) ensures that agricultural activity does not get positive profits anywhere. In equilibrium, no vacant land can exist in areas with positive land rents.[5] Thus, all land must be occupied either by housing or by agricultural activity, and it follows from (3.9)–(3.12) that

$$R(r) = \max\{\psi(Y - T(r), u^*), R_A\} \quad \text{at each} \quad r. \tag{3.13}$$

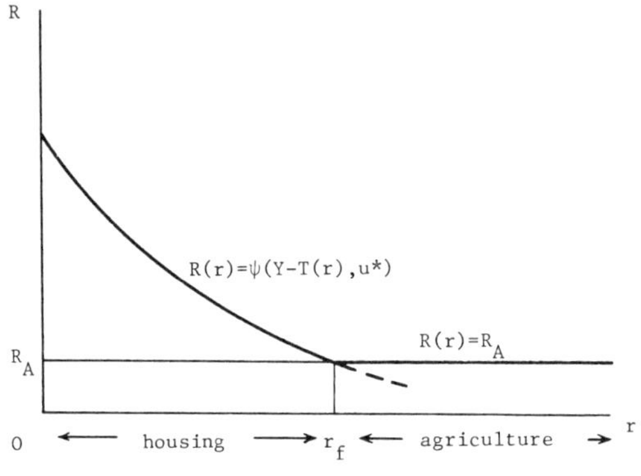

Figure 3.2. Competitive equilibrium land use pattern.

That is, *at each location the market land rent coincides with the maximum of the equilibrium bid rent and the agricultural rent*. As we can see from Figure 3.2, geometrically this means that *the market rent curve equals the upper envelope of the equilibrium bid rent curve and the agricultural rent line*. Since the equilibrium bid rent curve $\psi(Y - T(r), u^*)$ is decreasing in r, this implies that

$$R(r) = \begin{cases} \psi(Y - T(r), u^*) & \text{for} \quad r \leq r_f, \\ R_A & \text{for} \quad r \geq r_f, \end{cases} \tag{3.14}$$

where r_f is the *urban fringe distance*. In Figure 3.2, land to the left of r_f is used for housing, and that to the right is used for agriculture. In other words, *in equilibrium, each location is occupied by the activity with the highest (equilibrium) bid rent*.

At each distance $r \leq r_f$, the equilibrium lot size $s(r)$ for each household coincides with the bid-max lot size $s(Y - T(r), u^*)$:

$$s(r) = s(Y - T(r), u^*) \qquad \text{for} \quad r \leq r_f. \tag{3.15}$$

Since no land is left vacant at any $r < r_f$, we have

$$n(r)s(Y - T(r), u^*) = L(r).$$

Although the above equality is not required to hold at r_f (i.e., some amount of land may be left for agriculture at r_f), for mathematical convenience we can assume that it also holds at r_f. Hence, the equilibrium household distribution is given as

$$n(r) = \begin{cases} L(r)/s(Y - T(r), u^*) & \text{for} \quad r \leq r_f, \\ 0 & \text{for} \quad r > r_f. \end{cases} \tag{3.16}$$

Then since N households reside in the city, the population constraint is stated as

$$\int_0^{r_f} \frac{L(r)}{s(Y - T(r), u^*)} dr = N. \tag{3.17}$$

In summary, $R(r)$, $n(r)$, $s(r)$, u^*, and r_f together represent an equilibrium land use for the CCA model if and only if conditions (3.14)–(3.17) are satisfied.[6] Two real unknowns are the equilibrium utility u^* and fringe distance r_f. They can be determined from (3.17) and the next boundary rent condition derived from (3.14):

$$\psi(Y - T(r_f), u^*) = R_A . \tag{3.18}$$

Since the equilibrium bid rent curve $\psi(Y - T(r), u^*)$ is decreasing in r, from (3.14) it follows that *the market rent curve $R(r)$ is necessarily decreasing in r up to the urban fringe*. We can also conclude from Property 2.2 that *if the transport cost function $T(r)$ is linear or concave in r, then the market rent curve is strictly convex up to the urban fringe*. Let $\rho(r)$ be the *household density* (i.e., the number of households per unit of land) at distance r. Then, from (3.16) we have

$$\rho(r) = \frac{n(r)}{L(r)} = \begin{cases} 1/s(Y - T(r), u^*) & \text{for} \quad r \leq r_f, \\ 0 & \text{for} \quad r > r_f. \end{cases} \tag{3.19}$$

From Property 2.1, *lot size curve $s(Y - T(r), u^*)$ is increasing in r*. Hence, *the household density curve is decreasing in r up to the urban fringe*.

Now, the existence and uniqueness of the equilibrium solution can be demonstrated by using the concept of the *boundary rent curve*. Under each value of u, we solve the next equation for b,

$$\int_0^{b} \frac{L(r)}{s(Y - T(r), u)} dr = N, \tag{3.20}$$

and obtain the *outer boundary function $b(u)$* of the residential area. For each given u, $b(u)$ marks a distance on the corresponding bid rent curve $\psi(Y - T(r), u)$ such as point A in Figure 3.3. By changing u, we can obtain a curve $\hat{R}(r)$, called the *boundary rent curve,* as depicted in Figure 3.3. If the inverse function of $r = b(u)$ is denoted by $u = U(r)$, the boundary rent curve can be defined as

$$\hat{R}(r) = \psi(Y - T(r), U(r)). \tag{3.21}$$

By definition, $\hat{R}(r)$ represents a hypothetical market land rent at r such that if all N households are to be accommodated within distance r in

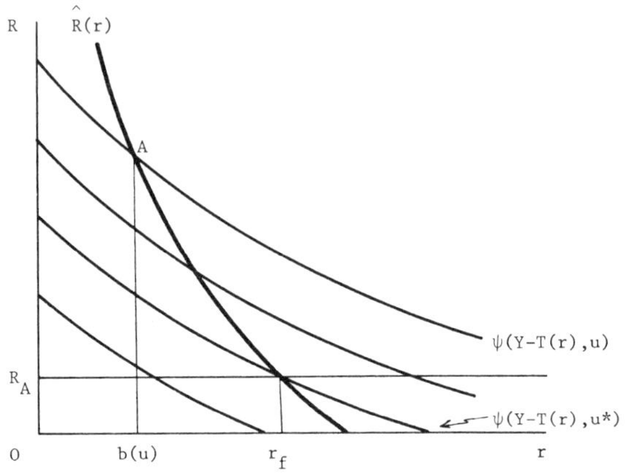

Figure 3.3. Boundary rent curve $\hat{R}(r)$ for equilibrium land use.

equilibrium, the market land rent at r must be equal to $\hat{R}(r)$. Suppose we have obtained the curve $\hat{R}(r)$. Then as depicted in Figure 3.3, the equilibrium residential boundary, or the urban fringe r_f, is given by the point at which curve $\hat{R}(r)$ meets the agricultural rent line:

$$\hat{R}(r_f) = R_A . \tag{3.22}$$

Once r_f has been determined, the equilibrium utility u^* can be obtained from the next relationship:

$$\psi(Y - T(r_f), u^*) = R_A . \tag{3.23}$$

That is, u^* is the utility level corresponding to the bid rent curve that passes through the intersection of the boundary rent curve $\hat{R}(r)$ and the agricultural rent line. By construction, this pair (r_f, u^*) satisfies the equilibrium conditions (3.17) and (3.18) simultaneously. Under Assumptions 2.1–2.3 and 3.1, it is not difficult to show that the boundary rent curve $\hat{R}(r)$ is continuously decreasing in r, becomes zero as r approaches a certain finite distance, and becomes infinitely high as r approaches zero.[7] Therefore, as demonstrated in Figure 3.3, we can conclude the following:

Proposition 3.1. Under any given income $Y > T(0)$ and population $N > 0$, there exists a unique equilibrium for the CCA model.

In closing the discussion of case 1, we present an example of equilibrium land use for case 1, which suggests that equations (3.17) and (3.18) can be explicitly solved only in very special instances. We have developed the boundary rent curve approach in order to explore, without tedious computation, the essential characteristics of equilibrium solutions.

Example 3.1. Suppose we have the log-linear utility function of Example 2.1. Then equations (3.17) and (3.18) can be rewritten as follows:

$$\int_0^{r_f} \alpha^{\alpha/\beta}(Y - T(r))^{\alpha/\beta} e^{-u^*/\beta} L(r)\, dr = N, \tag{3.24}$$

$$\alpha^{\alpha/\beta}\beta(Y - T(r_f))^{1/\beta} e^{-u^*/\beta} = R_A. \tag{3.25}$$

As a special case, assume that

$$R_A = 0, \qquad T(r) = ar, \qquad \alpha = \beta = \tfrac{1}{2}, \qquad L(r) = \theta r^{\lambda},$$

where a, θ, and λ are constants, and $a, \theta > 0$ (e.g., if $\theta = 2\pi$ and $\lambda = 1$, $L(r) = 2\pi r$, which means a circular city). From (3.25), $r_f = Y/a$, and hence from (3.24),

$$e^{-u^*/\beta} = 2(\lambda + 1)(\lambda + 2)a^{\lambda+1}N/(\theta Y^{\lambda+2}).$$

Thus, from (2.13) and (2.14), for $r \leq r_f = Y/a$,

$$\begin{aligned} R(r) = \Psi(r, u^*) &= \frac{(\lambda + 1)(\lambda + 2)a^{\lambda+1}}{2\theta} \frac{(Y - ar)^2}{Y^{\lambda+2}} N, \\ s(r) = S(r, u^*) &= \frac{\theta}{(\lambda + 1)(\lambda + 2)a^{\lambda+1}} \frac{Y^{\lambda+2}}{Y - ar} \frac{1}{N}. \end{aligned} \tag{3.26}$$

Case 2 describes the *open-city model under absentee landownership (OCA model)*. For this, let us assume that each household that chooses to reside in the city receives a constant income Y and behaves according to the basic model of (2.1).[8] Then the equilibrium is trivially simple to obtain. Given income Y, let $\tilde{u}(Y)$ be the *supreme utility level* defined from the relation

$$\psi(Y - T(0), \tilde{u}(Y)) = R_A. \tag{3.27}$$

If equation (3.27) does not have a finite solution for $\tilde{u}(Y)$ [i.e., if $Y \leq T(0)$], we define $\tilde{u}(Y) = -\infty$. Then if the national utility level is given by a constant u, the urban fringe distance r_f can be determined from the relation

$$\psi(Y - T(r_f), u) = R_A \qquad \text{if} \quad u < \tilde{u}(Y), \tag{3.28}$$

$$r_f = 0 \qquad \text{if} \quad u \geq \tilde{u}(Y). \tag{3.29}$$

Having obtained r_f, we can obtain the equilibrium land rent curve as

$$R(r) = \begin{cases} \psi(Y - T(r), u) & \text{for} \quad r \leq r_f, \\ R_A & \text{for} \quad r \geq r_f, \end{cases} \tag{3.30}$$

the equilibrium lot size as

$$s(r) = s(Y - T(r), u) \qquad \text{for} \quad r \leq r_f, \tag{3.31}$$

and the equilibrium household distribution as

$$n(r) = \begin{cases} L(r)/s(Y - T(r), u) & \text{for} \quad r \leq r_f, \\ 0 & \text{for} \quad r > r_f. \end{cases} \tag{3.32}$$

Finally, the equilibrium population N^* can be obtained as

$$N^* = \int_0^{r_f} \frac{L(r)}{s(Y - T(r), u)} dr. \tag{3.33}$$

Note that given any Y, equation (3.27) uniquely defines the supreme utility level $\tilde{u}(Y)$, and equations (3.28) and (3.29) in turn uniquely determine r_f. Therefore, we can conclude the following:

> ***Proposition 3.2.*** Under any given household income $Y > 0$ and national utility u, there exists a unique equilibrium for the OCA model. The equilibrium population of the city is positive if and only if $u < \tilde{u}(Y)$.

Next for case 3 let us consider the *closed-city model under public land-ownership (CCP model)*. The city residents are assumed to form a government, which rents the land for the city from rural landlords at agricultural rent R_A. The city government, in turn, subleases the land to city residents at the competitively determined rent $R(r)$ at each location. Define the *total differential rent* (TDR) from the city by

$$\text{TDR} = \int_0^{r_f} (R(r) - R_A)L(r)\, dr. \tag{3.34}$$

Assume that there are N identical households in the city. Then the income of each household is its nonland income Y^0 plus a share of differential land rent, TDR/N. Thus, the residential choice behavior of each household can be formulated as follows:

$$\max_{r,z,s} U(z, s), \qquad \text{subject to} \quad z + R(r)s = Y^0 + (\text{TDR}/N) - T(r). \tag{3.35}$$

Since the equilibrium value of TDR is unknown, let us represent it by TDR*. Then by substituting $Y^0 + (\text{TDR}^*/N) - T(r)$ for $Y - T(r)$, from the equilibrium conditions (3.14)–(3.17) of the CCA model we can obtain the equilibrium conditions of the CCP model as follows:

$$R(r) = \begin{cases} \psi(Y^0 + \mathrm{TDR}^*/N - T(r), u^*) & \text{for } r \le r_f, \\ R_A & \text{for } r \ge r_f, \end{cases} \tag{3.36}$$

$$s(r) = s(Y^0 + \mathrm{TDR}^*/N - T(r), u^*) \quad \text{for } r \le r_f, \tag{3.37}$$

$$n(r) = \begin{cases} L(r)/s(Y^0 + \mathrm{TDR}^*/N - T(r), u^*) & \text{for } r \le r_f, \\ 0 & \text{for } r > r_f, \end{cases} \tag{3.38}$$

$$\int_0^{r_f} L(r)/s(Y^0 + \mathrm{TDR}^*/N - T(r), u^*)\, dr = N. \tag{3.39}$$

Since TDR* is unknown, we cannot apply the boundary rent curve approach in order to examine the existence and uniqueness of the equilibrium. However, in Section 3.5, via the existence and uniqueness of the optimal land use we can show the following:

> ***Proposition 3.3.*** Under any nonland income $Y^0 > T(0)$ and population $N > 0$, there exists a unique equilibrium for the CCP model.

Case 4 is the *open-city model under public landownership (OCP model)*. As in case 3, each resident of the city gets a nonland income Y^0 plus a share of land rent TDR/N. The residential choice behavior of each household can be described, as before, by (3.35). However, both TDR and N are now unknown: The utility of residents is fixed at the national utility level u. Hence, by substituting N^* for N and u for u^* into equations (3.36)–(3.39), we can obtain the equilibrium conditions of the OCP model as follows:

$$R(r) = \begin{cases} \psi(Y^0 + \mathrm{TDR}^*/N^* - T(r), u) & \text{for } r \le r_f, \\ R_A & \text{for } r \ge r_f, \end{cases} \tag{3.40}$$

$$s(r) = s(Y^0 + \mathrm{TDR}^*/N^* - T(r), u) \quad \text{for } r \le r_f, \tag{3.41}$$

$$n(r) = \begin{cases} L(r)/s(Y^0 + \mathrm{TDR}^*/N^* - T(r), u) & \text{for } r \le r_f, \\ 0 & \text{for } r > r_f, \end{cases} \tag{3.42}$$

$$N^* = \int_0^{r_f} \frac{L(r)}{s(Y^0 + \mathrm{TDR}^*/N^* - T(r), u)}\, dr. \tag{3.43}$$

In Section 5.4, we will show the following:

> ***Proposition 3.4.*** Under any given nonland income $Y^0 > 0$ and national utility level u, there exists a unique equilibrium for the OCP model. The equilibrium population of the city is positive if and only if $u < \tilde{u}(Y^0)$.

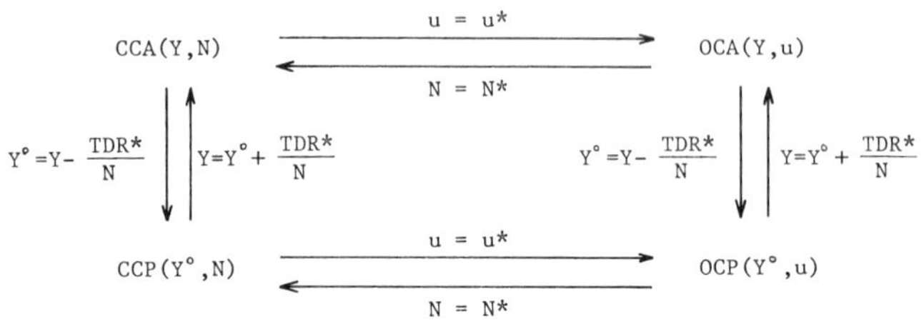

Figure 3.4. Relationships among four types of models.

We have introduced four types of equilibrium model. However, it is not difficult to observe that equilibrium land use patterns derived from the four types are all essentially the same. To make this point precise, let us introduce the following notation:

- CCA(Y, N): the CCA model under household income Y and population N, where $Y > T(0)$ and $N > 0$
- CCP(Y^0, N): the CCP model under nonland income Y^0 and population N, where $Y^0 > T(0)$ and $N > 0$
- OCA(Y, u): the OCA model under household income Y and national utility level u, where $Y > 0$ and $-\infty < u < \infty$
- OCP(Y^0, u): the OCP model under nonland income Y^0 and national utility level u, where $Y^0 > 0$ and $-\infty < u < \infty$

Then comparing equilibrium conditions for each pair of models, we can readily conclude as follows (see Figure 3.4):

Proposition 3.5. Let parameters Y, Y^0, N, and u be restricted such that $Y > T(0)$, $Y^0 > T(0)$, $N > 0$, $u < \tilde{u}(Y)$, and $u < \tilde{u}(Y^0)$.[9] Then we have the following:

(i) If u^* is the equilibrium utility of the CCA(Y, N) model [CCP(Y^0, N) model], then the solution of the CCA(Y, N) model [CCP(Y^0, N) model] is the solution of the OCA(Y, u^*) model [OCP(Y^0, u^*) model].[10]

(ii) Conversely, if N^* is the equilibrium population of the OCA(Y, u) model [OCP(Y^0, u) model], then the solution of the OCA(Y, u) model [OCP(Y^0, u) model] is the solution of the CCA(Y, N^*) model [CCP(Y^0, N^*) model].

(iii) If TDR* is the total differential rent at the solution of the CCA(Y, N) model [OCA(Y, u) model], then the solution of the CCA(Y, N) model [OCA(Y, u) model] is the solution of the CCP(Y − TDR*/N, N) model [OCP(Y − TDR*/N, u) model].

(iv) Conversely, if TDR* is the total differential rent at the solution of the CCP(Y^0, N) model [OCP(Y^0, u) model], then the solution of the CCP(Y^0, N) model [OCP(Y^0, u) model] is the solution of the CCA(Y^0 + TDR*/N, u) model [OCA(Y^0 + TDR*/N, u) model].

These relationships among the four types of model are summarized in Figure 3.4. For example, the arrow from CCA(Y, N) to OCA(Y, u) [from CCP(Y^0, N) to OCP(Y^0, u)] explains Proposition 3.5(i). Let us consider that each arrow in Figure 3.4 represents a mapping from one type of model to another. For example, the arrow labeled $u = u^*$ at the top center of Figure 3.4 represents a mapping from CCA models to OCA models such that if u^* is the equilibrium utility level of the CCA(Y, N) model, then the OCA(Y, u^*) model is associated with the CCA(Y, N) model; the domain of this mapping is $\{(Y, N) \mid Y > T(0), N > 0\}$, and its range $\{(Y, u) \mid Y > T(0), u < \tilde{u}(Y)\}$. Note that because of Propositions 3.1–3.4, each mapping is a well-defined, single-valued, and onto-mapping from one type of model to another. This implies, in particular, the following:

Proposition 3.6. Let parameters Y, Y^0, N, and u be restricted such that $Y > T(0)$, $Y^0 > T(0)$, $N > 0$, $u < \tilde{u}(Y)$, and $u < \tilde{u}(Y^0)$. Then the solution of any model of one type can also be obtained from an appropriate model of any other type. Hence, the four types of model have an identical set of solutions.

3.4 Optimal land use

Exactly what optimal land use is, of course, depends on how the objective function is specified. In spaceless economics, it is common to maximize a Benthamite social welfare function, which is the sum of utilities of individual households (an unweighted sum in the case of identical households). However, this is not the most convenient approach to land use problems, because the maximization of a Benthamite welfare function results in the assignment of different utility levels to identical households depending on their locations. Such a result is referred to as *Mirrlees' inequality* or *unequal treatment of equals* and is a unique phenomenon due to the nonconvexity introduced by space.[11] Since competitive markets treat all equals equally, it is clear that the maximization of a Benthamite welfare function is not the most appropriate approach to the investigation of the efficiency of land markets. A more convenient formulation of optimization problems for land use theory is the so-called Herbert–Stevens model (HS model). In this model, the objective is to maximize the surplus subject to a set of prespecified target utility levels for all household types. The model is designed so that its solution is always efficient, and all efficient allocations can be obtained by simply varying target utility levels.

In this section, we consider the HS model in the context of the closed city, where N identical households reside.[12] As before, the utility function of each household is given by $U(z, s)$, transport cost function by $T(r)$, and the land distribution function by $L(r)$. The land that is not occupied by households is used for agriculture, yielding a net revenue (or rent) R_A per unit of land. These functions, $U(z, s)$, $T(r)$, and $L(r)$, and constant R_A are assumed to be the same as those of the equilibrium models in Section 3.3. Hence, Assumptions 2.1–2.3 and 3.1 are also taken to be satisfied here. Since the utility function $U(z, s)$ is considered to be ordinal, without loss of generality we can assume that its range is from $-\infty$ to ∞:

$$\inf\{U(z, s) \mid z > 0, s > 0\} = -\infty, \qquad \sup\{U(z, s) \mid z > 0, s > 0\} = \infty. \tag{3.44}$$

Let us denote by $n(r)$ the number of households at distance r, by $(z(r), s(r))$ the consumption bundle by each household at r, and by r_f the urban fringe distance.

Suppose we choose a *target utility level* $\bar{u}$ and require that *regardless of their locations all households will attain this utility level*. This implies that each allocation, $(n(r), z(r), s(r); 0 \leq r \leq r_f)$, must satisfy the following restriction:

$$U(z(r), s(r)) = \bar{u} \qquad \text{if} \quad n(r) > 0.$$

Equivalently,

$$z(r) = Z(s(r), \bar{u}) \qquad \text{if} \quad n(r) > 0,$$

where $Z(s, \bar{u})$ is the solution of $\bar{u} = U(z, s)$ for z. Therefore, the *total cost* C under each allocation can be calculated as follows:

$$C = \text{transport costs} + \text{composite good costs} + \text{opportunity land costs}$$

$$= \int_0^{r_f} [T(r) + Z(s(r), \bar{u}) + R_A s(r)] n(r)\, dr. \tag{3.45}$$

Each allocation must also satisfy the following land and population constraints:

$$s(r)n(r) \leq L(r) \qquad \text{at each} \quad r \leq r_{\mathrm{f}}, \tag{3.46}$$

$$\int_0^{r_{\mathrm{f}}} n(r)\,dr = N. \tag{3.47}$$

The problem is to choose an allocation ($n(r)$, $s(r)$, r_{f}) that minimizes the total cost C subject to the land and population constraint:[13]

$$\min_{r_{\mathrm{f}}, n(r), s(r)} \quad C = \int_0^{r_{\mathrm{f}}} [T(r) + Z(s(r), \bar{u}) + R_{\mathrm{A}}s(r)]n(r)\,dr, \tag{3.48}$$

subject to constraints (3.46) and (3.47).

This problem can be more conveniently expressed in terms of surplus. If we assume that the per capita income of the city is given by Y^0, then the total income of the city is NY^0. Here Y^0 is assumed to be a fixed number determined independently of the residential land use pattern. Noting that $N = \int_0^{r_{\mathrm{f}}} n(r)\,dr$, we define *surplus* $\mathcal{S}$ from allocation ($n(r)$, $s(r)$, r_f) by

$$\begin{aligned} \mathcal{S} &= NY^0 - C \\ &= \int_0^{r_{\mathrm{f}}} (Y^0 - T(r) - Z(s(r), \bar{u}) - R_{\mathrm{A}}s(r))n(r)\,dr. \end{aligned} \tag{3.49}$$

Since NY^0 is assumed to be a constant, minimization of C is equivalent to maximization of $\mathcal{S}$, and the Herbert–Stevens model, HS(Y^0, $\bar{u}$, N), can be stated as follows:[14]

$$\max_{r_{\mathrm{f}}, n(r), s(r)} \quad \mathcal{S} = \int_0^{r_{\mathrm{f}}} (Y^0 - T(r) - Z(s(r), \bar{u}) - R_{\mathrm{A}}s(r))n(r)\,dr, \tag{3.50}$$

subject to constraints (3.46) and (3.47). Considering that $\mathcal{S}$ represents a benefit (or cost, if negative) for the rest of the economy, it is obvious that the solution to any HS model is efficient, and any efficient allocation under the equal-utility condition is a solution to some HS model.[15]

The next task is to obtain mathematical conditions for the solution to the HS model. For this, and also for examining the relationship between optimal land use and equilibrium land use in the next section, it is convenient to introduce here a new concept of market equilibrium, called *compensated equilibrium*. Let us recall the CCA(Y, N) model in Section 3.3 (case 1). In that model, the income of each household is fixed at a constant Y, and each household chooses its location and consumption bundle so as to maximize its utility. An equilibrium is reached when the land market clears everywhere and every household achieves the same maximum utility, which is endogenously determined. We can call this equilibrium an (ordinary) *competitive equilibrium*. In contrast, for the compensated equilibrium problem, we ask the following question: Suppose the government desires to achieve a certain fixed target utility $\bar{u}$ for all N households through the competitive land market. Although every household has the same pretax income Y^0, the government is free to impose a (lump-sum) income tax G on each household. Given an income tax G, the residential choice behavior of each household can be expressed as

$$\max_{r,z,s} U(z, s), \qquad \text{subject to} \quad z + R(r)s = Y^0 - G - T(r). \tag{3.51}$$

The question is, What income tax G (or income subsidy, if $G < 0$) will make the equilibrium utility just equal the target utility $\bar{u}$?

To answer this question, let us recall the Solow bid rent function $\psi(I, u)$ and bid-max lot size function $s(I, u)$ introduced in Section 3.2. Then since under our income tax G the net income at distance r equals $Y^0 - G - T(r)$, the bid rent and bid-max lot size at each distance r are given, respectively, as $\psi(Y^0 - G - T(r), u)$ and $s(Y^0 - G - T(r), u)$. From Property 3.1, we can readily conclude as follows:

Property 3.2

(i) $\psi(Y^0 - G - T(r), u)$ is continuously decreasing in r, G, and u (decreasing until ψ becomes zero).

(ii) $s(Y^0 - G - T(r), u)$ is continuously increasing in r, G, and u (increasing until s becomes infinite).

Now suppose $R(r)$, $n(r)$, $s(r)$, r_f, and G^* together represent a compensated equilibrium in which target utility $\bar{u}$ is achieved.[16] Then income tax G^* must be determined so that if some households reside at r [i.e., $n(r) > 0$], then the maximum utility attainable at r just equals the target utility $\bar{u}$, and nowhere can the maximum utility for households exceed the target utility $\bar{u}$:

$$\bar{u} = V(R(r), Y^0 - G^* - T(r)) \qquad \text{if} \quad n(r) > 0,$$

$$\bar{u} \geq V(R(r), Y^0 - G^* - T(r)) \qquad \text{for all} \quad r.$$

Hence, as with (3.9) and (3.10), it follows that

$$R(r) = \psi(Y^0 - G^* - T(r), \bar{u}) \qquad \text{if} \quad n(r) > 0,$$

$$R(r) \geq \psi(Y^0 - G^* - T(r), \bar{u}) \qquad \text{for all} \quad r.$$

Of course, relations (3.11) and (3.12) must be satisfied as before. Also, as before, bid rent $\psi(Y^0 - G^* - T(r), \bar{u})$ is decreasing in r. Therefore,

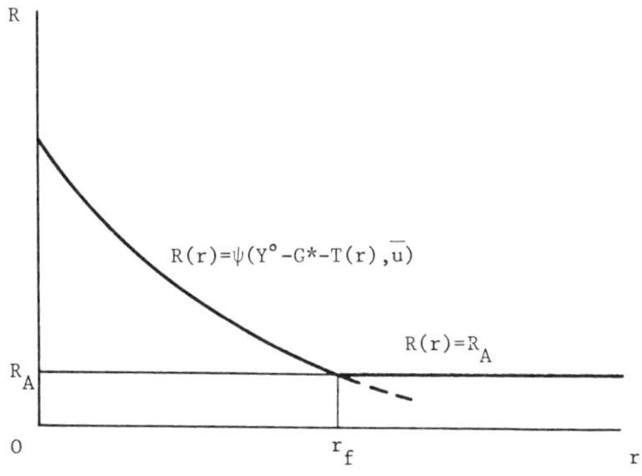

Figure 3.5. Compensated equilibrium/optimal land use pattern.

as with (3.14), we can obtain the following relationship:

$$R(r) = \begin{cases} \psi(Y^0 - G^* - T(r), \bar{u}) & \text{for} \quad r \leq r_f, \\ R_A & \text{for} \quad r \geq r_f. \end{cases} \tag{3.52}$$

Figure 3.5 depicts this relationship. By definition, the equilibrium lot size $s(r)$ equals the Marshallian demand for land, $\hat{s}(R(r), Y^0 - G^* - T(r))$. Hence, from relation (3.52) and from identity (3.5) it follows that

$$s(r) = s(Y^0 - G^* - T(r), \bar{u}) \qquad \text{for} \quad r \leq r_f. \tag{3.53}$$

As before, no agricultural land shall be left inside the urban fringe: $n(r)s(r) = L(r)$. Hence, from (3.53),

$$n(r) = \begin{cases} L(r)/s(Y^0 - G^* - T(r), \bar{u}) & \text{for} \quad r \leq r_f, \\ 0 & \text{for} \quad r > r_f. \end{cases} \tag{3.54}$$

Finally, the following population constraint must be met:

$$\int_0^{r_f} \frac{L(r)}{s(Y^0 - G^* - T(r), \bar{u})} dr = N. \tag{3.55}$$

In summary, we can conclude that $R(r)$, $n(r)$, $s(r)$, r_f, and G^* represent a compensated equilibrium if and only if conditions (3.52)–(3.55) are satisfied. Two real unknowns are G^* and r_f, which can be determined from condition (3.55) and the next boundary rent condition derived from (3.52):

$$\psi(Y^0 - G^* - T(r_f), \bar{u}) = R_A. \tag{3.56}$$

Now let us return to the HS model of optimal allocation, (3.50). The optimality conditions for this model can be obtained by applying the maximum principle of optimal control theory. As shown in Appendix C.2, it turns out that the conditions for optimal allocation are the same as conditions (3.52)–(3.55) for compensated equilibrium land use. That is, for an allocation $(n(r), s(r), r_f)$ to be optimal for the HS$(Y^0, \bar{u}, N)$ model, it is necessary and sufficient that there exist multipliers $R(r)$ and G^* under which conditions (3.52)–(3.55) are satisfied.

This can be informally shown as follows: Note that

$$\mathcal{S} = \int_0^{r_f} (Y^0 - T(r) - Z(s(r), \bar{u}) - R_A s(r))n(r)\, dr$$

$$= \int_0^{r_f} \left(\frac{Y^0 - T(r) - Z(s(r), \bar{u})}{s(r)} - R_A \right) s(r)n(r)\, dr. \tag{3.57}$$

Since land closer to the CBD is more valuable for housing than land farther from the CBD, at the optimal allocation all land within the urban fringe must be used for housing. Hence, $s(r)n(r) = L(r)$ for all $r \leq r_f$. Therefore, problem (3.50) can be restated as follows:

$$\max_{r_f, s(r)} \mathcal{S} = \int_0^{r_f} \left(\frac{Y^0 - T(r) - Z(s(r), \bar{u})}{s(r)} - R_A \right) L(r)\, dr,$$

$$\text{subject to population constraint} \qquad \int_0^{r_f} \frac{L(r)}{s(r)}\, dr = N.$$

First, let us neglect the population constraint. Then it is obvious that at each distance $r \leq r_f$, $s(r)$ must be chosen so as to maximize $(Y^0 - T(r) - Z(s(r), \bar{u}))/s(r)$. In terms of bid rent function (3.2), this means that $s(r)$ is optimal if and only if

$$\frac{Y^0 - T(r) - Z(s(r), \bar{u})}{s(r)} = \psi(Y^0 - T(r), \bar{u}) \qquad \text{at each} \quad r \leq r_f.$$

In terms of the bid-max lot size function $s(I, u)$, this means

$$s(r) = s(Y^0 - T(r), \bar{u}) \qquad \text{at each} \quad r \leq r_f.$$

And the urban fringe r_f must be chosen so that

$$\psi(Y^0 - T(r_f), \bar{u}) = R_A.$$

If $\int_0^{r_f} L(r)/s(Y^0 - T(r), \bar{u})\, dr$ happens to be equal to N, we have obtained the solution to the problem. This can happen, of course, only accidentally, and suppose $\int_0^{r_f} L(r)/s(Y^0 - T(r), \bar{u})\, dr - N \neq 0$. Then the Lagrangian multiplier method requires that some *penalty* G^* be introduced for violation of the population constraint. And now $s(r)$ and r_f must be chosen so as to maximize the Lagrangian function $\mathcal{L}$ defined as

$$\mathcal{L} = \int_0^{r_f} \left(\frac{Y^0 - T(r) - Z(s(r), \bar{u})}{s(r)} - R_A \right) L(r)\, dr - G^* \left(\int_0^{r_f} \frac{L(r)}{s(r)}\, dr - N \right)$$

$$= \int_0^{r_f} \left(\frac{Y^0 - G^* - T(r) - Z(s(r), \bar{u})}{s(r)} - R_A \right) L(r)\, dr + G^* N.$$

Hence, at each distance $r \leq r_f$, $s(r)$ is optimal if and only if it maximizes the function $(Y^0 - G^* - T(r) - Z(s, \bar{u}))/s$. In terms of the bid rent function (3.2), this means that $s(r)$ is optimal if and only if

$$\frac{Y^0 - G^* - T(r) - Z(s(r), \bar{u})}{s(r)} = \psi(Y^0 - G^* - T(r), \bar{u}) \qquad \text{at each} \quad r \leq r_f. \tag{3.58}$$

This in turn implies that

$$s(r) = s(Y^0 - G^* - T(r), \bar{u}) \qquad \text{at each} \quad r \leq r_f. \tag{3.59}$$

And the optimal r_f is determined from the condition

$$\psi(Y^0 - G^* - T(r_f), \bar{u}) = R_A. \tag{3.60}$$

Household distribution $n(r)$ is given as

$$n(r) = \begin{cases} L(r)/s(Y^0 - G^* - T(r), \bar{u}) & \text{for} \quad r \leq r_f, \\ 0 & \text{for} \quad r > r_f. \end{cases} \tag{3.61}$$

The correct penalty, or income tax G^*, must be chosen so as to satisfy the population constraint

$$\int_0^{r_f} \frac{L(r)}{s(Y^0 - G^* - T(r), \bar{u})}\, dr = N. \tag{3.62}$$

Notice now that if we define *shadow rent* $R(r)$ by

$$R(r) = \begin{cases} \psi(Y^0 - G^* - T(r), \bar{u}) & \text{for} \quad r \leq r_f, \\ R_A & \text{for} \quad r \geq r_f, \end{cases} \tag{3.63}$$

then conditions (3.59)–(3.63) are identical with (3.52)–(3.56). That is, the optimality conditions for the HS(Y^0, $\bar{u}$, N) model coincide with the conditions for compensated equilibrium under target utility $\bar{u}$. From this, we can conclude the following:

> ***Proposition 3.7.*** ($R(r)$, $n(r)$, $s(r)$, r_f, G^*) is a solution to the HS(Y^0, $\bar{u}$, N) model if and only if it is a compensated equilibrium under target utility $\bar{u}$.

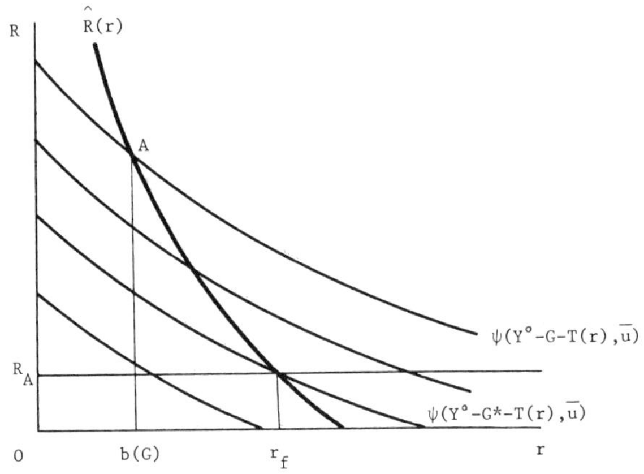

Figure 3.6. Boundary rent curve $\hat{R}(r)$ for optimal/compensated equilibrium land use.

For the HS(Y^0, $\bar{u}$, N) model, originally (3.52)–(3.56) [i.e., (3.59)–(3.63)] represent purely mathematical conditions for optimal allocation. However, we can now interpret that these conditions represent the equilibrium conditions for the competitive land market through which the government achieves target utility $\bar{u}$ via an income tax policy. Shadow rent $R(r)$ can be interpreted as the land rent at each r, and G^* the income tax in the compensated equilibrium.

Next, recalling the boundary rent curve approach, we can determine two unknowns G^* and r_f. Under each value of G, we solve the next equation for b,

$$\int_0^b \frac{L(r)}{s(Y^0 - G - T(r), \bar{u})} dr = N, \tag{3.64}$$

and obtain the outer boundary function $b(G)$. For each given G, $b(G)$ marks a distance on the corresponding bid rent curve $\psi(Y^0 - G - T(r), \bar{u})$, such as point A in Figure 3.6. By changing G, we can obtain the boundary rent curve $\hat{R}(r)$, as depicted in Figure 3.6. That is,

$$\hat{R}(r) = \psi(Y^0 - G(r) - T(r), \bar{u}), \tag{3.65}$$

where $G(r)$ is the inverse function of $r = b(G)$. With $\hat{R}(r)$, then, as depicted in Figure 3.6, r_f is determined from the relation $\hat{R}(r_f) = R_A$, and G^* from $\psi(Y^0 - G^* - T(r_f), \bar{u}) = R_A$.

In addition to Assumptions 2.1, 2.2, and 3.1, suppose the following assumption is satisfied:[17]

Assumption 3.2. z is perfectly substitutable for s. That is, on each indifference curve $u = U(z, s)$, s approaches zero as z approaches infinity.

Then, as before, $\hat{R}(r)$ is continuously decreasing in r, becomes zero as r approaches a certain finite distance, and becomes infinitely high as r approaches zero.[18] Therefore, as demonstrated in Figure 3.6, we can conclude the following:

Proposition 3.8. For any given Y^0, $\bar{u}$, and $N > 0$, the HS(Y^0, $\bar{u}$, N) model has a unique solution. Hence, there also exists a unique compensated equilibrium under each target utility $\bar{u}$.

3.5 Equilibrium versus optimal

In this section, we examine the relationship between optimal solutions of HS models in Section 3.4 and equilibrium solutions for the closed-city models CCA and CCP in Section 3.3.[19] For this, it is convenient to consider a market model that is a slight generalization of the CCA(Y, N) model. Keeping the context of the basic model (2.1), let us denote the original (pretax) income by Y^0, and introduce a new parameter $\bar{G}$, which represents an income tax per household. Here $\bar{G}$ is a fixed number predetermined by the government. Then the residential choice behavior of each household can be expressed as

$$\max_{r,z,s} U(z, s), \qquad \text{subject to} \quad z + R(r)s = Y^0 - \bar{G} - T(r). \tag{3.66}$$

Assuming that there are N identical households in the city, we denote by CCA($Y^0 - \bar{G}$, N) the closed-city model under absentee landownership with income tax $\bar{G}$. Then substituting $Y^0 - \bar{G}$ for Y in equilibrium conditions (3.14)–(3.17), we can see that ($R(r)$, $n(r)$, $s(r)$, r_f, u^*) represents an equilibrium of the CCA($Y^0 - \bar{G}$, N) model if and only if

$$R(r) = \begin{cases} \psi(Y^0 - \bar{G} - T(r), u^*) & \text{for} \quad r \leq r_f, \\ R_A & \text{for} \quad r \geq r_f, \end{cases} \tag{3.67}$$

$$s(r) = s(Y^0 - \bar{G} - T(r), u^*) \qquad \text{for} \quad r \leq r_f, \tag{3.68}$$

$$n(r) = \begin{cases} L(r)/s(Y^0 - \bar{G} - T(r), u^*) & \text{for} \quad r \leq r_f, \\ 0 & \text{for} \quad r > r_f, \end{cases} \tag{3.69}$$

$$\int_0^{r_f} \frac{L(r)}{s(Y^0 - \bar{G} - T(r), u^*)} dr = N. \tag{3.70}$$

As in Section 3.3, we can see that for each $\bar{G}$ such that $Y^0 - \bar{G} > T(0)$, the CCA($Y^0 - \bar{G}$, N) model has a unique solution.[20]

Next, let us recall from Section 3.4 that ($R(r)$, $n(r)$, $s(r)$, r_f, G^*) represents the solution to the HS(Y^0, $\bar{u}$, N) model if and only if

$$R(r) = \begin{cases} \psi(Y^0 - G^* - T(r), \bar{u}) & \text{for} \quad r \leq r_f, \\ R_A & \text{for} \quad r \geq r_f, \end{cases} \tag{3.71}$$

$$s(r) = s(Y^0 - G^* - T(r), \bar{u}) \qquad \text{for} \quad r \leq r_f, \tag{3.72}$$

$$n(r) = \begin{cases} L(r)/s(Y^0 - G^* - T(r), \bar{u}) & \text{for} \quad r \leq r_f, \\ 0 & \text{for} \quad r > r_f, \end{cases} \tag{3.73}$$

$$\int_0^{r_f} \frac{L(r)}{s(Y^0 - G^* - T(r), \bar{u})}\, dr = N. \tag{3.74}$$

For each $\bar{u}$, the HS(Y^0, $\bar{u}$, N) model has a unique solution.

We can now easily see the following:

Proposition 3.9. ($R(r)$, $n(r)$, $s(r)$, r_f, G^*) is the solution to the HS(Y^0, $\bar{u}$, N) model if and only if ($R(r)$, $n(r)$, $s(r)$, r_f, $\bar{u}$) is the solution to the CCA($Y^0 - G^*$, N) model.

To understand this, recall that ($R(r)$, $n(r)$, $s(r)$, r_f, G^*) is the solution to the HS(Y^0, $\bar{u}$, N) model if and only if it is the compensated equilibrium under target utility $\bar{u}$. That is, if the government sets income tax at G^*, the competitive market will achieve target utility $\bar{u}$ in equilibrium. This implies that if we set $\bar{G} = G^*$ in (3.66), all households will achieve utility level $\bar{u}$ at the competitive equilibrium. Therefore, ($R(r)$, $n(r)$, $s(r)$, r_f, $\bar{u}$) must be the solution to the CCA($Y^0 - G^*$, N) model. Conversely, if ($R(r)$, $n(r)$, $s(r)$, r_f, $\bar{u}$) is a solution to the CCA($Y^0 - G^*$, N) model, then ($R(r)$, $n(r)$, $s(r)$, r_f, G^*) is the compensated equilibrium under target utility $\bar{u}$. Hence, it must be the solution to the HS(Y^0, $\bar{u}$, N) model.[21]

Note that Proposition 3.9 is true for any combination of (G^*, $\bar{u}$). Hence, if we replace (G^*, $\bar{u}$) by ($\bar{G}$, u^*) in Proposition 3.9 we obtain the following conclusion:

Corollary. ($R(r)$, $n(r)$, $s(r)$, r_f, u^*) is the solution to the CCA($Y^0 - \bar{G}$, N) model if and only if ($R(r)$, $n(r)$, $s(r)$, r_f, $\bar{G}$) is the solution to the HS(Y^0, u^*, N) model.

Proposition 3.9 implies that the solution to any HS model can be achieved through the competitive market by the choice of an appropriate income tax (or subsidy). And the corollary implies that the competitive equilibrium for any CCA model can be obtained by solving an HS model with an appropriate target utility. Then since the solution of any HS model is efficient, Proposition 3.10 immediately follows.

> ***Proposition 3.10.*** The competitive equilibrium for any CCA model is efficient (*first welfare theorem*). And any efficient allocation under the equal-utility constraint can be achieved through the competitive market by the choice of an appropriate income tax or subsidy (*second welfare theorem*).[22]

Recall from Proposition 3.6 that the four types of model, CCA, CCP, OCA, and OCP, have an identical set of solutions (when parameters Y, Y^0, N, and u are restricted such that $Y > T(0)$, $Y^0 > T(0)$, $N > 0$, and $u < \tilde{u}(Y)$ and $u < \tilde{u}(Y^0)$). From Proposition 3.10, the solution to any CCA model is efficient. Therefore, we can conclude the following:

> ***Proposition 3.11.*** The solution to any equilibrium model of the four types (i.e., CCA, CCP, OCA, and OCP) is efficient.

The above results can be summarized graphically. Let $(R(r), n(r), s(r), r_{\mathrm{f}}, G^*)$ be the solution to the HS$(Y^0, \bar{u}, N)$ model. Then using (3.71)–(3.74), we have

$$\begin{aligned}
\mathcal{S} &= \int_0^{r_{\mathrm{f}}} (Y^0 - T(r) - Z(s(r), \bar{u}) - R_{\mathrm{A}} s(r)) n(r)\, dr \\
&= \int_0^{r_{\mathrm{f}}} \left(\frac{Y^0 - G^* - T(r) - Z(s(r), \bar{u})}{s(r)} - R_{\mathrm{A}} \right) s(r) n(r)\, dr + \int_0^{r_{\mathrm{f}}} G^* n(r)\, dr \\
&= \int_0^{r_{\mathrm{f}}} (R(r) - R_{\mathrm{A}}) L(r)\, dr + G^* \int_0^{r_{\mathrm{f}}} n(r)\, dr \\
&= \mathrm{TDR} + NG^*,
\end{aligned}$$

where TDR is the total differential rent defined by (3.34). In general, if we let $\mathcal{S}(Y^0, u, N)$, $\mathrm{TDR}(Y^0, u, N)$, and $G(Y^0, u, N)$ represent, respectively, the surplus, the total differential rent, and the (shadow) income tax at the solution to the HS(Y^0, u, N) model, then it holds that

$$\mathcal{S}(Y^0, u, N) = \mathrm{TDR}(Y^0, u, N) + NG(Y^0, u, N). \qquad (3.75)$$

Suppose $R_{\mathrm{A}} > 0$. Then about functions $\mathcal{S}(Y^0, u, N)$ and $G(Y^0, u, N)$, we can show the following:

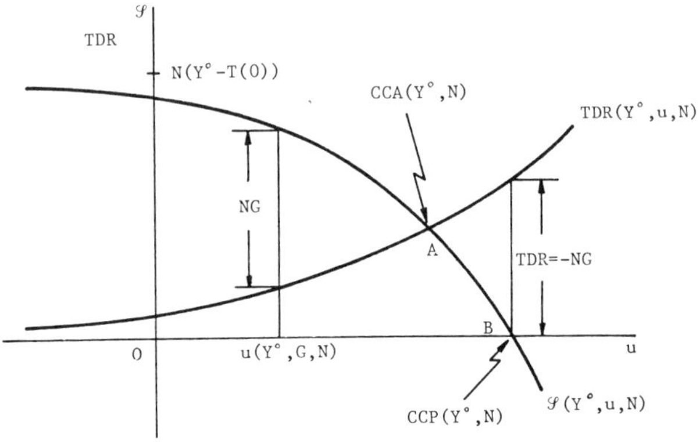

Figure 3.7. Relationship between optimal solutions and equilibrium solutions (Y^0 and N fixed).

Property 3.3

(i) $\mathcal{S}(Y^0, u, N)$ is continuously decreasing in u, where $\lim_{u\to-\infty} \mathcal{S}(Y^0, u, N) = N(Y^0 - T(0))$ and $\lim_{u\to\infty} \mathcal{S}(Y^0, u, N) = -\infty$.

(ii) $G(Y^0, u, N)$ is continuously decreasing in u, where $\lim_{u\to-\infty} G(Y^0, u, N) = Y^0 - T(0)$ and $\lim_{u\to\infty} G(Y^0, u, N) = -\infty$.

Since a higher target utility implies the need for a greater consumption of goods, both the surplus $\mathcal{S}(Y^0, u, N)$ and extractable income tax $G(Y^0, u, N)$ necessarily decrease with increasing u.[23]

Using Property 3.3, the relationship between the two curves $\mathcal{S}(Y^0, u, N)$ and $\text{TDR}(Y^0, u, N)$ can be depicted as in Figure 3.7. Note from (3.75) that the difference between the surplus and total differential rent equals the total income taxes:

$$NG(Y^0, u, N) = \mathcal{S}(Y^0, u, N) - \text{TDR}(Y^0, u, N). \tag{3.76}$$

Since $G(Y^0, u, N)$ is decreasing in u, before they intersect at point A the difference between the two curves, $NG(Y^0, u, N)$, is decreasing in u; after point A, the difference is increasing in u.[24] Let $u(Y^0, G, N)$ be the inverse function of $G = G(Y^0, u, N)$ with respect to u. From Proposition 3.9, $u(Y^0, G, N)$ represents the equilibrium utility at the solution to the $\text{CCA}(Y^0 - G, N)$ model. Now, given an income tax G (or subsidy), the equilibrium utility $u(Y^0, G, N)$ at the solution to the $\text{CCA}(Y^0 - G, N)$ model can be obtained as in Figure 3.7. In particular, G equals zero at point A. Hence, comparing (2.1) and (3.66), we can see that this point corresponds to the market equilibrium for the $\text{CCA}(Y^0, N)$ model in Section 3.3 (case 1). Since Property 3.3 ensures that point A exists uniquely, this reconfirms the validity of Proposition 3.1. Next, at point B, we have $\mathcal{S}(Y^0, u, N) = 0$ and hence $\text{TDR}/N = -G$. Thus, comparing (3.35) and (3.66), we can see that point B corresponds to the market equilibrium for the CCP(Y^0, N) model in Section 3.3 (case 3). Since curve $\mathcal{S}(Y^0, u, N)$ is continuously decreasing in u, positive for small u, and negative for large u, point B exists uniquely. Therefore, we can conclude as in Proposition 3.3.

3.6 Comparative statics

In this section, we examine how the equilibrium land use will be affected by changes in such exogenous parameters as the agricultural rent, population, transport costs, household income, land tax, and zoning. Throughout this section, we assume that the residential choice of each household is given by the basic model (2.1) and consider only the case of the closed-city model under absentee landownership [i.e., the CCA(Y, N) model in Section 3.3].[25] Assumptions 2.1–2.3 and 3.1 are taken to hold. Also keeping identities (3.3) and (3.4) in mind, for brevity of notation we use Alonso functions $\Psi(r, u)$ and $S(r, u)$ in place of Solow functions $\psi(Y - T(r), u)$ and $s(Y - T(r), u)$.

As we shall see, the boundary rent curve plays the central role. Many important conclusions follow from the observation that the boundary rent curve is decreasing in distance from the CBD. Recall that this characteristic of the boundary rent curve follows from the assumption of normality of land.

3.6.1 Effects of changes in agricultural rent and population

Agricultural rent increase. Suppose that agricultural rent changes from R_A^a to R_A^b such that

$$R_A^a < R_A^b .$$

All parameters are assumed to stay the same. Let us denote by r_f^a (r_f^b) and u_a^* (u_b^*), respectively, the urban fringe distance and equilibrium utility level under R_A^a (R_A^b). Since this change in agricultural rent affects neither the bid rent function nor the (bid-max) lot size function of individual households, the boundary rent curve $\hat{R}(r)$ remains the same. Hence, recalling Figure 3.3, we can depict the changes in equilibrium land use as in Figure 3.8.

Since the boundary rent curve $\hat{R}(r)$ is decreasing in r, we have that

$$r_f^a > r_f^b \qquad \text{and} \qquad \Psi(r, u_a^*) < \Psi(r, u_b^*) \qquad \text{for all} \quad r \leq r_f^a .$$

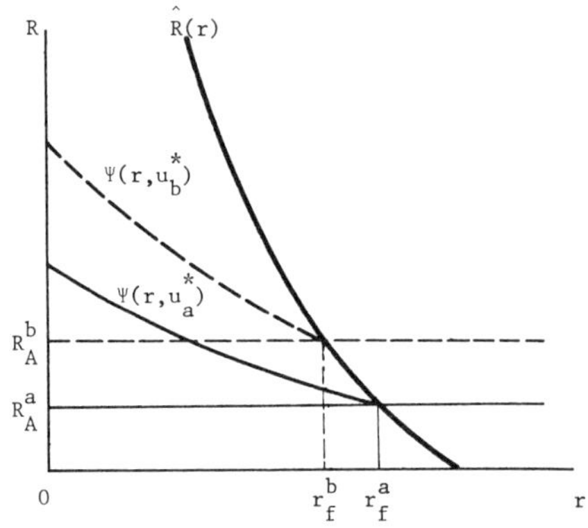

Figure 3.8. Effects of an increase in agricultural rent.

Since a higher bid rent curve implies a lower utility level, we have

$$u_a^* > u_b^* \, .$$

Then since the bid-max lot size function $S(r, u)$ is increasing in u,

$$S(r, u_a^*) > S(r, u_b^*) \qquad \text{for all} \quad r.$$

Therefore, recalling the equation of the market rent curve, (3.13), we can conclude as follows:

> ***Proposition 3.12.*** As the agricultural rent R_A increases,
>
> (i) urban fringe r_f will move inward,
> (ii) equilibrium utility u^* will become lower,
> (iii) land rent curve $R(r)$ will become higher everywhere,
> (iv) lot size $S(r, u^*)$ will become smaller everywhere, and hence the population density will increase everywhere within the new urban fringe.

In short, with the increase in the agricultural land rent, the market rent curve will be pushed upward everywhere, and hence the per capita land consumption will decrease everywhere.

Population increase. Suppose the city population (i.e., the number of households) changes from N_a to N_b such that

$$N_a < N_b \, .$$

Again, all other parameters are assumed to stay the same. Let us denote by r_f^a (r_f^b) and u_a^* (u_b^*), respectively, the urban fringe distance and equi-

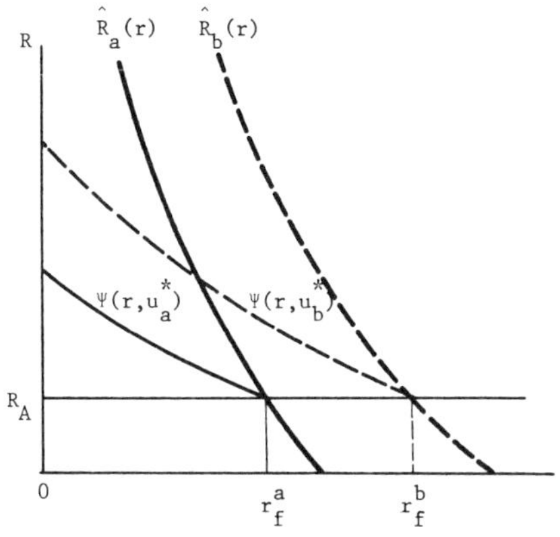

Figure 3.9. Effects of an increase in population.

librium utility level under N_a (N_b). This change in population does not affect the lot size function $S(r, u)$. Hence, we can see from (3.20) that an increasing N increases the boundary distance $b(u)$ under each value of u. Then since each bid rent curve stays the same, we can see from Figure 3.3 that with increasing N, the boundary rent curve $\hat{R}(r)$ will shift outward. The changes in equilibrium land use can be depicted as in Figure 3.9. Since R_A remains the same, we can see that

$$r_f^a < r_f^b \quad \text{and} \quad \Psi(r, u_a^*) < \Psi(r, u_b^*) \quad \text{for all} \quad r \leq r_f^b .$$

Therefore, as in the previous case of an agricultural rent increase, we have

$$u_a^* > u_b^* \quad \text{and} \quad S(r, u_a^*) > S(r, u_b^*) \quad \text{for all} \quad r \leq r_f^b .$$

Hence, we can conclude as follows:

Proposition 3.13. As the city population increases,

(i) urban fringe r_f will move outward,
(ii) equilibrium utility u^* will become lower,
(iii) land rent curve $R(r)$ will become higher everywhere up to the new fringe,
(iv) lot size $S(r, u^*)$ will become smaller everywhere, and hence population density will increase everywhere within the new urban fringe.

In short, an increasing population will increase the demand for residential land, which in turn will increase the land rent everywhere and push the urban fringe outward.

3.6.2 *Effects of changes in transport costs and income*

Here we are concerned with two separate cases. In case A, transport cost function changes from $T_a(r)$ to $T_b(r)$ such that[26]

$$T_a(0) = T_b(0) \qquad \text{and} \qquad T'_a(r) > T'_b(r) \qquad \text{for all} \quad r, \tag{3.77}$$

but the household income remains the same. That is, the marginal transport cost decreases everywhere. In case B, the household income changes from Y_a to Y_b such that

$$Y_a < Y_b, \tag{3.78}$$

but transport costs are the same. The effects of these two changes are more complex than before, because the bid rent and lot size functions also change. However, these two changes have very similar effects. So in this section, first the common effects of the two cases will be studied; then the two cases will be examined separately.

Let us begin by expressing parameter changes as

$$(T_a(r), Y_a) \rightarrow (T_b(r), Y_b).$$

Then case A means that condition (3.77) holds but $Y_a = Y_b$, and for case B condition (3.78) holds but $T_a(r) = T_b(r)$ for all r. Note that in either case, the net income increases at all positive distances:

$$I_a(r) \equiv Y_a - T_a(r) < Y_b - T_b(r) \equiv I_b(r) \qquad \text{for all} \quad r > 0. \tag{3.79}$$

This fact is crucial to the subsequent analysis. Let us denote the bid rent function, lot size function, boundary rent curve, urban fringe distance, and equilibrium utility level under parameter set $(T_a(r), Y_a)$ by $\Psi_a(r, u)$, $S_a(r, u)$, $\hat{R}_a(r)$, r_f^a, and u_a^*, respectively; and those under parameter set $(T_b(r), Y_b)$ by $\Psi_b(r, u)$, $S_b(r, u)$, $\hat{R}_b(r)$, r_f^b, and u_b^*. By definition, of course, $\Psi_a(r, u) = \psi(Y_a - T_a(r), u)$, $S_a(r, u) = s(Y_a - T_a(r), u)$, $\Psi_b(r, u) = \psi_b(Y_b - T_b(r), u)$, and $S_b(r, u) = s(Y_b - T_b(r), u)$.

First, we shall show that function Ψ_a is steeper than Ψ_b. Suppose that two bid rent curves, $\Psi_a(r, u_a)$ and $\Psi_b(r, u_b)$, intersect at distance x: $\Psi_a(x, u_a) = \Psi_b(x, u_b) = \bar{R} > 0$. Then recalling identity (2.19), from the normality of land and from (3.79) we have

$$S_a(x, u_a) = \hat{s}(\bar{R}, I_a(x)) \leq \hat{s}(\bar{R}, I_b(x)) = S_b(x, u_b),$$

where we have inequality if $x > 0$, and equality if $x = 0$ and $Y_a = Y_b$ (case A). Therefore, in either case A or case B, from (2.27) we have that

$$-\frac{\partial \Psi_a(x, u_a)}{\partial r} = \frac{T'_a(x)}{S_a(x, u_a)} > \frac{T'_b(x)}{S_b(x, u_b)} = -\frac{\partial \Psi_b(x, u_b)}{\partial r},$$

which implies that Ψ_a is steeper than Ψ_b (Definition 2.2′).

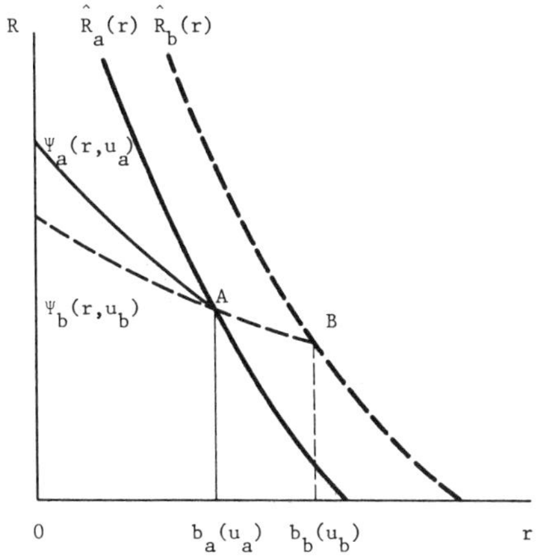

Figure 3.10. Shift of boundary rent curve with a decrease in transport costs and an increase in income.

Next, let us show that the *new boundary rent curve* $\hat{R}_b(r)$ *is located to the right of* $\hat{R}_a(r)$. For this, we take a point, for example, A, on the initial boundary rent curve $\hat{R}_a(r)$, as depicted in Figure 3.10. Let $\Psi_a(r, u_a)$ [$\Psi_b(r), u_b)$] be the bid rent curve of Ψ_a (Ψ_b), which passes point A. Then by definition of the boundary rent curve $\hat{R}_a(r)$, point A gives the outer boundary distance $b_a(u_a)$ such that

$$\int_0^{b_a(u_a)} \frac{L(r)}{S_a(r, u_a)} dr = N. \tag{3.80}$$

Next since curve $\Psi_a(r, u_a)$ is steeper than $\Psi_b(r, u_b)$,

$$\Psi_a(r, u_a) > \Psi_b(r, u_b) \qquad \text{for all} \quad r < b_a(u_a).$$

Then since $I_a(r) < I_b(r)$ for all $r > 0$, from the normality of land we have

$$\begin{aligned} S_a(r, u_a) &= \hat{s}(\Psi_a(r, u_a), I_a(r)) < \hat{s}(\Psi_b(r, u_b), I_b(r)) \\ &= S_b(r, u_b) \qquad \text{for all} \quad r < b_a(u_a). \end{aligned} \tag{3.81}$$

From (3.80) and (3.81) it follows that

$$N = \int_0^{b_a(u_a)} \frac{L(r)}{S_a(r, u_a)} dr > \int_0^{b_a(u_a)} \frac{L(r)}{S_b(r, u_b)} dr,$$

which implies that $b_b(u_b)$, the new outer boundary distance, is located to the right of $b_a(u_a)$, as depicted in Figure 3.10. Since this result is true for each point on curve $\hat{R}_a(r)$, we can conclude that the new boundary rent curve $\hat{R}_b(r)$ must be located to the right of $\hat{R}_a(r)$.

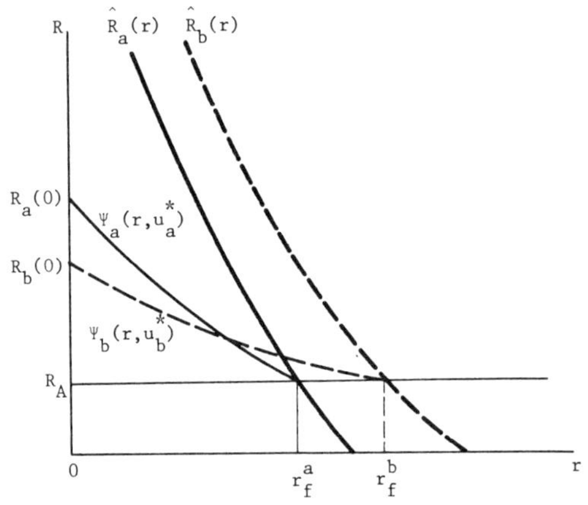

Figure 3.11. Effects of a decrease in transport costs and an increase in income.

Therefore, the effects of parameter changes from $(T_a(r), Y_a)$ to $(T_b(r), Y_b)$ can be depicted as in Figure 3.11. Since R_A remains the same, it is evident from the figure that

$$r_f^a < r_f^b. \tag{3.82}$$

An intuitive rationale is as follows: With parameter changes, the net income increases everywhere. Hence, demand for land increases everywhere, and the city boundary is pushed outward. Similarly, since with parameter changes the net income increases everywhere, it is intuitively evident that the equilibrium utility will become higher:[27]

$$u_a^* < u_b^*. \tag{3.83}$$

Thus far, we have seen that the effects of a decrease in transport cost and those of an increase in income are qualitatively the same. In fact, the only possible difference concerns the direction of land rent change at the city center. According to Figure 3.11, land rent at the city center decreases with parameter changes $[R_a(0) > R_b(0)]$. As shown below, this is always true in the case of a decrease in transport costs, but not always in the case of an increase in income.

Transport cost decrease. Suppose that the transport costs decreases, as indicated by (3.77), while income remains the same. Then

$$Y - T_a(0) = Y - T_b(0).$$

Since $u_a^* < u_b^*$, from identity (2.20) we have

$$V(\Psi_a(0, u_a^*), Y - T_a(0)) = u_a^* < u_b^* = V(\Psi_b(0, u_b^*), Y - T_b(0)).$$

Since the indirect utility function V is decreasing in R, the above two relations imply that

$$\Psi_a(0, u_a^*) > \Psi_b(0, u_b^*), \qquad \text{that is,} \quad R_a(0) > R_b(0). \tag{3.84}$$

In short, residents at the city center can achieve a higher utility [as required by (3.83)] only when land rent there becomes lower. This is because income at the city center does not change with a decrease in marginal transport cost.

Finally, notice that from identity (2.25), $S_a(0, u_a^*) = \tilde{s}(\Psi_a(0, u_a^*), u_a^*)$ and $S_b(0, u_b^*) = \tilde{s}(\Psi_b(0, u_b^*), u_b^*)$. Then since the compensated demand function $\tilde{s}(R, u)$ is decreasing in R and increasing in u, from (3.83) and (3.84) we can conclude that

$$S_a(0, u_a^*) < S_b(0, u_b^*). \tag{3.85}$$

Since lot size curve $S(r, u)$ is continuous in r, this implies that with a decrease in transport costs, lot size will become larger in an area close to the city center.

In summary, we can conclude as follows:

> ***Proposition 3.14.*** Suppose the marginal transport cost decreases at every distance, while the fixed transport cost remains the same. Then
>
> (i) urban fringe r_f will move outward,
> (ii) equilibrium utility u^* will become higher,
> (iii) land rent $R(r)$ will become lower in an area close to the CBD and higher in the suburbs,
> (iv) lot size $S(r, u^*)$ will become larger in an area close to the CBD, and hence population density $\rho(r) = 1/S(r, u^*)$ will become lower there.

In other words, a decrease in transport cost makes the lands in the suburbs less disadvantageous compared with lands close to the city center. Hence, some households move from the center to the suburbs, which expands the urban fringe, lowers land rent at the center, and increases land rent in the suburbs. Consequently, both the land rent curve and the population density curve will become flatter.

Increase in income. The effects of an increase in income on the land rent at the city center depend on the nature of the transport cost function and land distribution. This can be seen from the next example.

Example 3.2. In the context of Example 3.1, if we further assume that $\lambda = 1$ and hence $L(r) = \theta r$ (pie-shaped or circular), then from (3.26)

$$R(0) = \frac{3a^2}{\theta}\frac{N}{Y}.$$

Hence, if the city is pie-shaped or circular, the land rent at the city center decreases as income increases. If we assume, instead, that $\lambda = 0$ and hence $L(r) = \theta$ (a linear city), then

$$R(0) = \frac{a}{\theta}N.$$

Hence, in the case of a linear city, the land rent at the city center is independent of income level. Finally, if $\lambda = -0.5$ and hence $L(r) = \theta/\sqrt{r}$, then

$$R(0) = \frac{0.5 \times 1.5}{2\theta}\sqrt{a}\sqrt{Y}N.$$

Hence, if the amount of land is decreasing with the distance from the city center, the land rent at the city center increases as income increases. Note that in this example we have assumed that $T(r) = ar$ (constant marginal transport cost).

The results of Example 3.2 can be generalized in the context of the basic model (2.1) and stated as[28]

Property 3.4

(i) If $L(r)/T'(r)$ is increasing at all r, then $R(0)$ decreases as income increases.

(ii) If $L(r)/T'(r)$ is constant everywhere, then $R(0)$ is independent of Y.

(iii) If $L(r)/T'(r)$ is decreasing at all r, then $R(0)$ increases as income increases.

For example, suppose the marginal transport cost $T'(r)$ is constant. Then, if $L(r)$ is increasing in r, we have case (i); if $L(r)$ is constant, case (ii); and if $L(r)$ is decreasing, case (iii). In case (i), the effects of an increase in income can be depicted as in Figure 3.11. Recall that the bid rent function Ψ_a is steeper than Ψ_b. Hence, in cases (ii) and (iii), we have that $R_a(r) = \Psi_a(r, u_a^*) < \Psi_b(r, u_b^*) = R_b(r)$ for all $r > 0$. In most cities, the amount of land is increasing and marginal transport cost is decreasing with the distance from the city center. In practice, therefore, we are most likely to have case (i).

Finally, let us recall that the Marshallian demand for land, $\hat{s}(R, I)$, is decreasing in R and increasing in I. In both cases (i) and (ii), $\Psi_a(0, u_a^*) \geq \Psi_b(0, u_b^*)$; and $Y_a - T(0) < Y_b - T(0)$ by assumption. Therefore, we have

$$S_a(0, u_a^*) = \hat{s}(\Psi_a(0, u_a^*), Y_a - T(0))$$
$$< \hat{s}(\Psi_b(0, u_b^*), Y_b - T(0)) = S_b(0, u_b^*).$$

From the continuity of $S_a(r, u_a^*)$ and $S_b(r, u_b^*)$ in r, the equilibrium lot size $S_b(r, u_b^*)$ is greater than $S_a(r, u_a^*)$ in an area close to the CBD. This can be summarized as follows:

Proposition 3.15. As the household income increases,

(i) urban fringe r_f will move outward;
(ii) equilibrium utility u^* will become higher;
(iii) (a) if $L(r)/T'(r)$ is increasing at all r, then land rent $R(r)$ will become lower in an area close to the CBD, become higher in the suburbs; (b) if $L(r)/T'(r)$ is constant everywhere, then $R(r)$ will become higher at all $r > 0$; (c) if $L(r)/T'(r)$ is decreasing at all r, then $R(r)$ will become higher everywhere;
(iv) in both cases of (a) and (b) above, lot size $S(r, u^*)$ will become larger in an area close to the CBD.

In short, an increase in the household income causes an increase in demand for land at every distance. It also makes the transport cost relatively less important and hence makes the land in the suburbs less disadvantageous. Therefore, if a sufficient amount of land exists in the suburbs [case (i)], many households will move from the center to the suburbs. This will in turn decrease the land rent and population density at the center, and increase them in the suburbs. Consequently, both the land rent curve and the population density curve will become flatter. On the other hand, if there is not a sufficient amount of land in the suburbs [cases (ii) and (iii)], the increased demand for land will drive up the land rent everywhere in the city.

3.6.3 Effects of land tax and zoning

In this subsection, we consider the effects of land taxes and zoning. For the purpose of practical application, this part of the analysis may not be very useful, because, as it turns out, any land tax or zoning policy with effects different from those of (lump-sum) income taxation will necessarily undermine the efficiency of the competitive land market. This is because no element of market imperfection is involved in the present analysis.[29] Nevertheless, this analysis is important for several reasons. First, it is of theoretical interest. Second, the results can be usefully compared with a similar analysis in Part II where various externalities are introduced. Finally, when income taxation has limitations for political reasons, land taxation or zoning may be a useful tool for welfare redistribution.

Taxation on land usually takes the form of either *proportional tax* or *flat-rate tax*. In the case of proportional taxation, we denote by τ_R or τ_A the tax levied on each unit of money collected from residential land or agricultural land, respectively. In the case of flat-rate taxation, we denote by T_R or T_A the tax levied on each unit of residential land or agricultural land. Although many different zoning policies exist, we will consider only land use zoning, which restricts certain activities to certain zones.[30] In particular, we will consider *(urban) fringe zoning* in which residential land use is restricted within a certain radius from the city center. We will show that if appropriately chosen, the three policies, proportional taxation, flat-rate taxation, and fringe zoning, have exactly the same effects on equilibrium land use.

Land taxation. For convenience, let us assume that land taxes are paid by landowners.[31] Let us also assume that money collected from land (in the form of either tax or rent) is not recirculated into the urban economy. Then since land taxes affect neither the income nor the utility function of city residents, the bid rent function $\Psi(r, u)$ and lot size function $S(r, u)$ of each household remain the same. Hence, the boundary rent curve $\hat{R}(r)$ also remains the same. The maximum rent that farmers can bid per unit of land under the zero-profit condition, R_A, is also a constant independent of land tax. Let $R(r)$ be the market rent that tenants (households or farmers) pay the landowners per unit of land at each distance r. Then since the land within (beyond) the urban fringe r_f is used for housing (agriculture), as before it must hold in equilibrium that

$$R(r) = \Psi(r, u^*) \qquad \text{for} \quad r < r_f, \tag{3.86}$$

$$R(r) = R_A \qquad \text{for} \quad r > r_f, \tag{3.87}$$

where u^* is the equilibrium utility. In the case of proportional taxation, let τ_R (τ_A) be the tax on each unit of rents collected from residential land (agricultural land). At the urban fringe r_f, landowners must be indifferent between renting land to households or farmers. Hence, it must hold that

$$(1 - \tau_R)\Psi(r_f, u^*) = (1 - \tau_A)R_A. \tag{3.88a}$$

In the case of flat-rate taxation, let T_R (T_A) be the tax on each unit of residential land (agricultural land). Then similarly we have

$$\Psi(r_f, u^*) - T_R = R_A - T_A. \tag{3.88b}$$

Now, if the same tax rate is levied on residential land and agricultural land (i.e., $\tau_R = \tau_A$ or $T_R = T_A$), then both (3.88a) and (3.88b) reduce to

$$\Psi(r_f, u^*) = R_A.$$

Therefore, we have the same set of equilibrium conditions as before [i.e., (3.14)–(3.18)]. It is then clear that in the case of an equal tax rate, the equilibrium land use [including both land use pattern and land rent curve $R(r)$] is independent of land tax; it will remain as if there were no land tax. This implies that all land taxes are borne by landowners.

Next, in the case of differential tax rates, let

$$\Delta R = \Psi(r_f, u^*) - R_A, \tag{3.89}$$

which represents the gap in land rent at the urban fringe. Then from (3.88a) and (3.88b), we have, respectively,

$$\Delta R = \frac{\tau_R - \tau_A}{1 - \tau_R} R_A, \tag{3.90a}$$

or

$$\Delta R = T_R - T_A. \tag{3.90b}$$

If the tax rate is higher on residential land ($\tau_R > \tau_A$ or $T_R > T_A$), which is the usual case, then ΔR is positive and the equilibrium land use configuration can be depicted as in Figure 3.12. In this figure, r_f^0 represents the urban fringe that would occur in the absence of land taxation. If the tax rate is higher on agricultural land, then ΔR is negative and the urban fringe is to the right of r_f^0. Since equilibrium utility u^* is lower when bid rent curve $\Psi(r, u^*)$ locates higher, u^* becomes lower as ΔR becomes greater. Since the equilibrium land use is the same whenever ΔR is equal, the same equilibrium land use can be achieved either by proportional taxation or by flat-rate taxation.[32]

In summary, we can conclude as follows:

Proposition 3.16. In the case of either proportional land taxation or flat-rate land taxation,

(i) if the same tax rate is levied on residential land and agricultural land, land taxation will have no effect on the equilibrium land use pattern or market land rents;

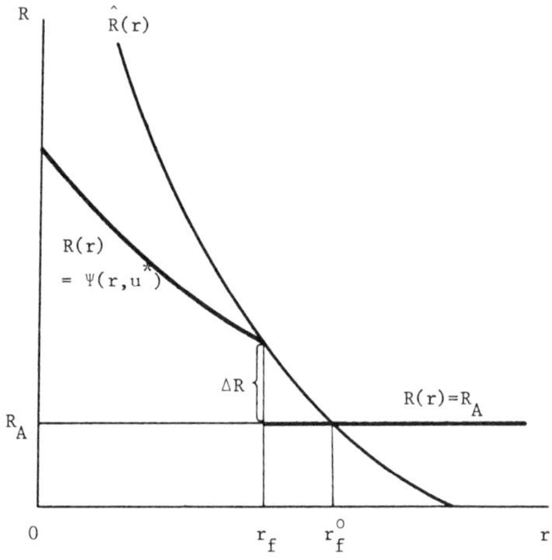

Figure 3.12. Effects of land taxation and urban fringe zoning.

(ii) in the cases of differential land taxation, as the land rent gap ΔR at the urban fringe [defined by (3.90a) or (3.90b)] increases, (a) urban fringe r will move inward, (b) equilibrium utility u^* will become lower, (c) land rent $R(r)$ will become higher everywhere within the new urban fringe, (d) lot size $S(r, u^*)$ will become smaller everywhere and hence population density will increase everywhere within the new urban fringe.

Urban fringe zoning. Let us consider a zoning ordinance that states that the land within (beyond) radius r_f shall be used for housing (agriculture). Here r_f is an arbitrarily chosen distance from the CBD. Suppose r_f happens to coincide with that in Figure 3.12. Then from the definition of boundary rent curve $\hat{R}(r)$, it is evident that the equilibrium land use configuration under this zoning ordinance coincides with the one depicted in Figure 3.12. The equilibrium bid rent curve $\Psi(r, u^*)$ is, as before, the one that passes through the intersection between the boundary rent curve $\hat{R}(r)$ and the vertical line at r_f. Beyond r_f, the land rent equals the agricultural rent R_A. Moreover, under any such urban fringe zoning, the corresponding rent gap ΔR is uniquely determined as in Figure 3.12. And for any such ΔR, we can find an appropriate set of land taxes (either proportional or flat rates) via equation (3.90a) or (3.90b). Hence, we can conclude as follows:

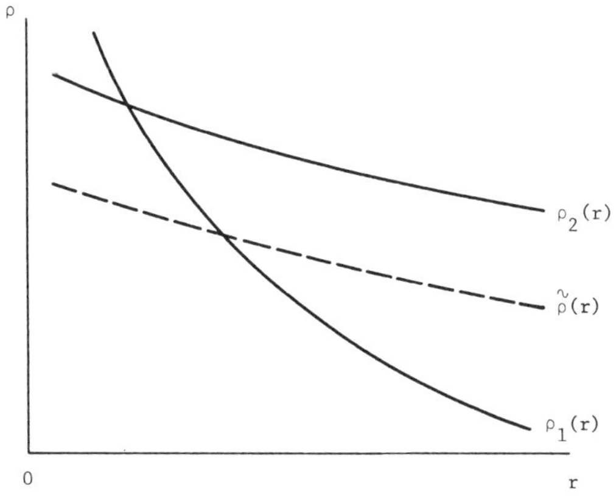

Figure 3.13. Flattening population density curve.

Proposition 3.17. For any urban fringe zoning, we can find an appropriate set of land taxes (either proportional or flat rates) such that they have the same effects on equilibrium land use.

Finally, let us observe that the equilibrium land use depicted in Figure 3.12 is not efficient. Recall that the efficient land use in which all households achieve the equilibrium utility level u^* is given by the solution of the HS(Y, u^*, N) model, which coincides with the compensated equilibrium under target utility u^*. If we compare the equilibrium land use depicted in Figure 3.12 with the compensated equilibrium land use pattern depicted in Figure 3.5, it is clear that the pattern in Figure 3.12 cannot be efficient.

In closing this section, we note that the results of this section have often been used to explain the trends in the residential land use pattern observed in the United States. It is well documented by many empirical studies that in large U.S. cities, population density curves have been getting flatter over many decades.[33] To explain this trend, let us recall other major phenomena in these cities, that is, the decrease in transport cost (in particular, commuting cost) due to railway and highway construction, increase in household incomes due to economic growth, and increase in population due to urbanization. Propositions 3.14(iv) and 3.15(iv) predict that both a decrease in transport cost and an increase in income will make flatter the population density curve of a city. In Figure 3.13, this effect can be depicted as the movement of the population density curve from $\rho_1(r)$ to $\tilde{\rho}(r)$. On the other hand, according to Proposition 3.13(iv), a population increase will make the density curve higher everywhere in the city. Hence, the overall effects will be the movement of the density curve from $\rho_1(r)$ to $\rho_2(r)$. Consequently, with the passage of time, the population density curve will become flatter and higher almost everywhere in the city.

3.7 Muth model continued: capital intensity on land

In actual cities, we can observe that as we get closer to the city center, not only the population density but also the capital intensity per square mile, or the height of building, increases. Since the Muth model of the housing industry (introduced in Section 2.5.3) considers both land and capital inputs in the production of housing service, it is useful for explaining this phenomenon.

We have already defined many elements of the problem. These include the residential choice behavior of each household (2.70), the bid *housing rent* function $\Psi_H(r, u)$ (2.76), and the behavior of the housing industry (2.71). Now, assuming that the production function F satisfies the standard neoclassical conditions,[34] we define the bid *land rent* function of the housing industry as

$$\Psi(r; R_H(r)) = \max_{L,K} \frac{R_H(r)F(L, K) - K}{L}, \tag{3.91}$$

which gives the maximum rent each housing firm could pay per unit of land at distance r while *maintaining the zero-profit condition*. Specifying zero profit follows from our assumption that the housing industry is competitive with constant returns to scale in production, so that in equilibrium the profit of each firm is zero.

In order to obtain conditions for equilibrium land use, it is convenient to rewrite (3.91) in terms of inputs and outputs per household. First, by using (2.72) and (2.73), the behavior of the housing industry, (2.71), can be rewritten as

$$\max_{s,k} R_H(r)F(s, k) - R(r)s - k, \qquad \text{at each} \quad r. \tag{3.92}$$

Then we can express the bid land rent function of the housing industry as

$$\Psi(r; R_H(r)) = \max_{s,k} \frac{R_H(r)F(s, k) - k}{s}. \tag{3.93}$$

Definitions (3.91) and (3.93) are, of course, identical because F has constant returns to scale.

Next, in equilibrium we have $R_H(r) = \Psi_H(r, u)$. Hence, upon substitution of (2.76) into (3.93), and newly expressing $\Psi(r; R_H(r)) \equiv \Psi(r, u)$, we obtain[35]

$$\Psi(r, u) = \max_{s,k} \frac{Y - T(r) - Z(F(s, k), u) - k}{s}. \tag{3.94}$$

This represents the maximum land rent each firm can bid *when the equilibrium household utility is expected to be u*. Solving the maximization problem of (3.94), we can obtain the *(bid-max) lot size function* $s(r, u)$ and *(bid-max) capital input function* $k(r, u)$.

Now suppose $R(r)$, $R_H(r)$, $n(r)$, $s(r)$, $k(r)$, u^*, and r_f together represent an equilibrium land use. Here, $k(r)$ represents the capital input per household at each distance r, and all other notation is the same as before. Then the equilibrium conditions can be summarized as follows:

$$R_H(r) = \Psi_H(r, u^*) \qquad \text{for} \quad r \leq r_f, \tag{3.95}$$

$$R(r) = \begin{cases} \Psi(r, u^*) & \text{for} \quad r \leq r_f, \\ R_A & \text{for} \quad r \geq r_f, \end{cases} \tag{3.96}$$

$$s(r) = s(r, u^*), \qquad k(r) = k(r, u^*) \qquad \text{for} \quad r \leq r_f, \tag{3.97}$$

$$n(r) = \begin{cases} L(r)/s(r, u^*) & \text{for} \quad r \leq r_f, \\ 0 & \text{for} \quad r > r_f, \end{cases} \tag{3.98}$$

$$\int_0^{r_f} \frac{L(r)}{s(r, u^*)} dr = N. \tag{3.99}$$

As before, the real unknowns are only u^* and r_f, and they can be determined from (3.99) and the next condition derived from (3.96):

$$\Psi(r_f, u^*) = R_A. \tag{3.100}$$

Therefore, the existence and uniqueness of equilibrium can be established, as before, by use of the boundary rent curve approach.

Next let us examine how the capital–land ratio $k(r)/s(r)$ varies with distance r. For this, we introduce the *(bid-max) housing service function* $q(r, u)$, defined as

$$q(r, u) = F(s(r, u), k(r, u)), \tag{3.101}$$

where $s(r, u)$ and $k(r, u)$ are defined from the solution to (3.94). The relationship among $s(r, u)$, $k(r, u)$, and $q(r, u)$ can be depicted as in Figure 3.14. As with Figure 2.2, it is not difficult to see that the isocost line,

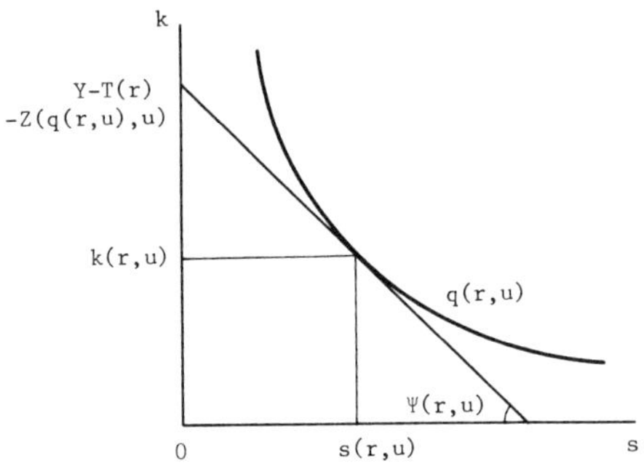

Figure 3.14. Bid rent and bid-max lot size and capital.

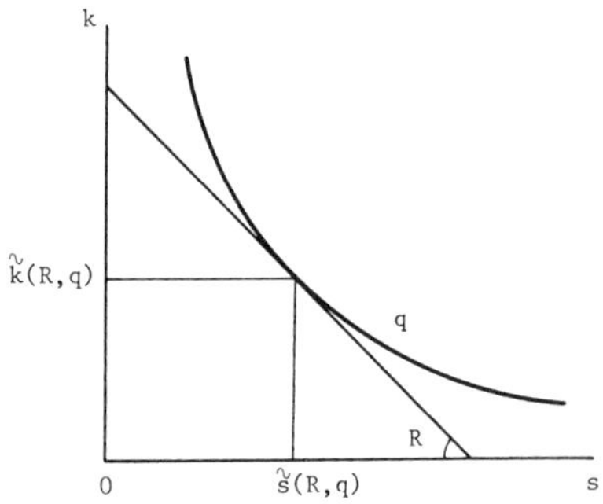

Figure 3.15. Conditional demands for land and capital.

$$k = (Y - T(r) - Z(q(r, u), u)) - \Psi(r, u)s,$$

is tangent to the isoquant $F(s, k) = q(r, u)$ at the optimal input combination $(s(r, u), k(r, u))$. Next, given arbitrary land rent R and output level q, let us consider the following *cost-minimization problem:*

$$\min_{s,k} Rs + k, \qquad \text{subject to} \quad F(s, k) = q. \tag{3.102}$$

The solution to this problem is denoted by $(\tilde{s}(R, q), \tilde{k}(R, q))$, which is a set of *conditional demands* for inputs. Graphically, as depicted in Figure 3.15, $(\tilde{s}(R, q), \tilde{k}(R, q))$ is determined at the point where an isocost line with slope R is tangent to the isoquant $q = F(s, k)$. Note that since F has constant returns to scale, *the ratio $\tilde{k}(R, q)/\tilde{s}(R, q)$ is independent of output level q* and determined only by land rent R. Hence, we can represent

$$\frac{\tilde{k}(R, q)}{\tilde{s}(R, q)} \equiv v(R), \tag{3.103}$$

which gives the input ratio as a function of R.

Now, observe that if we set R equal to $\Psi(r, u)$ and q equal to $q(r, u)$ Figure 3.15 becomes identical to Figure 3.14. This implies that the following identities hold:

$$s(r, u) = \tilde{s}(\Psi(r, u), q(r, u)), \; k(r, u) = \tilde{k}(\Psi(r, u), q(r, u)). \tag{3.104}$$

From (3.96), (3.97), (3.103), and (3.104), we have that

$$\frac{k(r)}{s(r)} = v(\Psi(r, u^*)). \tag{3.105}$$

From Figure 3.15, we can easily see that $v(R)$ increases as R increases:

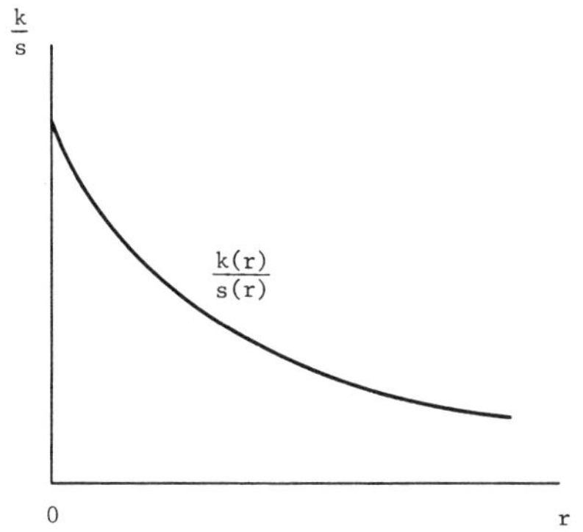

Figure 3.16. Capital–land ratio curve.

$$\frac{dv(R)}{dR} > 0.$$

And by applying the envelope theorem to (3.94), we have

$$\frac{\partial\Psi(r, u^*)}{\partial r} = -\frac{T'(r)}{s(r, u^*)} < 0. \qquad (3.106)$$

Therefore,

$$\frac{d(k(r)/s(r))}{dr} = \frac{dv(\Psi(r, u^*))}{dR} \frac{\partial\Psi(r, u^*)}{\partial r} < 0.$$

We can summarize as follows:

> ***Proposition 3.18.*** In the context of the Muth model, in equilibrium the capital–land ratio in housing service production $k(r)/s(r)$ decreases with the distance from the CBD.

This result is depicted in Figure 3.16. In practice, we can consider the capital–land ratio as a surrogate for building height. Hence, Proposition 3.18 suggests that the height of residential building decreases with the distance from the CBD.

Example 3.3. In the context of the Muth model, let us assume that

$$U(z, q) = \alpha \log z + \beta \log q, \qquad \alpha > 0, \quad \beta > 0, \quad \alpha + \beta = 1,$$

$$F(s, k) = As^a k^b, \qquad a > 0, \quad b > 0, \quad a + b = 1, A > 0.$$

Then $Z(F(s, k), u) = A^{-\beta/\alpha} s^{-a\beta/\alpha} k^{-b\beta/\alpha} e^{u/\alpha}$. Solving the maximization problem of (3.94), we have

$$\begin{aligned}
\Psi(r, u) &= A^{1/a} \alpha^{\alpha/a\beta} (a\beta)(b\beta)^{b/a} (Y - T(r))^{1/a\beta} e^{-u/a\beta}, \\
k(r, u) &= b\beta(Y - T(r)), \\
s(r, u) &= a\beta(Y - T(r))/\Psi(r, u) \\
&= A^{-1/a} \alpha^{-\alpha/a\beta} (b\beta)^{-b/a} (Y - T(r))^{-(1-a\beta)/a\beta} e^{u/a\beta}.
\end{aligned} \tag{3.107}$$

Hence, in equilibrium

$$\frac{k(r)}{s(r)} = \frac{b}{a} \Psi(r, u^*) = \frac{b}{a} R(r).$$

That is, the capital–land ratio is proportional to the land rent at each distance. If the transport cost $T(r)$ is linear or strictly concave in r, then from (3.107) bid rent curve $\Psi(r, u^*)$ is strictly convex. Hence, the capital land–rent ratio curve is also strictly convex in r, as depicted in Figure 3.16.

3.8 Conclusion

In this chapter, we have examined equilibrium land use patterns, compared them with optimal land use patterns, and concluded that competitive equilibria are socially efficient. We have also analyzed the effects on equilibrium land use of changes in various exogenous parameters such as population, transport costs, and income. Finally, we have examined how the capital intensity on land, or the height of residential building, varies with distance from the city center.

The results of this chapter are generally consistent with our casual observations of actual cities. Nevertheless, the analysis here is based on very simple models, and hence it requires many extensions. The introduction of multiple household types is the next natural extension, which will be accomplished in the next chapter.

Bibliographical notes

The equilibrium land use theory presented in Section 3.3 is essentially a simple version of neoclassical urban models, which were developed by Alonso (1964), Muth (1969), Casetti (1971), Mills (1972a,b), and Solow (1973), among others. Definitions of closed and open cities were introduced by Wheaton (1974a). The public landownership model was introduced by Solow (1973) and further studied by Kanemoto (1980, Ch. 1).

A concept similar to the boundary rent curve was introduced by Kanemoto (1980, Ch. 6) in his stability analysis of mixed cities. Fujita (1985, 1986a) generalized it to the case of variable lot size and used it for the study of the existence and uniqueness of the equilibrium and optimal land use.

The Benthamite optimal city was first analyzed by Mirrlees (1972). He discovered that at the Benthamite optimum, different utility levels are assigned to identical households at different locations. This result, called Mirrlees' inequality, was further analyzed by the authors cited in note 11. Another formulation of an optimal city in which the common utility is maximized subject to the resource constraint was introduced by Dixit (1973) and Oron, Pines, and Sheshinski (1973). The Herbert–Stevens problem explained in Section 3.4 is the dual to this equal-utility maximization problem. Originally, Herbert and Stevens (1960) formulated the problem in the context of discrete space and analyzed it by using the duality theorem of linear programming. The equivalence between the HS problem and the equilibrium land use problem was first studied by Britton Harris in his numerous unpublished papers, and formally shown by Wheaton (1974b) and Fujita and Kashiwadani (1976). The present continuous version of the HS problem was introduced by Ando (1981).

Comparative statics of equilibrium land use were studied first by Wheaton (1974a) in the case of the single household type and by Wheaton (1976), Hartwick, Schweizer, and Varaiya (1976), and Arnott, MacKinnon, and Wheaton (1978) in the case of multiple income classes. Their approach is based on the standard method based on differential calculus. Our boundary rent curve approach appears to be more intuitively appealing. The effects of land taxation and zoning were first studied by Alonso (1964, Ch. 6) and Henderson (1985). Wildasin (1985) presents comparative statics of income taxes with time allocation. Comparative statics of optimal land use were studied by Witchard (1984). Although all these studies focus on comparative statics of cities under absentee landownership, Pines and Sadka (1986), Arnott, Pines, and Sadka (1986), and Sasaki (1987) examined the case of public landownership. Comparative statics of equilibrium land use with endogenous wage income (due to returns to scale in production) was studied by Koide (1985). In discussing the flattening population density curve (Figure 3.13), the author benefited from Schweizer (1985).

Because of space limitations, we were unable to discuss several important topics. Although we have assumed that the transport cost is the same in every direction from the CBD, more realistic, nonuniform transport networks have been considered by Muth (1969, Ch. 4) and Anas and Moses (1979). Next, although we have assumed a single concentration of employment and shopping, the CBD, many works have introduced multiple, prespecified centers of employment or shopping. See, for example, Muth (1969), Papageorgiou and Casetti (1971), Hartwick and Hartwick (1974), Odland (1976), White (1976), Romanos (1977), and Sullivan (1986). Solow (1973) considered the spatial distribution of service workers. Finally, recall that a negative exponential function has often been used in the empirical analysis of urban population densities. For the theoretical derivation of a negative exponential population density function, see Muth (1969, Ch. 4), Niedercorn (1971), Mills (1972b), and Brueckner (1982).

Notes

1. As before, when there is no solution to the maximization problem of (3.2), we define $\psi(I, u) = 0$ and $s(I, u) = \infty$.
2. Recall that $\partial \bar{s}/\partial R$ is always negative, and $\partial \hat{s}/\partial R$ is negative from Assumption 2.3.
3. Since agricultural activity does not play an important role in urban land use theory, we assume that the agricultural bid rent is a constant independent of location.
4. By definition, $n(r)$ represents the number of households per unit of distance at r. As noted in Section 1.2, we assume that the number of households is so large that the distribution of households over the urban area can safely be treated in terms of density. Consequently, throughout this book, all equilibrium conditions and optimality conditions are stated in terms of *densities* of households and land consumptions at each location (or distance). For mathematical justification of this *density approach*, see Asami, Fujita, and Smith (1987) and Papageorgiou and Pines (1987).
5. Since land conversion cost is assumed to be zero, landowners who keep their lands idle simply miss an opportunity to earn rents. This contradicts the rationality of landowners.
6. As the reader may have noticed, landowners do not play an active role in the static theory of land use. For the reason explained in note 5, the only rational choice for landowners is to rent their lands at market prices.
7. These points will be proved in the formal analysis of the next chapter (see Property 4.10).
8. The case in which Y is a function of city population N is studied in Section 5.7 and in Chapter 8.
9. When $u \geq \tilde{u}(Y)$ $(u > \tilde{u}(Y^0))$, the equilibrium population of the OCA(Y, u) model [OCP(Y, u) model] is zero. And when $N = 0$, the CCA(Y, N) and CCP(Y, N) models are not defined. Of course, when $Y \leq T(0)$ or $Y^0 \leq T(0)$, no city can exist. Hence, these are not interesting cases.
10. More precisely, let $(R(r), n(r), s(r), r_f, u^*)$ represent the equilibrium solution of a CCA model and $(R(r), n(r), s(r), r_f, N^*)$ that of an OCA model. Then

Proposition 3.5(i) (outside brackets) means that if $(R(r), n(r), s(r), r_f, u^*)$ is the solution to the CCA(Y, N) model, then $(R(r), n(r), s(r), r_f, N)$ is the solution to the OCA(Y, u^*) model. Similar comments apply to the rest of Proposition 3.5.

11. This phenomenon was discovered by Mirrlees (1972). For an explanation and for further discussion of this subject, see Riley (1973, 1974), Arnott and Riley (1977), Levhari, Oron, and Pines (1978), Kanemoto (1980, App. I), and Wildasin (1986a).
12. For the HS model with variable population, see Section 5.4.
13. $(n(r), s(r), r_f)$ is the simplified expression of $(n(r), s(r), r_f: n(r) \geq 0, s(r) > 0$, at each $0 \leq r \leq r_f)$.
14. Each HS model is characterized by a per capita income Y^0, target utility $\bar{u}$, and population N; hence, we represent it by HS(Y^0, $\bar{u}$, N).
15. A feasible allocation is called *efficient (or Pareto optimal)* if and only if the following two conditions are met: (a) no feasible reallocation could increase the utility level of any group of households without lowering the utility level of some other group of households or without decreasing the surplus, and (b) no feasible reallocation could increase the surplus without lowering the utility level of some group of households. It is not difficult to see that the solution to any HS model is efficient in this sense.
16. As before, $R(r)$, $n(r)$, $s(r)$, and r_f represent, respectively, the market rent curve, population distribution, lot size function, and urban fringe distance; G^* is the income tax in the equilibrium.
17. Since u is fixed, Assumption 2.3 is not necessary for the existence and uniqueness of the solution to the HS(Y^0, $\bar{u}$, N) model. Note also that in Assumption 2.2, it is not necessary to assume that $T(0) < Y$. If we assume that the total amount of land $\int_0^\infty L(r)\,dr$ is infinite, then Assumption 3.2 is also unnecessary. However, if $\int_0^\infty L(r)\,dr < \infty$, then Assumption 3.2 is necessary in order to ensure the existence of a solution b to equation (3.64) under each value of G.
18. For the proof of these points, see Property 4.10 and the argument just before Proposition 4.3.
19. A similar comparison with open-city models (OCA and OCP) will be made in Section 5.4.
20. We assume throughout this section that Assumptions 2.1–2.3 and Assumptions 3.1 and 3.2 hold. We also assume that $N > 0$.
21. Mathematically, Proposition 3.9 is obvious. If we compare the set of conditions (3.67)–(3.70) with the set of conditions (3.71)–(3.74), it is evident that $(R(r), n(r), s(r), r_f, G^*)$ satisfies all conditions (3.71)–(3.74) if and only if it satisfies all conditions (3.67)–(3.70), with u^* and $\bar{G}$ being replaced by $\bar{u}$ and G^*, respectively. This means Proposition 3.9.
22. This conclusion is hardly surprising in light of traditional welfare economic theory. Nevertheless, it is worth reconfirming in the context of the model with continuous space. Notice also that we can partition the originally homogeneous households into any finite number of groups and assign different

target utility levels (if we wish to do so). Then we have a problem with multiple household types, which will be considered in Section 4.4.

23. For the proof of Property 3.3, see Appendix C.3. The assumption, $R_A > 0$ is necessary only to show that $\lim_{u\to\infty} \mathcal{S}(Y^0, u, N) = -\infty$ and $\lim_{u\to\infty} G(Y^0, u, N) = -\infty$.
24. Although the TDR(Y^0, u, N) curve is depicted in Figure 3.7 as if it is always increasing in u, this may not always be true. This point, however, is not important in the subsequent discussion.
25. Other cases can be studied similarly. In particular, the cases of the open-city model are much simpler. Comparative statics of optimal land use can also be studied in this way.
26. Since the change in the fixed transport cost $T(0)$ can be considered to be a change in gross income Y, we assume here that $T(0)$ remains the same.
27. For the formal proof of relation (3.83), see Appendix C.4.
28. For the proof of Property 3.4, see Appendix C.5.
29. Although this point will be explained later in detail, it is clear from Proposition 3.10, which says that any efficient allocation can be achieved through an appropriate income taxation.
30. Another popular type of zoning is density intensity zoning such as minimum lot zoning, maximum lot zoning, and building height zoning. Here we study only land use zoning because, as noted before, the study of zoning is not very important in the context of Part I.
31. This is merely a matter of convenience. We can easily see that whether we assume land taxes are paid by landowners or by tenants, no difference emerges in the main conclusions of this subsection.
32. Here, in the case of proportional land taxation, we are implicitly assuming that R_A is positive. When R_A is zero, ΔR is always zero, and hence proportional land taxation has no effect on equilibrium land use.
33. See, e.g., Muth (1969) and Mills and Hamilton (1984).
34. That is, F has the property of constant returns to scale, it is strictly quasi-concave and twice continuously differentiable, and $\partial F/\partial L > 0$, $\partial F/\partial K > 0$, $\partial^2 F/\partial L^2 < 0$, $\partial^2 F/\partial K^2 < 0$, $\partial F/\partial L \to \infty$ as $L \to 0$, and $\partial F/\partial K \to \infty$ as $K \to 0$.
35. Equation (3.94) can be obtained as follows: $\max_{s,k}(R_H(r)F(s, k) - k)/s = \max_{s,k}\{R_H(r)F(1, k/s) - k/s\} = \max_{s,k,q}\{[(Y - T(r) - Z(q, u))/q]F(1, k/s) - k/s\} = \max_{s,k,q}\{[(Y - T(r) - Z(q, u))/q]F(1, k/s) - k/s \mid q = F(s, k)\}$ (because of the freedom due to the constant returns to scale property of F) $= \max_{s,k}\{[(Y - T(r) - Z(F(s, k), u))/F(s, k)]F(s, k)/s - k/s\} = \max_{s,k}\{[Y - T(r) - Z(F(s, k), u)]/s - k/s\}$, which gives (3.94). Note also that in the context of the reduced-form model (2.75), this bid land rent function comes out in a straightforward way.

CHAPTER 4

Equilibrium land use and optimal land use: multiple household types

4.1 Introduction

In this chapter, we consider the case of multiple household types. The contents of the chapter are parallel to those of the preceding chapter. First, we introduce the concept of well-behaved bid rent functions and lot size functions in order to establish a rigorous mathematical base for the bid rent curve approach. Then in Section 4.3 we go on to define equilibrium land use in the context of the closed-city model under absentee landownership and demonstrate its existence and uniqueness. In Section 4.4 we define optimal land use and show its existence and uniqueness. As in Chapter 3, we use boundary rent curves, taking a graphical approach to the proof of the existence and uniqueness of equilibrium and optimal land use. This also leads to a simple algorithm for the computation of equilibrium and optimal land use. In Section 4.5 we compare equilibrium and optimal land use, and draw the conclusion that the competitive equilibrium is socially efficient. In Section 4.6, we conduct comparative static analyses of equilibrium land use. Again, by using the boundary rent curve approach, we examine the effects of population and income changes on equilibrium land use.

Although our boundary rent curve approach for the existence and uniqueness problem is mathematically simple and intuitively appealing, it requires a strong condition–that the set of bid rent functions involved in the problem can be ordered according to their steepness. Hence, this approach works only for a limited class of problems. It is therefore natural to ask whether we can prove the existence and/or uniqueness of equilibrium and optimal land use without the assumption of ordered bid functions. It turns out that although this assumption is essential for the uniqueness, it is not necessary for the existence. The existence proof without this assumption, however, requires complex mathematical analysis, and the reader is referred to Fujita and Smith (1987).

4.2 Well-behaved bid rent functions and lot size functions

In the subsequent sections, we define and analyze equilibrium land use in terms of bid rent functions and (bid-max) lot size functions. We simply assume that these functions have been derived from certain residential choice models, such as the basic model or time-extended model in Chapter 2. The specification of bid rent and lot size functions is unnecessary for our formal analysis in this chapter; all we need is to assume that the functions derived from residential choice models are *well behaved*. The definition of well-behaved functions is given later. To lay the foundation for the definition, let us first consider a simple example of a residential choice model.[1]

Let us consider the following model of residential choice by a household:

$$\max_{r,z,s} \alpha \log z + \beta \log s, \qquad \text{subject to} \quad z + R(r)s = Y - T(r), \tag{4.1}$$

which is obtained by specifying the log-linear utility function (2.12) in the basic model (2.1). Here, α and β are positive constants such that $\alpha + \beta = 1$, and all other notation is the same as in Chapter 2. Then as we learned in Example 2.1, the bid rent function and lot size function are given respectively as follows:

$$\Psi^0(r, u) = \alpha^{\alpha/\beta}\beta(Y - T(r))^{1/\beta}e^{-u/\beta}, \tag{4.2}$$

$$S^0(r, u) = \alpha^{-\alpha/\beta}(Y - T(r))^{-\alpha/\beta}e^{u/\beta}. \tag{4.3}$$

Here for a reason that will quickly become clear, we use expressions $\Psi^0(r, u)$ and $S^0(r, u)$ instead of $\Psi(r, u)$ and $S(r, u)$. Note that functions (4.2) and (4.3) are both well defined only on the domain $D^0 = \{(r, u) \mid 0 \leq r < \infty, T(r) < Y, -\infty < u < \infty\}$. For convenience, we want to extend the domain of each function on the set $D = \{(r, u) \mid 0 \leq r < \infty, -\infty < u < \infty\}$. This we can achieve by extending the functions as follows:

$$\Psi(r, u) = \begin{cases} \Psi^0(r, u) & \text{for} \quad (r, u) \in D^0, \\ 0 & \text{for} \quad (r, u) \in D - D^0, \end{cases} \tag{4.4}$$

$$S(r, u) = \begin{cases} S^0(r, u) & \text{for} \quad (r, u) \in D^0, \\ \infty & \text{for} \quad (r, u) \in D - D^0. \end{cases} \tag{4.5}$$

Then we have $\Psi: D \to [0, \infty)$ and $S: D \to (0, \infty]$.[2] When the distinction is necessary, we may call Ψ^0 and S^0 the *original functions*, and Ψ and S the *extended functions*. For this extended function S, it is also convenient to associate the (extended) *household density function* $\rho: D \to [0, \infty)$, defined by

$$\rho(r, u) = \frac{1}{S(r, u)} = \begin{cases} 1/S^0(r, u) & \text{for} \quad (r, u) \in D^0, \\ 0 & \text{for} \quad (r, u) \in D - D^0. \end{cases}$$

These extended functions have many desirable characteristics. By summarizing these characteristics, we obtain the following definitions of *well-behaved functions:*[3]

Definition 4.1. Let $D = \{(r, u) \mid 0 \leq r < \infty, -\infty < u < \infty\}$. A pair of functions, $\Psi: D \to [0, \infty)$ and $S: D \to (0, \infty]$, is *well behaved* if and only if the following set of conditions is satisfied:

(i) Ψ and $\rho \equiv 1/S$ are continuous on D.
(ii) $\{(r, u) \in D \mid \Psi(r, u) > 0\} = \{(r, u) \in D \mid \rho(r, u) > 0\} \neq \emptyset$. This nonempty set is denoted by D^0.
(iii) On D^0, Ψ and ρ are decreasing in both r and u.
(iv) D^0 is bounded in r. That is, there exists a finite distance $\bar{r} > 0$ such that if $(r, u) \in D^0$, then $r < \bar{r}$.
(v) There exists a finite distance $\tilde{r} > 0$ such that for any $r \in [0, \tilde{r}]$, $\Psi(r, u) \to \infty$ and $\rho(r, u) \to \infty$ as $u \to -\infty$.
(vi) $\Psi(0, u) \to 0$ and $\rho(0, u) \to 0$ as $u \to \infty$.

When functions Ψ and S are well behaved, we may call D^0 and D in Definition 4.1, respectively, the *effective domain* and the *extended domain* of Ψ and S. Condition (i) means that small changes in distance and utility level yield only small changes in bid rent and lot size, which is a natural mathematical requirement. Condition (ii) means that when bid rent $\Psi(r, u)$ is positive, lot size $S(r, u)$ is finite; in other words, when land price is positive, demand for land is finite. Condition (iii) is simply a restatement of Property 2.1. Condition (iv) means that beyond a certain distance from the CBD, bid rent becomes zero. Condition (v) means that in an area close to the CBD, bid rent (lot size) can be made as large (small) as desired by lowering the utility level. In the context of Figure 2.2, this means that indifference curve u approaches the origin as u decreases. Finally, condition (vi) means that the bid rent (lot size) at the CBD becomes zero (infinite) as utility level increases. Again, in the context of Figure 2.2, this means that as u increases, the indifference curve moves toward the northeast without limit.

When carefully defined in the context of monocentric cities, bid rent and lot size functions are almost always well behaved. For example, in the case of model (4.1), further suppose that the transport cost function $T(r)$ satisfies Assumption 2.2. Then we can easily see that functions Ψ and S defined by equations (4.2)–(4.5) are well behaved.[4] A more general example can be given as follows:

Example 4.1 (well-behaved bid rent and lot size functions). Let us recall the basic model of residential choice:

$$\max_{r,z,s} U(z, s), \qquad \text{subject to} \quad z + R(r)s = Y - T(r).$$

We assume that Assumptions 2.1–2.3 are satisfied. Without loss of generality, we can also assume that

$$\inf\{U(z, s) \mid z > 0, s > 0\} = -\infty, \qquad \sup\{U(z, s) \mid z > 0, s > 0\} = \infty.$$

We define the original bid rent function by (2.8), that is, by

$$\Psi^0(r, u) = \max_{s>0} \frac{Y - T(r) - Z(s, u)}{s}, \tag{4.6}$$

and the original lot size function $S^0(r, u)$ is defined as the optimal s for the maximization problem in the right-hand side. The domain of functions Ψ^0 and S^0 is given by

$$D^0 = \{(r, u) \mid 0 \leq r < \infty, -\infty < u < \infty, Y - T(r) > \lim_{s\to\infty} Z(s, u)\}.$$

We define the extended functions Ψ and S in the same way as (4.4) and (4.5). Then it is not difficult to see that functions Ψ and S are well behaved.[5] In particular, $\rho \equiv 1/S$ is decreasing in u because of the normality of land. Condition (iv) of Definition 4.1 is satisfied by any $\bar{r}$ such that $T(\bar{r}) > Y$, and condition (v) by any $\bar{r} > 0$ such that $T(\bar{r}) < Y$.

As we learned in Chapter 2, for each fixed u, $\Psi(\cdot, u)$ defines a bid rent curve in the r(distance) – R(rent) space, and $S(\cdot, u)$ a lot size curve in the $r - s$ space. Suppose functions Ψ and S are well behaved. Then it is not difficult to confirm the following properties of bid rent curves:[6]

Property 4.1. Bid rent curves (that belong to the same household) never intersect before reaching the r axis. That is, if $u \neq u'$, then $\Psi(r, u) \neq \Psi(r, u')$ whenever $\Psi(r, u) > 0$.

Property 4.2. For each point on the positive part of the R axis, there is one and only one bid rent curve that starts from that point.

Property 4.3. Each bid rent curve is continuous and decreasing in r up to the intersection with the r axis.

Property 4.4. As u increases, the positive part of the bid rent curve continuously shifts downward[7] and uniformly converges to the r axis.

Similarly, it is not difficult to confirm the following properties of lot size curves:

Property 4.5. Lot size curves (that belong to the same household) never intersect before reaching infinity. That is, if $u \neq u'$, then $S(r, u) \neq S(r, u')$ whenever $S(r, u) < \infty$.

Property 4.6. Each lot size curve $S(\cdot, u)$ is continuous and increasing in r and approaches infinity at the distance where the corresponding bid rent curve $\Psi(\cdot, u)$ intersects the r axis.

Property 4.7. As u decreases, the lot size curve continuously shifts downward. On $[0, \bar{r}]$, the lot size curve uniformly converges to the r axis as u approaches $-\infty$.

Therefore, as before, the general shape of bid rent curves can be depicted as in Figure 2.5; the general shape of lot size curves as in Figure 2.6.

4.3 Equilibrium land use

4.3.1 Definition of equilibrium land use

Suppose that the households in the city consist of m different types, $i = 1, 2, \ldots, m$. The number of household types i is exogenously given by a positive constant N_i. All households of type i have the same bid rent function Ψ_i and the same lot size function S_i such that

$$\Psi_i: D \to [0, \infty), \; S_i: D \to (0, \infty], \qquad i = 1, 2, \ldots, m, \tag{4.7}$$

where $D = \{(r, u) \mid 0 \leq r < \infty, -\infty < u < \infty\}$. We assume that all functions Ψ_i and $S_i (i = 1, 2, \ldots, m)$ are exogenously given.[8] As before, the amount of land available for residential use at each distance r is given by $L(r)$. Land that is not occupied by households is used for agriculture, yielding a constant rent $R_A \geq 0$. Now, generalizing the equilibrium conditions (3.13)–(3.17) to the present case with multiple household types, we define equilibrium land use as follows:[9]

Definition 4.2. An *equilibrium land use* consists of a set of utility levels u_i^*, nonnegative household distributions $n_i(r)$ $[i = 1, 2, \ldots, m, 0 \leq r < \infty]$, and a land rent curve $R(r)$ such that

(a) for land market at each $r \in [0, \infty)$,

$$R(r) = \max\{\max_i \Psi_i(r, u_i^*), R_A\}, \tag{4.8}$$

$$R(r) = \Psi_i(r, u_i^*) \qquad \text{if} \quad n_i(r) > 0, \tag{4.9}$$

$$\sum_{i=1}^{m} S_i(r, u_i^*) n_i(r) \leq L(r), \tag{4.10}$$

$$\sum_{i=1}^{m} S_i(r, u_i^*) n_i(r) = L(r) \qquad \text{if} \quad R(r) > R_A, \tag{4.11}$$

(b) for population constraint

$$\int_0^\infty n_i(r)\, dr = N_i, \qquad i = 1, 2, \ldots, m. \tag{4.12}$$

Condition (4.8) means that *the market rent curve $R(r)$ is the upper envelope of the equilibrium bid rent curves $\Psi_i(r, u_i^*)$ of all household types ($i = 1, 2, \ldots, m$) and the agricultural rent line R_A*. This ensures that no type i household can achieve a utility level higher than u_i^* ($i = 1, 2, \ldots, m$), and no farmers can make a positive profit. Condition (4.9) ensures that if some households of type i reside at distance r, they actually achieve the equilibrium utility u_i^*. Condition (4.10) means that at each r, the total demand for land cannot exceed the amount of land existing there. This is simply a physical constraint. Condition (4.11) means that if the market land rent at r exceeds the agricultural rent, all land there must be used for housing. Conditions (4.8), (4.9), and (4.11) together imply that whenever the equilibrium rent exceeds the agricultural rent, the land is used by the households with the highest equilibrium bid rent. In other words, they ensure that *each location is occupied by a highest-bidding activity*. Condition (4.12) ensures that every household resides somewhere in the city.[10]

Our subsequent analysis in this section is based on the following set of assumptions.[11]

> ***Assumption 4.1.*** Land distribution function $L(r)$ is continuous on $[0, \infty)$, and $L(r) > 0$ for all $r > 0$.
>
> ***Assumption 4.2.*** All bid rent functions Ψ_i and lot size functions S_i ($i = 1, 2, \ldots, m$) are well behaved.
>
> ***Assumption 4.3.*** The set of bid rent functions Ψ_i ($i = 1, 2, \ldots, m$) can be ordered by relative steepness. For convenience, let index i represent steepness in decreasing order. Thus, Ψ_1 is the steepest function, Ψ_2 is the next steepest, and so on.

Under Assumption 4.2, all equilibrium bid rent curves $\Psi_i(r, u_i^*)$, $i = 1, 2, \ldots, m$, are continuously decreasing in r (until they reach the r axis).

Then since the upper envelope of these curves is also continuously decreasing in r, Property 4.8 follows from equilibrium condition (4.8).

Property 4.8. In equilibrium under Assumption 4.2, the market rent curve $R(r)$ is continuously decreasing up to the urban fringe r_f, which is uniquely defined by $r_f = \min\{r \mid R(r) = R_A\}$.

Also, under Assumption 4.2, from Definition 4.1(ii), there is a nonempty subset of D_i^0 of D for each i such that

$$\begin{aligned} D_i^0 &= \{(r, u) \in D \mid \Psi_i(r, u) > 0\}, \\ &= \{(r, u) \in D \mid S_i(r, u) < \infty\}, \end{aligned} \tag{4.13}$$

which gives the *effective domain* of functions Ψ_i and S_i ($i = 1, 2, \ldots, m$). From equilibrium condition (4.10), if $n_i(r) > 0$, then $S_i(r, u_i^*) < \infty$; hence, from (4.13), $(r, u_i^*) \in D_i^0$, and $\Psi_i(r, u_i^*) > 0$. By definition, $\Psi_i(r, u) < \infty$ and $S_i(r, u) > 0$ for any u. Hence, we can conclude the following:

Property 4.9. In equilibrium under Assumption 4.2, if $n_i(r) > 0$, then $(r, u_i^*) \in D_i^0$, and hence $0 < \Psi_i(r, u_i^*) < \infty$ and $0 < S_i(r, u_i^*) < \infty$ ($i = 1, 2, \ldots, m$).

From a practical point of view, an equilibrium with zero lot size or infinite lot size for some households would not be acceptable. In this sense, Property 4.9 ensures that the equilibrium under Assumption 4.2 is practically meaningful.

Next, let us recall that the relative steepness among bid rent functions is characterized by Definition 2.2. From Rule 2.3, if bid rent function Ψ_i is steeper than Ψ_j, then all type i households reside closer to the city center than the households of type j. Therefore, under Assumption 4.3, it follows that in equilibrium all type 1 households reside closer to the city center than households of any other type, and so on. That is, *households of each type form a concentric ring, or zone, around the city center, and zones for all household types are ranked by the distance from the city center in the order of steepness of their bid rent functions.* And from Property 4.8 and equilibrium condition (4.11), no agricultural land should be left inside the urban fringe. Hence, zone J_i for each household type i can be expressed as

$$J_1 = [0, r_1^*), \qquad J_i = [r_{i-1}^*, r_i^*), \qquad i = 2, 3, \ldots, m,$$

where

$$0 < r_1^* < r_2^* < \cdots < r_m^* = r_f .$$

And each household distribution $n_i(r)$, $i = 1, 2, \ldots, m$, takes the next form:

$$n_i(r) = \begin{cases} L(r)/S_i(r, u_i^*) & \text{for} \quad r \in J_i , \\ 0 & \text{for} \quad r \notin J_i . \end{cases}$$

Therefore, under Assumptions 4.2 and 4.3, Definition 4.2 can be restated as follows:

Definition 4.2′. Suppose Assumptions 4.2 and 4.3 hold. Then an equilibrium land use consists of a set of utility levels u_i^*, $i = 1, 2, \ldots, m$, a set of distances r_i^*, $i = 0, 1, 2, \ldots, m$, where $r_0^* \equiv 0 < r_1^* < r_2^* < \cdots < r_m^*$, and a land rent curve $R(r)$ such that

$$\Psi_i(r_i^*, u_i^*) = \Psi_{i+1}(r_i^*, u_{i+1}^*), \qquad i = 1, 2, \ldots, m-1, \tag{4.14}$$

$$\Psi_m(r_m^*, u_m^*) = R_A , \tag{4.15}$$

$$R(r) = \begin{cases} \Psi_i(r, u_i^*) & \text{for} \quad r_{i-1}^* \leq r \leq r_i^*, \qquad i = 1, 2, \ldots, m, \\ R_A & \text{for} \quad r \geq r_m^*, \end{cases} \tag{4.16}$$

$$\int_{r_{i-1}^*}^{r_i^*} \frac{L(r)}{S_i(r, u_i^*)} dr = N_i , \qquad i = 1, 2, \ldots, m. \tag{4.17}$$

In Figure 4.1, the equilibrium land use configuration, as defined above, is depicted for the case of three household types ($m = 3$). In the upper half of the figure, the market rent curve is described by a set of kinked bold lines. In the two-dimensional picture of the lower half, the land use pattern is described as a set of *Thünen rings*.

4.3.2 Existence and uniqueness of the equilibrium

As might be inferred from the preceding chapter, the direct computation of an equilibrium land use for the case of multiple households would be very difficult, if not impossible. But as before, we do not have to obtain an exact description of equilibrium; knowledge of more general properties, such as existence, uniqueness, efficiency, and comparative statics, is sufficient for our purposes. To this end, therefore, and as in Chapter 3, we resort to the concept of boundary rent curves, which we now elaborate in order to explore the more general case. The basic difference between our method here and that of Chapter 3 is that now we must define a set of boundary rent curves, not just one.

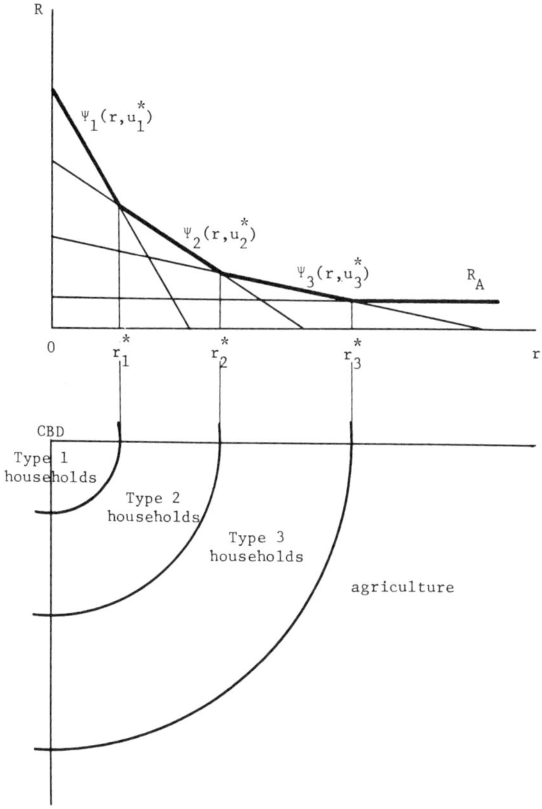

Figure 4.1. Equilibrium land use configuration ($m = 3$).

In this subsection, we show that the equilibrium land use uniquely exists under Assumptions 4.1–4.3. To do this, it is sufficient to show the existence and uniqueness of the set of pairs (r_i^*, u_i^*), $i = 1, 2, \ldots, m$ that satisfies equilibrium conditions (4.14)–(4.17). This can be achieved by a procedure that is similar to the recursive solution method of dynamic programming by Bellman (1957). The key part of the procedure is to obtain a set of boundary rent curves, denoted by $R_i(r)$, $i = 1, 2, \ldots, m$. Here we give an informal description of how to obtain these curves recursively. The formal procedure is explained in Appendix C.6.

The first boundary rent curve $R_1(r)$ is obtained in exactly the same manner as before. That is, under each value of u, we solve the following equation for b:

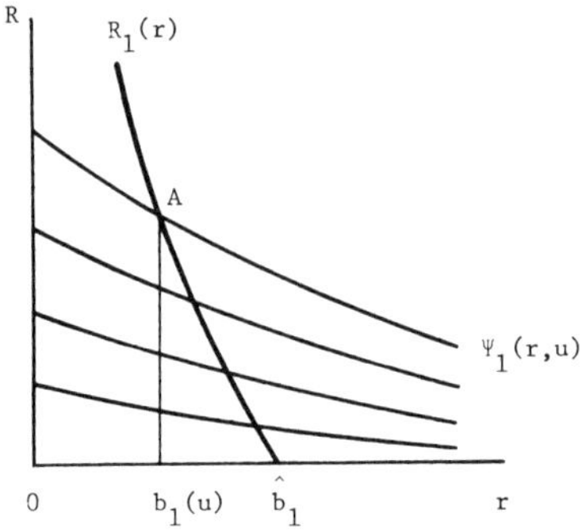

Figure 4.2. Boundary rent curve between zones 1 and 2.

$$\int_0^b \frac{L(r)}{S_1(r, u)}\, dr = N_1, \tag{4.18}$$

and obtain the *outer boundary function* $b_1(u)$ of zone 1. For each given u, $b_1(u)$ marks a distance on the corresponding bid rent curve $\Psi_1(r, u)$, such as point A in Figure 4.2. By changing u, we can obtain a curve $R_1(r)$, called the boundary rent curve, between zones 1 and 2. If the inverse of $r = b_1(u)$ is denoted by $U_1(r)$, this boundary rent curve can be defined as

$$R_1(r) = \Psi_1(r, U_1(r)). \tag{4.19}$$

By definition, $R_1(r)$ represents the market land rent at r when the boundary between zones 1 and 2 occurs at r. From condition (iii) of Definition 4.1, it is not difficult to see that curve $R_1(r)$ is decreasing in r.

Continuing, we solve the next equation for a under each value of u,

$$\Psi_2(a, u) = R_1(a),$$

and obtain the *inner boundary function* $a_2(u)$ of zone 2. That is, $a_2(u)$ denotes the distance at which the bid rent curve $\Psi_2(r, u)$ intersects the boundary rent curve $R_1(r)$ (see Figure 4.3 and let $i = 2$). Next, using this function $a_2(u)$, under each value of u, we solve the following equation for b,

$$\int_{a_2(u)}^b \frac{L(r)}{S_2(r, u)}\, dr = N_2,$$

and obtain the outer boundary function $b_2(u)$ of zone 2. Let $U_2(r)$ be the inverse function of $r = b_2(u)$. Then the boundary rent curve $R_2(r)$ between zones 2 and 3 can be defined as

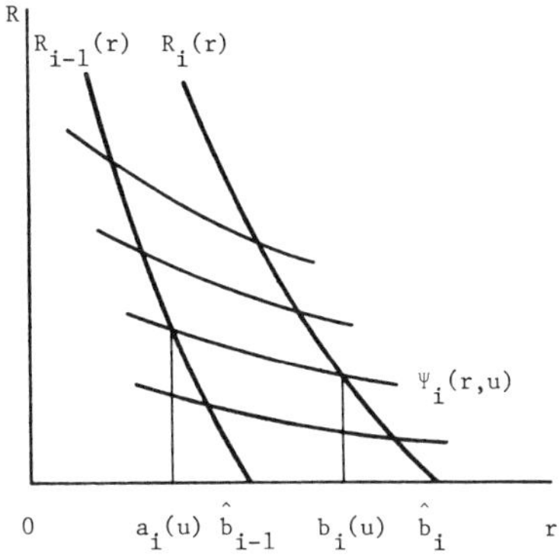

Figure 4.3. Determination of $R_i(r)$ from $R_{i-1}(r)$.

$$R_2(r) = \Psi_2(r, U_2(r)).$$

As before, we can see that $R_2(r)$ is decreasing in r.

Generally, given $R_{i-1}(r)$ via prior calculation ($i = 2, 3, \ldots,$ or m), the inner boundary function $a_i(u)$ of zone i is obtained by solving the next equation for a under each value of u:

$$\Psi_i(a, u) = R_{i-1}(a). \tag{4.20}$$

The outer boundary function $b_i(u)$ is given by solving

$$\int_{a_i(u)}^{b} \frac{L(r)}{S_i(r, u)}\, dr = N_i\,. \tag{4.21}$$

Finally, if the inverse function of $r = b_i(u)$ is denoted by $U_i(r)$, the boundary rent curve $R_i(r)$ between zones i and $i + 1$ is defined as

$$R_i(r) = \Psi_i(r, U_i(r)). \tag{4.22}$$

Figure 4.3 depicts the process for determining $R_i(r)$ from $R_{i-1}(r)$.

In this way, we can recursively determine a set of boundary rent curves $R_i(r)$, $i = 1, 2, \ldots, m$. By definition, $R_i(r)$ represents the market land rent at r when the boundary between zones i and $i + 1$ occurs at r. About these curves, we can show the following:

Property 4.10. Under Assumptions 4.1–4.3, the boundary rent curves $R_i(r)$, $i = 1, 2, \ldots, m$, have the following characteristics:

(i) There exists a distance $\hat{b}_i > 0$ such that $R_i(r)$ is defined on $(0, \hat{b}_i)$ and $\lim_{r\to 0} R_i(r) = \infty$, $\lim_{r\to \hat{b}_i} R_i(r) = 0$ ($i = 1, 2, \ldots, m$).

(ii) On $(0, \hat{b}_i)$, $R_i(r)$ is continuous and decreasing in r ($i = 1, 2, \ldots, m$).

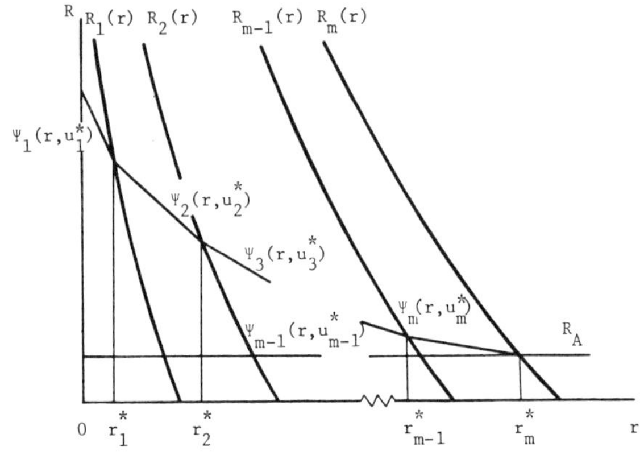

Figure 4.4. Determination of equilibrium land use.

(iii) $0 < \hat{b}_1 \leq \hat{b}_2 \leq \cdots \leq \hat{b}_m$, and no pair of boundary rent curves intersects one another.

(iv) $R_i(r)$ is *steeper* than all Ψ_j, $j = i, i + 1, \ldots, m$. That is, whenever $R_i(r) = \Psi_j(r, u)$ for some r and u, then $R_i(x) > \Psi_j(x, u)$ for all $x < r$, and $R_i(x) < \Psi_j(x, u)$ for all $r < x < \hat{b}_i$.

The proof of this property is given in Appendix C.6. From this, we can draw the set of boundary rent curves $R_i(r)$, $i = 1, 2, \ldots, m$, as in Figure 4.4.

Next, by using these boundary rent curves $R_i(r)$, $i = 1, 2, \ldots, m$, we can determine the equilibrium land use by the following *backward procedure* (see Figure 4.4). First, determine the urban fringe r_m^* by the relation[12]

$$R_m(r_m^*) = R_A. \tag{4.23}$$

That is, r_m^* is the distance at which boundary rent curve $R_m(r)$ intersects the agricultural rent line. Then determine the equilibrium utility level u_m^* by the relation

$$\Psi_m(r_m^*, u_m^*) = R_A. \tag{4.24}$$

Next, determine boundary distance r_{m-1}^* by the relation

$$\Psi_m(r_{m-1}^*, u_m^*) = R_{m-1}(r_{m-1}^*). \tag{4.25}$$

That is, r_{m-1}^* is the distance at which bid rent curve $\Psi_m(r, u_m^*)$ intersects the boundary rent curve $R_{m-1}(r)$. Then determine the equilibrium utility level u_{m-1}^* by the relation

$$\Psi_{m-1}(r^*_{m-1}, u^*_{m-1}) = R_{m-1}(r^*_{m-1}). \tag{4.26}$$

Recursively, having obtained u_i^* ($i = m, m-1, \ldots,$ or 2), determine boundary distance r^*_{i-1} by the relation

$$\Psi_i(r^*_{i-1}, u_i^*) = R_{i-1}(r^*_{i-1}). \tag{4.27}$$

Then determine the equilibrium utility level u^*_{i-1} ($i = m, m-1, \ldots,$ or 2) by the relation

$$\Psi_{i-1}(r^*_{i-1}, u^*_{i-1}) = R_{i-1}(r^*_{i-1}). \tag{4.28}$$

The procedure ends when (r_1^*, u_1^*) is determined.

From Property 4.10, it is not difficult to see the following:

Property 4.11. Under Assumptions 4.1–4.3,

(i) the above procedure uniquely determines a set of pairs (r_i^*, u_i^*), $i = 1, 2, \ldots, m$;

(ii) this set of pairs (r_i^*, u_i^*), $i = 1, 2, \ldots, m$, together with the market rent curve $R(r)$ defined by (4.16), constitutes an equilibrium land use;

(iii) there is no other equilibrium land use.

The proof is given in Appendix C.6. From Properties 4.9 and 4.11, we can conclude as follows:

> ***Proposition 4.1.*** Under Assumptions 4.1–4.3, the equilibrium land use exists uniquely. In equilibrium, whenever $n_i(r) > 0$, (r, u_i^*) belongs to the effective domain D_i^0, and hence $0 < \Psi_i(r, u_i^*) < \infty$ and $0 < S_i(r, u_i^*) < \infty$ ($i = 1, 2, \ldots, m$).

Note that in the case of a single household type ($m = 1$), Assumption 4.3 is not necessary for the existence and uniqueness of the equilibrium.

Finally, the above proof suggests the following algorithm for computing the equilibrium land use, which is described in Figure 4.5. In this algorithm, having obtained u_i ($i = 1, 2, \ldots,$ or m), we obtain r_i by solving the equation

$$\int_{r_{i-1}}^{r_i} \frac{L(r)}{S_i(r, u_i)}\, dr = N_i,$$

where $r_0 \equiv 0$. Then, u_{i+1} ($i = 1, 2, \ldots,$ or m) is determined by the relation $\Psi_i(r_i, u_i) = \Psi_{i+1}(r_i, u_{i+1})$. If we appropriately specify the step size in choosing a new value of u_1 at each round of computation, this

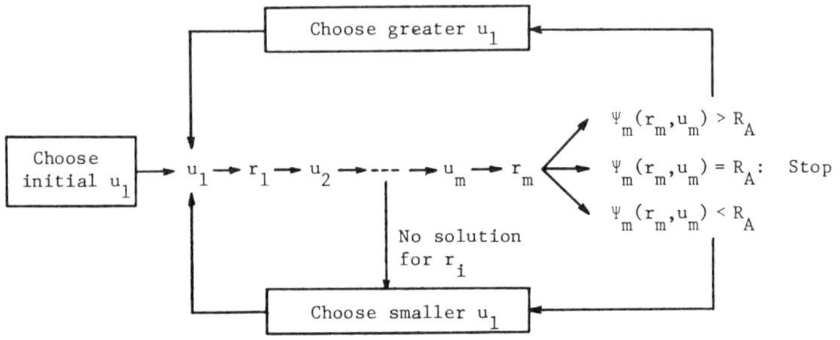

Figure 4.5. Computational algorithm.

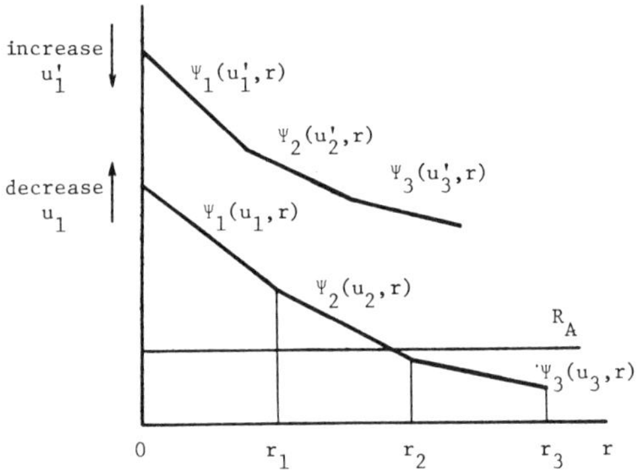

Figure 4.6. Graphical expression of the algorithm in Figure 4.5.

algorithm always converges to the equilibrium solution. Taking the case of $m = 3$, Figure 4.6 describes this algorithm in the urban space.

4.3.3 *Examples and discussion*

In order to apply Proposition 4.1, it is essential to know whether a set of bid rent functions can be ordered by the relative steepness. We learned in Chapter 2 that Rule 2.4 is useful for answering this question.

Example 4.2 (multiple income classes). Suppose all households in the city are identical except for their incomes. They can be grouped into m income classes such that $Y_1 < Y_2 < \cdots < Y_m$, where Y_i is the income for class i ($i = 1, 2, \ldots, m$). The residential choice behavior of each income class i can be expressed as

$$\max_{r,z,s} U(z, s), \qquad \text{subject to} \quad z + R(r)s = Y_i - T(r).$$

Assume that Assumptions 2.1–2.3 are satisfied by each $(U(\cdot), T(\cdot), Y_i)$, $i = 1, 2, \ldots, m$. As in Example 4.1, we obtain the bid rent function and lot size function for each class i, and express them as $\Psi_i(r, u) \equiv \psi(Y_i - T(r), u)$ and $S_i(r, u) \equiv s(Y_i - T(r), u)$. Then, as before, these functions are well behaved; and as we learned in Section 2.4, Ψ_1 is the steepest, Ψ_2 the next steepest, and Ψ_m the least steep.

Similar examples can be constructed by means of the time-extended model or family-structure model in Chapter 2. These examples suggest that although Assumption 4.3 seems a very strong requirement, it is actually satisfied in many land use problems.

Next, we briefly discuss how each of Assumptions 4.1–4.3 is important for the existence or uniqueness of the equilibrium. First, the purpose of Assumption 4.1 is mainly one of mathematical convenience. Actually, $L(r)$ can be any piecewise continuous function on $[0, \infty)$ such that $L(r) \geq 0$ on $[0, \infty)$, $L(r) > 0$ on $(0, r')$, and $L(r) \leq \tilde{L}(r)$ on $[0, \infty)$, where r' is any positive number and $\tilde{L}(r)$ is any continuous function on $[0, \infty)$. Then Proposition 4.1 still holds. Among conditions for well-behaved Ψ and S, the importance of (i) and (ii) of Definition 4.1 for the existence of the equilibrium is obvious. In condition (iii) of Definition 4.1, the monotonicity of Ψ and S in r is not important. With appropriate modifications to other conditions, we can obtain Proposition 4.1 without the monotonicity of Ψ and S in r.[13] Note, however, that in this case boundary rent curves may not be monotonically decreasing in r. Condition (iv) of Definition 4.1 is also not very important. This condition can be dropped if we assume that there exists a distance $\bar{r}$ such that $L(r) = 0$ for all $r > \bar{r}$. Conditions (v) and (vi) are necessary in order to ensure the existence of the intersections between boundary rent curves and the agricultural rent line. The next example illustrates the importance of condition (v) of Definition 4.1.

Example 4.3 (nonexistence of equilibrium). Suppose that the residential choice behavior of all N households of a city can be expressed as

$$\max_{r,z,s} \alpha \log z + \beta \log(s - \bar{s}), \qquad \text{subject to} \quad z + R(r)s = Y - ar,$$

where α, β, $\bar{s}$, and a are positive constants. In this context, we define bid rent function $\Psi(r, u)$ and lot size function $S(r, u)$ as in Example 4.1. Then it is not difficult to see that functions Ψ and S satisfy all conditions of Definition 4.1 except (v). That is,

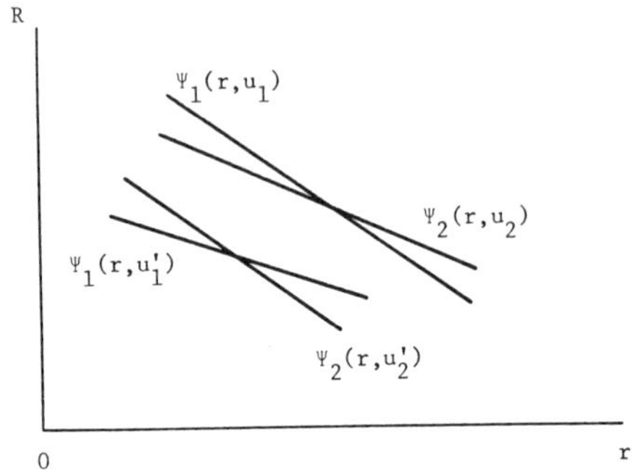

Figure 4.7. Possibility of multiple equilibria: case 1.

$$\lim_{u \to -\infty} \Psi(r, u) \leq Y/\bar{s} \quad \text{and} \quad \lim_{u \to -\infty} S(r, u) = \bar{s} \quad \text{for any} \quad r < Y/a.$$

Therefore, if $R_A > Y/\bar{s}$, then $\Psi(r, u) < R_A$ for any (r, u); hence, there is no equilibrium land use. Even in the case of $R_A = 0$, if $\int_0^{Y/a} L(r)\, dr < N\bar{s}$, there is no equilibrium land use.

Finally, in order to see that Assumption 4.3 is crucial for the uniqueness of equilibrium, let us consider the case of two household types ($m = 2$). Without Assumption 4.3, the possibility of multiple equilibria arises from two different causes. First, if the relative steepness of two bid rent functions changes with utility levels, multiple equilibria may happen. This possibility is illustrated in Figure 4.7, where bid rent curve $\Psi_1(r, u_1)$ is steeper than $\Psi_2(r, u_2)$, but bid rent curve $\Psi_1(r, u_1')$ is not as steep as $\Psi_2(r, u_2')$. Assumptions 4.1 and 4.2 alone cannot prevent the possibility that both (u_1, u_2) and (u_1', u_2') are equilibrium utility combinations. Second, if the relative steepness of two bid rent functions changes with distance, multiple equilibria may happen. This possibility is illustrated in Figure 4.8. In this figure, two bid rent curves, $\Psi_1(r, u_1)$ and $\Psi_2(r, u_2)$ [$\Psi_1(r, u_1')$ and $\Psi_2(r, u_2')$], intersect at distances x_1 and x_2 (y_1 and y_2), and interval (y_1, y_2) is not entirely contained in interval (x_1, x_2). Again, Assumptions 4.1 and 4.2 alone cannot prevent the possibility that both (u_1, u_2) and (u_1', u_2') are equilibrium utility combinations. These examples suggest that when the requirement of relative steepness (Assumption 4.3) is not satisfied, the condition for ensuring the uniqueness of equilibrium will take a complex form involving all parameter functions Ψ_i, S_i, and $L(\cdot)$ ($i = 1, 2, \ldots, m$).

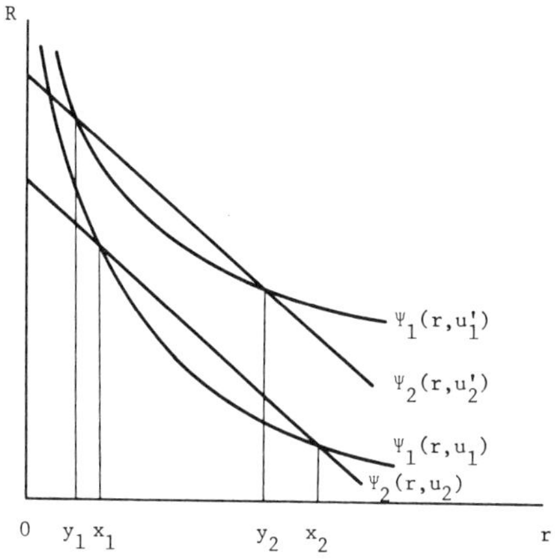

Figure 4.8. Possibility of multiple equilibria: case 2.

4.4 Optimal land use

Here we extend the Herbert–Stevens model (HS model) to the case of multiple household types. And we show that the same method developed in the preceding section (i.e., the boundary rent curve approach) can be applied to the study of the existence and uniqueness of the solution to the HS model.

Suppose that the residents of a city consist of households of m different types. Let $U_i(z, s)$ be the utility function of each type i household, where z and s are, as before, the amount of composite good and the lot size ($i = 1, 2, \ldots, m$). The working members of each household commute to the CBD with commuting costs $T_i(r)$ (per household), earning income Y_i^0 (per household). The number of type i households is given by N_i. All of $T_i(r)$, Y_i^0, and N_i are exogenously given. Let us denote by $n_i(r)$ the number of type i households at distance r, by $(z_i(r), s_i(r))$ the consumption bundle of each household of type i at r, and by r_f the urban fringe distance.

Suppose we choose a target utility level $\bar{u}_i$ for type i households ($i = 1, 2, \ldots, m$) and require that regardless of their locations all households of type i shall attain this utility level. This implies that each allocation $(n_i(r), z_i(r), s_i(r); i = 1, 2, \ldots, m, 0 \leq r \leq r_f)$ must satisfy the following restriction,

$$U_i(z_i(r), s_i(r)) = \bar{u}_i \qquad \text{if} \quad n_i(r) > 0$$

or

$$z_i(r) = Z(s_i(r), \bar{u}_i) \qquad \text{if} \quad n_i(r) > 0,$$

where $Z_i(s, u)$ is the solution to $u = U_i(z, s)$ for z. Therefore, the *total cost* C under each allocation can be calculated as follows:

$$\begin{aligned} C &= \text{transport costs} + \text{composite good costs} + \text{opportunity land costs} \\ &= \int_0^{r_f} \sum_{i=1}^{m} [T_i(r) + Z_i(s_i(r), \bar{u}_i) + R_A s_i(r)] n_i(r)\, dr, \end{aligned} \tag{4.29}$$

where R_A is the agricultural land rent exogenously given. Next, noting that $N_i = \int_0^{r_f} n_i(r)\, dr$, we define the *surplus* from an allocation as follows:

$$\begin{aligned} \mathcal{S} &= \text{total income} - \text{total cost} \\ &= \sum_{i=1}^{m} N_i Y_i^0 - \int_0^{r_f} \sum_{i=1}^{m} [T_i(r) + Z_i(s_i(r), \bar{u}_i) + R_A s_i(r)] n_i(r)\, dr \\ &= \int_0^{r_f} \sum_{i=1}^{m} [Y_i^0 - T_i(r) - Z_i(s_i(r), \bar{u}_i) - R_A s_i(r)] n_i(r)\, dr. \end{aligned}$$

As before, let $L(r)$ be the distribution of land around the CBD. Then given a *target utility vector*

$$\bar{\mathbf{u}} = (\bar{u}_1, \bar{u}_2, \ldots, \bar{u}_m),$$

an HS model of optimal land use can be formulated as follows:

HS($\bar{\mathbf{u}}$). Choose urban fringe distance r_f, household distribution $n_i(r)$, and lot size distribution $s_i(r)$ ($i = 1, 2, \ldots, m$, $0 \le r \le r_f$) so as to maximize the surplus

$$\mathcal{S} = \int_0^{r_f} \sum_{i=1}^{m} [Y_i^0 - T_i(r) - Z_i(s_i(r), \bar{u}_i) - R_A s_i(r)] n_i(r)\, dr, \tag{4.30}$$

subject to

(a) land constraint

$$\sum_{i=1}^{m} s_i(r) n_i(r) \le L(r) \qquad \text{at each} \quad r \le r_f, \tag{4.31}$$

(b) population constraint

$$\int_0^{r_f} n_i(r)\, dr = N_i, \qquad i = 1, 2, \ldots, m, \tag{4.32}$$

where $n_i(r) \ge 0$ and $s_i(r) > 0$ at each $r \in [0, r_f)$.

The problem is to determine the allocation of households and land so as to maximize the surplus subject to the land constraint and population constraint while satisfying the target utility levels.

Each HS model is characterized by a target utility vector $\bar{\mathbf{u}}$. As before, without loss of generality we can assume that $\inf\{U_i(z, s) \mid z > 0, s > 0\} = -\infty$ and $\sup\{U_i(z, s) \mid z > 0, s > 0\} = \infty$, $i = 1, 2, \ldots, m$. We set

$$\Lambda = \{(u_1, u_2, \ldots, u_m) \mid -\infty < u_i < \infty, i = 1, 2, \ldots, m\}.$$

For each $\bar{\mathbf{u}} \in \Lambda$, we denote the corresponding HS model by HS ($\bar{\mathbf{u}}$).[14] Considering that $\mathcal{S}$ represents a benefit (or cost, if negative) to the rest of the economy, it is obvious that the solution to any HS model is socially efficient, and any efficient allocation under the equal-utility condition is a solution to some HS model.

In the subsequent analysis, we assume that Assumption 4.1 and the following two assumptions are satisfied:

Assumption 4.4. Each $(U_i(\cdot), T_i(\cdot), Y_i^0)$ satisfies Assumptions 2.1–2.3 ($i = 1, 2, \ldots, m$).

Assumption 4.5. On each indifference curve $u = U_i(z, s)$, $s \to 0$ as $z \to \infty$ ($i = 1, 2, \ldots, m$).[15]

As before, the optimality conditions for the HS ($\bar{\mathbf{u}}$) model can be conveniently expressed by using bid rent functions and lot size functions.[16] For each $i = 1, 2, \ldots, m$, we define the original bid rent function as

$$\psi_i^0(I, u) = \max_{s>0} \frac{I - Z_i(s, u)}{s} \tag{4.33}$$

and represent the maximizing s of the above problem as $s_i^0(I, u)$. The domain of functions ψ_i^0 and s_i^0 is

$$D_i^0 = \{(I, u) \mid I > \lim_{s\to\infty} Z_i(s, u), -\infty < u < \infty\}. \tag{4.34}$$

We extend these functions on the domain

$$D = \{(I, u) \mid -\infty < I < \infty, -\infty < u < \infty\} \tag{4.35}$$

as follows:

$$\psi_i(I, u) = \begin{cases} \psi_i^0(I, u) & \text{for } (I, u) \in D_i^0, \\ 0 & \text{for } (I, u) \in D - D_i^0, \end{cases} \tag{4.36}$$

$$s_i(I, u) = \begin{cases} s_i^0(I, u) & \text{for } (I, u) \in D_i^0, \\ \infty & \text{for } (I, u) \in D - D_i^0. \end{cases} \tag{4.37}$$

Now, by using these functions, we can derive the optimality conditions for the HS($\bar{\mathbf{u}}$) model as follows.[17] First, the objective function (4.30) can be rewritten as

$$\mathcal{S} = \int_0^{r_f} \sum_{i=1}^{m} [Y_i^0 - T_i(r) - Z_i(s_i(r), \bar{u}_i) - R_A s_i(r)] n_i(r)\, dr$$

$$= \int_0^{r_f} \sum_{i=1}^{m} \left(\frac{Y_i^0 - T_i(r) - Z_i(s_i(r), \bar{u}_i)}{s_i(r)} - R_A \right) s_i(r) n_i(r)\, dr.$$

If there were no constraint, we would simply choose each $n_i(r)$, $s_i(r)$, and r_f so as to maximize this objective function. Actually, however, we must satisfy constraints (4.31) and (4.32). The Lagrange multiplier method requires that we introduce a *penalty* $DR(r)$ for violation of the land constraint at each r, and a *penalty* G_i^* for violation of each population constraint of (4.32) ($i = 1, 2, \ldots, m$). Then instead of the original objective function (4.30), we choose $n_i(r)$, $s_i(r)$, and r_f ($i = 1, 2, \ldots, m$) so as to maximize the following Lagrangian function:

$$\mathcal{L} = \mathcal{S} - \int_0^{r_f} DR(r) \left[\sum_{i=1}^{m} s_i(r) n_i(r) - L(r) \right] dr$$

$$- \sum_{i=1}^{m} G_i^* \left[\int_0^{r_f} n_i(r)\, dr - N_i \right]$$

$$= \int_0^{r_f} \sum_{i=1}^{m} \left[\frac{Y_i - G_i^* - T_i(r) - Z_i(s_i(r), \bar{u}_i)}{s_i(r)} - R(r) \right] n_i(r) s_i(r)\, dr$$

$$+ \int_0^{r_f} DR(r) L(r)\, dr + \sum_{i=1}^{m} G_i^* N_i,$$

where

$$R(r) \equiv DR(r) + R_A.$$

Each of G_i^*, $DR(r)$, and $R(r)$ has the implication of the *shadow income tax, shadow differential land rent* at r, and *shadow land rent* at r, respectively. Now it is obvious that in order to prevent $n_i(r)$ from becoming infinitely large, the following condition must be satisfied at each r and for each i:

$$R(r) \geq \frac{Y_i^0 - G_i^* - T_i(r) - Z_i(s, \bar{u}_i)}{s} \qquad \text{for any} \quad s > 0.$$

Then if $s_i(r)$ and $n_i(r)$ are the optimal choices at r, the following condition must hold

$$R(r) = \frac{Y_i^0 - G_i^* - T_i(r) - Z_i(s_i(r), \bar{u}_i)}{s_i(r)} \qquad \text{if} \quad n_i(r) > 0,$$

because otherwise $n_i(r)$ should be kept zero. In terms of bid rent functions and lot size functions defined previously, these two conditions can be equivalently expressed by the following set of conditions:

$$R(r) \geq \max_i \psi_i(Y_i^0 - G_i^* - T_i(r), \bar{u}_i) \qquad \text{at each} \quad r,$$

$$R(r) = \psi_i(Y_i^0 - G_i^* - T_i(r), \bar{u}_i) \qquad \text{if} \quad n_i(r) > 0,$$

$$s_i(r) = s_i(Y_i^0 - G_i^* - T_i(r), \bar{u}_i) \qquad \text{if} \quad n_i(r) > 0.$$

Because of inequality constraint (4.31), the associated penalty $DR(r)$ is always nonnegative, and hence $R(r) \geq R_A$ for all r. Furthermore, at a distance r if constraint (4.31) holds with a strict inequality (i.e., $\Sigma_i s_i(r)n_i(r) < L(r)$), then $DR(r)$ must equal zero, and hence $R(r) = R_A$. This implies that if $R(r) > R_A$ (i.e., $DR(r) > 0$), then $\Sigma_i s_i(r)n_i(r) = L_i(r)$ and thus $n_i(r) > 0$ for some i. Finally, notice that since each of $\psi_i(Y_i^0 - G_i^* - T_i(r), \bar{u}_i)$, $i = 1, 2, \ldots, m$, is decreasing in r, so is $\max_i \psi_i(Y_i^0 - G_i^* - T_i(r), \bar{u}_i)$. Therefore, we can readily see that in order to maximize $\mathcal{L}$, the optimal urban fringe distance must be chosen at r_f, where

$$R_A = \max_i \psi_i(Y_i^0 - G_i^* - T_i(r_f), \bar{u}_i),$$

and hence we have

$$R(r) = \begin{cases} \max_i \psi_i(Y_i^0 - G_i^* - T_i(r), \bar{u}_i) & \text{for} \quad r \leq r_f, \\ R_A & \text{for} \quad r \geq r_f. \end{cases}$$

Adding original constraints (4.31) and (4.32), we can summarize these conditions as follows:

Optimality conditions, OC($\bar{\mathbf{u}}$). Suppose we have Assumptions 4.1 and 4.4. Then for $(r_f, n_i(r), s_i(r); i = 1, 2, \ldots, m, 0 \leq r \leq r_f)$ to be a solution to the HS($\bar{\mathbf{u}}$) model, it is necessary and sufficient that there exists a set of multipliers $R(r)$ $(0 \leq r < \infty)$ and G_i^* $(i = 1, 2, \ldots, m)$ such that

(a) for land market,

$$R(r) = \begin{cases} \max_i \psi_i(Y_i^0 - G_i^* - T_i(r), \bar{u}_i) & \text{for} \quad r \leq r_f, \\ R_A & \text{for} \quad r \geq r_f, \end{cases} \tag{4.38}$$

$$R(r) = \psi_i(Y_i^0 - G_i^* - T_i(r), \bar{u}_i) \qquad \text{if} \quad n_i(r) > 0, \tag{4.39}$$

$$s_i(r) = s_i(Y_i^0 - G_i^* - T_i(r), \bar{u}_i) \quad \text{if} \quad n_i(r) > 0, \tag{4.40}$$

$$\sum_{i=1}^{m} s_i(r) n_i(r) = L(r) \quad \text{for} \quad r \leq r_f, \tag{4.41}$$

(b) for population constraint,

$$\int_0^{r_f} n_i(r)\, dr = N_i, \qquad i = 1, 2, \ldots, m, \tag{4.42}$$

where $n_i(r) \geq 0$ and $s_i(r) > 0$ at each r.[18]

As before, we can interpret that these optimality conditions represent the conditions for a *compensated equilibrium* under target utility vector $\bar{\mathbf{u}} = (\bar{u}_1, \bar{u}_2, \ldots, \bar{u}_m)$. That is, suppose that for households of each type i ($i = 1, 2, \ldots, m$) the government wants to achieve a target utility $\bar{u}_i$ through the competitive land market. Given an income tax G_i for type i households, the residential choice behavior of type i households ($i = 1, 2, \ldots, m$) can be expressed as

$$\max_{r,z,s} U_i(z, s), \qquad \text{subject to} \quad z + R(r)s = Y_i^0 - G_i - T_i(r). \tag{4.43}$$

The question is, What set of income taxes, $\mathbf{G} = (G_1, G_2, \ldots, G_m)$, will make the equilibrium utility levels of m household types just equal to the target utilities $\bar{u}_i$, $i = 1, 2, \ldots, m$? As in the case of a single household type in Chapter 3, it is not difficult to see that $(R(r), n_i(r), s_i(r), r_f, G_i^*; i = 1, 2, \ldots, m)$ *represents a compensated equilibrium under target utility vector* $\bar{\mathbf{u}} = (\bar{u}_1, \bar{u}_2, \ldots, \bar{u}_m)$ *if and only if conditions (4.38)–(4.42) are satisfied*. Condition (4.38) ensures that under the land rent curve $R(r)$ and income tax G_i^*, there is no location in the city where type i households can achieve a utility level higher than $\bar{u}_i$ ($i = 1, 2, \ldots, m$). Condition (4.39) ensures that if some type i households actually reside at r [i.e., $n_i(r) > 0$], then the maximum utility attainable for them at r under income tax G_i^* just equals $\bar{u}_i$. Also, conditions (4.39) and (4.40) together imply that each household chooses the optimal lot size under the land rent at its residence. Conditions (4.38) and (4.41) together ensure that within the urban fringe every location is occupied by households with the highest equilibrium bid rent. Finally, condition (4.42) ensures that every household resides somewhere in the city. This result implies the following:

Proposition 4.2. $(R(r), n_i(r), s_i(r), r_f, G_i^*; i = 1, 2, \ldots, m)$ is a solution to the HS($\bar{\mathbf{u}}$) model if and only if it is a compensated equilibrium under the target utility vector $\bar{\mathbf{u}}$.

Next, we arbitrarily fix a utility vector $\bar{\mathbf{u}} = (\bar{u}_1, \bar{u}_2, \ldots, \bar{u}_m) \in \Lambda$ and examine the existence and uniqueness of the solution to the HS($\bar{\mathbf{u}}$) model. Since each of Y_i, $T_i(\cdot)$, and $\bar{u}_i$ is fixed, it is convenient to use the following shorthand notation:

$$\psi_i(Y_i - G - T_i(r), \bar{u}_i) \equiv \Psi_i(r, G), \; s_i(Y_i^0 - G - T_i(r), \bar{u}_i) \equiv S_i(r, G),$$
$$i = 1, 2, \ldots, m. \quad (4.44)$$

We say that functions $\Psi_i(r, G)$ and $S_i(r, G)$ are *well behaved* if they satisfy all conditions of Definition 4.1, where parameter u should be replaced with G. It is not difficult to see the following:

Property 4.12. Under Assumptions 4.4 and 4.5, functions $\Psi_i(r, G)$ and $S_i(r, G)$ are well behaved ($i = 1, 2, \ldots, m$).

Note that under Assumption 4.2, the land rent curve $R(r)$ in Definition 4.2 is continuously decreasing in r (Property 4.8). Hence, if we define $r_f = \min\{r \,|\, R(r) = R_A\}$, we can see that the set of conditions of Definition 4.2 and those of OC($\bar{\mathbf{u}}$) [in the shorthand notation (4.44)] are the same except for the notational difference between u_i^* and G_i^*.[19] Therefore, if we replace parameters u_i with $G_i (i = 1, 2, \ldots, m)$, all the results of Section 4.3 can be applied to the HS($\bar{\mathbf{u}}$) model.

More specifically, let us define the relative steepness among bid rent functions $\Psi_i(r, G)$, $i = 1, 2, \ldots, m$ as Definition 2.2, where parameters u_i and u_j should be replaced by G_i and G_j. And suppose Assumption 4.3 holds in the present context. Then the solution to the HS($\bar{\mathbf{u}}$) model can be defined as Definition 4.2′, where each u_i^* should be replaced by G_i^* ($i = 1, 2, \ldots, m$). Therefore, if we repeat the same analysis of Section 4.3.2 by replacing parameters u_i with G_i ($i = 1, 2, \ldots, m$), we can conclude as follows:

> ***Proposition 4.3.*** Suppose Assumptions 4.1 and 4.3–4.5 hold in the context of the HS($\bar{\mathbf{u}}$) model. Then the solution to the HS($\bar{\mathbf{u}}$) model exists uniquely. In the solution, whenever $n_i(r) > 0$, then $0 < \Psi_i(r, G_i^*) < \infty$ and $0 < S_i(r, G_i^*) < \infty$ ($i = 1, 2, \ldots, m$).

The solution to the HS($\bar{\mathbf{u}}$) model can be calculated by the same algorithm depicted in Figure 4.5, where each u_i must be replaced by G_i ($i = 1, 2, \ldots, m$).

In applying Proposition 4.3, as before one must consider whether a set of bid rent functions can be ordered by the relative steepness. The next example demonstrates how to apply Rule 2.4 in the context of optimal land use in order to investigate this question.

Example 4.4 (multiple utility classes). Suppose all households in the city are identical. We arbitrarily classify them into m groups and assign a target utility $\bar{u}_i$ for each group i ($i = 1, 2, \ldots, m$). Without loss of generality, we can assume that

$$\bar{u}_1 < \bar{u}_2 < \cdots < \bar{u}_m .$$

Since all households are originally identical, we represent their common bid rent function and lot size function by $\psi(I, u)$ and $s(I, u)$, respectively. By definition, on the effective domain $D^0 = \{(I, u) \mid I > \lim_{s\to\infty} Z(s, u), -\infty < u < \infty\}$,

$$\psi(I, u) = \max_{s>0} \frac{I - Z(s, u)}{s}.$$

Then under the fixed target utility vector $\bar{\mathbf{u}} = (\bar{u}_1, \bar{u}_2, \ldots, \bar{u}_m)$, we have a set of ($u$-fixed) bid rent functions $\Psi(r, G; \bar{u}_i) \equiv \psi(Y^0 - G - T(r)), \bar{u}_i)$, $i = 1, 2, \ldots, m$ and a set of (u-fixed) lot size functions $S(r, G; \bar{u}_i) \equiv s(Y^0 - G - T(r), \bar{u}_i)$, $i = 1, 2, \ldots, m$. In order to rank these bid rent functions according to relative steepness, we examine how the relative steepness of the original bid rent function $\Psi(r, G; u) \equiv \psi(Y^0 - G - T(r), u)$ changes with u. For this, first from the envelope theorem,

$$\Psi_r \equiv \partial\Psi(r, G; u)/\partial r = -T'(r)/s(Y^0 - G - T(r), u).$$

Then since identity (3.5) holds on the effective domain D^0,

$$\begin{aligned} -\frac{\partial \Psi_r}{\partial u}\bigg|_{d\Psi=0} &= \frac{\partial[T'(r)/\tilde{s}(\psi(Y^0 - G - T(r), u), u)]}{\partial u}\bigg|_{\psi(Y^0-G-T(r),u)=\text{const}} \\ &= -\frac{T'(r)}{\tilde{s}^2}\frac{\partial \tilde{s}}{\partial u} < 0, \end{aligned} \tag{4.45}$$

which is negative since $\partial\tilde{s}/\partial u$ is positive from the normality of land. Therefore, from Rule 2.4 we can conclude that the bid rent function $\Psi(r, G; u)$ becomes less steep as u increases. That is, function $\Psi(r, G; \bar{u}_1)$ is the steepest, $\Psi(r, G; \bar{u}_2)$ is the next steepest, and so on.[20]

4.5 Equilibrium versus optimal

In order to examine the relationship between equilibrium land use and optimal land use, in the equilibrium land use model of Section 4.3 we must specify more explicitly the residential choice behavior of each household type. For this, we assume that the residential choice behavior of type i households ($i = 1, 2, \ldots, m$) can be expressed as

$$\max_{r,z,s} U_i(z, s), \qquad \text{subject to} \quad z + R(r)s = Y_i^0 - \bar{G}_i - T_i(r), \tag{4.46}$$

where $\bar{G}_i$ represents a prespecified income tax on type i households ($i = 1, 2, \ldots, m$). Throughout this section, we assume that Assumptions 4.1, 4.4, and 4.5 are satisfied. Then using the bid rent functions $\psi_i(I, u)$ and lot size functions $s_i(I, u)$ ($i = 1, 2, \ldots, m$) defined from (4.33)–(4.37), in the present context we can restate Definition 4.2 as follows:[21]

Equilibrium conditions, EC($\bar{\mathbf{G}}$). Under Assumptions 4.1 and 4.4, ($R(r)$, $n_i(r)$, $s_i(r)$, r_f, u_i^*; $i = 1, 2, \ldots, m$) represents a competitive equilibrium if and only if the following conditions are satisfied:

(a) for land market,

$$R(r) = \begin{cases} \max_i \psi_i(Y_i^0 - \bar{G}_i - T_i(r), u_i^*) & \text{for } r \leq r_f, \\ R_A & \text{for } r \geq r_f, \end{cases} \tag{4.47}$$

$$R(r) = \psi_i(Y_i^0 - \bar{G}_i - T_i(r), u_i^*) \qquad \text{if } n_i(r) > 0, \tag{4.48}$$

$$s_i(r) = s_i(Y_i^0 - \bar{G}_i - T_i(r), u_i^*) \qquad \text{if } n_i(r) > 0, \tag{4.49}$$

$$\sum_{i=1}^{m} s_i(r) n_i(r) = L(r) \qquad \text{for } r \leq r_f, \tag{4.50}$$

(b) for population constraint,

$$\int_0^{r_f} n_i(r)\, dr = N_i, \qquad i = 1, 2, \ldots, m, \tag{4.51}$$

where $n_i(r) \geq 0$ and $s_i(r) > 0$ at each r.

We call this market model the CCA model (the closed-city model under absentee landownership) under income tax vector $\bar{\mathbf{G}} = (\bar{G}_1, \bar{G}_2, \ldots, \bar{G}_m)$, and denote it by CCA($\bar{\mathbf{G}}$).

Comparing the optimality conditions $OC(\bar{\mathbf{u}})$ and the equilibrium conditions $EC(\bar{\mathbf{G}})$ we can, as before, easily see the following:[22]

Proposition 4.4. ($R(r)$, $n_i(r)$, $s_i(r)$, r_f, G_i^*; $i = 1, 2, \ldots, m$) is the solution to the HS($\bar{\mathbf{u}}$) model if and only if ($R(r)$, $n_i(r)$, $s_i(r)$, r_f, $\bar{u}_i$; $i = 1, 2, \ldots, m$) is the solution to the CCA($\mathbf{G}^*$) model, where $\mathbf{G}^* = (G_1^*, G_2^*, \ldots, G_m^*)$.

Since this proposition holds to be true for any combination of ($\mathbf{G}^*$, $\bar{\mathbf{u}}$), if we replace ($\mathbf{G}^*$, $\bar{\mathbf{u}}$) with ($\bar{\mathbf{G}}$, $\mathbf{u}^*$), we can also obtain the following conclusion:

Corollary. $(R(r), n_i(r), s_i(r), r_f, u_i^*; i = 1, 2, \ldots, m)$ is the solution to the CCA($\bar{\mathbf{G}}$) model if and only if $(R(r), n_i(r), s_i(r), r_f, \bar{G}_i; i = 1, 2, \ldots, m)$ is the solution to the HS($\mathbf{u}^*$) model, where $\mathbf{u}^* = (u_1^*, u_2^*, \ldots, u_m^*)$.

Proposition 4.4 implies that the solution to any HS model can be achieved through the competitive market by the choice of an appropriate income tax vector. And the corollary implies that the competitive equilibrium for any CCA model can be obtained by solving an HS model with an appropriate target utility vector. Then since the solution of any HS model is efficient, as before we can conclude as follows:

> ***Proposition 4.5***. The competitive equilibrium for any CCA model is efficient (*first welfare theorem*). And any efficient allocation under the equal utility constraint (for each household type) can be achieved through the competitive market by the choice of an appropriate set of income taxes or subsidies (*second welfare theorem*).

4.6 Comparative statics

Let us recall that we reached the following conclusion in Section 4.3.2: Under Assumptions 4.1–4.3, the equilibrium land use exists uniquely (Proposition 4.1). The equilibrium conditions are summarized in Definition 4.2′ and Figure 4.4 depicts the pattern of equilibrium land use. In this section, we examine how this equilibrium land use will be altered with changes in parameters. Since other cases can be similarly analyzed, here we examine only the two most interesting cases: the effects of a change in population and the effects of change in income.[23]

In both cases, we employ the following conventions: Attached to the first set of parameters is a superscript a, and to the second set a superscript b. And in the context of Definition 4.2′, the equilibrium land use under the first set of parameters is represented by $(R^a(r), u_i^a, r_i^a; i = 1, 2, \ldots, m)$, and the corresponding boundary rent curve by $R_i^a(r), i = 1, 2, \ldots, m$; similarly, the equilibrium land use under the second set of parameters is represented by $(R^b(r), u_i^b, r_i^b; i = 1, 2, \ldots, m)$, and the corresponding boundary rent curves by $R_i^b(r), i = 1, 2, \ldots, m$.[24]

4.6.1 Change in population

Suppose the population structure changes from

$$\mathbf{N}^a = (N_1, N_2, \ldots, N_{j-1}, N_j^a, N_{j+1}, \ldots, N_m)$$

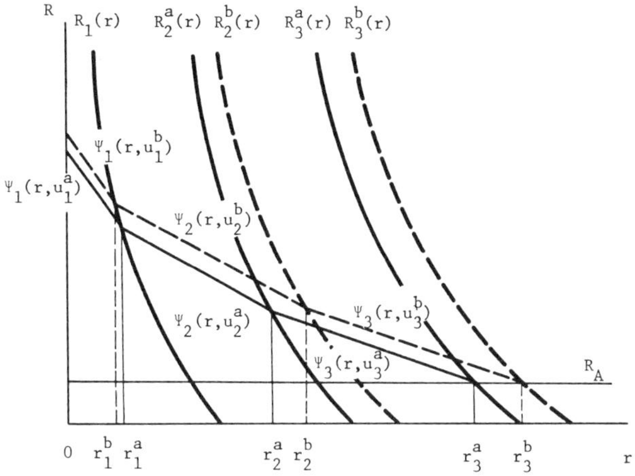

Figure 4.9. Effects of an increase in population of type 2 ($m = 3$, $j = 2$).

to

$$\mathbf{N}^b = (N_1, N_2, \ldots, N_{j-1}, N_j^b, N_{j+1}, \ldots, N_m),$$

such that

$$N_j^a < N_j^b.$$

That is, only the number of type j households increases. Let all other parameters also remain the same. Then since this change in population structure does not affect any bid rent function or lot size function, it is evident that *for each $i < j$, there is no change in the boundary rent curve:*

$$R_i^a(r) = R_i^b(r) \equiv R_i(r), \qquad i = 1, 2, \ldots, j-1.$$

If we recall the procedure of Section 4.3.2, it is also easy to see that *for each $i \geq j$, the boundary rent curve $R_i(r)$ moves outward with an increase in N_j.* Therefore, taking the case of three household types with a population increase for type 2 (i.e., $m = 3$ and $j = 2$), the change in equilibrium land use pattern can be depicted as in Figure 4.9. Since a higher bid rent curve implies a lower utility, it is evident from this figure that

$$r_m^a < r_m^b, \; u_m^a > u_m^b. \tag{4.52}$$

Then since N_m remains the same (assuming $m > j$), it must hold that

$$\int_{r_m^a}^{r_m^a} \frac{L(r)}{S_m(r, u_m^a)} \, dr = N_m = \int_{r_m^b}^{r_m^b} \frac{L(r)}{S_m(r, u_m^b)} \, dr. \tag{4.53}$$

Here $u_m^a > u_m^b$ implies that $S_m(r, u_m^a) > S_m(r, u_m^b)$ for all r. Hence, from (4.52) and (4.53) we can conclude that $r_{m-1}^a < r_{m-1}^b$. Since $\Psi_m(r, u_m^a) < \Psi_m(r, u_m^b)$ for all r, it also holds that $\Psi_{m-1}(r, u_{m-1}^a) < \Psi_{m-1}(r, u_{m-1}^b)$ for all r. Thus, $u_{m-1}^a > u_{m-1}^b$. Recursively, we can conclude that

$$r_i^a < r_i^b, \qquad u_i^a > u_i^b \qquad \text{for all} \quad i \geq j.$$

Since $R_{j-1}(r)$ remains the same and $\Psi_j(r, u_j^a) < \Psi_j(r, u_j^b)$ for all r, it follows that $r_{j-1}^a > r_{j-1}^b$ and $u_{j-1}^a > u_{j-1}^b$. Recursively, we can conclude that

$$r_i^a > r_i^b, \qquad u_i^a > u_i^b \qquad \text{for all} \quad i < j.$$

In summary, we have the following:

> ***Proposition 4.6.*** As the household number increases for type j while it remains the same for all other types,
>
> (i) equilibrium utility u_i^* will become lower for all i;
>
> (ii) for each $i < j$, the boundary distance r_i^* will move inward, whereas for each $i \geq j$, r_i^* will move outward;
>
> (iii) land rent curve $R(r)$ will become higher everywhere within the new urban fringe.

In other words, if type j population increases, demand for land in zone j increases. Consequently, all outside zones $(j, j+1, \ldots, m)$ are pushed away from the CBD, whereas all inside zones $(1, 2, \ldots, j-1)$ are squeezed toward it, and every household lowers its utility level.

This result on the effects of an increase in population is not surprising. The effects of an increase in income, however, are much more complex and interesting, as shown next.

4.6.2 *Change in income*

A change in the income level of one household type alters its bid rent function and lot size function. Therefore, in order to examine the effects of income changes on equilibrium land use, we must specify the residential choice behavior of each household type. As an example, we consider the multiple-income model of Example 4.2. Also, for simplicity, we analyze only the case of two income classes.

Suppose the residential choice behavior of each income class can be expressed as

$$\max_{r,z,s} U(z, s), \qquad \text{subject to} \quad z + R(r)s = Y_i - T(r), \qquad i = 1, 2, \tag{4.54}$$

where

$$Y_1 < Y_2. \tag{4.55}$$

The bid rent functions and lot size functions of each class are expressed as $\Psi_i(r, u) \equiv \psi(Y_i - T(r), u)$ and $S_i(r, u) \equiv s(Y_i - T(r), u)$, $i = 1, 2$. We assume that Assumptions 2.1–2.3 are satisfied by each $(U(\cdot), T(\cdot), Y_i)$, $i = 1, 2$. Then, as explained before, for each i, functions Ψ_i and S_i are well behaved, and Ψ_1 is steeper than Ψ_2.

There are the following two basic cases:

(A) Income remains the same for class 1 (the poor class), whereas class 2 (the rich class) becomes richer:

$$Y_1^a = Y_1^b, \qquad Y_2^a < Y_2^b. \tag{4.56}$$

(B) Income remains the same for class 2. Class 1's income increases, but it does not exceed that of class 2:[25]

$$Y_1^a < Y_1^b < Y_2^a = Y_2^b. \tag{4.57}$$

Let us first consider case (A). Since class 1's income remains the same, there is no change for functions Ψ_1 and S_1, and hence the first boundary rent curve remains the same:

$$R_1^a(r) = R_1^b(r) \equiv R_1(r).$$

By using this result, as in Section 3.6.2 we can show that the new second boundry rent curve $R_2^b(r)$ is located to the right of the initial curve $R_2^a(r)$. That is, as a consequence of an increase in income for class 2, demands for land by class 2 households increase in zone 2, and the second boundary rent curve is pushed outward. The result is depicted in Figure 4.10. Then it is evident from Figure 4.10 that the urban fringe is also pushed outward:

$$r_2^a < r_2^b. \tag{4.58}$$

Next, since Y_2 increases, it is intuitively evident that the equilibrium utility for class 2 households will increase:[26]

$$u_2^a < u_2^b. \tag{4.59}$$

In Figure 4.10, as Y_2 increases, the boundary between zone 1 and zone 2 moves outward ($r_1^a < r_1^b$) and the land rent at the boundary becomes lower ($R_1(r_1^a) > R_1(r_1^b)$). Actually, as shown in the next property, this result depends on the nature of the transport cost function and land distribution.[27]

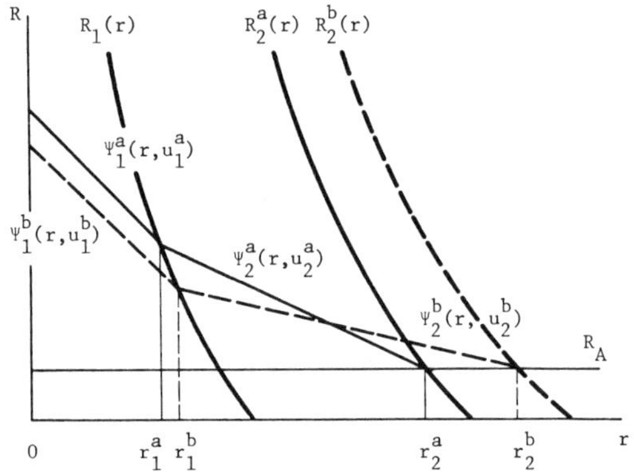

Figure 4.10. Effects of an increase in income for the rich class.

Property 4.13. As the income of class 2 increases, we have that

(i) if $L(r)/T'(r)$ is increasing at all r, then $r_1^a < r_1^b$ and $R_1(r_1^a) > R_1(r_1^b)$,

(ii) if $L(r)/T'(r)$ is constant everywhere, then $r_1^a = r_1^b$ and $R_1(r_1^a) = R_1(r_1^b)$,

(iii) if $L(r)/T'(r)$ is decreasing at all r, then $r_1^a > r_1^b$ and $R_1(r_1^a) < R_1(r_1^b)$.

Suppose, for example, the transport cost function is linear [$T(r) = ar$], and hence $T'(r)$ is constant. Then depending on whether $L(r)$ is increasing, constant, or decreasing, we have, respectively, situation (i), (ii), or (iii). As noted before, since in most cities the amount of land increases and marginal transport cost decreases with the distance from the city center, we are most likely to have situation (i). Since the bid rent function of class 1 households is not altered, a higher bid rent curve implies a lower utility. Therefore, from Property 4.13, we can immediately conclude as follows:

Property 4.14. As the income of class 2 increases, we have

(i) if $L(r)/T'(r)$ is increasing at all r, then $u_1^a < u_1^b$,

(ii) if $L(r)/T'(r)$ is constant everywhere, then $u_1^a = u_1^b$,

(iii) if $L(r)/T'(r)$ is decreasing at all r, then $u_1^a > u_1^b$.

A rationale for Properties 4.13 and 4.14 is as follows. An increase in income for the rich class further increases its demand for land. If there remains a sufficient amount of agricultural land in the suburbs [situation

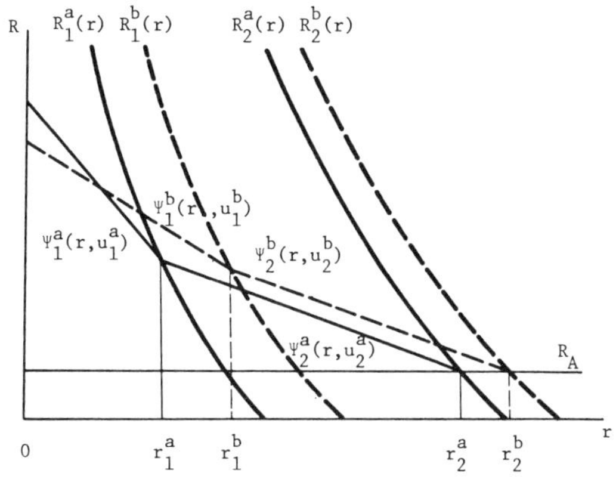

Figure 4.11. Effects of an increase in income for the poor class.

(i)], this increase in demand for land will be absorbed by further suburbanization of the rich class. This in turn diminishes the pressure toward the land market in zone 1; consequently, zone 1 expands, land rents in zone 1 decrease, and the equilibrium utility of the poor class also becomes higher. On the other hand, without a sufficient amount of agricultural land left in the suburbs [situation (iii)], an increase in demand for land by the rich class aggravates the pressure toward the land market in zone 1, and the results are the opposite.

In summary we can conclude as follows:

Proposition 4.7. As the income of the rich class further increases (while the income of the poor class remains the same),

(i) the urban fringe will move outward;
(ii) the equilibrium utility for the rich class will become higher;
(iii) (a) if $L(r)/T'(r)$ is increasing at all r, the (inner) zone for the poor class will expand outward, land rents will decrease there, and the equilibrium utility of the poor class will also become higher, (b) if $L(r)/T'(r)$ is constant everywhere, nothing will change within the zone for the poor class (i.e., the size of the zone, land rents there, and the equilibrium utility of the poor class will remain the same), or (c) if $L(r)/T'(r)$ is decreasing at all r, the zone for the poor class will shrink inward, land rents will increase there, and the equilibrium utility of the poor class will become lower.

Next, let us examine case (B) under assumption (4.57). In Figure 4.11, the equilibrium land use configuration under the initial set of incomes

(Y_1^a, Y_2^a) is depicted by solid lines; that under the new set of incomes (Y_1^b, Y_2^b) by dashed lines. As class 1's income increases from Y_1^a to Y_1^b, in the first zone the demand for land increases; consequently, the first boundary rent curve moves outward from $R_1^a(r)$ to $R_1^b(r)$. This in turn pushes the second boundary rent curve outward from $R_2^a(r)$ to $R_2^b(r)$. Therefore, the urban fringe also expands outward:

$$r_2^a < r_2^b. \tag{4.60}$$

Since the bid rent function of class 2 households does not change, a higher bid rent curve implies a lower utility level. Hence, it is evident from Figure 4.11 that

$$u_2^a > u_2^b. \tag{4.61}$$

Then, since $S_2(r, u_2^a) > S_2(r, u_2^b)$, it follows immediately that the new boundary between the two classes must be located to the right of the initial boundary:[28]

$$r_1^a < r_1^b. \tag{4.62}$$

Finally, since Y_1 increases, it is also intuitively evident that the equilibrium utility for class 1 households will increase.[29]

In summary we can conclude as follows:

> ***Proposition 4.8.*** As income increases for the poor class (while it remains the same for the rich class),
>
> (i) the inner zone for the poor class will expand outward,
> (ii) the outer zone for the rich class will be pushed further out,
> (iii) the equilibrium utility of the poor class will become higher, whereas that of the rich class will become lower.

In short, as the income of the poor class (located inside) increases, its zone expands outward, and its equilibrium utility becomes higher. This in turn pushes the zone of the rich class (located outside) further out, and the equilibrium utility of the rich class becomes lower.[30]

Propositions 4.7 and 4.8 exhibit a stark asymmetry. Suppose there remains a sufficient amount of agricultural land in the suburbs [i.e., $L(r)/T'(r)$ is increasing in r]. Then, an increase in income for the rich class will make both classes better off (Proposition 4.7), whereas an increase in income for the poor class will make the poor class better off but make the rich class worse (Proposition 4.8). This asymmetry arises solely from the locational relation between the two classes. This result also suggests a potential conflict between the two classes. That is, the poor class may not find any objection to the rich class becoming richer. However, the rich class may find itself better off by keeping the poor class poor (or, more cruelly, making the poor class poorer). This may induce the rich class to practice discrimination, perhaps in the form of restrictive zoning policies against the poor class. It suggests that even without racial or ethnic conflicts, income difference alone may produce conflicts between the two classes.

4.7 Conclusion

In this chapter we looked at the character of equilibrium and optimal land use in the context of multiple household types. Assuming that the set of bid rent functions can be ordered according to their steepness, we obtained neat results: Both the equilibrium land use and optimal land use exist uniquely, and they can be depicted by a set of Thünen rings surrounding the CBD. In Chapter 7, we will use the results of this chapter and examine the impact of racial externalities on urban land markets.

Bibliographical notes

The existence of equilibrium land use has been studied by MacKinnon (1974), Schweizer, Varaiya, and Hartwick (1976), King (1980), Richter (1980), and Karmann (1982) by using fixed-point methods. However, all of them are concerned with the case of discrete space. Our boundary rent curve approach for the existence and uniqueness proof is based on Fujita (1985). Without the assumption of ordered bid rent functions, the existence of equilibrium land use was established by Fujita and Smith (1987), which provides a general existence proof in the context of n-dimensional space. Ando (1981) studied the existence and uniqueness problem by a different approach. He first obtained the existence of the optimal land use by relying on an existence theorem in optimal control theory. Then he obtained the existence of the equilibrium land use by examining the relationship between the optimal land use and equilibrium land use. A similar approach was taken by Scotchmer (1982, 1985).

As noted before, comparative statics in the case of multiple income classes were studied by Wheaton (1976), Hartwick, Schweizer, and Varaiya (1976), Arnott, MacKinnon, and Wheaton (1978), and Miyao (1981, Ch. 2). In particular, Hartwick et al. (1976) achieved a complete characterization of comparative statics for a general, m-income-class case. They introduced the condition that $L(r)/T'(r)$ is increasing at all r, which was also used in our analysis in Section 4.6.2. A stability analysis of equilibrium land use with multiple household types was conducted by Miyao (1981, Ch. 2).

Finally, although in this chapter we have studied only theoretical models with continuous space, many simulation models (both equilibrium and optimum models) were developed using discrete space. For such simulation models, the reader is referred to the survey articles of Anas (1987) and Kain (1987).

Notes

1. In this and the next section, we use the Alonso functions $\Psi(r, u)$ and $S(r, u)$. This is because we cannot specify the functional forms of Solow bid rent and bid-max lot size functions without giving a concrete model of residential choice.
2. For example, $\Psi: D \to [0, \infty)$ means that Ψ is a function that is defined on *domain* D and takes values in the *range* $[0, \infty)$.
3. In Definition 4.1, we can alternatively specify the domain of Ψ as $D = \{(r, u) \mid 0 \leq r < \infty, \underline{u} < u < \bar{u}\}$, where $\underline{u}$ and $\bar{u}$ are some constants such that $-\infty \leq \underline{u} < \bar{u} \leq \infty$. However, as noted before, since any utility function in this book is assumed to be ordinal, without loss of generality we can specify the domain of Ψ as in Definition 4.1.
4. Condition (iv) can be satisfied by any $\bar{r}$ such that $T(\bar{r}) > Y$. Condition (v) can be satisfied by any $\bar{r} > 0$ such that $T(\bar{r}) < Y$. Other conditions are obviously satisfied.
5. For the proof, see Appendix 3 of Fujita and Smith (1985).
6. The following properties of bid rent curves and lot size curves are merely a restatement of those properties that have been confirmed in the context of the basic model in Section 2.3.
7. That is, for each $u_1 < u_2$, $\Psi(r, u_1) > \Psi(r, u_2)$ at all r such that $\Psi(r, u_2) > 0$; and for each fixed r, function $\Psi(r, \cdot)$ is continuous on $(-\infty, \infty)$.
8. In practice, this implies that all land in the city is owned by absentee landlords, and hence the income of each household does not include any revenue from land. Therefore, in the terminology of Section 3.3, here we are dealing with an equilibrium land use problem in the context of the closed-city model with absentee landlords. We focus on this case because this is the most basic case and other cases can be examined similarly.
9. Throughout this book, we adopt the following rules of arithmetic involving ∞:

$$0 \cdot \infty = \infty \cdot 0 = 0, \qquad a/\infty = 0 \qquad \text{for} \quad -\infty < a < \infty.$$

For example, in (4.10), if $S_i(r, u_i^*) = \infty$ and $n_i(r) = 0$, then $S_i(r, u_i^*)n_i(r) = 0$. Note that in Definition 4.2, all conditions involving densities are required to hold only for *almost all* r (i.e., for all $r \geq 0$, except possibly for a set of r with zero Lebesgue measure). However, this measure-theoretic consideration plays no significant role in the present analysis. Hence, we choose for simplicity to require that these conditions be satisfied for all $r \geq 0$.

10. As shown by Fujita and Smith (1987) in order to ensure the existence of equilibrium land use for general problems, the integral in the population constraint (4.12) must be considered to be a Lebesgue integral. However, in this book, we analyze those problems that involve only Riemann integrable functions. Therefore, in this book we can always consider that $\int$ denotes the sign of a Riemann integral.
11. In Section 4.3.3 we will discuss how each condition in the following set of assumptions is critical (or not critical) to the existence or uniqueness of the equilibrium land use.
12. When $R_A = 0$, we must replace condition (4.23) with the relation $r_m^* = \hat{b}_m$, and condition (4.24) should be changed as $u_m^* = \lim_{r \to \hat{b}_m} U_m(r)$.
13. For a general existence theorem without this monotonicity assumption, see Fujita and Smith (1987).
14. Throughout this section, income vector $\mathbf{Y} = (Y_1, Y_2, \ldots, Y_m)$ and population vector $\mathbf{N} = (N_1, N_2, \ldots, N_m)$ are fixed. Hence, for simplicity, we represent each HS model by HS($\bar{\mathbf{u}}$).
15. This means that z is completely substitutable for s. If we assume that the amount of land $\int_0^\infty L(r)\, dr$ is infinite, this assumption is not necessary for the existence and uniqueness of the optimal solution.
16. For convenience of comparison between optimal models and equilibrium models, in this and the next section we use Solow bid rent and lot size functions.
17. In the following, we explain the derivation of optimality conditions for the HS($\bar{\mathbf{u}}$) model in an informal manner. For a formal derivation of these conditions, see Appendix C.7.
18. Since each $\psi_i(Y_i^0 - G_i^* - T_i(r), \bar{u}_i)$ is decreasing in r up to the urban fringe, from (4.38) $R(r) > R_A$ for all $r < r_f$. Hence, in condition (4.41), we have an equality sign (rather than an inequality sign). For the sufficiency of these optimality conditions, see Appendix C.7.
19. Actually, there is a minor difference. That is, in $OC(\bar{\mathbf{u}})$, when $n_i(r) = 0$, $s_i(r)$ may not equal $S_i(r, G_i^*)$. However, when $n_i(r) = 0$, the value of $s_i(r)$ does not matter in practice; and at the level of Definition 4.2′, even this minor difference disappears.
20. In this example, we may be uncomfortable with the assumption that identical households are assigned with different utility levels. Therefore, alternatively, we may assume that all households are identical except for their original incomes (reflecting their productivity differences); each household of type i receives (original) income Y_i and is assigned target utility $\bar{u}_i$. We can easily see, however, that this change in scenario does not alter the conclusion of this example at all. That is, we can easily see from calculation (4.45) that the relative steepness of the u-fixed bid rent function is not affected by the original income level. Hence, regardless of their original incomes, the household group assigned to the lowest target utility has the steepest u-fixed bid rent function, and so on.
21. As we can see from Example 4.1, under any fixed $\bar{G}_i$, functions $\Psi_i(r, u) \equiv \psi_i(Y_i^0 - \bar{G}_i - T_i(r), u)$ and $S_i(r, u) \equiv s_i(Y_i^0 - \bar{G}_i - T_i(r), u)$ are well

behaved ($i = 1, 2, \ldots, m$). Hence, from Property 4.8, urban fringe distance r_f can be uniquely defined by $r_f = \min\{r \mid R(r) = R_A\}$. Using this result, we can restate Definition 4.2 as EC($\bar{\mathbf{G}}$).

22. Proposition 4.4 is merely a restatement of Proposition 3.9 in the context of multiple household types. For the derivation of Proposition 4.4, see the explanation just after Proposition 3.9.
23. These two cases have also been studied by Hartwick, Schweizer, and Varaiya (1976). It is interesting to contrast their standard differential calculus approach with our intuitive boundary rent curve approach.
24. Obviously, u_i^a (u_i^b) represents the equilibrium utility for type i households under the first (second) set of parameters, and $r_i^a(r_i^b)$ represents the equilibrium boundary distance between zone $i - 1$ and i.
25. The third case, $Y_1^a < Y_2^a = Y_2^b < Y_1^b$, can be analyzed in the same way as case (A) (by exchanging index 1 and 2 after income change). Hence, we omit it.
26. For the proof of relation (4.59), see Appendix C.8.
27. The proof of Property 4.13 is given in Appendix C.9.
28. To obtain this result, in equation (4.53) set m equal to 2 and use relations (4.60) and (4.61).
29. The proof is quite similar to that of relation (4.59).
30. Figure 4.11 depicts $\Psi_1(0, u_1^a) > \Psi_1(0, u_1^b)$ and $\Psi_1(r_1^a, u_1^a) > \Psi_1(r_1^b, u_1^b)$. Actually in a treatment similar to the one of Property 3.4 we can show the following:

    (i) If $L(r)/T'(r)$ is increasing at all r, then $\Psi_1(0, u_1^a) > \Psi_1(0, u_1^b)$ and $\Psi_1(r_1^a, u_1^a) > \Psi_1(r_1^b, u_1^b)$.
    (ii) If $L(r)/T'(r)$ is constant everywhere, then $\Psi_1(0, u_1^a) = \Psi_1(0, u_1^b)$ and $\Psi_1(r_1^a, u_1^a) = \Psi_1(r_1^b, u_1^b)$.
    (iii) If $L(r)/T'(r)$ is decreasing at all r, then $\Psi_1(0, u_1^a) < \Psi_1(0, u_1^b)$ and $\Psi_1(r_1^a, u_1^a) < \Psi_1(r_1^b, u_1^b)$.

CHAPTER 5

Urban aggregates and city sizes

5.1 Introduction

In the preceding three chapters, we examined the spatial structure of cities. We now turn our attention from spatial structure to *urban aggregates*. That is, within the same context of monocentric cities, we examine the relations among urban macrovariables such as the population, total income, total land rent, and total transport cost of a city. We also examine, in various contexts, the equilibrium city size and optimal city size. This chapter, therefore, provides a connection between urban land use theory and city-system theory. It deals with a simple case in which all households of the economy are assumed to be identical.

In the study of equilibrium and optimal city sizes, it is essential first to know why cities exist. Thus, in Section 5.2 we discuss various causes of urban agglomeration. In general, the equilibrium city size is determined at the intersection between the *population supply curve* and *population demand curve* of the city. And in determining the optimal city size, the *surplus function* of the city must be maximized. In deriving these curves and function, we need to know the relationships among economic aggregates in the city. Hence, in Section 5.3 we obtain some general accounting relationships among urban aggregates. Then, in Section 5.4, on the basis of these accounting relationships, we obtain the population supply function and population cost function. After these preliminary analyses, in Sections 5.5 to 5.7 we examine the equilibrium and optimal city sizes in different contexts.

It must be noted that under a set of reasonable assumptions on the transport cost function and land distribution, some simple and general relationships hold between the total transport cost and total land rent of a city. However, since these relationships are not used in the following analysis, we discuss them separately in Appendix B.

5.2 Causes of urban agglomeration

Let us suppose as before that a city takes a monocentric form. Then due to the increase in commuting distance, the total transport cost of a city increases more than proportionally to its population. In order to have cities, therefore, we must have technological advantages in production or consumption that exceed the transport cost increase. It is commonly agreed that the basic sources of such technological advantages are

1. resource and transport advantages,
2. indivisibility and economies of scale,
3. externalities and nonprice interactions, and
4. preference for variety in consumption and production.

Cities may arise due to appropriate combinations of these basic factors.[1]

Interregional differences in resource endowments provide a base for interregional trade.[2] In this context, for example, the location of an economical coal bed will lead to the development of a mining industry there; then such industries as steel and chemicals, which use coal heavily, will locate nearby to save transport costs. In turn, these *basic industries* and their workers will attract suppliers of related manufactures and services for home consumption. Eventually, a city will be developed around these basic industries. As another example, a region with fertile land for wheat production may start exporting wheat to other regions and nations. Then owing to *scale economies in transport technologies,* a transport node, or port, will have to be developed. The port, in turn, will attract many export-related businesses and manufacturers. Moreover, suppliers of manufactured goods for agricultural production and farmers' consumption will tend to locate near the port, partly because of scale economies in production and distribution and partly because of saving in transport costs for inputs that are imported through the port. Eventually, a port city will develop, surrounded by its hinterland.

Perhaps the most fundamental reason for the existence of cities stems from *economies of scale* in production and consumption, which are, in turn due largely to the *indivisibility* of some commodities (such as persons, residences, plants, equipment, and public facilities).[3] The indivisibility of persons leads to the specialization of labor, and some equipment can be effectively used only on a larger scale. Moreover, the efficient coordination of many specialized persons, equipment, and production processes requires them to locate nearby – due partly to the facility of communication and partly to transport cost savings in various production processes. Therefore, the average total cost of the production of a good will be smaller (to a certain extent) if it is performed at a *larger scale* and at a *contiguous location*. In addition, if the production of one firm uses an output of another firm, the two firms may find it economical to locate near each other. Hence, through *input–output linkages,* many large firms may find it economical to locate closely, and these firms will provide the basic sectors of a large city. Moreover, the provision of many *public services and facilities* (such as schools, hospitals, utilities, and highways) typically exhibits the characteristic of economies of scale. This provides another important reason for the formation of cities. Finally, in many societies, males are primary workers. However, because of the indivisibility of families and residences, the concentration of male workers in a city also results in the concentration of potential female labor. This, in turn, attracts many industries that make heavy use of (unskilled) female labor. The garment industry is an example.

(Technological) externalities are those consequences of human activity that affect others without passing through the market mechanism.[4] From the viewpoint of city formation, the most important classes of externalities are those of *(local) public goods* that are jointly consumed by many agents in a city. Local radio and television programs enhance the utilities of all people in a city; the same can be said of many cultural and social events in a city. Services from various *public facilities* (schools, museums, police services, streets, and sewerages) have the nature of public goods. If we broadly define externalities to include the effects of all *nonprice interactions* among agents, then externalities represent a major cause of cities. Business firms locate in large cities mainly because of the facility of *communication* with other firms and customers. Many people are also attracted to large cities because of enhanced *social interactions*.

Finally, the *preference for variety* in consumption also contributes to the formation of large cities. A simple example will illustrate this point. Suppose that a consumer has a fixed budget for dining in restaurants. Furthermore, suppose that in city 1 there is only one (Chinese) restaurant. In Figure 5.1, let x_1 represent the number of Chinese restaurant meals consumed per year. Let point A denote the number of meals afforded under the consumer's budget constraint in city 1. Then the consumer will achieve the utility level corresponding to the indifference curve AB. Now, suppose city 2 has two restaurants, one Chinese and one French. Then if line CD represents an equivalent budget and x_1 and x_2 denote the annual number of Chinese and French meals, respectively, the same consumer will achieve a higher utility level ($A'B'$) in city 2 by eating at both restaurants.[5] This example suggests that *other things being equal, the greater the variety of consumption goods available in a city, the higher is the real income of each consumer*. This effect was first emphasized by Stahl (1983) in explaining the spatial agglomeration of activities.

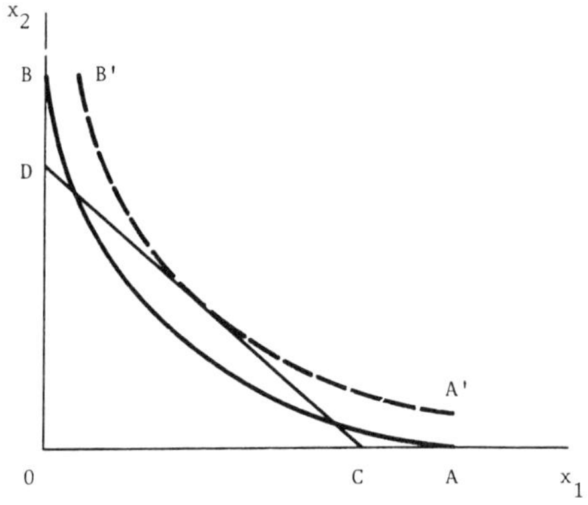

Figure 5.1. Complementarity effects in consumption and in production.

Similarly, in Figure 5.1 if we consider x_1 and x_2 to represent the amount of each good used in the production of a good by a firm (or a public agent), we can apply the same argument and conclude that *other things being equal, the greater the variety of inputs available in a city, the higher is the productivity of the firm in a city*. Although these *complementarity effects* (among consumption goods and among production inputs) alone cannot explain the existence of cities, the formation of large cities can be explained only when this factor is combined with other factors (in particular, with indivisibility and economies of scale).[6]

We can also consider the complementarity effects among output goods. For example, if two goods can be produced more efficiently than when each good is produced separately, we say that *economies of joint production* exist for the production of the two goods. Economies of joint production are closely related to the concept of *economies of scope,* which was introduced into urban economics by Goldstein and Gronberg (1984). For example, Goldstein and Gronberg state that if two goods can be produced more efficiently at the same location than when each good is produced at a separate location, economies of scope exist in the production of the two goods. Economies of scope, therefore, include both economies of joint production and savings in transport costs of intermediate inputs (including communication costs). Note that these complementarity effects emphasize the role of *convexity* in production and consumption technologies (on spatial agglomeration of activities), whereas economies of scale emphasize the role of *nonconvexity* in these technologies. Thus, both convexity and nonconvexity in production and consumption technologies play important roles in the formation of cities.

Following the preliminary analyses in Sections 5.3 and 5.4, we examine equilibrium and optimal city sizes in each specific context. In section 5.5 we discuss city formation as a result of resource and transport advantages. In Section 5.6, we examine the role of fixed costs in city formation. Finally, in Section 5.7, we analyze the scale economies in production and city sizes.[7] In each section we employ a simple example to illustrate the trade-off between technological advantages and disadvantages in determining city sizes. In all of these examples, we assume for simplicity that firms do not use any land; the only variable input of firms is labor. Also for simplicity, we consider only the case of monocentric cities, where it is assumed *a priori* that all production activities take place at the CBD.

5.3 Urban accounts

In this section, we obtain general accounting relationships among urban aggregates that hold in both equilibrium cities and optimal cities. Throughout the discussion in the rest of this chapter, we always assume that Assumptions 2.1–2.3, 3.1, and 3.2 hold and that $R_A > 0$. To begin with, let us recall the CCA model with income tax $\bar{G}$, which was introduced in Section 3.5. In equilibrium, it follows immediately from conditions (3.67) and (3.68) that

$$R(r) = \frac{Y^0 - \bar{G} - T(r) - Z(s(r), u^*)}{s(r)} \qquad \text{for} \quad r \leq r_f, \tag{5.1}$$

where $s(r) = s(Y^0 - \bar{G} - T(r), u^*)$ represents the bid-max lot size under equilibrium utility u^* and exogenous income tax $\bar{G}$. Rearranging equation (5.1), we have

$$Y^0 = T(r) + Z(s(r), u^*) + R(r)s(r) + \bar{G} \qquad \text{for} \quad r \leq r_f. \tag{5.2}$$

This simply represents the budget equation of each household in an equilibrium city. Similarly, from conditions (3.71) and (3.72), we can see that the following budget equation holds in an optimal city,

$$Y^0 = T(r) + Z(s(r), \bar{u}) + R(r)s(r) + G^* \qquad \text{for} \quad r \leq r_f, \tag{5.3}$$

where $s(r) = s(Y^0 - G^* - T(r), \bar{u})$ represents the bid-max lot size under target utility $\bar{u}$ and shadow income tax G^*; $R(r)$ is the shadow land rent at r. We can also see from Proposition 3.7 that relation (5.3) holds in a compensated equilibrium city under target utility $\bar{u}$. Let us represent both u^* and $\bar{u}$ simply by u, and G^* and $\bar{G}$ by G. Then, relations (5.2) and (5.3) can be commonly expressed as

$$Y^0 = T(r) + Z(s(r), u) + R(r)s(r) + G \qquad \text{for} \quad r \leq r_f. \tag{5.4}$$

Multiplying both sides of equation (5.4) by equilibrium (or optimal) population $n(r)$ at each $r \leq r_f$, we have

$$\begin{aligned} Y^0 n(r) &= [T(r) + Z(s(r), u) + R(r)s(r) + G]n(r) \\ &= [T(r) + Z(s(r), u) + R_A s(r)]n(r) \\ &\quad + (R(r) - R_A)s(r)n(r) + Gn(r), \end{aligned}$$

where R_A represents the agricultural land rent. It follows, by integrations, that

$$\begin{aligned} Y^0 \int_0^{r_f} n(r)\,dr = &\int_0^{r_f} [T(r) + Z(s(r), u) + R_A s(r)]n(r)\,dr \\ &+ \int_0^{r_f} (R(r) - R_A)s(r)n(r)\,dr + G\int_0^{r_f} n(r)\,dr. \end{aligned}$$

Since

$$\int_0^{r_f} n(r)\,dr = N \qquad \text{and} \qquad s(r)n(r) = L(r) \qquad \text{for} \quad r \leq r_f,$$

finally we have

$$NY^0 = C + \text{TDR} + NG, \tag{5.5}$$

where

$$\begin{aligned} Y^0 &= \text{(pretax) income per household}, \\ N &= \text{population}, \\ C &= \int_0^{r_f} [T(r) + Z(s(r), u) + R_A s(r)]n(r)\,dr \\ &= \text{total residential cost (population cost)}, \qquad (5.6) \\ \text{TDR} &= \int_0^{r_f} (R(r) - R_A)L(r)\,dr \\ &= \text{total differential rent}, \\ G &= \text{income tax per household}. \qquad (5.7) \end{aligned}$$

Equation (5.5) gives a simple accounting relation, stating that the total income for the residential sector, NY^0, breaks up into three expenditure items, that is, total residential cost C, total differential rent TDR, and total income tax NG.

Next, let $C(u, N)$ be the *minimum residential cost* for achieving common utility u for all N residents. Cost $C(u, N)$ is obtained from the solution of problem (3.48), by setting $\bar{u} = u$. Then in the case of optimal cities, by definition it holds in equation (5.5), that

$$C = C(u, N). \tag{5.8}$$

From Proposition 3.11, every competitive equilibrium is efficient. Hence, we can see that relation (5.8) also holds in equilibrium in the CCA model.[8] Thus, from (5.5) and (5.8), it holds that[9]

$$NY^0 = C(u, N) + \text{TDR} + NG. \tag{5.9}$$

Next, in the case of the CCP model of Section 3.3, the share of revenue (for each household) from city land, TDR/N, should be considered a negative tax, and it must be included in G. Then we can see that relation (5.9) holds also for the CCP model as $NY^0 = C(u, N)$. Finally, in the case of the OCA model and OCP model of Section 3.3, we interpret u to represent the given national utility level and N the equilibrium population derived from equation (3.33) and (3.43). Then we can readily see that relation (5.9) also holds for these open-city models.

Therefore, we can conclude that with appropriate interpretation of u, N, and G, relation (5.9) holds for any city model examined in Chapter 3. It is convenient, however, to summarize the specific form of relation (5.9) for each specific group of city models.

1. In the HS(Y^0, u, N) model and for the compensated equilibrium of Section 3.4, we have

$$NY^0 = C(u, N) + \text{TDR} + NG, \tag{5.10}$$

where u is the target utility and G the shadow income tax (for the optimal allocation) or equilibrium income tax (for the compensated equilibrium).

2. In the CCA(Y, N) model and OCA(Y, u) model of Section 3.3, it has been assumed that

$$G = 0, \qquad Y = Y^0, \tag{5.11}$$

and hence we have

$$NY = C(u, N) + \text{TDR}, \tag{5.12}$$

where G is the exogenous income tax, u the equilibrium utility (for CCA) or given national utility (for OCA), and N the given population (for CCA) or equilibrium population (for OCA).

Table 5.1. *Notation in urban accounts*

Symbol	Definition
W	Wage per household
G	Tax (if positive) or subsidy (if negative) per household (the share of production profits and TDR from the city in question is treated as a subsidy)
Y^0	Pretax/subsidy income ≡ nonland income per household ≡ W + other incomes (if any) from outside the city in question
Y	(Posttax/subsidy) income ≡ $Y^0 - G$
$I(r)$	$Y - T(r) \equiv Y^0 - G - T(r)$ ≡ net income at r
N	Population of the city
$F(N)$	Aggregate production function of the city
δ	Marginal product and average product of labor [if $F(N) = \delta N$]
K	Fixed costs or local public good costs of the city
$C(u, N)$	Population cost function ≡ minimum residential cost (excluding K)
$\mathcal{S}$	(Gross) surplus (or profit) of the city ≡ $F(N) - C(u, N)$
Π	Net surplus (or profit) of the city ≡ $\mathcal{S} - K$
TDR	Total differential rent of the city
$N(Y, u)$	Population supply function
$Y(u, N)$	Inverse population supply function ≡ (population) supply–income function

3. In the CCP(Y^0, N) model and OCP(Y^0, u) model of Section 3.3, by definition,

$$G = -\text{TDR}/N, \tag{5.13}$$

and hence we have

$$NY^0 = C(u, N), \tag{5.14}$$

where G is the per capita share of differential land rent, u the equilibrium utility (for CCP) or national utility (for OCP), and N the given population (for CCP) or equilibrium population (for OCP). Table 5.1 summarizes the notation in urban accounts.

5.4 Population supply function and population cost function

In the study of city sizes, population supply function and population cost function play central roles. In this section, we introduce these functions and examine their characteristics.

Recall the OCA(Y, u) model introduced in Chapter 3. When we compare equilibrium city sizes with optimal city sizes, this model turns out to play the key role. Hence, we first examine how the equilibrium solution to this model changes with respect to two parameters, household income Y and national utility u. Recall that given Y, the supreme utility

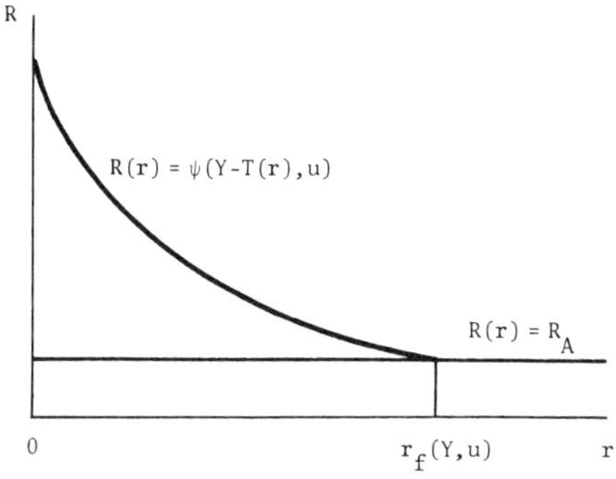

Figure 5.2. Equilibrium land use pattern for OCA(Y, u).

level $\tilde{u}(Y)$ is defined by relation (3.27). Given (Y, u), we denote the equilibrium urban fringe distance by $r_f(Y, u)$ and the equilibrium population by $N(Y, u)$ for the OCA(Y, u) model, respectively. Assuming that $u < \tilde{u}(Y)$, the equilibrium land rent curve can be depicted from (3.30) as in Figure 5.2, where $r_f(Y, u)$ is determined from (3.28). If $u \geq \tilde{u}(Y)$, of course, $r_f(Y, u) = 0$ and no city exists. From (3.33) the equilibrium population can be derived as

$$N(Y, u) = \int_0^{r_f(Y,u)} \frac{L(r)}{s(Y - T(r), u)} dr \tag{5.15}$$

We can consider $N(Y, u)$ to represent the number of households that will migrate from the rest of the nation into the city when each household in the city receives income Y and the national utility is u. Hence, we call $N(Y, u)$ the *population supply function* from the national economy to the city. In Figure 5.2, since the bid rent curve $\psi(Y - T(r), u)$ moves upward (downward) when Y (u) increases, urban fringe $r_f(Y, u)$ also moves outward (inward) when Y (u) increases. Moreover, the lot size function $s(Y - T(r), u)$ is decreasing in Y and increasing in u. Hence, from (5.15) we can readily conclude as follows:

Property 5.1. The population supply function $N(Y, u)$, which is defined at each $Y \in (0, \infty)$ and $u \in (-\infty, \infty)$, has the following characteristics:

(i) $N(Y, u) > 0$ for $u < \tilde{u}(Y)$, $N(Y, u) = 0$ for $u \geq \tilde{u}(Y)$, where $\tilde{u}(Y)$ is the supreme utility function defined by (3.27).

(ii) At each $u < \tilde{u}(Y)$, $N(Y, u)$ is increasing in Y and decreasing in u: $\partial N(Y, u)/\partial Y > 0$, $\partial N(Y, u)/\partial u < 0$.

(iii) $\lim_{Y\to\infty} N(Y, u) = \infty$; for each $Y > T(0)$ we have $\lim_{u\to-\infty} N(Y, u) = \infty$.[10]

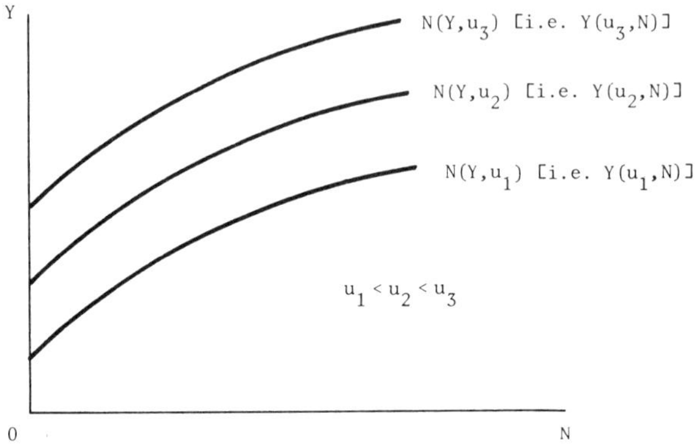

Figure 5.3. Population supply curves $N(Y, u_i)$ [i.e., population supply–income curves $Y(u_i, N)$].

On the basis of this property, we can draw a set of *population supply curves* $N(Y, u_i)$, $i = 1, 2, 3$, as depicted in Figure 5.3. For example, given the national utility level u_1, curve $N(Y, u_1)$ shows the population supply (i.e., equilibrium population of the city) when the household income is given at each point on the Y axis.

Next, let $Y(u, N)$ be the solution to equation $N(Y, u) = N$ for Y under each value of N. Given u, $Y(u, N)$ represents the household income (in the city) that is necessary to have N households supplied from the national economy into the city. We call $Y(u, N)$ the *inverse population supply function* or the *(population) supply–income function*. In Figure 5.3, by definition, each curve also represents a *supply–income curve*.[11] From Property 5.1 and (5.15), we can readily conclude as follows:

Property 5.2. Population supply–income function $Y(u, N)$ has the following characteristics: At each $u \in (-\infty, \infty)$ and $N > 0$,

(i) $Y(u, N) > 0$, and $\lim_{N\to 0} Y(u, N) > 0$;

(ii) $Y(u, N)$ is increasing in both N and u: $\partial Y(u, N)/\partial N > 0$, $\partial Y(u, N)/\partial u > 0$;

(iii) $\lim_{N\to\infty} Y(u, N) = \infty$, $\lim_{u\to\infty} Y(u, N) = \infty$, $\lim_{u\to-\infty} Y(u, N) = T(0)$.

That is, to attract any positive population N, the household income Y in the city must be positive. Hence, $Y(u, N) > 0$ for any $N > 0$. Moreover, since $R_A > 0$, no good is free for households. Hence, $Y(u, N) > 0$ even at an infinitely small N [i.e., $\lim_{N\to 0} Y(u, N) > 0$]. Since $N(Y, u)$ and Y move in the same direction, supply–income $Y(u, N)$ is an increasing function of N; and from Property 5.1(iii), $Y(u, N)$ approaches ∞ as N becomes infinitely large. Finally, since $N(Y, u)$ is decreasing in u, in order to maintain the same size of population supply $N(Y, u)$ when u is increasing, the household income Y must be increased. Hence, $Y(u, N)$ is an increasing function of u.

Example 5.1. Suppose we have the log-linear utility function of Example 2.1 and the following additional specifications,

$$T(r) = ar \qquad \text{and} \qquad L(r) = \theta \qquad \text{for all} \quad r \geq 0, \tag{5.16}$$

where a and θ are positive constants. Then using (3.28) and the bid rent function (2.13), we have $r_f(Y, u) = (Y - \alpha^{-\alpha}\beta^{-\beta}e^u R_A^\beta)/a$. Substituting this urban fringe distance and bid-max lot size function (2.14) into (5.15), we can obtain the population supply function as

$$N(Y, u) = (\alpha^{\alpha/\beta}\beta e^{-u/\beta}Y^{1/\beta} - R_A)\theta a^{-1} \tag{5.17}$$

for each $u < \tilde{u}(Y) \equiv \log \alpha^\alpha\beta^\beta R_A^{-\beta}Y$. Solving the equation $N(Y, u) = N$ for Y, we obtain the supply–income function as

$$Y(u, N) = D(N + E)^\beta e^u, \tag{5.18}$$

where

$$D = \alpha^{-\alpha}\beta^{-\beta}\theta^{-\beta}a^\beta, \qquad E = \theta a^{-1}R_A. \tag{5.19}$$

It can be readily confirmed that functions (5.17) and (5.18) satisfy all conditions of Properties 5.1 and 5.2.

It turns out that supply–income function $Y(u, N)$ has a very close relationship to the minimum residential cost function $C(u, N)$. To examine this relationship, recall from (3.48) that the minimum residential cost $C(u, N)$ for achieving common utility u for all N households in the city can be defined as

$$C(u, N) \equiv \min_{r_f, n(r), s(r)} \int_0^{r_f} [T(r) + Z(s(r), u) + R_A s(r)]n(r)\, dr,$$

$$\text{subject to} \qquad s(r)n(r) \leq L(r) \qquad \text{at each} \quad r \leq r_f,$$

$$\int_0^{r_f} n(r)\, dr = N. \tag{5.20}$$

We simply call $C(u, N)$ the *population cost function*. Now, let $N(Y, u)$ and $\mathrm{TDR}(Y, u)$ be, respectively, the equilibrium population and total differential rent for the OCA(Y, u) model. Then from (5.12) it holds identically that

$$N(Y, u)Y = C(u, N(Y, u)) + \text{TDR}(Y, u). \tag{5.21}$$

Equivalently, if we set Y equal to $Y(u, N)$ in (5.21), then since $N(Y(u, N), u) \equiv N$, it follows that

$$NY(u, N) = C(u, N) + \text{TDR}(Y(u, N), u). \tag{5.22}$$

Differentiating both sides of equation (5.22) by N, we have

$$Y(u, N) + N\frac{\partial Y(u, N)}{\partial N} = \frac{\partial C(u, N)}{\partial N} + \frac{\partial \text{TDR}}{\partial N}. \tag{5.23}$$

A simple calculation reveals that[12]

$$N\frac{\partial Y(u, N)}{\partial N} = \frac{\partial \text{TDR}}{\partial N}. \tag{5.24}$$

Hence, we can conclude that

$$Y(u, N) = \frac{\partial C(u, N)}{\partial N}.$$

Equivalently, since $Y(u, N(Y, u)) \equiv Y$, it follows that

$$Y = \frac{\partial C(u, N)}{\partial N} \quad \text{at} \quad N = N(Y, u).$$

In summary, we can conclude as follows:

Property 5.3. At each $u \in (-\infty, \infty)$ and $N > 0$, the supply–income $Y(u, N)$ equals the marginal population cost:

$$Y(u, N) = \frac{\partial C(u, N)}{\partial N}. \tag{5.25}$$

Equivalently, at each equilibrium population $N(Y, u) > 0$, the household income Y equals the marginal population cost:

$$Y = \frac{\partial C(u, N)}{\partial N} \quad \text{at} \quad N = N(Y, u). \tag{5.26}$$

Similarly, starting from relation (5.22), we can readily obtain the following result:

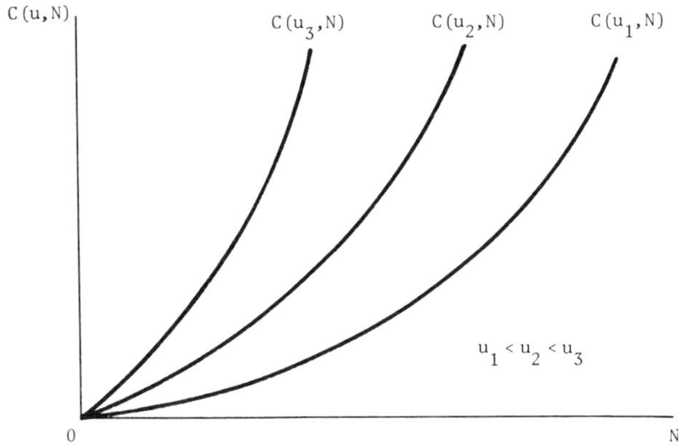

Figure 5.4. Population cost curves.

Property 5.4. Given $u < \tilde{u}(Y)$, let $(s(r), n(r), r_f)$ be the equilibrium solution to the OCA(Y, u) model. Then it holds that

$$\frac{\partial C(u, N)}{\partial u} = \int_0^{r_f} \frac{\partial Z(s(r), u)}{\partial u} n(r)\, dr > 0. \tag{5.27}$$

Utilizing relations (5.25) and (5.27) and Property 5.2, we can derive the following characteristics of population cost function $C(u, N)$ (see Appendix C.10 for the proof):

Property 5.5. At each $u \in (-\infty, \infty)$ and $N > 0$,

(i) $\partial C(u, N)/\partial u > 0$, $\lim_{u\to-\infty} C(u, N) = NT(0)$, and $\lim_{u\to\infty} C(u, N) = \infty$; that is, population cost is increasing in u, and it becomes $NT(0)$ (infinitely large) as u approaches $-\infty$ (∞);

(ii) $\partial C(u, N)/\partial N > 0$, $C(u, 0) \equiv \lim_{N\to 0} C(u, N) = 0$, and $\lim_{N\to\infty} C(u, N) = \infty$; that is, population cost is increasing in N, and it becomes zero (infinitely large) as N approaches 0 (∞).

(iii) $\partial^2 C(u, N)/\partial N^2 > 0$ and $\lim_{N\to\infty} \partial C(u, N)/\partial N = \infty$; that is, each population cost curve is strictly convex in N, and its slope becomes infinitely large as N approaches ∞;

(iv) $\partial^2 C(u, N)/\partial N \partial u > 0$; that is, the population cost curve becomes steeper as u increases.

On the basis of Property 5.5, the behavior of the population cost function can be depicted as in Figure 5.4. An increasing population or utility level causes more consumption of resources. Hence, the population cost function is naturally increasing in N and u. This means that each population cost curve is upward-sloped everywhere, and it shifts upward as u increases. Moreover, from Property 5.2 and (5.25), the following relation can be obtained,

$$\frac{\partial^2 C(u, N)}{\partial N^2} = \frac{\partial Y(u, N)}{\partial N} > 0, \tag{5.28}$$

which means [as indicated in Property (5.5)(iii)] that each population cost curve is strictly convex. An economic rationale for this result is as follows: Due to increases in commuting distance, the total transport cost of the city increases more than in direct proportion to population size. This causes the population cost $C(u, N)$ to increase at an increasing rate with population N, which means mathematically that each population curve is strictly convex. Similarly, utilizing relation (5.25), we can derive the following additional characteristics of the population cost function at $N = 0$ (see Appendix C.10 for the proof):

Property 5.6. At each $u \in (-\infty, \infty)$,

(i) $C_N(u, 0) \equiv \lim_{N\to 0} \partial C(u, N)/\partial N > 0$; that is, each population cost curve has a positive slope at the origin;
(ii) $\partial C_N(u, 0)/\partial u > 0$; that is, at the origin, the population cost curve becomes steeper as u increases;
(iii) $\lim_{u\to -\infty} C_N(u, 0) = T(0)$; that is, as u decreases, the slope of the population cost curve at the origin eventually approaches $T(0)$;
(iv) $\lim_{u\to\infty} C_N(u, 0) = \infty$; that is, as u increases, the population cost curve eventually becomes infinitely steep at the origin.

Example 5.2. In the context of Example 5.1 [with the log-linear utility function (2.12) and additional specifications of (5.16)], let us obtain the population cost function $C(u, N)$. Recall that the minimization problem (5.20) is equivalent to problem (3.50). Substituting (2.13) and (2.14) into (3.55) and (3.56), we have

$$N = \int_0^{r_f} \alpha^{\alpha/\beta}(Y^0 - G^* - ar)^{\alpha/\beta} e^{-u/\beta} \theta \, dr,$$

$$\alpha^{\alpha/\beta}\beta(Y^0 - G^* - ar_f)^{1/\beta} e^{-u/\beta} = R_A,$$

which yield

$$G^* = Y^0 - De^u(N + E)^\beta, \qquad r_f = a^{-1}De^u\{(N + E)^\beta - E^\beta\}, \tag{5.29}$$

where D and E are parameters defined by (5.19). Substituting G^* and r_f into the Lagrangian function $\mathcal{L}$ in Section 3.4, we have by integration that

$$\mathcal{L} = NY^0 - (1 + \beta)^{-1}D\{(N + E)^{1+\beta} - E^{1+\beta}\}e^u.$$

Since $\mathcal{L} = \mathcal{S} = NY^0 - C(u, N)$ at the optimal solution, it follows that

$$C(u, N) = (1 + \beta)^{-1}D\{(N + E)^{1+\beta} - E^{1+\beta}\}e^u. \tag{5.30}$$

It can be readily confirmed that this population cost function satisfies all conditions of Properties 5.5 and 5.6. Recalling (5.18), we can also see that relation (5.25) holds.

Next, let $F(N)$ be the *aggregate production function* of the city, which represents the net ouput of the city (in terms of value under fixed national or international prices) produced using each total labor force (i.e., population) N. Here, for simplicity, we assume that the production in the city requires only labor (all other costs are treated as fixed costs). Then the *(gross) surplus* of the city is given by

$$\mathcal{S} = F(N) - C(u, N), \tag{5.31}$$

and the *net surplus* is given by

$$\begin{aligned} \Pi &= \mathcal{S} - K \\ &= F(N) - C(u, N) - K, \end{aligned} \tag{5.32}$$

where K represents the fixed costs (or local public good costs) of the city.

As a special case, suppose that $F(N)$ is linear,

$$F(N) = \delta N, \tag{5.33}$$

where the positive constant δ represents the *marginal (value) product* and the *average (value) product of labor* for the city under study. In this case, we denote the surplus function of the city as follows:

$$\mathcal{S}(\delta, u, N) = \delta N - C(u, N). \tag{5.34}$$

By definition, $\mathcal{S}(\delta, u, N)$ equals the maximum surplus obtained from the solution of the HS(δ, u, N) model (i.e., the HS model under household income δ, target utility u, and city population N). Recalling (3.48) and (3.49), we can define $\mathcal{S}(\delta, u, N)$ in more detail as

$$\mathcal{S}(\delta, u, N) \equiv \max_{r_f, n(r), s(r)} \int_0^{r_f} [\delta - T(r) - Z(s(r), u) - R_A s(r)]n(r)\, dr,$$

$$\text{subject to} \quad s(r)n(r) \leq L(r) \quad \text{at each} \quad r \leq r_f,$$

$$\int_0^{r_f} n(r)\, dr = N. \tag{5.35}$$

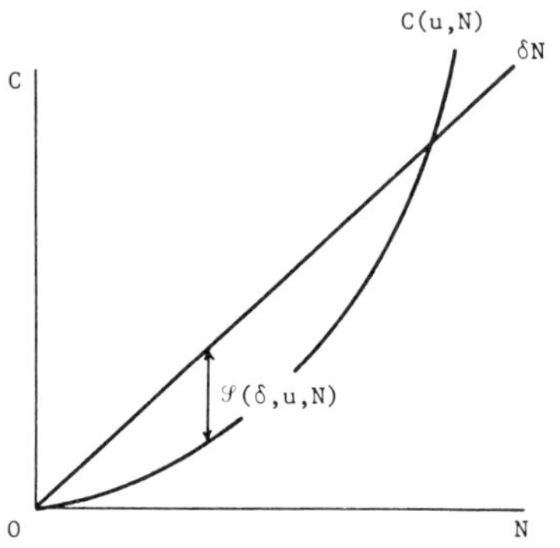

Figure 5.5. Population cost curve $C(u, N)$ and income line δN.

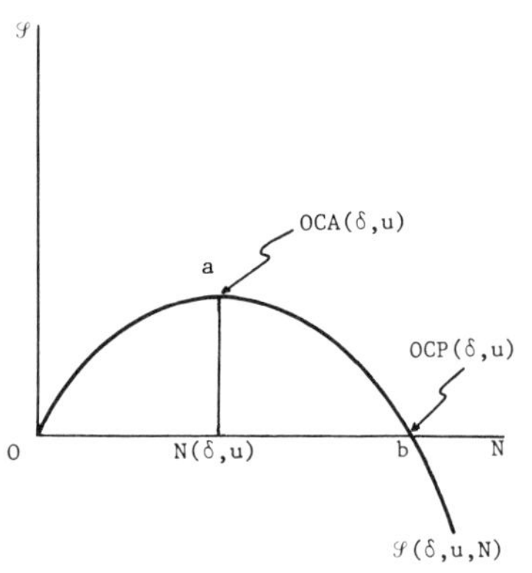

Figure 5.6. Surplus curve $\mathcal{S}(\delta, u, N)$.

Graphically, given target utility u, the population cost curve $C(u, N)$ can be depicted as in Figure 5.5 (δN represents a straight line). Hence, it becomes clear that at each population N the surplus $\mathcal{S}(\delta, u, N)$ equals the vertical distance between income line δN and population cost curve $C(u, N)$. Moreover, from Property 5.5(ii), $C(u, 0) = 0$.[13] From Property 5.5(iii), curve $C(u, N)$ is strictly convex, and its slope becomes infinitely large as N approaches ∞. By definition, $N(\delta, \tilde{u}(\delta)) = 0$. Hence, from (5.26),

$$\delta = \frac{\partial C(\tilde{u}(\delta), N)}{\partial N} \quad \text{at} \quad N = 0. \tag{5.36}$$

From Property 5.6(ii), at the origin, the population cost curve becomes steeper as u increases. Therefore, from (5.36), we can conclude that

$$\delta > \frac{\partial C(u, N)}{\partial N} \quad \text{at} \quad N = 0 \qquad \text{if and only if} \quad u < \tilde{u}(\delta). \tag{5.37}$$

That is, at the origin, population cost curve $C(u, N)$ is less steep than income line δN if and only if $u < \tilde{u}(\delta)$. Therefore, given (δ, u) such that $u < \tilde{u}(\delta)$, the *surplus curve* $\mathcal{S}(\delta, u, N)$ can be depicted as in Figure 5.6. The surplus curve $\mathcal{S}(\delta, u, N)$ is strictly concave; it is positive for $0 < N < b$, and negative for $N > b$. The maximum surplus point a can be identified as follows: From definition (5.34) at the maximum surplus point a we have

$$0 = \frac{\partial \mathcal{S}(\delta, u, N)}{\partial N} = \delta - \frac{\partial C(u, N)}{\partial N}, \qquad \text{i.e.,} \quad \delta = \frac{\partial C(u, N)}{\partial N}, \tag{5.38}$$

which means that *the surplus is maximum when the marginal product of labor equals the marginal population cost for the city*. On the other hand, setting Y equal to δ in (5.26), it follows that $\delta = \partial C(u, N)/\partial N$ at $N = N(\delta, u)$. Therefore, we can conclude from (5.38) that

$$\frac{\partial \mathcal{S}(\delta, u, N)}{\partial N} = 0 \qquad \text{at} \quad N = N(\delta, u), \tag{5.39}$$

which means that the surplus curve $\mathcal{S}(\delta, u, N)$ attains the maximum when N equals the equilibrium population $N(\delta, u)$ of the OCA(δ, u) model. In Figure 5.6, this means that *point a corresponds to the equilibrium solution of the OCA(δ, u) model*. We can also see from (5.21) and (5.34) that

$$\mathcal{S}(\delta, u, N(\delta, u)) = \text{TDR}(\delta, u). \tag{5.40}$$

Namely, the maximum surplus $\mathcal{S}(\delta, u, N(\delta, u))$ equals the total differential rent of the OCA(δ, u) model. Notice also that when $u \geq \tilde{u}(\delta)$, $\delta \leq \partial C(u, N)/\partial N$ at $N = 0$; hence, $\mathcal{S}$ is maximum at $N = 0$. On the other hand, when $u \geq \tilde{u}(\delta)$, from Property 5.1(i) we have $N(\delta, u) = 0$. Therefore, we can generally conclude as follows:

Proposition 5.1. Given any (δ, u) such that $\delta > 0$,

(i) surplus $\mathcal{S}(\delta, u, N)$ is maximum when N equals the equilibrium population $N(\delta, u)$ of the OCA(δ, u) model;
(ii) hence, at $N = N(\delta, u)$, the solution to the HS(δ, u, N) model coincides with the equilibrium solution to the OCA(δ, u) model;
(iii) the maximum surplus $\mathcal{S}(\delta, u, N(\delta, u))$ equals the total differential rent TDR(δ, u) of the OCA(δ, u) model.

In particular, (i) and (ii) of Proposition 5.1 imply that *one can achieve the maximum surplus of the city simply by keeping migration free and paying each household its marginal product δ, while letting all residential allocation be determined by the competitive market.*

Finally, let $N_P(\delta, u)$ be the equilibrium population of the OCP(δ, u) model. Then from (5.14),

$$N_P(\delta, u)\delta = C(u, N_P(\delta, u)). \tag{5.41}$$

Hence, from (5.34),

$$\mathcal{S}(\delta, u, N_P(\delta, u)) = 0. \tag{5.42}$$

In Figure 5.6, this implies that *point b corresponds to the equilibrium solution to the OCP(δ, u) model*. As noted above, whenever $u < \tilde{u}(\delta)$, point b uniquely exists. When $u \geq \tilde{u}(\delta)$, the equilibrium population of the OCP(δ, u) model is, of course, zero. Hence, in either case there exists a unique equilibrium for any OCP(δ, u) model. Replacing δ by Y, we can see that this provides the proof of Proposition 3.4.

5.5 Resource and transport advantages

Suppose a city develops at the location of an economical mine (or at an advantageous port site). The city produces a single final product (or a composite of final products) by using a single input, labor. Let p be the unit price of the output at the representative market in the national (or world) economy, and t the transport cost per unit of the output from the city to the market, where $t < p$. The production technology has constant returns to scale; hence, the aggregate production function of the city (in terms of net value) can be described as

$$F(N) = (p - t)aN, \tag{5.43}$$

where a represents the marginal product of labor, and $(p - t)a \equiv \delta$ gives the marginal value product of labor. The total profit π for all firms in the city equals

$$\pi = (p - t)aN - WN, \tag{5.44}$$

where W is the wage rate in the city. Assuming that the labor market of the city is perfectly competitive, the wage rate equals the marginal value product of labor,

$$W = (p - t)a, \tag{5.45}$$

and the profit of each firm is zero. The *wage line W* depicted in Figure 5.7 represents the *demand curve of labor* in the city.[14] That is, for each additional one unit of labor, the city's firms are willing to pay $(p - t)a$.

Suppose the national utility level is given at a constant u, and households can move freely from the rest of the nation into the city. We also assume that the city's land belongs to absentee landowners. Hence, the income of each household in the city equals its wage: $Y = W = (p - t)a$. Therefore, substituting $Y = (p - t)a$ into the population supply function $N(Y, u)$ from Section 5.4, the equilibrium population of the city is given as $N[(p - t)a, u]$. That is, in Figure 5.7 the equilibrium population of the city is determined at the intersection between the wage line W and population supply curve $N(Y, u)$. Of course, the equilibrium population of the city is positive only when national utility u is sufficiently low or, equivalently, only when the marginal value product $(p - t)a$ of labor in the city is sufficiently large. More precisely, from Property 5.1(i), $N[(p - t)a, u] > 0$ if and only if $u < \tilde{u}[(p - t)a]$.

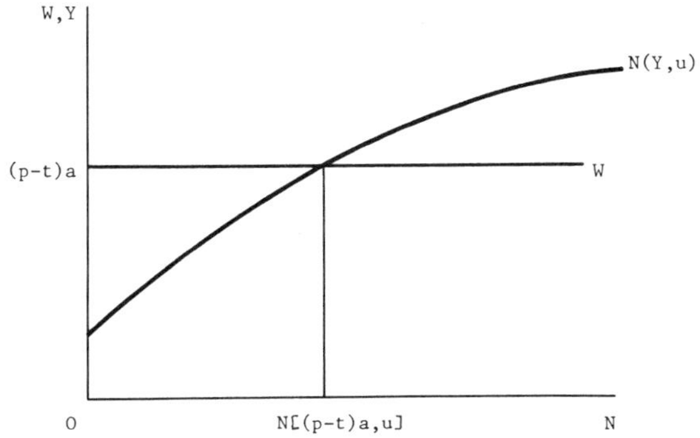

Figure 5.7. Determination of equilibrium population $N[(p - t)a, u]$.

From Proposition 5.1(i) and (ii), the *equilibrium population* $N[(p - t)a, u]$ *of the city is also optimal* in the sense that the city's surplus $\mathcal{S}[(p - t)a, u, N]$ is maximum when N equals $N[(p - t)a, u]$. And from Proposition 5.1(iii), in equilibrium the city's surplus equals the total differential rent; namely, the entire surplus of the city is absorbed by the differential land rents. It is also evident from Figure 5.7 that the equilibrium population of the city is larger as

1. the marginal product a of labor in the city is greater (e.g., minerals are more economically extractable);
2. the transport cost t to the market is smaller (e.g., the port city is more accessible to the major national or world markets);
3. the output price p is higher; or
4. the national utility u is lower.

Finally, suppose we have two cities, $i = 1, 2$, at different locations. The two cities are identical in terms of production and transport conditions, and hence they have the same value of marginal value product of labor, $(p - t)a$. However, in terms of *natural amenities* such as climate, city 1 is situated at a better location than city 2. This implies, as depicted in Figure 5.8, that given the same national utility u, at each household income Y, city 1's population supply $N_1(Y, u)$ is greater than city 2's population supply $N_2(Y, u)$.[15] Hence, not surprisingly, we can conclude from Figure 5.8 that city 1 (with better natural amenities) has a greater equilibrium population.

5.6 Fixed costs and city sizes

In this section, we assume that the formation of a city requires a certain amount of fixed costs K. For example, K may include construction costs

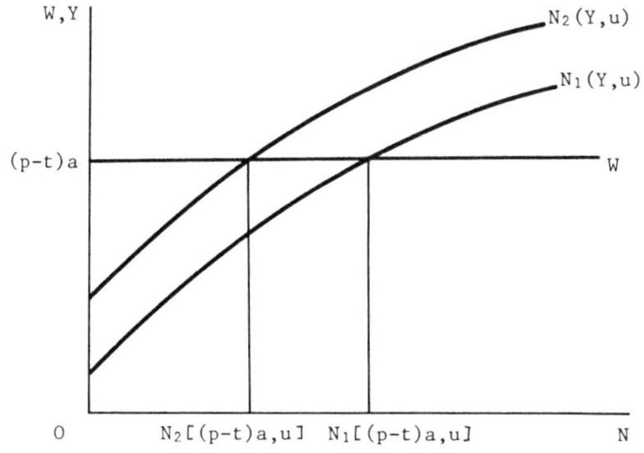

Figure 5.8. Effects of natural amenities on city sizes.

of basic public facilities such as transport and water systems. Since the per capita fixed costs become smaller as the population increases, the existence of fixed costs provides an incentive for city formation. As before, we assume that all production activity takes place at the center of the city, and the aggregate production function of the city has constant returns to scale, which is described by (5.33).[16] As noted before, the export price of the output is assumed to be given exogenously, and for simplicity it is normalized at unity. We also assume that all land in the city is owned by absentee landlords.

Given these basic assumptions, we can conceive of many different types of city organization. In Section 5.6.1, we assume that everything except the provision of basic public facilities is determined by competitive markets. In Section 5.6.2, we show that the city size determined by competitive markets is the same as the one chosen by a *profit-maximizing developer*. In Section 5.6.3 we consider the formation of a city by a *utility-maximizing community*. Finally, in Section 5.6.4, we examine the *equilibrium city system* of the nation that will result from the competition among profit-maximizing developers or among utility-maximizing communities. In this way, we develop in these four subsections an introductory theory on city systems.

5.6.1 *Market city size*

Let us assume that the city government first carries out the groundwork of city formation implied by the fixed costs K. Then everything else is left free to be determined by competitive markets. No taxes are collected from households or firms in the city. Fixed costs K are later confiscated from the differential land rents that initially belong to absentee landlords.

Observe that the competitive labor market sets the wage per unit of labor (i.e., per unit of household) equal to the marginal product of labor δ. Since no tax is collected from households, the income Y of every household in the city equals its wage δ:

$$Y = \delta. \tag{5.46}$$

Households are free to migrate into the city from the rest of the nation, where each household is attaining the (national) utility level u. Therefore, once the groundwork of city formation has been laid, *the market city model here is identical with the OCA(δ, u) model* (the open-city model under absentee landownership with income δ and national utility u). Hence, substituting $Y = \delta$ into the population supply function $N(Y, u)$ introduced in Section 5.4, we have the equilibrium population of the city as $N(\delta, u)$, which is positive assuming that $u < \tilde{u}(\delta)$.

The surplus of the city (before fixed costs K are deducted) is given by (5.34). As in Figure 5.6, we can draw the surplus curve $\mathcal{S}(\delta, u, N)$ shown in Figure 5.9. Then the equilibrium population $N(\delta, u)$ corresponds to the maximum surplus point a in the figure. From (5.40), we can also see that at the equilibrium population $N(\delta, u)$, the surplus equals the total differential rent of the city. Therefore, if the total differential rent TDR(δ, u) exceeds fixed costs K, the city can finance fixed costs K by confiscating a part of differential land rents from absentee landlords. Otherwise, the net surplus (after deducting fixed costs K) from the city formation becomes negative, and hence the development of the city should not be undertaken at all.[17]

5.6.2 *Profit-maximizing city size*

Next, let us assume that a city will be formed by a developer whose objective is to earn maximum profit from the development. The developer rents the land for the city at the unit price of agricultural land rent R_A and organizes the formation of the city.[18] There are two ways for the developer to organize the city. One way is for the developer to plan and manage every aspect of city formation, including production activity and residential allocation. The other, which is simpler for the developer, is to introduce competitive markets into the city.

The former can be explained as follows: Notice that the developer can induce as many workers (i.e., households) as desired to live in the city if he or she ensures for them the national utility u. Suppose the developer chooses a population size N. Then the optimal residential allocation problem for the developer can be represented by the HS(δ, u, N) model, and the maximum surplus from the city development is given by (5.34). De-

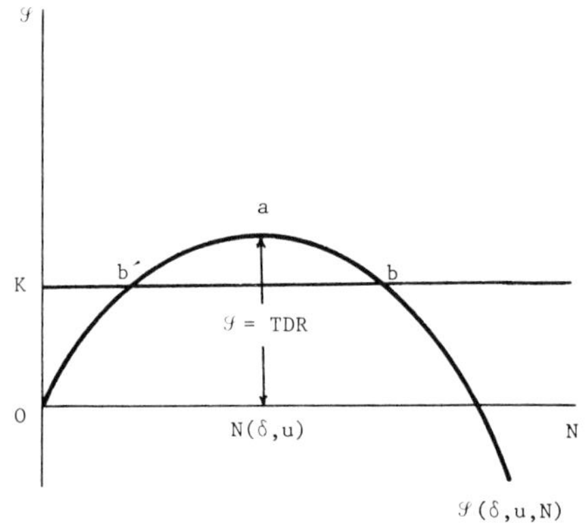

Figure 5.9. Surplus curve $\mathcal{S}(\delta, u, N)$ and fixed costs K.

ducting the fixed costs K, then, the net profit Π from the city development equals

$$\begin{aligned}\Pi &= \mathcal{S}(\delta, u, N) - K \\ &= \delta N - C(u, N) - K.\end{aligned} \tag{5.47}$$

The developer will choose, of course, population N so as to maximize the net profit Π. However, since K is a constant, the maximization of Π is equivalent to the maximization of surplus $\mathcal{S}(\delta, u, N)$. Hence, given the surplus curve $\mathcal{S}(\delta, u, N)$ in Figure 5.9, the developer will choose the population that corresponds to the peak point a on that curve. This means, again, that *the optimal population for the profit-maximizing developer equals the equilibrium population* $N(\delta, u)$ *of the OCA*(δ, u) *model*. Of course, as before, the developer will actually develop the city only when the maximum surplus $\mathcal{S}(\delta, u, N(\delta, u))$ exceeds fixed costs K.

In practice, however, if the developer were to plan and manage every aspect of city formation, it would involve a prohibitive amount of action. Fortunately, the above conclusion suggests that there is another, simpler way for the developer to realize the optimal city, as already suggested. That is, suppose the developer rents the land for the city at the agricultural land rent R_A and lays the groundwork of city formation (implied by the fixed costs K). Then everything else is left free to be determined by competitive markets. In particular, the city's land will be subleased to the city residents at the competitive market rent. Then the market city model under study coincides with that in Section 5.6.1. Hence, as we saw in that section, the optimal city (i.e., the profit-maximizing city) will be achieved in equilibrium. As indicated by equation (5.40), the surplus from the city development is embodied in the total differential rent TDR(δ, u). Hence, from (5.47), the net profit from the city development is given as

$$\Pi = \mathrm{TDR}(\delta, u) - K. \tag{5.48}$$

We can summarize the result as follows:

> ***Proposition 5.2.*** In the context of the city model with fixed costs K, when the national utility equals u,
>
> (i) the optimal population for the profit-maximizing developer equals the equilibrium population $N(\delta, u)$ of the OCA(δ, u) model, and
> (ii) the net profit from the city development is given as $\Pi = \mathrm{TDR}(\delta, u) - K$;
> (iii) hence, the city will be actually developed only when TDR(δ, u) $\geq K$.

5.6.3 *Utility-maximizing city size*

Let us consider the development of the city by a utility-maximizing community. That is, suppose a certain number of households form a community (or club) and develop the city. All households in the community (i.e., in the city) are to enjoy the same utility level, and the community's objective is to maximize its common utility level. The community must, of course, meet its budget constraint.

As before, we assume that the community can rent the land for the city from absentee landlords at the unit price of agricultural rent R_A. Suppose the community chooses a certain population size N. Then if the community wishes to achieve a common utility u, its surplus (before deducting the fixed costs K) is given, as before, by (5.34). Therefore, considering the fixed costs K, the *community's budget constraint* can be expressed as

$$\mathcal{S}(\delta, u, N) \equiv \delta N - C(u, N) \geq K. \tag{5.49}$$

Now, the *community's problem* is to achieve the highest common utility by appropriately choosing its population N, while satisfying the above budget constraint.

We can examine this community's problem graphically, as shown in Figure 5.10. Here a set of surplus curves is drawn across the horizontal fixed-cost line K. In order to meet the budget constraint (5.49), a surplus curve must pass the region above the fixed-cost line K. Since surplus curves move downward as u increases, *the community achieves the highest utility when the corresponding surplus curve is tangent to the fixed-*

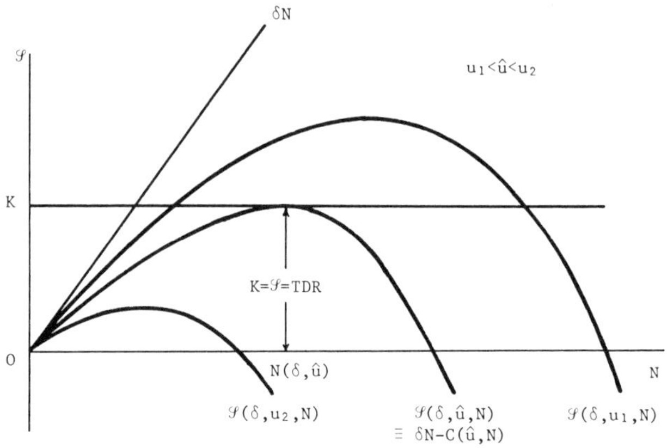

Figure 5.10. The community's problem.

cost line K from below. Hence, in Figure 5.10, $\hat{u}$ represents the highest utility attainable for the community. The optimal population of the community is the one that corresponds to the peak point of the surplus curve $\mathcal{S}(\delta, \hat{u}, N)$. Thus, setting $Y = \delta$ and $u = \hat{u}$, we can conclude from Proposition 5.1(i) that *the optimal population of the community equals $N(\delta, \hat{u})$, which is the equilibrium population of the OCA$(\delta, \hat{u})$ model*. Since the surplus curve $\mathcal{S}(\delta, \hat{u}, N)$ is tangent to the fixed-cost line K at the optimal population $N(\delta, \hat{u})$, the maximum surplus equals the fixed costs:

$$\mathcal{S}(\delta, \hat{u}, N) = K \qquad \text{at} \quad N = N(\delta, \hat{u}). \tag{5.50}$$

Suppose the national utility equals u. Then, of course, this community is viable only when $\hat{u} \geq u$; otherwise, no household would agree to move into the community. However, when $\hat{u} \geq u$ (in particular, when $\hat{u} > u$), the community must be "closed" so that the optimal number $N(\delta, \hat{u})$ of households is to be maintained. Therefore, we can see that once the optimal population $N(\delta, \hat{u})$ has been known, the optimal allocation within the community can be achieved through the following competitive market mechanism.

Suppose $N(\delta, \hat{u})$ households agree to form a community and set up the *community government*. The (community) government rents the city's land from absentee landlords at the unit price of agricultural rent R_A and lays the groundwork of the city formation that is implied by the fixed costs K. Then the only role of the government is to keep the city "closed" and let everything else be determined by competitive markets. The competitive labor market will set the wage per household equal to its marginal product δ. Then assuming no tax is collected from households, the income of each household equals δ. Notice that given household income δ, the competitive residential market under study coincides with the CCA(δ, $N(\delta, \hat{u})$) model [i.e., the closed-city model under absentee landownership with household income δ and population $N(\delta, \hat{u})$]. From Proposition 3.5(i), we know that the solution to the CCA(δ, $N(\delta, \hat{u})$) model coincides, mathematically, with the solution to the OCA(δ, $\hat{u}$) model.[19] And from Proposition 5.1(ii), the solution to the OCA(δ, $\hat{u}$) model coincides with the solution to the HS(δ, $\hat{u}$, $N(\delta, \hat{u})$) model, which, by definition, represents the optimal residential allocation of the community. Therefore, we can conclude that the optimal allocation within the community will be achieved at the equilibrium of the competitive market system described above.

Let TDR(δ, N) be the total differential rent in the equilibrium of the CCA(δ, N) model. Then since the solution to the CCA(δ, $N(\delta, \hat{u})$) model coincides with the solution to the OCA(δ, $\hat{u}$) model, recalling Proposition 5.1(iii) we can conclude that at the optimal population $N = N(\delta, \hat{u})$, the surplus of the community equals the total differential rent of the community:

$$\mathcal{S}(\delta, \hat{u}, N) = \mathrm{TDR}(\delta, N) \qquad \text{at} \quad N = N(\delta, \hat{u}). \tag{5.51}$$

Hence, from (5.50) and (5.51) we can conclude that *at the optimal population $N(\delta, \hat{u})$, the total differential rent of the community equals the fixed cost K:*

$$\mathrm{TDR}(\delta, N) = K \qquad \text{at} \quad N = N(\delta, \hat{u}). \tag{5.52}$$

If the fixed costs K are considered to represent the expenditure on local public goods, relation (5.52) represents a familiar result in the literature of public finance, called the *Henry George theorem* or the *golden rule of local public finance*. That is, in a city of optimal size, a confiscatory tax on differential land rents would by itself finance the local public goods.[20]

Finally, it is apparent from Figure 5.10 that under any given fixed costs $K > 0$, the highest utility $\hat{u}$ and optimal population $N(\delta, \hat{u})$ can be determined uniquely.[21] Let $\hat{u}(K)$ be the highest utility of the community when the fixed costs equal K. Then in Figure 5.10, since a surplus curve $\mathcal{S}(\delta, u, N)$ moves downward as u increases, we can conclude that $\hat{u}(K)$ is a decreasing function of K:

$$\frac{d\hat{u}(K)}{dK} < 0. \tag{5.53}$$

When u exceeds the supreme utility level $\tilde{u}(\delta)$, $\mathcal{S}(\delta, u, N) \leq 0$ for any N. This implies that given any $K > 0$, $\hat{u}(K)$ is lower than $\tilde{u}(\delta)$:

$$-\infty < \hat{u}(K) < \tilde{u}(\delta). \tag{5.54}$$

From Property 5.1(ii), $N(\delta, u)$ is decreasing in u. Hence, the optimal population $N(\delta, \hat{u}(K))$ is increasing in K:

$$\frac{\partial N(\delta, \hat{u}(K))}{\partial K} = \left(\frac{\partial N(\delta, u)}{\partial u} \bigg|_{u=\hat{u}(K)} \right) \frac{d\hat{u}(K)}{dK} > 0. \tag{5.55}$$

It is also apparent from Figure 5.10 that

$$N(\delta, \hat{u}(K)) \to 0 \qquad \text{as} \quad K \to 0. \tag{5.56}$$

We can summarize the results of this subsection as follows:

> ***Proposition 5.3.*** In the context of the city model with fixed costs K, let $\hat{u}$ be the highest utility the utility-maximizing community can achieve. Then
>
> (i) under any $K > 0$, $\hat{u}$ exists uniquely, and $-\infty < \hat{u} < \tilde{u}(\delta)$;
> (ii) the highest utility $\hat{u}$ is achieved when the community's population is equal to the equilibrium population $N(\delta, \hat{u})$ of the OCA(δ, $\hat{u}$) model;
> (iii) the optimal residential allocation of the (optimal) community coincides with the equilibrium solution of the CCA(δ, $N(\delta, \hat{u})$) model;
> (iv) the TDR at the equilibrium of CCA(δ, $N(\delta, \hat{u})$) model equals the fixed costs K.

5.6.4 *System of cities*

We now consider the system of cities in the nation that will result from competition among utility-maximizing communities or among profit-maximizing developers. Suppose the national economy consists of an urban sector with many cities and a rural sector with an insignificant population. For simplicity, we assume that the total population of the urban sector is exogenously given by a constant M. Since the national economy is closely tied with the world economy, both the output price of the urban sector and that of the rural sector are assumed to be exogenously given and fixed. As before, the output price of the urban sector is normalized as unity.

Wherever a city is to be developed in the nation, the aggregate production function of the city is the same, and it is represented by (5.33). As before, it is assumed that the formation of a city requires a certain amount of fixed costs K. Since the nation has a sufficient amount of land, each community or developer can rent the land for a city at a fixed agricultural land rent R_A.

First, the city system that will result from competition among utility-maximizing communities can be simply determined as follows: Let $\hat{u}$ be the highest common utility attainable for a community, which has been determined in Section 5.6.3. Then as we saw in that section, the optimal population of each community equals $N(\delta, \hat{u})$. Hence, the equilibrium number of total cities in the nation is given by

$$M/N(\delta, \hat{u}), \tag{5.57}$$

and each household in every city is achieving utility level $\hat{u}$. Here we are assuming that the total population M is so large that the number of cities determined by (5.57) can be safely treated as continuous. Note that by forming a community of any size, no group of households can achieve a common utility level higher than $\hat{u}$. Since in the city system above every household is enjoying this highest utility $\hat{u}$, we call it the *optimal city system*.[22]

Now let us consider the city system that will result from competition among profit-maximizing developers. We assume that no developer is able to form more than one city. As a result, since the size of each city to be developed is so small compared with the national economy, each developer will take the national utility level as a given constant. As we have seen in Section 5.6.2, given a national utility level u, the gross profit of each developer equals the surplus $\mathcal{S}(\delta, u, N)$ given by (5.34), which can be depicted as in Figure 5.9.[23] If this surplus curve passes the area above the fixed-cost line K, a developer can earn a positive profit by choosing the optimal population size $N(\delta, u)$. This implies that an infinite number of developers would want to form (an infinite number of) cities, and the total demand for population exceeds the national population M. On the contrary, if the surplus curve $\mathcal{S}(\delta, u, N)$ lies in the area below the fixed-cost line K in Figure 5.9, then a developer earns a negative profit from forming a city of any size. Hence, no city will be developed, and the total demand for population becomes zero. Therefore, we can conclude that if u^* is the utility level associated with an equilibrium city system, the corresponding surplus curve $\mathcal{S}(\delta, u^*, N)$ must be tangent to the fixed-cost line K from below. As is evident from Figure 5.10, this implies that the equilibrium utility u^* equals the highest utility $\hat{u}$. Given $\hat{u}$ as the national utility level, each developer earns zero net profit by choosing the optimal population size $N(\delta, \hat{u})$. The equilibrium number of cities is then given, as before, by (5.57).[24] This means that the equilibrium city system coincides with the optimal city system.

As we have seen in Section 5.6.2, given national utility $\hat{u}$, each developer can achieve a profit-maximizing city by the following simple open-city scheme. That is, after laying the groundwork for city formation implied by the fixed costs K, the developer lets everything else be determined by competitive markets. This implies, in particular, that each household is paid its marginal product δ and that the city's land (which was originally rented at the agricultural rent R_A) is subleased to the city's residents at the competitive market rent. Let TDR(δ, $\hat{u}$) be the total differential rent of the city in equilibrium. Then since the net profit Π is zero in equilibrium, from Proposition 5.2(ii) we can see that

$$\mathrm{TDR}(\delta, \hat{u}) = K.$$

This means that the Henry George theorem holds in every city of the equilibrium city system.

From (5.55) and (5.57), we can also conclude that the number of cities in the equilibrium and optimal city system increases as K decreases and M increases. We can summarize the results of this subsection as follows:

Proposition 5.4. In the context of the city model with fixed costs K, we can conclude that

(i) the equilibrium city system (which results from competition among profit-maximizing developers) is identical with the optimal city system (which consists of a set of utility-maximizing communities);
(ii) under any set of fixed costs $K > 0$ and national population $M > 0$, the equilibrium/optimal city system exists uniquely;
(iii) in every city of the equilibrium/optimal city system, the total differential rent equals the fixed costs K;
(iv) the number of cities in the equilibrium/optimal city system increases as K decreases and as total population M increases.

5.7 Production scale economies and city sizes

In this section, as an alternative cause of city formation, we introduce *scale economies in production.*[25] Let us assume that the aggregate production function $F(N)$ of the city has the following characteristics:

$$F(0) = 0, \tag{5.58}$$

$$F(N) > 0 \quad \text{for all} \quad N > 0, \tag{5.59}$$

$$F'(N) \gtreqless F(N)/N \quad \text{as} \quad N \lesseqgtr N_a, \tag{5.60}$$

where $F'(N) = dF(N)/dN$ represents the marginal product of labor and N_a is a positive constant.[26] Figure 5.11a shows an example of such a production function, which satisfies all the conditions of (5.58)–(5.60).[27] The condition (5.60) means that the marginal product of labor is greater

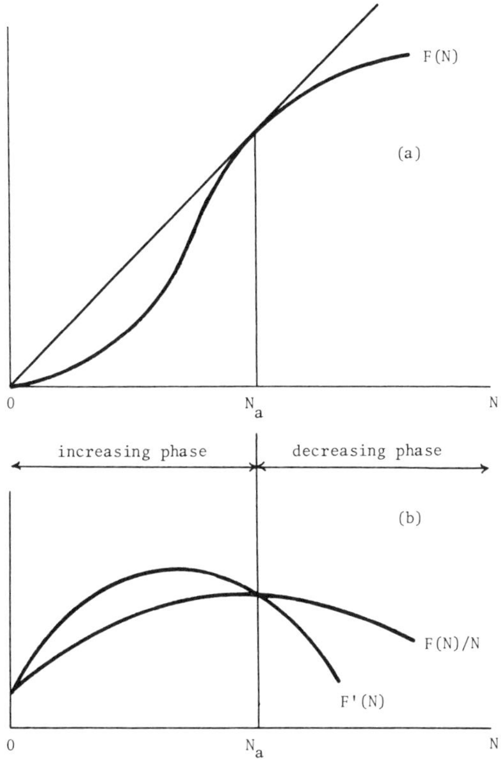

Figure 5.11. Urban production function.

than (equal to or less than) the average product of labor as N is less than (equal to or greater than) N_a. This relationship is depicted in Figure 5.11b. At N_a, the marginal product of labor equals the average product of labor. For the interval between 0 and N_a, scale economies are dominating scale diseconomies, while once N goes beyond N_a, scale diseconomies become dominating scale economies. We call the interval between 0 and N_a the *increasing (returns to scale) phase,* and the interval beyond N_a the *decreasing (returns to scale) phase*. In order to distinguish this section from the preceding section, we assume here that the formation of a city does not involve any fixed costs (i.e., $K = 0$).

First, we consider the formation of a city by a utility-maximizing community. Other than the above assumptions on the city's production function and fixed costs, the context is the same as in Section 5.6.3. In particular, it is assumed that the export price of the city's output is exogenously given and normalized as unity, and the city's land is rented from absentee

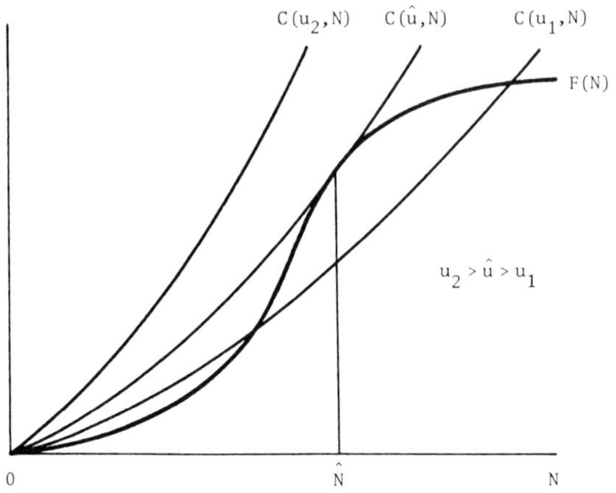

Figure 5.12. Determination of the optimal community size.

landlords at the unit price of agricultural rent R_A. Then the budget constraint of the community can be expressed as

$$F(N) - C(u, N) \geq 0, \tag{5.61}$$

where $C(u, N)$ represents, as usual, the population cost function defined by (5.20). The *community's problem* is then to achieve the highest common utility by appropriately choosing its population N while satisfying the budget constraint:

$$\max_{N>0} u, \qquad \text{subject to} \quad F(N) - C(u, N) \geq 0. \tag{5.62}$$

In this problem, it is essential to restrict N to be strictly positive. Otherwise, since $F(0) - C(u, 0) = 0$ for any u, the community could achieve an infinitely high utility by choosing zero population; but a community with zero population is practically no longer a community.

We can examine the community's problem, again graphically, as shown in Figure 5.12. Here a set of population cost curves is superimposed on the urban production curve $F(N)$. By inspection, it is evident from the figure that *the optimal community size is $\hat{N}$, at which a population cost curve $C(\hat{u}, N)$ is tangent to the urban production curve $F(N)$ from above.* In order to satisfy the budget constraint, a population cost curve must have a common point with the urban production curve at some positive population. At the same time, the community will maximize its common utility. Note that utility increases as one moves to the left in the family of population cost curves shown in Figure 5.12. Hence, the highest utility $\hat{u}$ will be achieved at population $\hat{N}$ at which a population cost curve is tangent to the urban production curve from above.

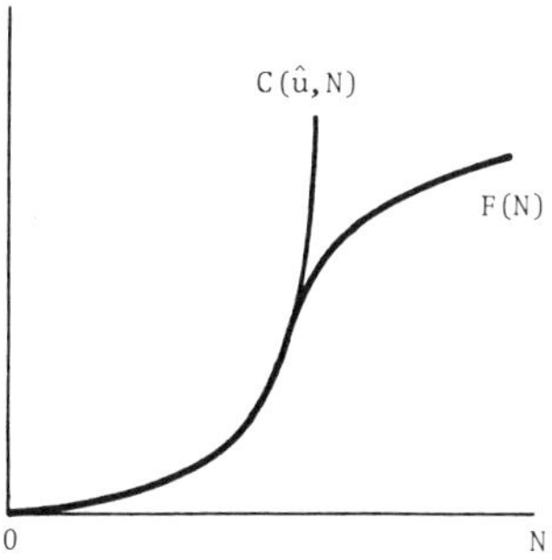

Figure 5.13. Infinitely many solutions to city size.

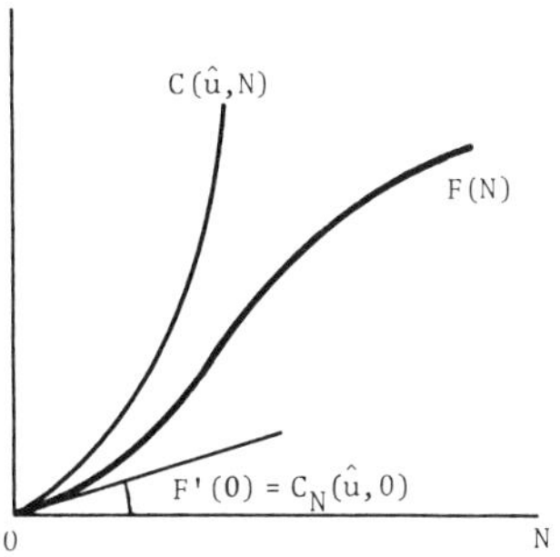

Figure 5.14. Nonexistence of optimal city size.

The tangency of two curves $F(N)$ and $C(\hat{u}, N)$ at point $\hat{N}$ implies that

$$\left.\begin{aligned} F(N) &= C(\hat{u}, N) \\ F'(N) &= \frac{\partial C(\hat{u}, N)}{\partial N} \end{aligned}\right\} \quad \text{at} \quad N = \hat{N}. \tag{5.63}$$

At the same time, the strict convexity of curve $C(\hat{u}, N)$ implies that at any $N > 0$, marginal cost exceeds average cost:

$$\frac{\partial C(\hat{u}, N)}{\partial N} > \frac{C(\hat{u}, N)}{N}. \tag{5.64}$$

From the above two conditions, it follows that

$$F'(N) > F(N)/N \quad \text{at} \quad N = \hat{N}. \tag{5.65}$$

That is, at the optimal city (or community) size, the marginal product of labor exceeds the average product of labor. From (5.60), this implies

$$\hat{N} < N_a. \tag{5.66}$$

Therefore, we can conclude as follows:

Property 5.7. The optimal city size for the utility-maximizing community occurs in the phase of increasing returns to scale.

Note that although the highest utility $\hat{u}$ is unique by definition, there may exist more than one optimal city size. For example, in the case of Figure 5.13, where two curves $C(\hat{u}, N)$ and $F(N)$, overlap on an interval, there are infinitely many solutions to optimal city size. In contrast, in the case of Figure 5.14, where curves $C(\hat{u}, N)$ and $F(N)$ are tangent at the origin, there is no optimal city size. In this case, for any $u < \hat{u}$, there exists N'

such that curve $F(N)$ dominates curve $C(u, N)$ in the range $(0, N')$. Hence, u is not the highest utility attainable for the community. At the same time, since two curves $F(N)$ and $C(\hat{u}, N)$ have only one common point at the origin, $\hat{u}$ is not achievable at any positive N. Hence, the community's problem (5.62) does not have a solution. The next property characterizes the necessary and sufficient condition for the existence of an optimal city size.

Property 5.8. The community's problem (5.62) has a solution if and only if there exist u' and $N' > 0$ such that

$$F(N') = C(u', N') \quad \text{and} \quad F(N) \leq C(u', N) \quad \text{for all} \quad N \in [0, N']. \tag{5.67}$$

The necessity of condition (5.67) is clear because any solution $(\hat{u}, \hat{N})$ to problem (5.62) satisfies this condition. For the sufficiency, see Appendix C.11. Condition (5.67) means that the urban production function is strongly S-shaped; that is, the marginal product of labor is very low when the city size is small, but it increases sharply with increasing city size.[28]

Let M be the total population of the urban sector, and let $(\hat{u}, \hat{N})$ be a solution to the community's problem, (5.62). Then if we form $(M/\hat{N})$ cities of population $\hat{N}$, all households in the urban sector can achieve the highest common utility $\hat{u}$.[29] As before, we call it an *optimal city system*. Of course, when there is more than one solution to problem (5.62), we can conceive of many different optimal city systems; but the highest common utility in any such system is the same.

Next, let us consider a competitive scheme through which an optimal city system will be achieved. Recall from the preceding section that in the case of constant returns to scale in production, if each developer pays households the marginal product of labor, the competition among developers will lead to the optimal city system. In the present context, however, the marginal product of labor is not constant, and hence developers do not know *a priori* how much to pay households. Recall also from Property 5.7 that if $\hat{N}$ is an optimal city size, it locates in the increasing phase. Hence, if developers pay households the marginal product of labor $F'(N)$, the profit derived from production activity, $F(\hat{N})–\hat{N}F'(\hat{N})$, becomes negative. Therefore, if developers try to maximize profits from production activity, they cannot pay households the marginal product of labor. However, it is well known from welfare economics that equality of wage and marginal product of labor is a necessary condition for achieving any social optimum. It turns out that *if each developer chooses a wage that maximizes the sum of the profit from production activity and the total differential rents from the city, then the competition among developers will lead to an optimal city system.*

To see this, we assume as before that each developer can rent the land for his or her city at the unit price of given agricultural rent R_A. Suppose that after renting the city's land, a developer adopts the following competitive scheme in managing the city:

1. Each household in the city is paid a wage W.
2. The city's land is subleased to the residents at the competitive market rent.
3. The migration between the city and the rest of the nation is kept free.

We call this scheme the *open-city scheme with wage W*. Note that if the utility level of households in the rest of the nation equals u, the environment of this scheme precisely coincides with that of the OCA(W, u) model (open-city model under absentee landlords with household income W and national utility u).[30] Hence, the equilibrium population of the city equals $N(W, u)$, which is the equilibrium population of the OCA(W, u) model. Thus, the *surplus* from the city development equals

$$\mathcal{S} \equiv F(N(W, u)) - N(W, u)W + \mathrm{TDR}(W, u), \tag{5.68}$$

where TDR(W, u) represents the total differential rent of the city at the equilibrium of the OCA(W, u) model. If we further define the *production profit* as

$$\pi(N, W) = F(N) - NW, \tag{5.69}$$

then

$$\mathcal{S} = \pi(N(W, u), W) + \mathrm{TDR}(W, u). \tag{5.70}$$

That is, under the open-city scheme, *the surplus from development of a city equals the sum of the production profit and total differential rents from the city*. Therefore, given national utility u, the *developer's problem* (under the open-city scheme) is to choose wage W so as to maximize the sum of production profit and total differential rent:

$$\max_W \pi(N(W, u), W) + \mathrm{TDR}(W, u). \tag{5.71}$$

Let us assume that every developer adopts the open-city scheme described above. Then assuming the free entry and exit of developers, in equilibrium the surplus of each developer must be zero. Hence, if u^* is the equilibrium national utility level, it must hold in every city that

$$\max_W \{\pi(N(W, u^*), W) + \mathrm{TDR}(W, u^*)\} = 0. \tag{5.72}$$

The other equilibrium condition, that is, the population constraint on the urban sector, can be generally stated as[31]

$$\text{the total population from all cities} = M. \tag{5.73}$$

When the zero-surplus condition (5.72) holds in every city and population constraint (5.73) is met as a whole, we say that the city system is in equilibrium.

Note that since the maximization problem of (5.72) may have more than one optimal W, in an equilibrium city system all cities need not be of equal size. This also suggests that there may exist more than one equilibrium city system. We can show, however, that *every equilibrium city system is an optimal city system.*

To see this, recall that when the national utility equals u and a developer adopts the open-city scheme with wage W, the equilibrium configuration of his or her city coincides with the solution to the OCA(W, u) model. Hence, setting N equal to $N(W, u)$ and Y equal to W in equation (5.12), the following relationship holds in the city:

$$N(W, u)W = C(u, N(W, u)) + \text{TDR}(W, u).$$

Hence, recalling (5.68) and (5.70), we have that

$$\mathcal{S} = \pi(N(W, u), W) + \text{TDR}(W, u) = F(N(W, u)) - C(u, N(W, u)). \tag{5.74}$$

Thus, the developer's problem (5.71) is mathematically identical with the following problem:[32]

$$\max_W F(N(W, u)) - C(u, N(W, u)). \tag{5.75}$$

Next, recall from Property 5.1 that under any given national utility u, the value of population supply function $N(W, u)$ continuously increases from zero to infinity as W increases from zero to infinity. Therefore, problem (5.75) is mathematically equivalent to the following problem[33]:

$$\max_N F(N) - C(u, N). \tag{5.76}$$

In short, we can conclude that

$$\begin{aligned} &\max_W \pi(N(W, u), W) + \text{TDR}(W, u) \\ &\quad = \max_W F(N(W, u)) - C(u, N(W, u)) \\ &\quad = \max_N F(N) - C(u, N). \end{aligned} \tag{5.77}$$

That is, for each developer, *adopting the open-city scheme and choosing an optimal wage rate W is equivalent to choosing an optimal population N directly, so as to maximize its surplus*. Now suppose u^* is the national utility level of an equilibrium city system. And suppose W^* is an optimal wage under national utility u^*, and $N(W^*, u^*)$ is the corresponding optimal city size, where $N(W^*, u^*)$ is assumed to be positive. Then from (5.72) and (5.77) it must hold that

$$\begin{aligned} 0 &= F(N(W^*, u^*)) - C(u^*, N(W^*, u^*)) \\ &= \max_N F(N) - C(u^*, N). \end{aligned} \tag{5.78}$$

This implies that

$$\begin{aligned} C(u^*, N) &\geq F(N) \qquad \text{for all} \quad N \geq 0 \\ C(u^*, N) &= F(N) \qquad \text{at} \quad N = N(W^*, u^*) > 0. \end{aligned} \tag{5.79}$$

In terms of Figure 5.12, this means that at $N = N(W^*, u^*)$, population cost curve $C(u^*, N)$ is tangent to production curve $F(N)$ from above. Hence, u^* must equal the highest utility $\hat{u}$, and $N(W^*, u^*)$ must be an optimal city size for utility-maximizing communities. Therefore, we can conclude that every equilibrium city system must be an optimal city. It is also not difficult to see that any optimal city system coincides with an equilibrium city system. Then since the existence of an optimal city system is assured under condition (5.67), the existence of an equilibrium city system is also assured.

Condition (5.72) implies that if W^* is an optimal wage in an equilibrium city system, then

$$\text{TDR}(W^*, u^*) = -\pi(N(W^*, u^*), W^*). \tag{5.80}$$

That is, *in every city of an equilibrium city system, the loss from production operation is just covered by the total differential rent*. Next, from the definition of the population supply–income function $Y(u, N)$ in Section 5.4, it holds identically that $Y(u^*, N(W^*, u^*)) = W^*$. Hence, it follows from (5.25) that

$$W^* = \frac{\partial C(u^*, N)}{\partial N} \qquad \text{at} \quad N = N(W^*, u^*). \tag{5.81}$$

Then since relation (5.79) implies that two curves, $C(u^*, N)$ and $F(N)$, are tangent at $N = N(W^*, u^*)$, it also follows that

$$W^* = \frac{dF(N)}{dN} \qquad \text{at} \quad N = N(W^*, u^*). \tag{5.82}$$

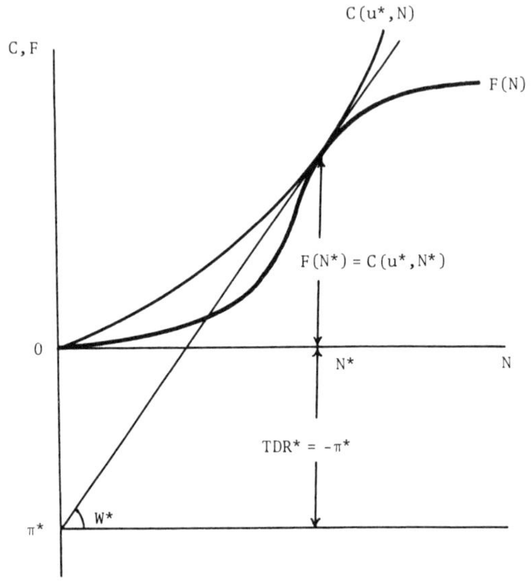

Figure 5.15. Relationship between N^* and other variables in an equilibrium city system.

That is, *in every city of an equilibrium city system, the wage equals the marginal population cost and marginal product of labor,* which is a prerequisite for any social optimal allocation. Graphically, relations (5.79)–(5.82) can be depicted as in Figure 5.15, where $u^* = \hat{u}$, $N^* \equiv N(W^*, u^*)$, $\pi^* \equiv \pi(N^*, W^*)$, and $\text{TDR}^* \equiv \text{TDR}(W^*, u^*)$.

We can summarize the results of this section as follows:

Proposition 5.5. In the context of the city model with scale economies in production, we can conclude that

(i) every equilibrium city system (which will result from competition among profit-maximizing developers) is an optimal city system (which consists of a set of utility-maximizing communities), and vice versa;
(ii) under the condition of (5.67), there exists at least one equilibrium/optimal city system;
(iii) in every city of an equilibrium/optimal city system, the total differential rent just covers the loss from production activity, and the wage equals the marginal population cost and marginal product of labor.

5.8 Conclusion

In this chapter, we have examined the relations among urban aggregates. Since no externalities are involved, competitive equilibria of residential land markets are socially efficient. This causes simple relationships to hold among urban aggregates both in equilibrium cities and in optimal cities. We have also examined equilibrium and optimal city sizes in various contexts as determined by the trade-off between technological advantages of agglomeration and disadvantages of increased commuting distance.

Two notes are in order: First, we have not yet considered the effects of externalities among urban aggregates and on city sizes. This will be done in Part II. Second, we have *a priori* assumed that cities always take on the monocentric form. In practice, however, this is not always the case; cities may have many different patterns, depending on the environment. However, for the simultaneous determination of urban patterns and city sizes, we must explicitly consider the land use by production activity. This extension will be achieved in our planned second book.

Bibliographical notes

In the development of this chapter, the author owes much to Arnott (1979), Kanemoto (1980, Ch. 2), Schweizer (1983), and Koide (1985). In the context of optimal cities, Arnott (1979) examined relationships among urban aggregates in various contexts, including the cases of public goods and congestion. Causes of city formation were discussed by Mills (1972b, Ch. 1), Mills and Hamilton (1984), and Kanemoto (1980, Ch. 2). Cities and systems of cities were studied, among others, by Henderson (1977, 1986, 1987), Arnott (1979), Kanemoto (1980), Schweizer (1983, 1985, 1986), Koide (1985), and Abdel-Rahman (in press). Our discussion of cities with fixed costs (Section 5.6) is a spatial version of Schweizer (1983), with land use by households being explicitly considered. In the discussion of cities with production scale economies in Section 5.7, the competitive procedure for achieving the optimal system of cities was introduced by Kanemoto (1980, Ch. 2). Although Kanemoto's discussion is based on the first-order conditions for equilibrium and optimum, our analyses are based on global conditions [see formulations (5.71), (5.75), and (5.76)]. This is because first-order conditions are hardly sufficient for determining optimal cities due to the nonconvexity of the production set. For the discrete treatment of city numbers, see Schweizer (1985, 1986). For the study of city systems with multiple goods and multiple city types, see Henderson (1982, 1986) and Abdel-Rahman (in press).

Notes

1. As explained below, the existence of any one of the first three factors may generate a city. In contrast, the fourth factor alone cannot generate a city; it is an amplifying factor that promotes the formation of larger cities in conjunction with the other three factors.
2. In the literature of international trade theory, *comparative advantage* (i.e., relative advantage) among nations (in producing different goods) has been emphasized as a major reason for trade (e.g., Ricardo 1817; Takayama 1972). Notice, however, that the concept of comparative advantage is meaningful only when some production factors (in particular, labor) are immobile among trade partners; otherwise, only absolute advantage provides a reason for trade. In the present context, where the static theory of city formation is concerned all agents (households and firms) are assumed to be freely movable within a nation. Hence, in the present context, only immobile land may provide a reason for interregional trade based on comparative advantage. It is interesting that von Thünen's land use theory (and all its extensions) is based on comparative advantage due to the immobility of land.
3. For a discussion of the relationship between indivisibility and economies of scale and its implications for urban location problems, see Koopmans (1957, pp. 150–4). Koopmans maintains that "without recognizing indivisibilities – in the human person, in residences, plants, equipment, and in transportation – urban location problems, down to those of the smallest village, cannot be understood" (p. 154).
4. More precisely, Baumol and Oates (1975) define externalities as follows: "An externality is present whenever some individual's (say A's) *utility* or *production* relationships include real (that is, nonmonetary) variables, whose values are chosen by others (persons, corporations, governments) without particular attention to the effects on A's welfare."
5. The intersection of budget line *CD* with indifference curve *AB* implies that the price of x_1 in city 2 is not too much higher than the price of the same good in city 1. Of course, if the price of x_1 in city 2 is the same as (or lower than) the price of the same good in city 1, the consumer can always achieve a higher utility in city 2.
6. Notice, however, that without economies of scale in production (and interurban transport costs) of these goods, the same number of goods would be produced in every city (or at every location). Only with scale economies in production will we be able to determine the equilibrium (or optimal) number of goods provided in a city. For elaboration of this topic, see Chapter 8.
7. Part II continues the discussion of city sizes in more complex contexts, including public goods, externalities, and product variety.
8. We can see later that the accounting relation (5.5) holds for all city models, including those in Part II with spatial externalities. However, in the context of market models, relation (5.8) holds only when market equilibria are efficient.

9. Note that equation (5.9) is an alternative expression of relation (3.75).
10. From Assumption 2.1, $\lim_{u \to -\infty} s(Y - T(r), u) = 0$ at each r such that $T(r) < Y$. And from Assumption 3.2, $\lim_{Y \to \infty} s(Y - T(r), u) = 0$. Hence, from (5.15) we can conclude as in Property 5.1(iii).
11. That is, in Figure 5.3, if we consider N to be the independent variable, $Y(u_i, N)$ represents the supply–income curve under u_i. If, however, we consider Y to be the independent variable, the same curve represents the population supply curve $N(Y, u_i)$.
12. $\mathrm{TDR}(Y, u) = \int_0^{r_f(Y,u)} [\psi(Y - T(r), u) - R_A] L(r)\, dr$ and $\psi(Y - T(r), u) = R_A$ at $r = r_f(Y, u)$. Hence

$$\frac{\partial \mathrm{TDR}(Y(u,N),u)}{\partial N} = 0 \cdot L(r_f)\frac{\partial r_f}{\partial N} + \int_0^{r_f} \frac{\partial \psi}{\partial I}\frac{\partial(Y(u,N)-T(r))}{\partial N} L(r)\, dr$$

$$= \frac{\partial Y(u,N)}{\partial N}\int_0^{r_f} \frac{1}{s[Y(u,N)-T(r),u]} L(r)\, dr$$

$$= \frac{\partial Y(u,N)}{\partial N} N.$$

13. Originally, the value of function $C(u, N)$ is not defined when $N = 0$. However, since $\lim_{N \to 0} C(u, N) = 0$, it is convenient to define $C(u, 0) = 0$.
14. More precisely, if we consider N as the independent variable, wage line W in Figure 5.7 represents the *inverse* labor-demand curve.
15. Actually, in order to derive this result from a utility function that has amenity level as a parameter, we must assume that amenity E is substitutable for land consumption s (for this point, see Assumption 6.4).
16. In order to justify the assumption of central concentration of all production activities under another assumption of the constant-returns-to-scale production technology, we can assume that K also includes common basic facilities for production activities, and they have to be supplied at a common location, the center of the city. Alternatively, we can assume that the city's production activity actually consists of many different processes, which must locate near one another so as to save transport costs for the exchange of intermediate inputs; the production function (5.33) describes the net output of all processes as a function of total labor N.
17. By definition (5.35), $\mathcal{S}(\delta, u, N(\delta, u))$ represents the maximum surplus attainable under the optimal organization of the city. Hence, if $\mathcal{S}(\delta, u, N(\delta, u)) < K$, no other tax system (such as income taxes or profit taxes) can finance the fixed costs K.
18. Here we are implicitly assuming that (a) the production function (5.33) and fixed costs K are independent of location, and (b) the area of the city under study is negligible compared with the total amount of agricultural land in the nation. Hence, the city can be developed at any location, and the developer can rent the land for the city at the unit price of agricultural rent R_A.

19. Notice that this is only a mathematical coincidence. Since $\hat{u} \geq u$, the OCA(δ, $\hat{u}$) model cannot be implemented in practice.
20. On the Henry George theorem, see Flatters, Henderson, and Mieszkowski (1974), Stiglitz (1977), and Arnott (1979) and Wildasin (1986b). Notice that although these articles emphasize only the case of optimal city size, we can see from Proposition 5.2(iii) that the Henry George theorem holds for any viable city; that is, a city will actually be developed only when TDR(δ, u) $\geq K$.
21. It is not difficult to show this result mathematically by using Property 5.5.
22. In this optimal city system, absentee landlords receive no differential land rent. We can also readily see that since the budget is balanced (i.e., TDR $= K$) in each community, no coalition between a group of landlords and households can yield a positive share of differential land rents to the landlords while maintaining the highest common utility to the households. In terms of game theory, this implies that the optimal city system belongs to the *core* of the economy under study. Recall that an allocation belongs to a core when no group of individuals can improve their situation by forming a different coalition. Since no individual's welfare can be increased at a core allocation, a core is always Pareto optimal (i.e., efficient).
23. Here we are assuming that the net profits of city developers do not belong to the residents of cities (e.g., profits go to absentee landlords). Hence, the residents of each city have no other income except that provided by the developer. This implies that given national utility u, all of the population cost $C(u, N)$ must be borne by the developer of each city; hence, the gross profit of each developer equals the surplus $\mathcal{S}(\delta, u, N)$ given by (5.34). Alternatively, we can assume that the net profits of developers are equally distributed among all M households in the nation. In this case, let us further assume that each city is so small compared with the whole economy in the sense that the action of a city developer affects the subsidies received by its residents only negligibly; hence, each developer considers the subsidy level of its residents (as well as the national utility level) as given. Then since the net profit of each developer is zero in equilibrium (as shown below), the subsidy is also zero in equilibrium. Therefore, in both cases we obtain the same equilibrium city system (which is explained below).
24. When the number of cities is determined by (5.57), it will be an integer only by coincidence. Considering this point, it is more appropriate to say that u^* and n^* (an integer) are in equilibrium if and only if there exists u' such that

$$n^*N(\delta, u^*) = M, \qquad \mathcal{S}(\delta, u^*, N(\delta, u^*)) \geq K,$$

$$(n^* + 1)N(\delta, u') = M, \qquad \mathcal{S}(\delta, u', N(\delta, u')) < K.$$

That is, n^* is the largest number of cities that is compatible with nonnegative profits. It is not difficult to see that given any $M > 0$, such (u^*, n^*, u') exists uniquely, which we represent by $(u^*(M), n^*(M), u'(M))$. We can also see that $u^*(M) \leq \hat{u} < u'(M)$, $0 \leq (M/N(\delta, u')) - n^*(M) \leq 1$,

$\lim_{M\to\infty} u^*(M) = \hat{u}$, and $\lim_{M\to\infty} [(M/N(\delta, \hat{u})) - n^*(M)]/n^*(M) = 0$. Therefore, assuming that M is sufficiently large, we can safely represent the equilibrium number of cities by (5.57) and the equilibrium utility level by $\hat{u}$.

25. In this section, we are not concerned with the causes of scale economies in production. If the scale economies are due to the increasing returns to scale of a *single firm's* production process, the model of this section represents the so-called *factory town model*. If the scale economies are due to *externalities among many firms*, the present model corresponds to a *(Marshallian) external economy model*. Since this section is concerned with only the optimal city system, we are not required to distinguish the two models. In Chapter 8, we examine the equilibrium city system in the context of the external economy model.
26. We can allow the case in which $N_a = \infty$. In this case, we must introduce an additional constraint such that $\sup_N F(N)/N < \infty$. Then it is not difficult to see that even in this case, all the results of this section still hold true as they are.
27. The S-shaped production function depicted in Figure 5.11 does satisfy all conditions of (5.58)–(5.60). Notice, however, that conditions (5.58)–(5.60) do not require that the production function always be S-shaped.
28. Since $C_N(u, 0)$ is positive under any u [Property 5.6(i)], Property 5.8 implies that if $F'(0) = 0$, the community's problem (5.62) always has a solution.
29. Again, we are assuming here that M is so large that the number of cities can be safely treated as continuous.
30. See note 23.
31. If the optimal wage is the same in every city and is denoted by W^*, population constraint (5.73) can be simply stated as

$$n^*N(W^*, u^*) = M,$$

where n^* is the equilibrium number of cities. However, the solution to the maximization problem of (5.72) need not always be unique. Hence, we keep this general expression.
32. Note that two expressions, (5.71) and (5.75), have very different economic contents. In (5.75), in order to know the form of population cost function $C(u, N)$, developers must know, among other things, the utility function of households and must also perform complex calculations implied by the minimization problem of (5.20). In contrast, in the context of (5.71), the calculation of profit function $\pi(N, W)$ is simple, and developers can know the value of total differential rent $\text{TDR}(W, u)$ simply by observing the land market (while setting wage W at various levels).
33. See note 32. In addition, when determining an optimal population by solving problem (5.76), the developer cannot be sure how to implement it under the condition of free migration.

PART II

Extensions with externalities

CHAPTER 6

Local public goods

6.1 Introduction

Starting in this chapter, we introduce various kinds of urban externalities and extend the basic theory of Part I. First, we introduce public goods and discuss how to achieve the efficient provision of public goods among cities or within a city.

Public goods are, in short, those goods whose benefits are realized mainly in the form of externalities, and hence they are collectively consumed by a large number of individuals. In considering the decentralized mechanisms for the efficient provision of such goods, we find that their *spatial characteristics* are crucial. Therefore, in this chapter we focus on the spatial dimension of public goods and categorize them as in Figure 6.1.[1] If the service level of a public good is virtually constant over a nation, we call it a *national good* (e.g., national defense). If, in contrast, the benefits of a public good are confined within a city (within a neighborhood), and its service level is invariant within a city (within a neighborhood), we call it a *city good* (*neighborhood good*).[2] If the benefits of a public good are confined within a city but vary among neighborhoods in the city, we call it a *superneighborhood good* (e.g., a large green park or a museum). As a group, city, neighborhood, and superneighborhood goods are referred to as *local public goods*.[3]

As has been shown by Samuelson (1954), it is extremely difficult to achieve the efficient provision of national goods by any decentralized market-type mechanism. This is because once provided, the same amount of a national good is consumed by every individual (in the nation); hence, a "rational" individual would misreveal his or her preferences in order to avoid being assessed his or her full share of the cost of providing the good. This difficulty is often called the *free-rider problem*.[4]

In the case of local public goods, however, the situation is more promising. Tiebout (1956) proposed the ingenious idea that one can utilize the competition among communities as a vehicle for achieving the efficient

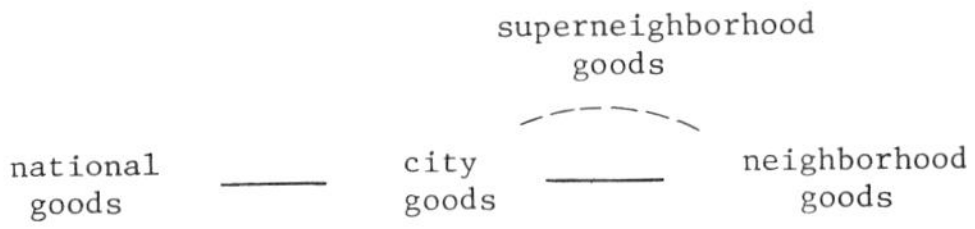

Figure 6.1. A categorization of public goods.

provision of local public goods (like the competition among firms for the efficient provision of private goods). Namely, if we assume that individuals can move costlessly among communities, each individual will choose the community that most fits his or her preferences. Thus, if each community competes for individuals by providing its own package of public goods, such competition among communities and "voting with the feet" of individuals may lead to the efficient provision of local public goods. This idea triggered the development of a rich field, namely the economics of local public goods. In this chapter, through simple examples, we study the basic principles of the efficient provision of local public goods. With our emphasis on the spatial dimension of the problem, the discussion in this chapter is limited to the case of *homogeneous households*. To focus on the problem of local public goods, we also assume that the aggregate production function of each city has *constant returns to scale*.[5]

However, before starting the discussion of local public goods, in Section 6.2 we extend the basic model of residential choice (Chapter 2) by introducing externalities in a general form and develop the *externality model* of residential choice. This preparation enables us to present the analyses of Part II in a unified manner.

Then, in Section 6.3 we start with a simple case of the *pure city good*, which is free of congestion. Each household can freely choose not only a city, but also a location (or a neighborhood) within a city. Hence, in equilibrium, every household in every city at every location should achieve the same utility level. The competition among households for location in a city forces them to reveal their benefit from city goods in the land market. In particular, if there are a large number of cities in the nation, the equilibrium utility level of households in the nation is virtually independent of a marginal change in the supply of city goods in a city; hence, the marginal benefit of such change is completely reflected in the total land rent change in that city. Therefore, if each city developer (or city government) behaves as a *utility taker* and aims to maximize the total differential land rent minus the cost of providing city goods, competition among such developers will lead to the efficient provision of city goods.

In Section 6.4, we introduce congestion in the supply of city goods. That is, the benefit of each household from a given supply of city goods depends on the population size of the city. In this case, when a household moves into a city, all existing households suffer from the marginal increase in the congestion level of city goods. Hence, each city developer needs to impose a congestion tax on each household. If each city developer aims to maximize the sum of the total differential land rent and congestion tax minus the cost of city goods, competition among such developers will lead to the efficient provision of city goods.

In Section 6.5, we study the problem of the efficient provision of neighborhood goods in a city. If we replace the competition among cities with that among neighborhoods, not surprisingly we reach essentially the same conclusion as before. Namely, assuming that the city consists of many small neighborhoods, if each neighborhood developer aims to maximize the sum of the total differential land rent and congestion tax minus the cost of providing neighborhood goods, then competition among such neighborhood developers will lead to the efficient provision of neighborhood goods in a city.

In the case of superneighborhood goods, however, the situation is more difficult. Since the benefits of a superneighborhood good are enjoyed by the residents of many neighborhoods, we cannot divide the city into a large number of regions in which the benefits of such a good are self-contained. In other words, if the city is divided into a large number of jurisdictions, there will be *spillover effects* of the superneighborhood good among jurisdictions. This causes difficulties in devising a decentralized mechanism for the efficient provision of superneighborhood goods. We study this problem in Section 6.6.

Finally, in Section 6.7, we briefly discuss the same topic (i.e., the efficient provision of local public goods) in more general contexts, including the cases of heterogeneous households and production functions with increasing returns to scale.

6.2 A preliminary analysis: the externality model of residential choice

Recall that in the basic model (2.1) of Chapter 2, the utility function of the household is assumed to be independent of location. This implies that residential environments are the same everywhere in the city. In this part, we introduce locational variation in environmental amenities and denote the utility function of a household by $U(z, s, E(x))$. As usual, z represents the amount of the composite good and s the lot size of the house; $E(x)$ represents the *environmental quality level* at each location x.[6] In general, $E(x)$ could be a vector, with each component representing a particular kind of environmental amenity. In most of the following discussion, however, we consider one kind of environmental amenity at a time. Hence, unless otherwise noted, $E(x)$ is a single number. We could also consider that $E(x)$ reflects the spatial variation in both the natural environment and man-made environment. However, in order to focus on the latter, we assume throughout Part II that the natural environment is the same everywhere in the city and consider the spatial variation of $E(x)$ to be due to *externalities* caused by economic agents or public goods.

On the basis of these considerations, we generalize the basic model (2.1) as follows:

$$\max_{x,z,s} U(z, s, E(x)), \qquad \text{subject to} \quad z + R(x)s = Y^0 - G(x) - T(x), \tag{6.1}$$

where Y^0 represents the pretax income of a household and $G(x)$ the lump-sum tax per household at each location x; the rest of notation is the same as that in (2.1). We introduce $G(x)$ because it turns out that the attainment of an efficient allocation under the presence of externalities may require location-dependent corrective taxation. We will call (6.1) the *externality model* of residential choice.

Without loss of generality, we can assume that at each location x, the value of $E(x)$ is always positive and finite. Furthermore, the utility is assumed to increase as E increases:

$$\partial U(z, s, E)/\partial E > 0. \tag{6.2}$$

We also assume that all goods, z, s, and E, are essential [i.e., $U(z, s, E) = -\infty$ if any one of z, s, or E is zero). Considering this, in parallel with Assumptions 2.1–2.3, we introduce the following set of assumptions:

Assumption 6.1 (well-behaved utility function). The utility function is continuous and increasing at all $z > 0$, $s > 0$, and $E > 0$, and it satisfies the following conditions:

(i) Under each fixed value of $E > 0$, all indifference curves in the z–s space are strictly convex and smooth, and they do not cut axes.

(ii) Given any $z > 0$ and $s > 0$,

$$\lim_{E \to 0} U(z, s, E) = -\infty, \tag{6.3}$$

$$\lim_{E \to \infty} \partial Z(s, u, E)/\partial E = 0, \tag{6.4}$$

where $Z(s, u, E)$ is the solution to $U(z, s, E) = u$ for z.[7]

Assumption 6.2 (increasing transport cost). $T(x) = T(|x|)$ and $T(|x|)$ is increasing in $|x|$, where $|x|$ represents the distance between each location x and the CBD.[8] In addition, $0 \leq T(0) < Y^0$ and $T(\infty) = \infty$.

Assumption 6.3 (normality of land). Under each fixed value of $E > 0$, the income effect on the Marshallian demand for land is positive.

Note that given u, function $Z(\cdot, u, \cdot)$ represents the equation of an indifference surface in z–s–E space. And (6.4) means that the marginal contribution of E (measured in terms of the composite good z) eventually becomes zero as E approaches infinity. Note also that Assumptions 6.1 and 6.3 imply that Assumptions 2.1 and 2.3 are satisfied under each fixed value of E. Throughout the analyses of Part II, Assumptions 6.1–6.3 are assumed to hold. In each of following discussions, the externality model (6.1) will take a specific form.

Next, in the context of model (6.1), we define the bid rent and bid-max lot size functions. We will start using Solow's form because it is conceptually more fundamental. To do so, let us introduce the following utility-maximization problem: Given a combination of E, R (land rent), and I (net income),

$$\max_{z,s} U(z, s, E), \qquad \text{subject to} \quad z + Rs = I. \tag{6.5}$$

Then the (Solow's) bid rent function can be defined as

$$\psi(I, u, E) = \max_{s} \frac{I - Z(s, u, E)}{s}, \tag{6.6}$$

where $Z(s, u, E)$ is the solution to $U(z, s, E) = u$ for z. By definition, $\psi(I, u, E)$ represents the maximum land rent (per unit land), which the household with net income I can pay under the presence of externality E; the household must also enjoy the given utility level u. We denote the optimal lot size for the maximization problem of (6.6) as $s(I, u, E)$, which is called the (Solow's) bid-max lot size function.[9] As described in Figure 6.2, bid rent $\psi(I, u, E)$ is given by the slope of the budget line, which is just tangent to the indifference curve $u = U(z, s, E)$, and bid-max lot size $s(I, u, E)$ is determined from the tangency point.

Similarly, in the context of model (6.1), the bid rent function in Alonso's form can be defined as

$$\Psi(x, u) = \max_{s} \frac{Y^0 - G(x) - T(x) - Z(s, u, E(x))}{s}. \tag{6.7}$$

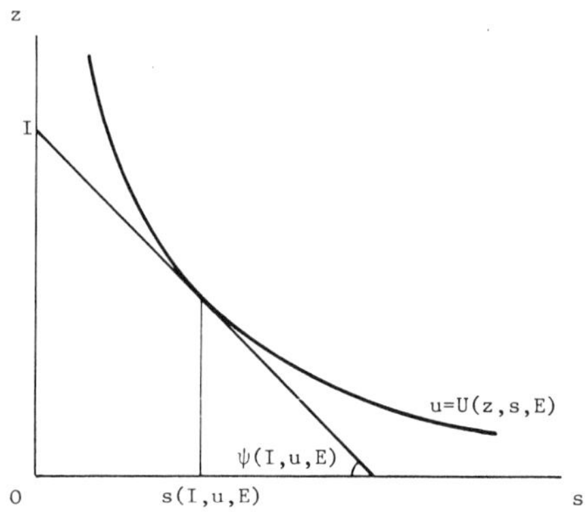

Figure 6.2. Bid rent $\psi(I, u, E)$ and bid-max lot size $s(I, u, E)$.

Solving the maximization problem of (6.7), we obtain the optimal lot size $S(x, u)$, which is called the (Alonso's) bid-max lot size. From definitions (6.6) and (6.7), we can immediately obtain the following identities:

$$\Psi(x, u) \equiv \psi(Y^0 - G(x) - T(x), u, E(x)), \tag{6.8}$$

$$S(x, u) \equiv s(Y^0 - G(x) - T(x), u, E(x)). \tag{6.9}$$

Example 6.1. Consider the following log-linear utility function:

$$U(z, s, E) = \alpha \log z + \beta \log s + \gamma \log E, \tag{6.10}$$

where α, β, and γ are positive constants such that $\alpha + \beta = 1$. We can readily confirm that this utility function satisfies all conditions of Assumptions 6.1 and 6.3. Since $Z(s, u, E) = s^{-\beta/\alpha}E^{-\gamma/\alpha}e^{u/\alpha}$, from (6.6) we have

$$\psi(I, u, E) = \alpha^{\alpha/\beta}\beta I^{1/\beta}E^{\gamma/\beta}e^{-u/\beta}, \tag{6.11}$$

$$s(I, u, E) = \beta I/\psi(I, u, E) = \alpha^{-\alpha/\beta}I^{-\alpha/\beta}E^{-\gamma/\beta}e^{u/\beta}. \tag{6.12}$$

Hence, from (6.8) and (6.9) we have

$$\Psi(x, u) = \alpha^{\alpha/\beta}\beta(Y^0 - G(x) - T(x))^{1/\beta}E(x)^{\gamma/\beta}e^{-u/\beta}, \tag{6.13}$$

$$S(x, u) = \alpha^{-\alpha/\beta}(Y^0 - G(x) - T(x))^{-\alpha/\beta}E(x)^{-\gamma/\beta}e^{u/\beta}. \tag{6.14}$$

Next, in order to facilitate the characterization of the bid rent and bid-max lot size functions, we derive several identities as in Chapters 2 and 3. Let $\hat{s}(R, I, E)$ be the *Marshallian demand for land,* which represents the optimal lot size for the utility-maximization problem of (6.5). Then, in the same way as we derived (3.5) from Figure 2.2, we can immediately derive the following identity from Figure 6.2:

$$s(I, u, E) \equiv \hat{s}(\psi(I, u, E), I, E). \tag{6.15}$$

From (6.9) and (6.15), we can also obtain the following identity:

$$S(x, u) \equiv \hat{s}(\psi(Y^0 - G(x) - T(x), u, E(x)), Y^0 - G(x) - T(x), E(x)). \tag{6.16}$$

Next, let $\tilde{s}(R, u, E)$ be the *Hicksian demand for land,* which is defined as the optimal lot size for the following expenditure-minimization problem:

$$\min_{z,s}\ z + Rs = I, \qquad \text{subject to} \quad U(z, s, E) = u. \tag{6.17}$$

Then again in the same way as we derived (3.5) from Figure 2.2, we can obtain the following identity from Figure 6.2:

$$s(I, u, E) \equiv \tilde{s}(\psi(I, u, E), u, E). \tag{6.18}$$

From (6.9) and (6.18), it follows that

$$S(x, u) \equiv \tilde{s}(\psi(Y^0 - G(x) - T(x), u, E(x)), u, E(x)). \tag{6.19}$$

With respect to parameters I and u, the properties of Solow functions ψ and s remain the same as Property 3.1. That is, since $\partial U/\partial z > 0$ implies that $\partial Z/\partial u > 0$, by applying the envelope theorem to (6.6) we have

$$\frac{\partial\psi}{\partial I} = \frac{1}{s} > 0, \qquad \frac{\partial\psi}{\partial u} = -\frac{1}{s}\frac{\partial Z}{\partial u} < 0. \tag{6.20}$$

Therefore, using identities (6.15) and (6.18), we have[10]

$$\frac{\partial s}{\partial I} = \frac{\partial\tilde{s}}{\partial R}\frac{\partial\psi}{\partial I} < 0, \qquad \frac{\partial s}{\partial u} = \frac{\partial\hat{s}}{\partial R}\frac{\partial\psi}{\partial u} > 0. \tag{6.21}$$

As for the Alonso functions Ψ and S, using identities (6.8) and (6.9) we can conclude that[11]

$$\frac{\partial\Psi}{\partial u} = \frac{\partial\psi}{\partial u} < 0, \qquad \frac{\partial S}{\partial u} = \frac{\partial s}{\partial u} > 0. \tag{6.22}$$

Notice that since the marginal utilities of z and E are respectively positive, it holds that

$$\partial Z(s, u, E)/\partial E < 0, \tag{6.23}$$

which means that in a better environment, the same utility can be achieved with a smaller amount of composite good. From (6.6) and (6.23), we have that

$$\frac{\partial \psi}{\partial E} = -\frac{1}{s}\frac{\partial Z}{\partial E} > 0. \tag{6.24}$$

That is, the bid rent increases as the environmental quality level increases. This result is illustrated in Figure 6.3. Note that (6.23) implies that indifference curves move downward as E increases. Hence, in Figure 6.3, the lower indifference curve corresponds to a better environment. Therefore, as shown in Figure 6.3, the household can bid a higher land rent in a better environment. However, the sign of the effects of E on the bid-max lot size cannot be determined by *a priori* considerations alone.[12] It is empirically reasonable to assume as follows:

> ***Assumption 6.4 (substitutability between land and environment).*** The bid-max lot size $s(I, u, E)$ is decreasing in E:
>
> $\partial s(I, u, E)/\partial E < 0.$

This assumption means that in order to sustain a constant utility level, a smaller lot size is necessary in a better environment. This assumption turns out to be crucial to the following analysis. It is not difficult to see that most familiar utility functions (including the log-linear utility function of Example 6.1) satisfy this assumption.

6.3 Pure city goods

In this section we consider the problem of the efficient provision of a *pure city good* that is jointly consumed by all residents of a city with no congestion effect. This can be achieved by slightly extending the fixed-cost model of Section 5.6. We keep all basic assumptions of the fixed-cost model, except the assumption that K is a fixed constant. Here we consider K to represent the cost for the provision of a pure city good, which is a policy variable to be chosen by a city government or a city developer.[13]

Each city is assumed to be monocentric, with its aggregate production function being given by (5.33).[14] Without loss of generality, we can consider K to represent both the *supply cost* and *service level* of a pure city good. That is, we measure the service level of the city good by its cost. Then assuming that the environmental quality level of a city is a function of K, we denote it by $E(K)$. Note that since the city good is assumed to be consumed jointly by all residents in a city, $E(K)$ is independent of

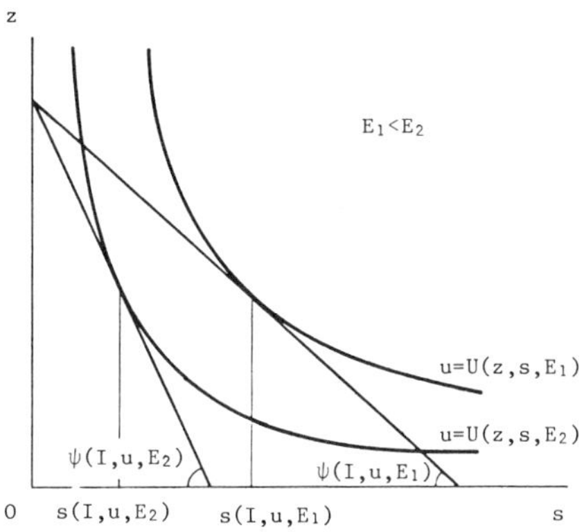

Figure 6.3. Effects of E on ψ and s.

location in the city. It is natural to assume that the environmental quality level of the city is increasing in K:

$$dE(K)/dK \equiv E'(K) > 0. \tag{6.25}$$

Now, in the externality model of (6.1), let us replace the location index x by r (the distance from the CBD), and $E(x)$ by $E(K)$. Then, given K, the residential choice behavior of each household can now be expressed as

$$\max_{r,z,s} U(z, s, E(K)), \qquad \text{subject to} \quad z + R(r)s = Y^0 - G(r) - T(r). \tag{6.26}$$

In order to emphasize the importance of the public good, we assume that K is indispensable:

$$U(z, s, E(K = 0)) = -\infty. \tag{6.27}$$

Next, as in (5.20), the *population cost function* $C(u, N, K)$ under a given K can be defined as

$$C(u, N, K) \equiv \min_{r_f, n(r), s(r)} \int_0^{r_f} [T(r) + Z(s(r), u, E(K)) + R_A s(r)] n(r)\, dr,$$

$$\text{subject to} \quad s(r)n(r) \leq L(r) \quad \text{at each} \quad r \leq r_f,$$

$$\int_0^{r_f} n(r)\, dr = N, \tag{6.28}$$

which represents the minimum residential cost for achieving common utility u for all N households under a given K. Note that $C(u, N, K)$ does not include the cost of the city good K. Then, as in (5.34), given u, N, K, and δ (marginal and average product of labor), the maximum (gross) surplus from city development can be obtained as

$$\mathcal{S}(\delta, u, N, K) \equiv \delta N - C(u, N, K). \tag{6.29}$$

Given the basic framework above, we first study the system of cities that will result from competition among profit-maximizing developers (or surplus-maximizing local governments). We then examine the system of cities that will result from competition among utility-maximizing communities. The two systems turn out to be identical, and both are efficient.

6.3.1 *Profit-maximizing developers and the system of cities*

We first examine the optimal formation of a city by a profit-maximizing developer (equivalently, by a surplus-maximizing city government). The developer takes the national utility level u as a given parameter and optimally chooses the city's population N and service level K of the city good so as to maximize the net profit (i.e., net surplus) from the city development:

$$\max_{N \geq 0, K \geq 0} \ \Pi \equiv \mathcal{S}(\delta, u, N, K) - K. \tag{6.30}$$

We can solve this developer's problem in two steps. In the first step, the developer may choose the optimal population N under each fixed value of K. Then in the second step, the developer may choose the optimal service level K of the city good.

The developer's problem in the first step can be formulated as follows: Given each value of $K \geq 0$,

$$\max_{N \geq 0} \mathcal{S}(\delta, u, N, K) \equiv \delta N - C(u, N, K). \tag{6.31}$$

Since K is fixed, this problem is identical to that in Section 5.6.2. Therefore, we can see that this part of the developer's problem can be solved by a simple decentralized scheme. That is, suppose the developer rents the land for the city from absentee landlords at the agricultural land rent R_A, and everything else is left free to be determined by competitive markets. In particular, each household will receive wage δ (marginal product of labor) and pay no tax $[G(r) = 0]$, the city's land will be subleased to the residents at the competitive market rent, and the migration between the city and the rest of the economy will be kept free. Then from Section 5.6.2 we can conclude that the profit-maximizing city (under given K)

will be achieved at equilibrium. More precisely, notice that given K, the open-city scheme described above is identical with the OCA(δ, u) model under K (the open-city model under absentee landownership with income δ, national utility u, and city-good level K), which we denote by OCA(δ, u, K). Therefore, from Proposition 5.1(i) we can conclude that given any K, the surplus $\mathcal{S}(\delta, u, N, K)$ is maximized when N equals the equilibrium population $N(\delta, u, K)$ of the OCA(δ, u, K) model; and from Proposition 5.1(iii), when the land market is in equilibrium, the (gross) surplus equals the total differential rent,

$$\mathcal{S}(\delta, u, N(\delta, u, K), K) = \mathrm{TDR}(\delta, u, K), \tag{6.32}$$

where TDR(δ, u, K) represents the total differential rent from the solution to the OCA(δ, u, K) model. Since relation (6.32) holds under any level of K, it implies that the benefits of the city good are entirely embodied in the differential land rents. This happens because the city is open and hence the utility level of the residents is held constant at the national utility level. The net profit from the city development can be obtained as

$$\begin{aligned} \Pi &= \mathcal{S}(\delta, u, N(\delta, u, K), K) - K \\ &= \mathrm{TDR}(\delta, u, K) - K. \end{aligned} \tag{6.33}$$

The equilibrium population $N(\delta, u, K)$ of the OCA(δ, u, K) model can be calculated as follows: Let ψ be the bid rent function and s the bid-max lot size function from Section 6.2. As in (3.27), we define the *supreme utility level* $\tilde{u}(\delta, K)$ from the relation

$$\psi(\delta - T(0), \tilde{u}(\delta, K), E(K)) = R_{\mathrm{A}}. \tag{6.34}$$

If $u \geq \tilde{u}(\delta, K)$, no household would move into the city and $N(\delta, u, K) = 0$. If $u < \tilde{u}(\delta, K)$, the equilibrium population can be obtained as

$$N(\delta, u, K) = \int_0^{r_{\mathrm{f}}(\delta, u, K)} \frac{L(r)}{s(\delta - T(r), u, E(K))}\, dr, \tag{6.35}$$

where the urban fringe distance $r_{\mathrm{f}} \equiv r_{\mathrm{f}}(\delta, u, K)$ is determined from the boundary condition,

$$\psi(\delta - T(r_{\mathrm{f}}), u, E(K)) = R_{\mathrm{A}}. \tag{6.36}$$

Given δ, u, and K such that $u < \tilde{u}(\delta, K)$, the surplus curve $\mathcal{S}(\delta, u, N, K)$ can be similarly drawn as in Figure 5.9. And from Proposition 5.1(i), the surplus curve $\mathcal{S}(\delta, u, N, K)$ achieves the maximum at the equilibrium population $N(\delta, u, K)$.

A change in supply level K of the city good will result in changes in the city population $N(\delta, u, K)$ and net profit Π. Therefore, in the second step, the developer may choose K so as to maximize the net profit:[15]

$$\max_{K \geq 0} \Pi \equiv \mathcal{S}(\delta, u, N(\delta, u, K), K) - K. \tag{6.37}$$

We can approach this problem graphically. In Figure 6.4, the 45° line K represents the supply cost line of the city good. Given a national utility level u, the surplus curve $\mathcal{S}(\delta, u, N(\delta, u, K), K)$ can be depicted as in Figure 6.4.[16] The net surplus $\Pi = \mathcal{S} - K$ is maximum at $K(u)$, where the vertical difference between $\mathcal{S}$ and K is largest.[17] This implies, analytically, that the $\mathcal{S}$ curve and K line have the same slope of unity at the optimal $K(u)$:

$$d\mathcal{S}(\delta, u, N(\delta, u, K), K)/dK = 1 \quad \text{at} \quad K = K(u). \tag{6.38}$$

In other words, the marginal benefit of the city good equals its marginal cost ($\equiv 1$). Using relation (6.32), we can restate (6.38) as follows:[18]

$$\int_0^{r_f(\delta,u,K)} -\frac{\partial Z(s(r), u, E(K))}{\partial K} n(r)\, dr = 1, \tag{6.39}$$

which is a spatial version of the *Samuelson condition* for optimal provision of a public good: The sum of the marginal benefits (measured by the rate of substitution $-\partial Z/\partial K$) over all households in the city must equal the marginal cost of the public good.

Although the direct implementation of the Samuelson condition (6.39) requires a prohibitive amount of information, the task of the developer (or the city government) becomes much easier in the present context of the open-city model. From (6.32), the developer's problem in the second step, (6.37), can be restated as follows:

$$\max_{K \geq 0} \Pi = \text{TDR}(\delta, u, K) - K. \tag{6.40}$$

Namely, since the entire benefit of the city good is reflected in the differential land rents, all the developer must do is choose the K that maximizes the net revenue from the land, TDR $-$ K. To achieve this, the developer may follow the next decision rule:[19]

$$\begin{Bmatrix} \text{increase} \\ \text{decrease} \end{Bmatrix} K \quad \text{as} \quad \frac{\partial \text{TDR}}{\partial K} \begin{Bmatrix} >1 \\ <1 \end{Bmatrix}. \tag{6.41}$$

Note that if TDR is less than K at the optimal $K(u)$, the net profit from the city formation is negative; and hence the development of the city should not be undertaken.

Next, we consider the city system of the nation that will result from

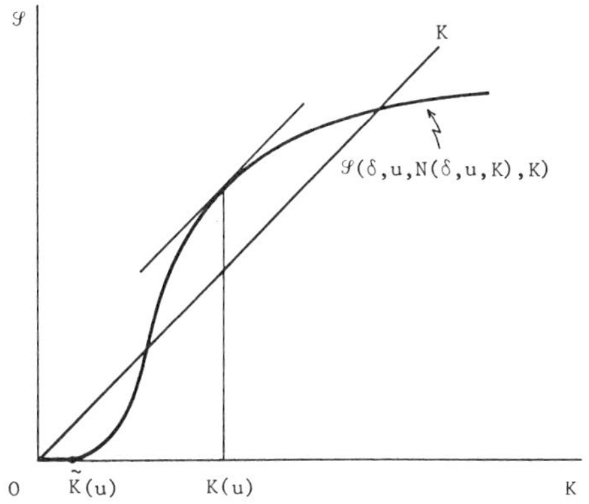

Figure 6.4. Determination of optimal K under given u.

competition among profit-maximizing developers (or surplus-maximizing local governments). We keep the basic assumptions of Section 5.6.4. In particular, the nation consists of M identical (urban) households. And wherever a city is to be developed in the nation, the aggregate production function of the city is the same, and it is given by (5.33).

We can obtain the equilibrium city system graphically. First, note that given an appropriate u, the corresponding surplus curve $\mathcal{S}(\delta, u, N(\delta, u, K), K)$ can be drawn as in Figure 6.4.[20] This surplus curve will move downward (upward) as u increases (decreases).[21] Therefore, by appropriately changing u, we can obtain a set of surplus curves as in Figure 6.5. If a surplus curve passes the region above the city-good cost line K, a developer can earn a positive net profit Π $(= \mathcal{S} - K)$ by appropriately choosing K. This will induce the entry of new developers, and hence the existing city system cannot be in equilibrium.[22] If the surplus curve lies entirely in the region below the K line, a developer earns a negative net profit. Thus, no city will be developed, and the total demand for population is zero. Therefore, we can conclude that the surplus curve corresponding to an equilibrium city system must be tangent to the K line from below. In Figure 6.5, u^* represents the equilibrium utility level, and the optimal supply level of the city good is given at point $K(u^*)$ in the same figure.[23] Thus, in the equilibrium city system, the population of each city equals $N(\delta, u^*, K(u^*))$, and the total number of cities in the nation is given by[24]

$$M/N(\delta, u^*, K(u^*)). \tag{6.42}$$

Finally, it is evident from Figure 6.5 that in the equilibrium city system, the surplus from each city equals the city-good cost:

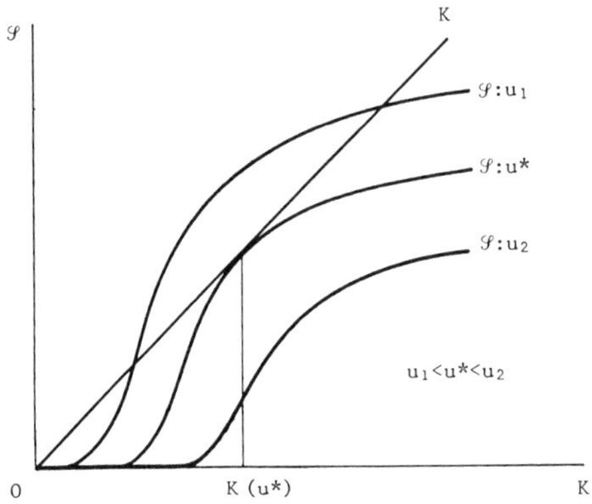

Figure 6.5. Optimal K in the equilibrium city system.

$$\mathcal{S}(\delta, u^*, N(\delta, u^*, K(u^*)), K(u^*)) = K(u^*). \tag{6.43}$$

And since relation (6.32) holds under any (u, K), in each city of the equilibrium city system, we have

$$\mathcal{S} = \text{TDR} = K, \tag{6.44}$$

which implies that the Henry George theorem holds in each city.

6.3.2 Utility-maximizing communities and the system of cities

Next, suppose a certain number of households form a community (or club) and develop a city. The community rents the land for the city from absentee landlords at the agriculture land rent R_A. All households in the community (i.e., in the city) are to enjoy the same utility level. Then, as in (5.49), the budget constraint of the community can be expressed as

$$\mathcal{S}(\delta, u, N, K) \equiv \delta N - C(u, N, K) \geq K. \tag{6.45}$$

The community's problem is to choose its population N and public service level K, while satisfying the budget constraint, so as to maximize the common utility level:[25]

$$\max_{N>0, K\geq 0} u \quad \text{subject to} \quad \mathcal{S}(\delta, u, N, K) \geq K. \tag{6.46}$$

Suppose that $(\hat{u}, \hat{N}, \hat{K})$ is a solution to this community's problem, where $\hat{N} > 0$ by definition, and $\hat{K} > 0$ from assumption (6.27). Then, since Proposition 5.3 holds under any $K > 0$, we can immediately conclude as follows: From Proposition 5.3(ii) the optimal population $\hat{N}$ of the community must be equal to the equilibrium population $N(\delta, \hat{u}, \hat{K})$ of the OCA(δ, $\hat{u}$, $\hat{K}$) model:

$$\hat{N} = N(\delta, \hat{u}, \hat{K}). \tag{6.47}$$

Furthermore, from Proposition 5.1(i) (which also holds under any fixed $K > 0$), we can see that whatever ($\hat{u}$, $\hat{K}$) are, the surplus function $\mathcal{S}(\delta, \hat{u}, N, \hat{K})$ achieves the maximum when N equals $N(\delta, \hat{u}, \hat{K})$.

This observation suggests that we can solve the community's problem (6.46) in two steps. Although we do not yet know the optimal values of $\hat{u}$ and $\hat{K}$, the optimal population $\hat{N}$ should maximize the surplus function $\mathcal{S}(\delta, \hat{u}, N, \hat{K})$ with respect to N. Therefore, in the first step, we may solve the next surplus-maximizing problem under each combination of u and K:

$$\max_{N \geq 0} \mathcal{S}(\delta, u, N, K). \tag{6.48}$$

Applying Proposition 5.1(i) again, we can see that the optimal N to problem (6.48) equals $N(\delta, u, K)$, which is the equilibrium population of the OCA(δ, u, K) model.

Having obtained the surplus-maximizing population function $N(\delta, u, K)$, we proceed to the second step:[26]

$$\max_{K \geq 0} u, \qquad \text{subject to} \quad \mathcal{S}(\delta, u, N(\delta, u, K), K) \geq K. \tag{6.49}$$

That is, we choose the supply level K of the city good so as to attain the highest common utility. We can approach this problem of the second step graphically. Recall that given an appropriate u, the corresponding surplus curve $\mathcal{S}(\delta, u, N(\delta, u, K), K)$ can be drawn as in Figure 6.4. And by changing u, we can obtain a set of surplus curves as in Figure 6.5. In order to meet the budget constraint, a surplus curve must pass the region above the public-good cost line K. Since surplus curves move downward as u increases, the community achieves the highest utility $\hat{u}$ when the corresponding surplus curve is tangent to the K line from below. As is evident from Figure 6.5, this implies that

$$\hat{u} = u^*, \qquad \hat{K} = K(u^*), \qquad \hat{N} = N(\delta, u^*, K(u^*)). \tag{6.50}$$

And the total number of communities (i.e., cities) in the nation is given, as before, by (6.42). Therefore, we can conclude that *the system of cities that will result from competition among utility-maximizing communities is identical with that which will result from competition among profit-maximizing developers*. In this city system, each household in every city is enjoying the highest utility $\hat{u}$; and by forming a city (or community) of any size, no group of households can achieve a common utility level higher than $\hat{u}$ (recall note 22, Chapter 5). Therefore, it represents an efficient (i.e., Pareto-optimal) system of cities.

As we have seen in Section 5.6.3, the internal allocation problem of each optimal community can be solved through competitive markets. That is, once $N(\delta, \hat{u}, \hat{K})$ households have agreed to form a community and set the service level of the city good at $\hat{K}$, everything else can be optimally achieved by competitive markets. In particular, each household receives wage δ (the marginal product of labor), and the optimal residential allocation of the community coincides with the equilibrium solution of the CCA(δ, $N(\delta, \hat{u}, \hat{K})$, $\hat{K}$) model. And from Proposition 5.3(iv), the total differential land rent equals the supply cost $\hat{K}$ of the city good. Also, from Figure 6.5, $\mathcal{S}$ equals $K(u^*) \equiv \hat{K}$. Hence, relation (6.44) also holds in each optimal community.

6.4 Congestible city goods

In this section, we introduce congestion effects into the pure city good model of the previous section and examine the problem of the efficient provision of *congestible city goods*. Although in the preceding section we neglected congestion effects, in practice the provision of city goods is often accompanied by significant congestion effects. For example, given a public library of a certain capacity, the benefit a person can derive from it usually decreases with an increasing number of users.

As before, we measure the supply level, or *capacity*, of a city good by its *cost* K. We now assume, however, that the *service level* of the city good that is actually enjoyed by each household in the city depends on the capacity K and the number of households N in the city, and denote it by $E(K, N)$. As before, it is assumed that the value of $E(K, N)$ is independent of the location in the city. It is natural to assume that the service level $E(K, N)$ is increasing in K and decreasing in N:

$$\partial E(K, N)/\partial K > 0, \qquad \partial E(K, N)/\partial N < 0. \tag{6.51}$$

Replacing $E(K)$ with $E(K, N)$ in the pure city good model of (6.26), the residential choice behavior of each household in the city can be expressed as

$$\max_{r,z,s} U(z, s, E(K, N)), \qquad \text{subject to} \quad z + R(r)s = Y^0 - G(r) - T(r). \tag{6.52}$$

As before, we assume that the public good is indispensable:

$$U(z, s, E(K = 0, N)) = -\infty. \tag{6.53}$$

As in (6.28) the *population cost function* can now be defined as

$$C(u, N, E(K, N)) \equiv \min_{r_f, n(r), s(r)} \int_0^{r_f} [T(r) + Z(s, u, E(K, N)) + R_A s(r)] n(r) dr,$$

$$\text{subject to} \quad s(r)n(r) \leq L(r) \quad \text{at each} \quad r \leq r_f,$$

$$\int_0^{r_f} n(r) dr = N. \tag{6.54}$$

Then, given u, N, δ, and K, the maximum (gross) surplus from the city development can be obtained as

$$\mathcal{S}(\delta, u, N, E(K, N)) \equiv \delta N - C(u, N, E(K, N)). \tag{6.55}$$

In this new context, we reexamine the problems of the optimal city size and efficient provision of city goods. It turns out that with the introduction of congestion effects, we have significant changes in the results from the preceding section. First, when a household plans to migrate into a city, it will consider only the benefits it can derive from the city. The addition of that extra one household, however, will magnify the congestion level in the consumption of the city goods in that city; hence, all existing households in the city will be adversely affected. This suggests that in achieving the optimal city size, the developer (or the city government) must impose a congestion tax on each household in the city. Second, this implies that the surplus from the development of a city is now the sum of the total differential rents and congestion taxes. Therefore, in achieving a profit-maximizing city, the developer should maximize the sum of the total differential rents and congestion taxes.

6.4.1 Developer's problem

Given the national utility level u, a developer (or a city government) will choose the population N and city-good capacity K so as to maximize the net profit from the city development:

$$\max_{N \geq 0, K \geq 0} \Pi \equiv \mathcal{S}(\delta, u, N, E(K, N)) - K. \tag{6.56}$$

As usual, we may solve this developer's problem in two steps. In the first step, given each value of K, the developer may choose population N so as to maximize the surplus ($\equiv$ the gross profit):

$$\max_{N \geq 0} \mathcal{S}(\delta, u, N, E(K, N)) \equiv \delta N - C(u, N, E(K, N)). \tag{6.57}$$

The first-order condition for the optimal population (assuming that it is positive) is given by

$$\frac{\partial \mathcal{S}}{\partial N} = 0: \qquad \delta = \frac{\partial C}{\partial N} + \frac{\partial C}{\partial E}\frac{\partial E}{\partial N}, \tag{6.58}$$

which means that the marginal product of labor δ equals the sum of the direct marginal cost of population, $\partial C/\partial N$, and the marginal congestion cost of population, $\partial C/\partial E \cdot \partial E/\partial N$. Solving equation (6.58) for N, we obtain the surplus-maximizing population $\hat{N}(u, K)$ under each value of K(and u).[27] A change in K will result in a change in $\hat{N}(u, K)$. Therefore, in the second step, the developer may choose K so as to maximize the net profit:

$$\max_{K \geq 0} \Pi \equiv \mathcal{S}(\delta, u, \hat{N}(u, K), E[K, \hat{N}(u, K)]) - K. \tag{6.59}$$

The first-order condition for the optimal K (assuming that it is positive) is given by

$$d\mathcal{S}(\delta, u, \hat{N}(u, K), E[K, \hat{N}(u, K)])/dK = 1. \tag{6.60}$$

Solving equation (6.60) for K, we can obtain the profit-maximizing capacity $K(u)$ of the city good under each value of u.[28] The relationship between the surplus curve $\mathcal{S}(\delta, u, \hat{N}(u, K), E[K, \hat{N}(u, K)])$ and optimal capacity $K(u)$ can be drawn as in Figure 6.4 [where $\mathcal{S}(\delta, u, N(\delta, u, K), K)$ must be replaced by $\mathcal{S}(\delta, u, \hat{N}(u, K), E[K, \hat{N}(u, K)])$]. Applying the envelope theorem to (6.57) and (6.54), we restate condition (6.60) as follows:

$$\int_0^{r_f} - \left(\frac{\partial Z(s(r), u, E(K, N))}{\partial K} \right) \Bigg|_{N=\hat{N}(u, K)} n(r)\, dr = 1, \tag{6.61}$$

which is, again, a spatial version of the Samuelson condition: The sum of marginal benefits (of the city good) over all households in the city equals the marginal cost of the city good.

Again, the direct implementation of these optimality conditions will require a prohibitive amount of information on the part of the developer. Hence, we next consider how the developer will be able to achieve the profit-maximizing city through a decentralized scheme. To do so, we need to obtain the *population supply function* in the context of the present problem. Because of congestion effects in the provision of the public good, we can no longer use the previous population supply function given by (6.35). Since the utility of each household now depends on the population of the city, it is necessary to solve the following *fixed-point problem* in order to obtain the equilibrium population of the city.

Let N^e represent the *expected population* of the city. Given an arbitrary combination of (Y, u, K, N^e), we consider the OCA$(Y, u, E(K, N^e))$ model (the open-city model under absentee landlords with posttax income Y, national utility u, and public-good service level $E(K, N^e)$). Recalling the bid rent function ψ and bid-max lot size function s defined by (6.6), we obtain the *realized population* of the OCA$(Y, u, E(K, N^e))$ model as

$$N(Y, u, E(K, N^e)) \equiv \int_0^{r_f} \frac{L(r)}{s(Y - T(r), u, E(K, N^e))} \, dr, \qquad (6.62)$$

where the fringe distance $r_f \equiv r_f(Y, u, E(K, N^e))$ is determined from the boundary condition

$$\psi(Y - T(r_f), u, E(K, N^e)) = R_A. \qquad (6.63)$$

In equilibrium, the realized population must equal the expected population:

$$N(Y, u, E(K, N^e)) = N^e. \qquad (6.64)$$

Solving this equation for N^e, we can obtain the *equilibrium population,* which is denoted by $N(Y, u, K)$.

Let $\tilde{u}(Y, K)$ be the *supreme utility level* defined from the relation

$$\psi(Y - T(0), \tilde{u}(Y, K), E(K, 0)) = R_A. \qquad (6.65)$$

Then, at $N^e = 0$, the value of realized population $N(Y, u, E(K, 0))$ is positive if and only if $u < \tilde{u}(Y, K)$. And since $\partial N(Y, u, E)/\partial E > 0$ [which follows from (6.62) and (6.63)] and $\partial E(K, N)/\partial N < 0$, function $N(Y, u, E(K, N^e))$ is continuously decreasing in N^e (before reaching zero). Therefore, it is evident from Figure 6.6 that the equilibrium population $N(Y, u, K)$ uniquely exists under each combination of (Y, u, K), and we have

$$N(Y, u, K) > 0 \quad \text{if and only if} \quad u < \tilde{u}(Y, K). \qquad (6.66)$$

In Figure 6.6, curve $N(Y, u\ E(K, N^e))$ shifts upward as Y increases (as u decreases or as K increases). Hence, given (Y, u, K) such that $u < \tilde{u}(Y, K)$, it is evident from Figure 6.6 that the (equilibrium) *population supply function* $N(Y, u, K)$ is increasing in Y and K and decreasing in u:

$$\partial N(Y, u, K)/\partial Y > 0, \qquad \partial N(Y, u, K)/\partial u < 0, \qquad \partial N(Y, u, K)/\partial K > 0. \qquad (6.67)$$

Next, solving the equation $N(Y, u, K) = N$ for Y under each combination of (u, K), we can obtain the *(population) supply–income function* $Y(u, N, K)$. From (6.67), we can readily see that $Y(u, N, K)$ is increasing in u and N and decreasing in K:

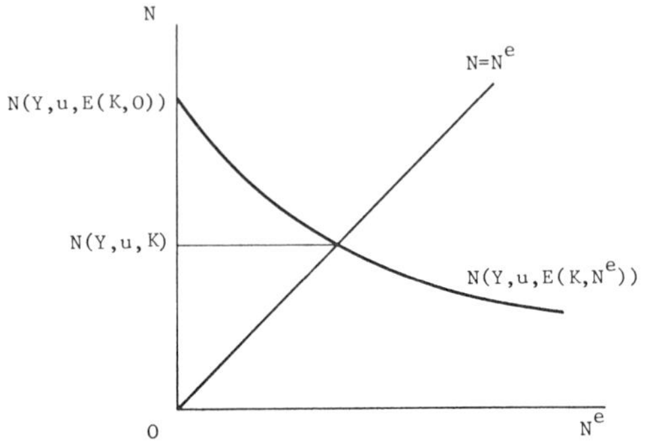

Figure 6.6. Equilibrium population supply $N(Y, u, K)$.

$$\partial Y(u, N, K)/\partial u > 0, \qquad \partial Y(u, N, K)/\partial N > 0, \qquad \partial Y(u, N, K)/\partial K < 0. \tag{6.68}$$

Finally, by using the population supply function above, we can derive a useful accounting relationship. We denote the OCA(Y, u, $E[K, N(Y, u, K)]$) model simply as OCA(Y, u, K). Note that given the equilibrium population $N(Y, u, K)$, the residential land market of the OCA(Y, u, K) model itself does not incorporate any source of market failure, and its equilibrium is efficient. Therefore, as in (5.21), we can derive the following identity:

$$N(Y, u, K)Y = C(u, N(Y, u, K), E[K, N(Y, u, K)]) + \mathrm{TDR}(Y, u, K), \tag{6.69}$$

where C is the population cost function from (6.54) and TDR(Y, u, K) the total differential land rent at the equilibrium of the OCA(Y, u, K) model. Equivalently, since $N(Y(u, N, K), u, K) \equiv N$, setting Y equal to $Y(u, N, K)$ in (6.69), we have

$$NY(u, N, K) = C(u, N, E(K, N)) + \mathrm{TDR}(Y(u, N, K), u, K). \tag{6.70}$$

From this identity, as in (5.25), we can derive the following relationship:[29] At each given $N > 0$,

$$Y(u, N, K) = \frac{\partial C(u, N, E)}{\partial N} \quad \text{at} \quad E = E(K, N). \tag{6.71}$$

Namely, *the supply–income $Y(u, N, K)$ equals the direct marginal cost of population*. Equivalently, since $Y(u, N(Y, u, K), K) \equiv Y$, at each equilibrium population $N(Y, u, K) > 0$, it follows from (6.71) that

$$Y = \frac{\partial C(u, N, E)}{\partial N} \quad \text{at} \quad N = N(Y, u, k) \quad \text{and} \quad E = E(K, N(Y, u, K)). \tag{6.72}$$

Now, we go back to the decentralization scheme for achieving the profit-maximizing city for the developer. The competitive labor market in the city will set the wage rate equal to the marginal product of labor, δ. On the other hand, substituting (6.72) into (6.58), we can see that the following condition must be met to achieve the profit-maximizing city:

$$Y = \delta - \frac{\partial C}{\partial E}\frac{\partial E}{\partial N}. \tag{6.73}$$

This means that the developer (or city government) must impose a *congestion tax,*

$$G \equiv \frac{\partial C}{\partial E}\frac{\partial E}{\partial N}, \tag{6.74}$$

on each household in the city. Using the other optimality condition (6.60), we can restate (6.74) as follows:[30]

$$G = -\left(\frac{\partial E}{\partial K}\right)^{-1}\frac{\partial E}{\partial N} \equiv \left.\frac{dK}{dN}\right|_{E(K,N)=\text{const}} \tag{6.75}$$

That is, the congestion tax G equals the amount of increase in the city-good cost K due to the addition of one more household to the city, while maintaining the service level of the public good in the city at the optimal level $E(K, N)$.

Example 6.2. Let us suppose the service level function $E(K, N)$ of the city good takes the form

$$E(K, N) = f(K/N^{\lambda}), \tag{6.76}$$

where f is an increasing function of K/N^{λ}.[31] The parameter λ represents the degree of the congestibility of the city good. When $\lambda = 0$, $E(K, N) = f(K)$, which represents the case of the *pure city good* in the preceding section. When $\lambda = 1$, $E(K, N) = f(K/N)$, and the publicly provided good resembles a *pure private good* since a doubling of population N results in a halving of potential benefits received by each household. From (6.75), the optimal congestion tax can be obtained as

$$G = \lambda K/N. \tag{6.77}$$

When $\lambda = 0$, we have $G = 0$; and when $\lambda = 1$, $G = K/N$, as expected.

Although equation (6.75) provides a rule for determining the optimal congestion tax, its value cannot be determined without knowledge of the optimal population N and optimal city-good capacity K. In order to avoid this difficulty, we next consider how to determine the optimal congestion tax G without requiring an excess amount of information on the part of the developer. Suppose the developer chooses a certain congestion tax G and city-good capacity K, and let everything else be determined by competitive markets. Then, the (posttax) income Y of each household in the city equals wage δ minus G. Hence, if we set Y equal to $\delta - G$ in the OCA(Y, u, K) model, the equilibrium population of the city equals $N(\delta - G, u, K)$; and from (6.55), the surplus from the city equals

$$\mathcal{S} \equiv \delta N(\delta - G, u, K) - C(u, N(\delta - G, u, K), E[K, N(\delta - G, u, K)]). \tag{6.78}$$

If we set Y equal to $\delta - G$ in (6.69), the following relation also holds at the equilibrium of the residential land market:

$$N(\delta - G, u, K)(\delta - G) = C(u, N(\delta - G, u, K), E[K, N(\delta - G, u, K)]) + \mathrm{TDR}(\delta - G, u, K). \tag{6.79}$$

From (6.78) and (6.79), it follows that

$$\mathcal{S} = \mathrm{TDR}(\delta - G, u, K) + N(\delta - G, u, K)G. \tag{6.80}$$

Therefore, the developer's problem (6.56) can now be restated as

$$\max_{G,K \geq 0} \Pi = \mathrm{TDR}(\delta - G, u, K) + N(\delta - G, u, K)G - K. \tag{6.81}$$

That is, *in order to achieve a profit-maximizing city, the developer may choose the congestion tax G and city-good capacity K so as to maximize the sum of the total differential rents and total congestion taxes minus the public-good cost*. This decentralized scheme requires only observable information on TDR, N, G, and K, and hence it is operational.

6.4.2 *System of cities*

Let us consider the city system that will result from competition among profit-maximizing developers (or surplus-maximizing city governments). As usual, we assume that the nation consists of M identical (urban) households. And wherever a city is to be developed in the nation, the aggregate production function of the city is the same, and it is given by (5.33). Then the equilibrium city system can be obtained as in Section 6.3.1. Recall from the second step of the developer's problem in the preceding subsection, a surplus curve $\mathcal{S}(\delta, u, \hat{N}(u, K), E[K, \hat{N}(u, K)])$ can be depicted as in Figure 6.4. This surplus curve will shift downward as u increases.[32] Hence, by appropriately changing u, we can obtain a set of surplus curves as in Figure 6.5. Since the net profit $\mathcal{S} - K$ must be zero in equilibrium, it is apparent from Figure 6.5 that u^* represents the equilibrium utility level and $K(u^*)$ the optimal public-good capacity in each city.[33] Thus, in the equilibrium city system, the population of each city equals $\hat{N}(u^*, K(u^*))$, and the total number of cities in the nation is given by

$$M/\hat{N}(u^*, K(u^*)). \tag{6.82}$$

When each developer achieves the profit-maximizing city through the decentralized scheme from the preceding subsection, the surplus of each city is given by (6.80). And the net profit $\Pi \equiv \mathcal{S} - K$ equals zero in each city. Therefore, in each city of the equilibrium city system, it holds that

$$\text{TDR} + NG = K. \tag{6.83}$$

Namely, the city-good cost can be financed from the total differential rents and congestion taxes.

Example 6.3. Recall that under specification (6.76), we have $G = \lambda K/N$. Substituting this into (6.83), we have

$$\text{TDR} + \lambda K = K, \qquad \text{or} \quad \text{TDR} = (1 - \lambda)K. \tag{6.84}$$

That is, in each city of the equilibrium city system, $(1 - \lambda) \times 100\%$ of the city-good cost is financed from the total differential rents, and $\lambda \times 100\%$ is financed from congestion taxes.[34] As the degree of the congestibility of the city good increases (i.e., the privateness of the good increases), an increasing proportion of its cost is financed from congestion taxes.

We now turn to the city system that will result from competition among utility-maximizing communities. First, in the present context, the *community's problem* can be formulated as follows:

$$\max_{N>0, K\geq 0} u, \qquad \text{subject to} \quad \mathcal{S}(\delta, u, N, E(K, N)) \geq K. \tag{6.85}$$

Suppose that $(\hat{u}, \hat{N}, \hat{K})$ is the solution to this problem. Then the relationship between $\hat{u}$, $\hat{N}$, and $\hat{K}$ can be depicted as in Figure 6.7. The surplus curve $\mathcal{S}(\delta, \hat{u}, N, E(\hat{K}, N))$ must be tangent to the horizontal $\hat{K}$ line from below.[35] This implies that $\hat{N}$ must be the solution to the following problem:

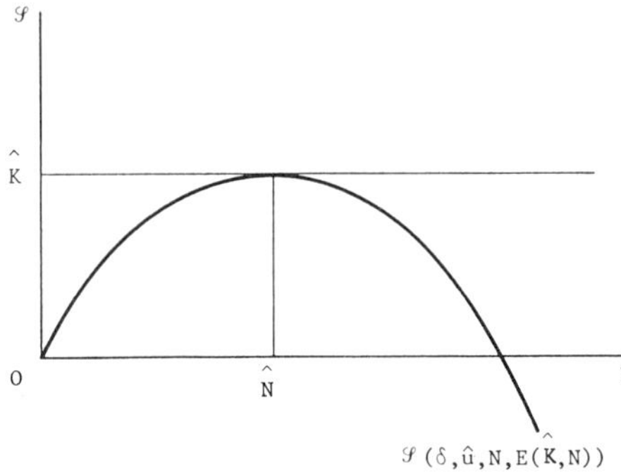

Figure 6.7. Relationship between $\hat{u}$, $\hat{N}$, and $\hat{K}$.

$$\max_{N \geq 0} \mathcal{S}(\delta, \hat{u}, N, E(\hat{K}, N)).$$

This observation suggests that we can solve the community's problem in two steps, as in Section 6.3.2. Since we do not yet know the optimal $\hat{u}$ and $\hat{K}$, in the first step we can solve the following surplus-maximizing problem under each combination of u and K,

$$\max_{N \geq 0} \mathcal{S}(\delta, u, N, E(K, N)), \tag{6.86}$$

which is identical to problem (6.57) in the first step of the developer's problem. Hence, as before, the solution to this problem is given by $\hat{N}(u, K)$. In the second step, we solve the next problem:

$$\max_{K \geq 0} u, \qquad \text{subject to} \quad \mathcal{S}(\delta, u, \hat{N}(u, K), E[K, \hat{N}(u, K)]) \geq K. \tag{6.87}$$

As before, by appropriately changing u, we can obtain a set of surplus curves as in Figure 6.5. Then since the surplus curves shift downward as u increases, it is again apparent from Figure 6.5 that the highest utility achievable by the community equals u^*, which is the equilibrium utility level obtained before. From this, we can immediately conclude that

$$\hat{u} = u^*, \qquad \hat{K} = K(u^*), \qquad \hat{N} = \hat{N}(u^*, K(u^*)), \tag{6.88}$$

and the total number of communities in the nation is given by (6.82). Therefore, we can also conclude that *the two systems of cities are identical, and both are efficient.*

6.5 Neighborhood goods

In the two preceding sections, it was assumed that the level of benefits from local public goods does not vary over space in a city. In practice, however, the benefits from most local public goods do vary over space. This is because most local public goods are supplied from public facilities with fixed location, and households can derive more benefits from a public facility as they reside closer to it.

In this section, we consider public goods that are local to a small neighborhood in a city. That is, public goods are assumed to be provided from public facilities that are densely located in a city and whose benefits belong only to those households located close to them. Examples are street lights, neighborhood beautification, and public parking places. We call such local public goods *neighborhood goods*.[36] In Section 6.5.1, we examine the optimal allocation of neighborhood goods in the context of the Herbert–Stevens model. In Section 6.5.2, we consider the decentralized mechanism for achieving that optimal allocation.

Not surprisingly, the decentralized mechanism for achieving the efficient provision of neighborhood goods in a city is essentially the same as for providing city goods in a nation. Namely, in the previous case of city goods, the developer of each city was able to achieve a profit-maximizing city by adopting an open-city scheme and maximizing the sum of the total differential rents and congestion taxes minus the city-good cost; and the competition among such developers led to the formation of an efficient city system. In the present case of neighborhood goods, suppose that each (small) neighborhood of a city is to be developed by a profit-maximizing developer. It turns out that the developer of each neighborhood can maximize its profit by choosing a congestion tax rate and supply level of public goods (in the neighborhood) so as to maximize the sum of the total differential rents and congestion taxes minus the neighborhood-good cost; and the competition among such developers will lead to the formation of an efficient city. There is, however, one significant difference between the two cases. In the case of city goods, we assumed that cities were to be developed on a *uniform plane,* with no overlapping of their boundaries; and the differential land rent at each location was equal to the residential land rent minus the agriculture land rent. In the present case, however, each neighborhood locates at a different distance from the CBD, and *a neighborhood is economically more advantageous if it is closer to the CBD*. Hence, the competition among neighborhood developers for an advantageous location will lead to a nonuniform distribution of rents on the original agricultural lands, or *raw lands*. Therefore, in counting the profit for each developer, we must now define the *differential land rent* at a location as the difference between the *residential land rent* (i.e., rent on the improved land with neighborhood goods, paid by households to a developer) and the *raw-land rent* (i.e., rent on the raw land, paid by a developer to landowners). In this way, we can guarantee that in equilibrium all developers in the city will earn zero profit.

6.5.1 *Optimal allocation*

Let us consider a neighborhood good that is to be efficiently provided over space in a monocentric city.[37] For simplicity, we consider only the case in which the spatial distribution of the neighborhood good is symmetric with respect to the CBD. Let r be the distance from the CBD, and $k(r)$ be the *neighborhood good density* at r, which represents the supply level, or *capacity*, of the neighborhood good *per unit area* at r. As usual, capacity $k(r)$ is measured by its cost. Similarly, if we let $n(r)$ and $L(r)$, respectively, be the number of households and amount of land per unit distance at r, then $\rho(r) \equiv n(r)/L(r)$ represents the *population density* at r. In this context, we assume that the *service level* $E(r)$ of the neighborhood good at r is a function of $k(r)$ and $\rho(r)$:

$$E(r) = E(k(r), \rho(r)). \tag{6.89}$$

It is natural to assume that the service level $E(r)$ is increasing in $k(r)$ and decreasing or constant in $\rho(r)$:

$$\partial E(k, \rho)/\partial k > 0, \qquad \partial E(k, \rho)/\partial \rho \leq 0. \tag{6.90}$$

The neighborhood good is congestible (noncongestible) when $\partial E/\partial \rho < 0$ ($\partial E/\partial \rho = 0$). All households in the city are assumed to have the same utility function $U(z, s, E(k, \rho))$, which satisfies Assumptions 6.1, 6.3, and 6.4. To emphasize the importance of the neighborhood good, we assume as usual that k is essential:

$$U(z, s, E(0, \rho)) = -\infty. \tag{6.91}$$

In this context, the minimum residential costs $C(u, N)$ for achieving the common target utility level u to N households can be defined as follows:

$$C(u, N) \equiv \min_{\substack{r_f, s(r), n(r),\\ k(r), \rho(r)}} \int_0^{r_f} \{T(r) + Z(s(r), u, E[k(r), \rho(r)]) + R_A s(r)\} n(r)\, dr$$

$$+ \int_0^{r_f} k(r) L(r)\, dr, \tag{6.92}$$

$$\text{subject to} \qquad \rho(r) = n(r)/L(r), \qquad r \leq r_f, \tag{6.93}$$

$$s(r)n(r) = L(r), \qquad r \le r_f, \tag{6.94}$$

$$\int_0^{r_f} n(r)\,dr = N, \tag{6.95}$$

where the terms $T(r)$, $Z(s, u, E)$, R_A, and r_f are defined as before. The solution to this problem gives an optimal (i.e., efficient) residential land use of the city. As usual, we call $C(u, N)$ the *population cost function*. But unlike before, $C(u, N)$ includes the cost of the public good $\int_0^{r_f} k(r)L(r)\,dr$.

As in Chapter 5, for convenience we restate the cost-minimization problem above as a surplus-maximization problem. Let Y^0 be the per capita income of the city, which is considered a given constant (or a parameter). Then the maximum surplus $\mathcal{S}(Y^0, u, N)$ from the residential development can be obtained by solving the following Herbert–Stevens problem (HS problem):

$$\mathcal{S}(Y^0, u, N) \equiv \max_{\substack{r_f, s(r), n(r),\\ k(r), \rho(r)}} \int_0^{r_f} \{Y^0 - T(r) - Z(s(r), u, E[k(r), \rho(r)])$$

$$- R_A s(r)\} n(r)dr - \int_0^{r_f} k(r)L(r)\,dr,$$

$$\text{subject to constraints (6.93)–(6.95).} \tag{6.96}$$

Since $\int_0^{r_f} n(r)\,dr = N$, it holds identically that

$$\mathcal{S}(Y^0, u, N) = NY^0 - C(u, N), \tag{6.97}$$

and hence the maximization of $\mathcal{S}$ is equivalent to the minimization of C. Upon appropriate substitutions of variables, we can simply restate the HS problem as follows:

$$\max_{\substack{r_f, s(r),\\ k(r), \rho(r)}} \int_0^{r_f} \left\{ \frac{Y^0 - T(r) - Z(s(r), u, E[k(r), \rho(r)])}{s(r)} - k(r) - R_A \right\} L(r)\,dr, \tag{6.98}$$

$$\text{subject to} \quad \rho(r) = 1/s(r), \qquad r \le r_f, \tag{6.99}$$

$$\int_0^{r_f} L(r)/s(r)\,dr = N, \tag{6.100}$$

where the first constraint represents the *density constraint,* and the second the *population constraint*. The *Lagrangian function* associated with this maximization problem is given by[38]

$$\mathscr{L} \equiv \int_0^{r_f} \left\{ \frac{Y^0 - T(r) - Z(s(r), u, E[k(r), \rho(r)])}{s(r)} - k(r) - R_A \right\} L(r)\, dr$$
$$- \int_0^{r_f} \tau(r) \left(\frac{1}{s(r)} - \rho(r) \right) L(r)\, dr - g \left(\int_0^{r_f} \frac{L(r)}{s(r)}\, dr - N \right)$$
$$= \int_0^{r_f} \left\{ \frac{Y^0 - g - \tau(r) - T(r) - Z(s(r), u, E[k(r), \rho(r)])}{s(r)} \right.$$
$$\left. + \tau(r)\rho(r) - k(r) - R_A \right\} L(r)\, dr + gN, \qquad (6.101)$$

where the Lagrangian multiplier $\tau(r)$ has the economic implication of the *(shadow) congestion tax* per household at r, which represents the marginal congestion cost of a household at location r; similarly, multiplier g has the implication of the *(shadow) population tax* per household in the city, which represents the marginal net cost of a household for the city. In terms of the bid rent function ψ and bid-max lot size function s defined by (6.6), the optimality conditions for the HS problem can be summarized as follows: For $(s(r), n(r), k(r), \rho(r);\ r \le r_f)$ to be the solution of the HS problem, it is necessary that there exist a set of multipliers $(g, \tau(r), R(r);\ r \le r_f)$ such that[39]

$$R(r) = \begin{cases} \psi(Y^0 - g - \tau(r) - T(r), u, E[k(r), \rho(r)]) & \text{for} \quad r \le r_f, & (6.102) \\ R_A + k(r) - \tau(r)\rho(r) \quad \text{at} \quad r = r_f: & \textit{boundary condition}, & (6.103) \\ R_A \quad \text{for} \quad r > r_f, & & (6.104) \end{cases}$$

$$s(r) = s(Y^0 - g - \tau(r) - T(r), u, E[k(r), \rho(r)]) \quad \text{for} \quad r \le r_f, \qquad (6.105)$$

$$\rho(r) = 1/s(r) \quad \text{for} \quad r \le r_f: \quad \textit{density constraint}, \qquad (6.106)$$

$$\rho(r)\left(-\frac{\partial Z}{\partial E}\frac{\partial E}{\partial k} \right) = 1 \quad \text{for} \quad r \le r_f: \quad \textit{Samuelson condition}, \qquad (6.107)$$

$$\tau(r) = \rho(r)\frac{\partial Z}{\partial E}\frac{\partial E}{\partial \rho} \quad \text{for} \quad r \le r_f: \quad \textit{congestion tax rule}, \qquad (6.108)$$

$$n(r) = \begin{cases} L(r)/s(Y^0 - g - \tau(r) - T(r), u, E[k(r), \rho(r)]) & \text{for } r \le r_f, \\ 0 & \text{for } r > r_f, \end{cases} \qquad (6.109)$$

$$\int_0^{r_f} n(r)\,dr = N. \qquad (6.110)$$

As usual, we can interpret these optimality conditions to represent the conditions of the *compensated equilibrium* in which the target utility u is achieved with the aid of congestion tax and population tax policies. To see this, first note that given a set of population tax g, congestion tax $\tau(r)$, public-good density $k(r)$, and population density $\rho(r)$ at each $r \leq r_f$, the residential choice behavior of each household in the competitive land market can be expressed as

$$\max_{r,z,s} U(z, s, E[k(r), \rho(r)]), \qquad \text{s.t.} \quad z + R(r)s = Y^0 - g - \tau(r) - T(r), \qquad (6.111)$$

where $R(r)$ is the land rent at each r, and $Y^0 - g - \tau(r) - T(r)$ gives the net income of a household at r. In this context, condition (6.102) means that at each distance $r \leq r_f$, the equilibrium land rent $R(r)$ equals the bid rent under the target utility u. Condition (6.103) states the zero-profit condition at the urban fringe: On each unit of land at r_f, the sum of revenues [i.e., residential land rent $R(r_f)$ plus congestion taxes $\tau(r_f)\rho(r_f)$] equals the sum of costs [i.e., opportunity cost of land R_A plus neighborhood-good cost $k(r_f)$]. Condition (6.105) means that at each $r \leq r_f$, the equilibrium lot size equals the bid-max lot size. Conditions (6.102) and (6.105) together imply that at each $r \leq r_f$, each household has chosen the optimal lot size $s(r)$ under the land rent $R(r)$. Condition (6.106) represents an obvious physical relationship. Condition (6.107) means that on each unit of land at $r \leq r_f$, the sum of the marginal benefits of the neighborhood good [over $\rho(r)$ households] equals the marginal cost of the neighborhood good. Condition (6.108) means that at each $r \leq r_f$, the optimal congestion tax $\tau(r)$ (per household at r) must equal the sum of the marginal congestion costs over $\rho(r)$ households. Condition (6.109) also represents an obvious physical relationship. Finally, (6.110) represents the population constraint.

Note that in order to achieve the fixed target utility level u, the income of each household must be adjusted by a lump-sum tax (or subsidy) g. In addition, to prevent the neighborhood good from experiencing excess congestion, an appropriate congestion tax $\tau(r)$ must be imposed at each r. Note also that the boundary condition (6.103) means

$$R(r_f) - R_A = k(r_f) - \tau(r_f)\rho(r_f). \qquad (6.112)$$

Hence, unlike before, the land rent at the urban fringe may not equal the agriculture land rent. This is because the neighborhood good is needed to convert the agricultural land to a residential land, and congestion taxes constitute a part of the revenue at each r. Finally, note that by using (6.107) we can restate the congestion tax rule (6.108) as follows:

$$\tau(r) = -\left(\frac{\partial E}{\partial k}\right)^{-1} \frac{\partial E}{\partial \rho} \equiv \frac{dk}{d\rho}\bigg|_{E(k,\rho)=\text{const}} \tag{6.113}$$

Example 6.4. As in Example 6.2, suppose we have

$$E(k, \rho) = f(k/\rho^{\lambda}), \tag{6.114}$$

where f is an increasing function of k/ρ^{λ}. When $\lambda = 0$, $E(k, \rho) = f(k)$, and hence the neighborhood good is uncongestible. When $\lambda = 1$, $E(k, \rho) = f(k/\rho)$, and hence the neighborhood good resembles a pure private good. From (6.113), the optimal congestion tax at each distance can be obtained as

$$\tau(r) = \lambda k(r)/\rho(r). \tag{6.115}$$

When $\lambda = 0$, $\tau(r) = 0$; when $\lambda = 1$, $\tau(r) = k(r)/\rho(r)$, as expected.

6.5.2 *Decentralized mechanism*

As noted before, in the system of equations (6.102)–(6.110), if we consider u to be fixed and g a variable, they represent the conditions of the *compensated equilibrium* under the target utility u. Or in these equations, if we consider g to be fixed and u a variable, they now represent the conditions of the *competitive equilibrium* under the population tax rate g. In either context, if the city government chooses $k(r)$ and $\tau(r)$ at each r so that conditions (6.107) and (6.108) are satisfied,[40] then the equilibrium allocation is efficient.[41]

In either context of the compensated equilibrium or competitive equilibrium, however, a direct implementation of optimality conditions (6.107) and (6.108) will require a prohibitive amount of information on the part of the city government. Therefore, we now consider a more operational decentralized scheme for achieving the efficient allocation.

Suppose that each unit of land in the city is to be developed by a (small) developer.[42] Figure 6.8 summarizes the relationship among landowners, developers, and households in the city. A developer at distance r rents a unit of raw land from a landowner there at the market *raw-land rent* $R_0(r)$. The developer, in turn, invests a certain amount $k(r)$ of the neighborhood good into the land. Then the developer rents that improved land to households at the market *residential land rent* $R(r)$ and collects $\tau(r)$ of conges-

Figure 6.8. Relationship among agents at r.

tion tax from each household there. Thus, the profit of the developer (per unit of land) at r is given by

$$\pi(r) = \text{differential rent} + \text{congestion taxes} - \text{neighborhood good cost}$$
$$= (R(r) - R_0(r)) + \tau(r)\rho(r) - k(r), \tag{6.116}$$

where $\rho(r)$ is the number of households per unit of land at r. By definition, $\rho(r) = 1/s(r)$, where $s(r)$ is the lot size chosen by each household at r. Note that since the raw-land rent $R_0(r)$ at each r is competitively determined by all developers, the value of $R_0(r)$ in equation (6.116) is outside the control of the developer in question. The developer, however, can influence the values of $R(r)$ and $\rho(r)$ in equation (6.116) by appropriately choosing $\tau(r)$ and $k(r)$. To see this relation more precisely, let us first examine how the equilibrium lot size $s(r)$ will be determined through the competitive land market.

Given $\tau(r)$ and $k(r)$ (chosen by the developer) and g (chosen by the government), if u were the equilibrium utility level and $\rho(r)$ were the equilibrium household density at r, the equilibrium lot size $s(r)$ would be given by (6.105). However, it must also hold by definition that $\rho(r) = 1/s(r)$. Hence, substituting this relation into (6.105), we will determine the equilibrium lot size $s(r)$ by solving the following fixed-point problem for $s(r)$:

$$s(r) = s(Y^0 - g - \tau(r) - T(r), u, E[k(r), 1/s(r)]), \; r \leq r_f. \tag{6.117}$$

Let $s^*(Y^0 - g - \tau(r) - T(r), u, k(r))$ be the solution to this equation, and call it the *equilibrium lot size function*. If we let s^e be the *expected lot size*, then as demonstrated in Figure 6.9, $s^*(Y^0 - g - \tau(r) - T(r), u, k(r))$ is uniquely determined at the intersection between the curve $s(Y^0 - g - \tau(r) - T(r), u, E[k(r), 1/s^e])$ and the 45° line, $s = s^e$. For simplicity, we often represent $s^*(Y^0 - g - \tau(r) - T(r), u, k(r))$ by $s^*(r)$:

$$s^*(r) \equiv s^*(Y^0 - g - \tau(r) - T(r), u, k(r)). \tag{6.118}$$

Now, substituting $1/s^*(r)$ into $\rho(r)$ in equation (6.102), we determine the equilibrium land rent $R(r)$ as

$$R(r) = \psi(Y^0 - g - \tau(r) - T(r), u, E[k(r), 1/s^*(r)]). \tag{6.119}$$

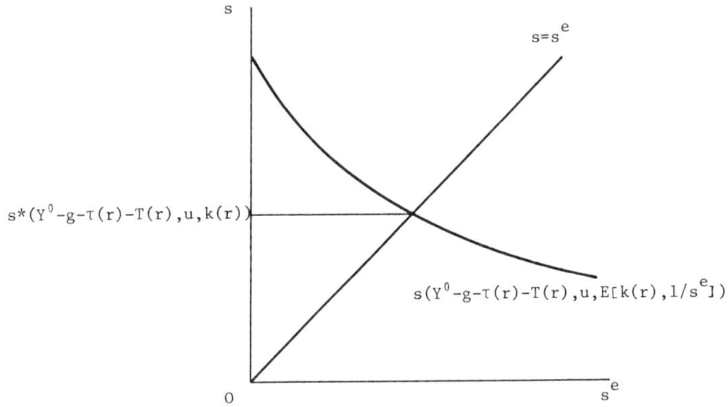

Figure 6.9. Determination of the equilibrium lot size s^*.

Therefore, from (6.106), (6.116), and (6.119), the *developer's problem* at r is to choose k and τ so as to maximize the profit $\pi(r)$:

$$\max_{k,\tau} \pi(r) = \psi(Y^0 - g - \tau - T(r), u, E[k, 1/s^*(r)]) - R_0(r) + \tau/s^*(r) - k, \tag{6.120}$$

where $s^*(r)$ is given by (6.118) (in which $\tau(r)$ and $k(r)$ should be replaced by τ and k, respectively). It turns out that the first-order conditions for this maximization problem are identical with the Samuelson condition, (6.107), and the congestion tax rule (6.108).[43] In equilibrium, of course, every developer obtains zero profit. In particular, since $R_0(r_f) = R_A$ at the urban fringe r_f, this implies that the boundary condition (6.103) must hold in equilibrium. Therefore, we can conclude that *given any population tax rate g, if each developer chooses the public-good capacity $k(r)$ (per unit of land) and congestion tax rate $\tau(r)$ so as to maximize the sum of the differential rent and congestion tax revenue minus the public-good cost (per unit of land), then an efficient land use will be achieved in equilibrium.*

Note that all variables in the profit function (6.120) are *observable* for the developer. In this sense, the decentralized scheme described above is operational. Note also that since each developer earns a zero profit in equilibrium, it holds from (6.116) that

$$(R(r) - R_0(r)) + \tau(r)\rho(r) = k(r), \qquad r \leq r_f. \tag{6.121}$$

Namely, *at each distance r, the sum of the differential rent and congestion tax revenue equals the neighborhood-good cost*. Therefore, the equi-

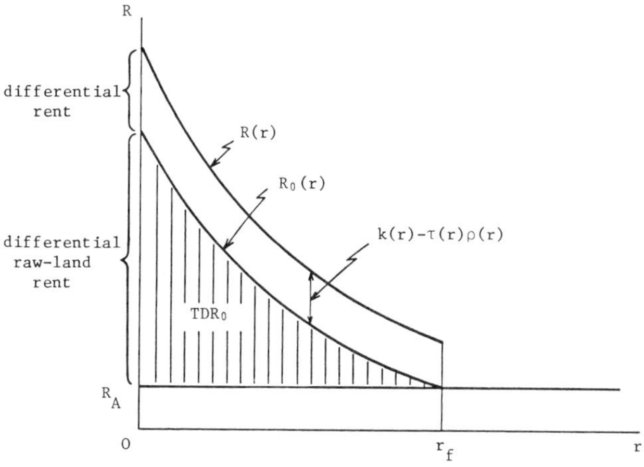

Figure 6.10. The equilibrium/efficient land use pattern.

librium (i.e., efficient) land use pattern can be depicted as in Figure 6.10. In particular, since

$$dR_0(r)/dr = -T'(r)/s^*(r), \tag{6.122}$$

the raw-land rent curve is decreasing in distance r.[44]

Example 6.5. Recall that under the specification (6.114), we have $\tau(r) = \lambda k(r)/\rho(r)$. Substituting this relation into (6.121), we have that

$$(R(r) - R_0(r)) + \lambda k(r) = k(r), \qquad \text{or} \qquad R(r) - R_0(r) = (1 - \lambda)k(r). \tag{6.123}$$

Hence, in an efficient city, at each distance r, $(1 - \lambda) \times 100\%$ of the public-good cost is financed from the differential rent, and $\lambda \times 100\%$ from congestion taxes.[45] As λ increases (i.e., the neighborhood good is more congestible), an increasing proportion of its cost is financed from the congestion taxes.

Finally, notice that in either context of the compensated equilibrium or the competitive equilibrium, if one appropriately changes u or g, all efficient allocations can be obtained. Let us briefly examine the relationship among urban aggregates prevailing in these efficient allocations. For any HS problem, at the optimal solution the value of surplus $\mathcal{S}$ [defined by (6.96)] equals the value of the Langrangian function $\mathcal{L}$ [defined by (6.101)]. And as we have seen before, at the solution it holds that $(Y^0 -$

$g - \tau(r) - T(r) - Z(s(r), u, E[k(r), \rho(r)]))/s(r) = \psi(Y^0 - g - \tau(r) - T(r), u, E[k(r), \rho(r)]) = R(r)$. Therefore, from (6.101) we have that

$$\begin{aligned}\mathcal{S}(Y^0, u, N) &= \int_0^{r_f} (R(r) + \tau(r)\rho(r) - k(r) - R_A)L(r)\,dr + gN \\ &\equiv \int_0^{r_f} [(R_0(r) - R_A) + (R(r) - R_0(r)) \\ &\quad + \tau(r)\rho(r) - k(r)]L(r)\,dr + gN \\ &= \int_0^{r_f} (R_0(r) - R_A)L(r)\,dr + gN, \qquad \text{from (6.121).}\end{aligned}$$

Hence, if we define the *total differential raw-land rent* by

$$\text{TDR}_0 = \int_0^{r_f} (R_0(r) - R_A)L(r)\,dr, \tag{6.124}$$

then

$$\mathcal{S}(Y^0, u, N) = \text{TDR}_0 + gN. \tag{6.125}$$

In Figure 6.10, TDR_0 equals the shaded area. Since at each distance r the net benefit of the neighborhood good $R(r) - R_0(r)$ equals its net cost $k(r) - \tau(r)\rho(r)$, in aggregation the surplus from the residential development equals TDR_0 plus the population tax revenue gN.

6.6 Superneighborhood goods

In the case of a city good (neighborhood good), its benefits are assumed to be uniform within a city (neighborhood), and no spillover effect is assumed to exist among cities (neighborhoods). In this situation, as was shown in previous sections, competition among many cities (neighborhoods) will lead to the efficient provision of such a good. In the case of a *superneighborhood good (SN good)*, however, its benefits are enjoyed by residents of many neighborhoods; hence, we cannot divide the city into a large number of regions in which the benefits of such a good are self-contained. In practice, benefits of many SN goods (e.g., major museums and green parks) are enjoyed by most residents in a city; but each resident receives a different amount of benefit, depending on his or her location in the city. Therefore, it is more difficult to devise a decentralized mechanism for the efficient provision of such goods.

In order to examine this problem more precisely, let us consider the following simple example involving a linear city. Suppose a city is to be developed on a long, narrow strip of land with unit width. All city residents are assumed to work at the CBD, the location of which is predetermined. Let the coordinate x denote each location in the city, where its origin O coincides with the location of the CBD (Figure 6.11). In this city, an SN good is to be provided from two public facilities, which are located respectively at y_1 and y_2. For simplicity, we assume that both facilities are free of congestion and that they do not use land. The *size* of each facility i is measured by its *costs* K_i ($i = 1, 2$). Although the two facilities are similar, they may provide different services; hence, each household in the city may receive benefits from both facilities. Let us assume that the total benefit $E(x)$ received from the two facilities by each household at location x is given as

$$E(x) = \Phi[f(K_1)g(|x - y_1|), f(K_2)g(|x - y_2|)]. \tag{6.126}$$

Here $f(K)$ is an increasing function of facility size K, which represents the potential benefit of a facility with size K, enjoyed by a household residing at its site. Function $g(r)$ is decreasing in distance r, representing the spatial decay nature of the benefit from a facility. Φ is an appropriate function, and the following two special cases are noteworthy:

(a) $E(x) = \max\{f(K_1)g(|x - y_1|), f(K_2)g(|x - y_2|)\}$.

(b) $E(x) = f(K_1)g(|x - y_1|) + f(K_2)g(|x - y_2|)$.

In case (a), each household chooses the facility with a greater benefit (e.g., primary schools). In case (b), the total benefit of each household is the sum of benefit from each facility; namely, each household receives a spillover-like benefit from each facility (e.g., green parks or museums). It turns out that case (b) poses more difficult problems in devising a decentralization scheme. Hence, in the following let us focus on case (b).[46] To be explicit, let us assume that

$$E(x) = f(K_1)e^{-\omega|x-y_1|} + f(k_2)e^{-\omega|x-y_2|}, \tag{6.127}$$

where the positive constant ω represents a *spatial discount rate,* which reflects the degree of localness of the SN good. Notice that

$$\lim_{\omega \to 0} E(x) = f(K_1) + f(K_2) \qquad \text{for all} \quad x,$$

which corresponds to the case of a pure city good in Section 6.3.

The residential choice behavior of each household in the city is assumed to be described by the externality model of (6.1). We further assume that the utility function of each household is given by the log-linear function of Example 6.1, that is, by

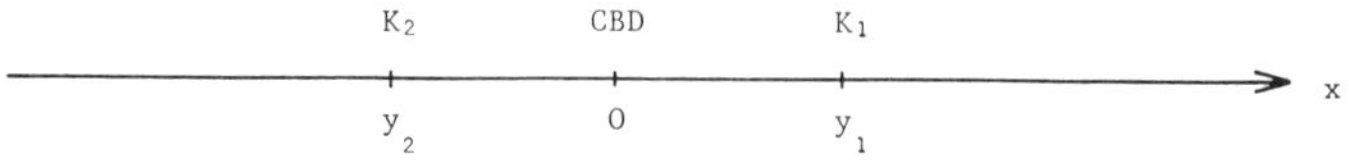

Figure 6.11. A linear city.

$$U(z, s, E(x)) = \alpha \log z + \beta \log s + \gamma \log E(x), \tag{6.128}$$

where $\alpha, \beta, \gamma > 0$ and $\alpha + \beta = 1$.

In the subsequent analysis of the optimal location of the two facilities, we confine ourselves to the cases of a symmetric situation such that[47]

$$K_1 = K_2 \equiv K/2, \tag{6.129}$$

$$y_1 = -y_2 \equiv y \geq 0. \tag{6.130}$$

Then (6.127) becomes

$$E(x) \equiv E(x; y, K) = \begin{cases} f\left(\dfrac{K}{2}\right) e^{-\omega x}\{e^{\omega y} + e^{-\omega y}\} & \text{for} \quad x \geq y, \\ f\left(\dfrac{K}{2}\right) e^{-\omega y}\{e^{\omega x} + e^{-\omega x}\} & \text{for} \quad -y < x < y, \\ f\left(\dfrac{K}{2}\right) e^{\omega x}\{e^{-\omega y} + e^{\omega y}\} & \text{for} \quad x \leq -y. \end{cases} \tag{6.131}$$

Figure 6.12 depicts the $E(x)$ curve for a given K.

It turns out that given a certain condition for the two parameters β and γ in the utility function (6.128), the optimal location of the two facilities can be determined independently of the values of all other parameters; that is, both locate at the center of the city. To show this, *in the first stage,* we arbitrarily fix u (the target utility level), N(city population), K, and y, and examine the optimal land/resource allocation (of the city) in the context of the HS model. Then *in the second stage,* we determine the optimal location y [for a given set of (u, N, K)].

To begin with the first stage, let us define the *population cost function* $C(u, N, K; y)$ as follows:

$$C(u, N, K; y) \equiv \min_{r_f, n(x), s(x)} \int_{-r_f}^{r_f} \{T(x) + Z[s(x), u, E(x; y, K)] + R_A s(x)\} n(x)\, dx,$$

$$\text{subject to} \qquad s(x) n(x) \leq 1, \qquad -r_f \leq x \leq r_f, \tag{6.132}$$

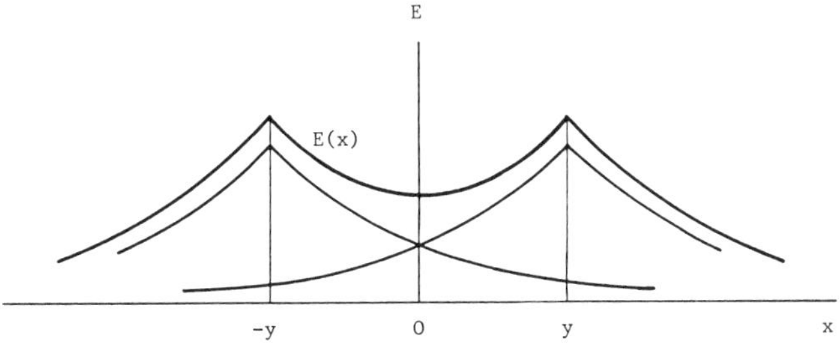

Figure 6.12. The $E(x)$ curve when $K_1 = K_2$.

$$\int_{-r_f}^{r_f} n(x)\, dx = N. \tag{6.133}$$

Then given the per capita income Y^0 of the city, the surplus function $\mathcal{S}(Y^0, u, N, K; y)$ can be defined as

$$\begin{aligned}\mathcal{S}(Y^0, u, N, K; y) &\equiv NY^0 - C(u, N, K; y)\\ &= \max_{r_f, n(x), s(x)} \int_{-r_f}^{r_f} \{Y^0 - T(x) - Z[s(x), u, E(x; y, K)]\\ &\qquad - R_A s(x)\} n(x)\, dx,\\ &\qquad \text{subject to} \quad (6.132) \text{ and } (6.133).\end{aligned}$$

The solution to the maximization problem above, called the HS(Y^0, u, N, K; y) problem, gives the optimal land/resource allocation (of the city) for each given set of (u, N, K, y).[48] Notice that at the optimal allocation, the land constraint (6.132) will be met with equality everywhere.[49] Considering this, the Lagrangian function associated with the HS problem above can be represented as

$$\begin{aligned}\mathcal{L} &\equiv \int_{-r_f}^{r_f} \{Y^0 - T(x) - Z[s(x), u, E(x; y, K)]\\ &\qquad - R_A s(x)\} \frac{1}{s(x)}\, dx - G^* \left(\int_{-r_f}^{r_f} \frac{1}{s(x)}\, dx - N \right)\\ &= \int_{-r_f}^{r_f} \left\{ \frac{Y^0 - G^* - T(x) - Z[s(x), u, E(x; y, K)]}{s(x)} - R_A \right\} dx + G^* N,\end{aligned} \tag{6.134}$$

where the multiplier G^* has, as before, the economic implication of the shadow income tax (or subsidy). The optimal r_f and $s(x)$ should be chosen so as to maximize $\mathcal{L}$. Hence, recalling the bid rent function $\psi(I, u, E)$ and bid-max lot size function $s(I, u, E)$ from Section 6.2, as with (3.59)–(3.63) [i.e., (3.71)–(3.74)], we can obtain the following optimality conditions:[50]

$$R(x) = \begin{cases} \psi(Y^0 - G^* - T(r), u, E(x)) & \text{for} \quad -r_f \le x \le r_f, \\ R_A & \text{for} \quad x \le -r_f, x \ge r_f, \end{cases} \tag{6.135}$$

$$s(x) = s(Y^0 - G^* - T(x), u, E(x)) \qquad \text{for} \quad -r_f \le x \le r_f, \tag{6.136}$$

$$n(x) = \begin{cases} 1/s(Y^0 - G^* - T(x), u, E(x)) & \text{for} \quad -r_f \le x \le r_f, \\ 0 & \text{for} \quad x < -r_f, x > r_f, \end{cases} \tag{6.137}$$

$$\int_{-r_f}^{r_f} 1/s(Y^0 - G^* - T(x), u, E(x))\, dx = N. \tag{6.138}$$

As before, we can interpret these optimality conditions as representing the conditions of the *compensated equilibrium* in which the target utility u is achieved with the aid of population tax G^* (recall the explanation in Section 3.4). In this context, $R(x)$ denotes the land rent at each x. Notice that except for $E(x)$, these optimality conditions are identical to (3.71)–(3.74).

From (6.11) and (6.12), we have

$$\psi(Y^0 - G^* - T(x), u, E(x)) = \alpha^{\alpha/\beta}\beta(Y^0 - G^* - T(x))^{1/\beta}E(x)^{\gamma/\beta}e^{-u/\beta}, \tag{6.139}$$

$$s(Y^0 - G^* - T(x), u, E(x)) = \alpha^{-\alpha/\beta}(Y^0 - G^* - T(x))^{-\alpha/\beta}E(x)^{-\gamma/\beta}e^{u/\beta}. \tag{6.140}$$

Suppose that $f(K/2) > 0$, $R_A > 0$, and $T(x) = T(|x|)$ as noted in Assumption 6.2. Then combining (6.139) and (6.140) with (6.131), we can depict the optimal spatial configuration (i.e., the compensated equilibrium) for given y as in Figure 6.13, which is symmetric with respect to 0.[51] Because of the benefits from the two public facilities, the land rent curve given by (6.135) and (6.139) may be locally peaked at y and $-y$.

Now turning to the second stage, to determine the optimal location y, let us examine the effect of a change in y on the surplus $\mathcal{S}$. Applying the envelope theorem, we have[52]

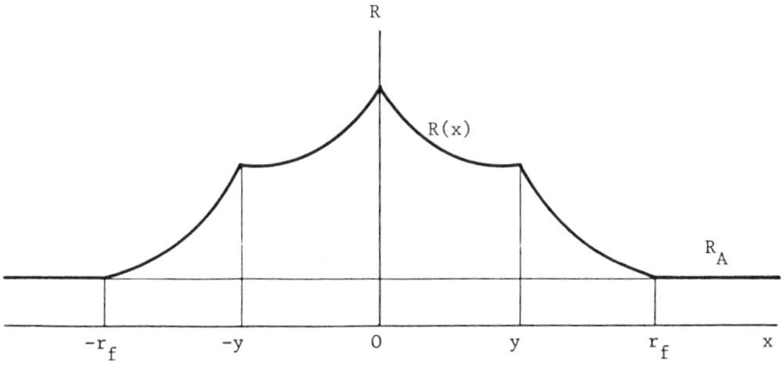

Figure 6.13. Optimal spatial configuration for a given facility location $(y, -y)$.

$$\frac{\partial \mathcal{S}}{\partial y} = \frac{\partial \mathcal{L}}{\partial y}$$
$$= \int_{-r_f}^{r_f} \frac{\partial}{\partial y}\left(\frac{Y_0 - G^* - T(x) - Z[s(x), u, E(x; y, K)]}{s(x)}\right) dx. \tag{6.141}$$

Since it holds at the optimal choice of $s(x)$ that

$$\frac{Y_0 - G^* - T(x) - Z[s(x), u, E(x; y, K)]}{s(x)}$$
$$= \psi(Y^0 - G^* - T(x), u, E(x; y, K)),$$

from (6.139) and (6.140) it follows that

$$\frac{\partial \mathcal{S}}{\partial y} = \int_{-r_f}^{r_f} \frac{\partial \psi(Y^0 - G^* - T(x), u, E(x; y, K))}{\partial y} dx \tag{6.142}$$

$$= 2\int_0^{r_f} \gamma \alpha^{\alpha/\beta}(Y^0 - G^* - T(x))^{1/\beta} E(x)^{(\gamma-\beta)/\beta} \frac{\partial E(x)}{\partial y} e^{-u/\beta}\, dx, \tag{6.143}$$

where $E(x) \equiv E(x; y, K)$, and from (6.131) we have

$$\frac{\partial E(x)}{\partial y} = \begin{cases} \omega f\left(\frac{K}{2}\right) e^{-\omega x}\{e^{\omega y} - e^{-\omega y}\} > 0 & \text{for } x > y, \\ -\omega f\left(\frac{K}{2}\right) e^{-\omega y}\{e^{\omega x} + e^{-\omega x}\} < 0 & \text{for } -y < x < y, \\ \omega f\left(\frac{K}{2}\right) e^{\omega x}\{e^{\omega y} - e^{-\omega y}\} > 0 & \text{for } x < -y. \end{cases} \tag{6.144}$$

The relation (6.142) indicates that *the benefits (in terms of $\mathcal{S}$) of a marginal change in y are entirely embodied in the change in the total (shadow) land rents.*[53] Thus, given $y > 0$, if $\partial\mathcal{S}/\partial y$ is positive (negative), both facilities must be moved outward (inward). In the following, we examine how $\partial\mathcal{S}/\partial y$ behaves for three different cases (according to relative magnitudes of β and γ) and then determine the corresponding optimal location y. Notice that $y \geq r_f$ never happens at the optimum.

Case 1: $\beta = \gamma$. When $\beta = \gamma$, we can see from (6.143) that the sign of $\partial\mathcal{S}/\partial y$ depends only on that of

$$\int_0^{r_f} (Y^0 - G^* - T(x))^{1/\beta} \frac{\partial E(x)}{\partial y}\, dx. \tag{6.145}$$

Recalling (6.144), we can see that for any $y \in (0, r_f)$,

$$\int_0^{y} (Y^0 - G^* - T(x))^{1/\beta} \frac{\partial E(x)}{\partial y}\, dx \leq (Y^0 - G^* - T(y))^{1/\beta} \int_0^{y} \frac{\partial E(x)}{\partial y}\, dx,$$

$$\int_y^{r_f} (Y^0 - G^* - T(x))^{1/\beta} \frac{\partial E(x)}{\partial y}\, dx \leq (Y^0 - G^* - T(y))^{1/\beta} \int_y^{r_f} \frac{\partial E(x)}{\partial y}\, dx,$$

so

$$\int_0^{r_f} (Y^0 - G^* - T(x))^{1/\beta} \frac{\partial E(x)}{\partial y}\, dx \leq (Y^0 - G^* - T(y))^{1/\beta} \int_0^{r_f} \frac{\partial E(x)}{\partial y}\, dx. \tag{6.146}$$

On the other hand, it follows from (6.144) that

$$\int_0^{r_f} \frac{\partial E(x)}{\partial y}\, dx = -f\left(\frac{K}{2}\right)\{e^{\omega y} - e^{-\omega y}\}e^{-\omega r_f} < 0. \tag{6.147}$$

Therefore, we can conclude from (6.145)–(6.147) that $\partial\mathcal{S}/\partial y$ is negative for all $y \in (0, r_f)$, and hence $\mathcal{S}$ is maximized when the two facilities locate at the center.

Case 2: $\beta < \gamma$. By the same argument as in Case 1, the following inequality can be seen to hold for any $y \in (0, r_f)$.

$$\int_0^{r_f} (Y^0 - G^* - T(x))^{1/\beta} E(x)^{(\gamma-\beta)/\beta} \frac{\partial E(x)}{\partial y}\, dx$$

$$\leq (Y^0 - G^* - T(y))^{1/\beta} \int_0^{r_f} E(x)^{(\gamma-\beta)/\beta} \frac{\partial E(x)}{\partial y}\, dx.$$

Hence, by showing that

$$\int_0^{r_f} E(x)^{(\gamma-\beta)/\beta} \frac{\partial E(x)}{\partial y}\, dx < 0, \tag{6.148}$$

we can obtain the same conclusion that $\mathcal{S}$ is maximized when the two facilities locate at the center.[54]

Case 3: $\beta > \gamma$. In this case, the problem is more subtle and requires more complex analyses. It can be shown that if γ is not too small compared with β, then the $\mathcal{S}$ is still maximized when the two facilities locate at the center. Therefore, the optimal sites of the two facilities are not at the center only when the ratio γ/β is sufficiently small compared with the spatial discount rate ω (i.e., ω is sufficiently large compared with γ/β).[55]

To summarize the three cases, we can conclude that *if the SN good is relatively more important than land (i.e., the ratio γ/β is sufficiently large), it is optimal to locate both facilities at the center of the city;* this is because it is more efficient to sacrifice the consumption of land by households and to provide the *SN* good at the city center so that more households can enjoy a higher service level of the *SN* good. If the opposite is true, the *SN* good is provided at two noncentral sites, and the distribution of households is more dispersed so that they can consume more land.

These results suggest that it is very difficult to achieve the efficient provision of an *SN* good by a decentralized mechanism. To see this, let us assume that the optimal sites of the two facilities are at the city center. Let us further suppose, for example, that the city is divided into two jurisdictions, the right of the center and the left of the center. Then if each local government independently chooses the optimal site of one facility (for provision of the *SN* good under study) within its own jurisdiction, the two facilities will never be located at the city center. This is because if a local government locates its facility at the city center (i.e., at the fringe of its jurisdiction), only half of the potential benefits from the facility can be received by residents of that jurisdiction. Hence, without introducing an appropriate coordination scheme, the optimal location of the two facilities will never be realized by the two local governments. On the other hand, if the city is divided into three jurisdictions – the center, the right, and the left – and if both facilities are to be provided by the local government of the central jurisdiction, then the optimal location (i.e., central location) of the two facilities may be realized. However, in this situation, the residents of the central jurisdictions receive only a part of the total benefits from the two facilities, while the two fringe jurisdictions enjoy spillover-like benefits from them. Therefore, even if the location of the two facilities were optimal, without an appropriate cost-sharing scheme among the three jurisdictions, the *size* of the two facilities would be smaller than the (citywide) optimum.[56] This suggests that the efficient provision of *SN* goods (with spillover-like benefits) requires either citywide planning by the city government or an appropriate coordination scheme among local jurisdictions.[57]

6.7 Summary and extensions

In this chapter, we have examined through simple examples the basic principles of the efficient provision of local public goods. It has been shown, in particular, that in the case of city goods or neighborhood goods, competition among surplus-maximizing developers (or local governments) will lead to an efficient provision of these goods. However, this encouraging result has been derived under a set of strong assumptions; hence, it is important to recognize the limitations of such a result. Let us briefly examine how the relaxation of each assumption will affect this result (for a thorough discussion of the following problems, see the articles referred to in the bibliographical notes below). First, the assumption that the aggregate production function of each city has constant returns to scale can be relaxed without affecting the result. For example, in the context of Section 6.4 (congestible city goods), let us now assume that the aggregate production function $F(N)$ of each city has increasing returns to scale (at least for small N). Then the surplus function Π in equation (6.81) now becomes

$$\Pi = \pi(W - G, u) + \text{TDR}(W - G, u, K) + N(W - G, u, K)G - K,$$

where W is the wage rate and π represents the production profit given by

$$\pi(W - G, u) \equiv F(N(W - G, u, K)) - N(W - G, u, K)W.$$

Recalling the analyses of Section 5.7, it is not difficult to show that if each city developer chooses the wage rate W, population tax rate G, and capacity K of the city good so as to maximize the net surplus Π (which is the sum of the production profit, total differential rent, and congestion tax revenue minus the city-good cost), then competition among such developers (combined with the free migration of households) will result in an optimal city system; and in each city, the following generalized version of the Henry George theorem holds:

$$\pi + \text{TDR} + NG = K.$$

In contrast, the assumption of homogeneous households is more fundamental. Suppose now that the national economy consists of many different types of household. As long as the number of household types is relatively small compared with the total number of cities in the nation (i.e., the households of each type spread themselves among many cities), then the competition among surplus-maximizing developers (or local governments) will still result in an efficient city system. However, if the number of household types is so large that the households of each type reside in only a few cities, then efficient city systems are difficult to achieve through a decentralized mechanism. This is because if the households of the same type reside in only a few cities, the developer of these cities will recognize that their policies will affect the common utility level of that household type; thus, each developer will no longer behave as a *utility taker*. Similarly, when the number of (potential) cities is relatively small compared with the total population of the nation, city developers will not behave as utility takers; thus, competition among such developers may not result in an efficient city system.

Next, recall that efficient allocations of local public goods require that each developer or local government behave as a *surplus maximizer*. However, when cities are managed by city governments, they may not behave as surplus maximizers. They may have different objectives such as the maximization of the population of their cities or winning the next mayoral election. Finally, it has been shown in Section 6.6 that spillover effects of local public goods among jurisdictions will create difficulties in the efficient provision of these goods. In the face of these limitations of our theory, in the real world we can say at best that competition among developers or local governments may significantly contribute to the efficient provision of local public goods. If we notice, however, that there is no perfect alternative mechanism, the ingenious idea of Tiebout is worth serious consideration.

Bibliographical notes

In developing this chapter, the author owes much to Arnott (1979), Kanemoto (1980, Ch. 3), Berglas and Pines (1981), Hochman (1982a,b), and Koide (1985, Ch. 4). This chapter has by no means been intended to provide a comprehensive theory of local public goods (for a review of recent literature on local public goods, see, e.g., Zodrow 1983, Cornes and Sandler 1986, and Wildasin 1986b). Rather, the emphasis of this chapter has been on the spatial dimension of problems in the efficient provision of local public goods. For further studies from this point of view, see Schuler (1974, 1976), Helpman, Pines, and Borukhov (1976), Fisch (1976), Helpman and Pines (1980), Brueckner (1979, 1981), Yang and Fujita (1983), Fujita (1986b), and Sakashita (1987a,b). Finally, Scotchmer (1986) studied equilibrium provision of local public goods by a finite number of jurisdictions.

Notes

1. Public goods are categorized in this way for the purpose of the theoretical development of this chapter. In practice, of course, there are many in-between public goods. For example, there is the category of *supercity goods* (e.g., interstate highways). However, the role of such goods in the national economy is theoretically the same as that of superneighborhood goods in a city economy.
2. In this chapter, a neighborhood is taken to be the smallest spatial unit of efficient residential development. In practice, we may consider a neighborhood to represent a few city blocks.
3. In the standard terminology of the literature, these local public goods belong to the category of *impure public goods*. Recall that a *pure public good* (or Samuelsonian public good) is collectively consumed by all members of the society (which is implicitly assumed to be a nation). Its consumption is *nonrivalry* in the sense that "each individual's consumption of such a good leads to no subtraction from any other individual's consumption of that good" (Samuelson 1954). Its benefits are also *nonexcludable* in the sense that once the good is provided it is virtually impossible to exclude any individual from the benefits. Therefore, once provided, a pure public good is consumed by every individual in the same amount, and it is free of congestion. In this chapter, we consider both noncongestible (i.e., pure) local public goods and congestible local public goods.
4. For a discussion of free-rider problems, see, e.g., Cornes and Sandler (1986).
5. For a discussion of the problem in more general contexts, see the summary in Section 6.7.
6. Note that in the equilibrium or optimal allocation, the distribution of environmental amenities may not be symmetric with respect to the CBD. Thus, instead of using r (the distance from the CBD), we use a general location index x, where the origin of the location coordinate coincides with the CBD.
7. As usual, whenever differential calculi are involved, we are also implicitly

assuming that the utility function is continuously differentiable in each component as many times as desired.

8. Here the notation is not very precise: $T(x)$ is a function of *location* x, whereas $T(|x|)$ is a function of *distance* $|x|$. Hence, it would be preferable to use different functional notation. In practice, however, this will cause no confusion in the following discussions.
9. As before, when there is no solution to the maximization problem of (6.6), we define $\psi(I, u, E) = 0$ and $s(I, u, E) = \infty$. The same applies to the maximization problem of (6.7).
10. Recall that $\partial\tilde{s}/\partial R$ is always negative, and $\partial\hat{s}/\partial R$ is negative from Assumption 6.3.
11. In order to examine the properties of the Alonso functions Ψ and S with respect to parameter x, we must specify the characteristics of functions $E(x)$, $G(x)$, and $T(x)$, which will be done later in each specific context.
12. According to Figure 6.3, we have $s(I, u, E_1) > s(I, u, E_2)$. This result, however, does not always hold true without some additional assumptions. From identities (6.15) and (6.18),

$$\frac{\partial s}{\partial E} = \frac{\partial \hat{s}}{\partial R}\frac{\partial \psi}{\partial E} + \frac{\partial \hat{s}}{\partial E} = \frac{\partial \tilde{s}}{\partial R}\frac{\partial \psi}{\partial E} + \frac{\partial \tilde{s}}{\partial E}.$$

Since we know that $\partial\psi/\partial E$ is positive from (6.24), a sufficient condition for negative $\partial s/\partial E$ is to assume that $\partial\hat{s}/\partial R < 0$ (i.e., land is a non-Giffen good) and $\partial\hat{s}/\partial E \leq 0$. Alternatively, since $\partial\tilde{s}/\partial R$ is always negative, $\partial s/\partial E$ is negative if we assume that $\partial\tilde{s}/\partial E \leq 0$. Neither is, however, the necessary condition. Therefore, we directly introduce Assumption 6.4.
13. We may consider K to represent a vector of costs for various city goods. In the present context of one-class households, this does not generate any essentially new result, and hence we keep the model simple.
14. For the case of a more general production function, see Section 6.7.
15. In the case of a developer, this behavior of net profit maximization is natural. When the city is managed by the city government, the city-good cost K is assumed to be paid by confiscating a part of TDR; hence, the net differential rent to be distributed among absentee landlords equals TDR $- K = \mathcal{G}(\delta, u, N(\delta, u, K), K) - K$ [from (6.33)]. Therefore, we can consider that the net-surplus-maximizing behavior of the city government is the result of political pressure from absentee landlords. Or we may simply assume that the maximization of the net surplus is a constitutional mandate imposed on each city government.
16. Let $\tilde{K}(u)$ ($\equiv \tilde{K}(\delta, u)$) be the solution to $\tilde{u}(\delta, K) = u$ for K. Then from Assumption 6.1, $\tilde{K}(u) > 0$ for all $u > -\infty$. Since $\tilde{u}(\delta, K)$ is increasing in K, $\tilde{K}(u)$ is increasing in u, and $N(\delta, u, K) = 0$ for all $K \leq \tilde{K}(u)$. Hence, $\mathcal{G}(\delta, u, N(\delta, u, K), K) = 0$ for all $K \leq \tilde{K}(u)$, as depicted in Figure 6.4. Since $d\mathcal{G}/dK = (\partial\mathcal{G}/\partial N)(\partial N/\partial K) + \partial\mathcal{G}/\partial K = 0 + \partial\mathcal{G}/\partial K$ at $N = N(\delta, u, K)$, $d\mathcal{G}(\delta, u, N(\delta, u, K), K)/dK = -\partial C(u, N, K)/\partial K$ at $N = N(\delta, u, K)$.

From (6.2) and (6.25), $\partial C/\partial K < 0$ and hence $d\mathcal{S}/dK > 0$. Therefore, the $\mathcal{S}$ ($\equiv$ TDR) curve is increasing in K.

17. If the $\mathcal{S}$ curve is S-shaped as in Figure 6.4, the optimal level $K(u)$ uniquely exists [note that since $d\mathcal{S}/dK = 0$ at $K = \tilde{K}(u)$, the $\mathcal{S}$ curve cannot be globally concave]. However, this may not always be the case. If we assume that $\partial Z(s, u, E(K))/\partial K = 0$ for all $K > \bar{K}(u)$, where $\bar{K}(u)$ is a some positive function of u, then the existence of an optimal K is assured. In the following discussion, we simply assume the unique existence of optimal $K(u)$.
18. By definition, TDR $= \int_0^{r_f}\{\max_s[(\delta - T(r) - Z(s, u, E(K)))/s] - R_A\}L(r)\,dr$, where $r_f \equiv r_f(\delta, u, K)$. Using the envelope theorem, take the derivative of this TDR with respect to K, and recall definition (6.6) and (6.36). Then we can obtain the left-hand side of (6.39).
19. Note that this gives a *local* decision rule that may apply only near the optimal point.
20. Note 23 of Chapter 5 applies here.
21. Since $\mathcal{S}$ is maximized at $N(\delta, u, K)$, $d\mathcal{S}(\delta, u, N(\delta, u, K), K)/du = \partial\mathcal{S}/\partial u + (\partial\mathcal{S}/\partial N)(\partial N/\partial u) = \partial\mathcal{S}/\partial u = -\partial C/\partial u < 0$.
22. In the present context of competition among profit-maximizing developers, this assumption of formation of new cities under a positive-profit environment is quite natural. This assumption may be less convincing in the case of surplus-maximizing city governments. Without this assumption, however, the equilibrium city system cannot be uniquely determined.
23. For simplicity of discussion, we assume that the optimal $K(u^*)$ is unique. The existence of equilibrium utility level u^* (which is unique whenever it exists) can be assured if we introduce a reasonable condition [in addition to Assumptions 6.1–6.4 and condition (6.25)]. Note that given any $K > 0$, the value of $\mathcal{S}(\delta, u, N(\delta, u, K), K)$ continuously increases from 0 to ∞ as u decreases from $\tilde{u}(\delta, K)$ to $-\infty$. Therefore, if we assume, as in note 17, that $\partial Z(s, u, E(K))/\partial K = 0$ for all $K \geq \bar{K}(u)$ (where $\bar{K}$ is some positive function of u), there exists the equilibrium utility level u^* under which the surplus curve $\mathcal{S}(\delta, u^*, N(\delta, u^*, K), K)$ is tangent to the K line from below.
24. We assume as usual that the total population M is so large that the number determined by (6.42) can be safely treated as a continuous number.
25. Again, in problem (6.46) it is essential to restrict N to be strictly positive. Otherwise, if we choose $N = 0$, problem (6.46) gives the solution $u = \infty$; but if $N = 0$, it is no longer a community.
26. To be exact, in problem (6.49) we must add a restriction on K such that $K \geq \tilde{K}(u)$, where function $\tilde{K}(u)$ is defined in note 16. Otherwise, if we set K equal to 0 and hence $N(\delta, u, K) = 0$, u can become infinitely large.
27. In the equilibrium of competition among developers (which is examined later), the surplus-maximizing population of each city must be positive. Hence, in the following, we are concerned only with the case in which $\hat{N}(u, K)$ is positive. Furthermore, for simplicity of discussion, we assume that the surplus-maximizing population $\hat{N}(u, K)$ is always unique.
28. Again, in the equilibrium of competition among developers, the profit-maximizing K must be positive because of assumption (6.53). Therefore, in

the following, we are concerned only with the case in which $K(u)$ is positive. Furthermore, again for simplicity of discussion, we assume that the optimal $K(u)$ exists uniquely under each u.

29. First, we differentiate both sides of (6.70) by N. Next, using the envelope theorem and the boundary rent condition, we can show that

$$\partial \mathrm{TDR}/\partial N = (\partial Y(u, N, K)/\partial N)N - \int_0^{r_f} \frac{\partial Z}{\partial E}\frac{\partial E}{\partial N}\, n(r)\, dr$$

and

$$\frac{\partial C}{\partial E}\frac{\partial E}{\partial N} = \int_0^{r_f} \frac{\partial Z}{\partial E}\frac{\partial E}{\partial N}\, n(r)\, dr.$$

Then (6.71) follows immediately.

30. Applying the envelope theorem to (6.57), we see that condition (6.60) means that $-\partial C/\partial E \cdot \partial E/\partial K = 1$. From this relation and (6.74), we have the first equality of (6.75). And since $dE = \partial E/\partial K \cdot dK + \partial E/\partial N \cdot dN$, setting dE equal to 0 [i.e., $E(K, N) = \text{const}$], we have the second equality of (6.75).
31. A similar specification was introduced by Arnott (1979) and Hochman (1982a).
32. This can be confirmed as in note 21.
33. Mathematically, we can determine u^* uniquely by solving the next equation for u: $\mathcal{S}(\delta, u, \hat{N}(u, K(u)), E[K(u), \hat{N}(u, K(u))]) = K(u)$, where $K(u)$ is the optimal K for (6.59) under each u.
34. The same relation as (6.84) was obtained by Arnott (1979).
35. Since the surplus curve shifts downward as u increases, if the curve $\mathcal{S}(\delta, \hat{u}, N, E(\hat{K}, N))$ passes the region above the $\hat{K}$ line, then $\hat{u}$ is not the highest utility achievable for the community. If the curve lies entirely below the $\hat{K}$ line, then $\hat{u}$ is not feasible within the budget constraint.
36. Hochman (1982a) calls neighborhood goods *dispersed local public goods,* whereas Kanemoto (1980) calls them *extremely local public goods,* and Yang (1980) refers to them as *spatially continuous local public goods.*
37. Although we consider only one neighborhood good for notational simplicity, the main results of this section are valid for any number of goods.
38. Since $L(r) > 0$ at each r, the density constraint (6.99) is equivalent to $(1/s(r) - \rho(r))L(r) = 0$. In the definition of the Lagrangian function (6.101), we used this new form of density constraint for convenience.
39. Let us define $\mathfrak{S}(s, k, \rho; r, g, \tau(r)) \equiv \{Y^0 - g - \tau(r) - T(r) - Z(s, u, E(k, \rho))\}/s + \tau(r)\rho - k - R_A$. The optimal allocation $(s(r), k(r), \rho(r); r \leq r_f)$ must be chosen so as to maximize the Lagrangian function $\mathcal{L}$. This implies that at each $r \leq r_f$, $(s(r), k(r), \rho(r))$ must maximize $\mathfrak{S}$. From the maximization of $\mathfrak{S}$ with respect to s, we have (6.105). In addition, $(k(r), \rho(r))$ must be the solution to the next maximization problem:

$$\max_{k,\rho} \mathfrak{S}(s(r), k, \rho; r, g, \tau(r)). \qquad (*)$$

Conditions (6.107) and (6.108) are the first-order conditions for this problem. Equations (6.102) and (6.104) give the definition of $R(r)$ at each r. The equality of (6.102) and (6.103) at r_f follows from the optimal choice of r_f so as to maximize $\mathcal{L}$. The rest of the conditions represent obvious physical relationships. Note that if we replace the first-order conditions (6.107) and (6.108) with the original decision rule (*) above, then (6.102)–(6.110) represent the necessary and sufficient conditions for the HS problem. We can show that under Assumptions 6.1–6.4 and (6.90) and (6.91), there exists a unique solution to each HS problem.

40. When the first-order conditions (6.107) and (6.108) are not sufficient, we must replace them with the original decision rule (*) in note 39.
41. This can be shown in a similar way to Proposition 3.9. That is, suppose $u^*(g)$ is the equilibrium utility level at the competitive equilibrium under tax level g. Then we can easily see that the competitive equilibrium is the solution to the *HS* model with target utility level $u^*(g)$, and hence it is efficient.
42. In practice, this means that a few city blocks will be formed by each developer. Each developer should be sufficiently small so that he or she will take the common utility level of the households in the city as given. That is, all developers in the city are assumed to be *utility takers*.
43. From (6.6), $\psi(Y^0 - g - \tau - T(r), u, E[k, \rho(r)]) = \max_s (Y^0 - g - \tau - T(r) - Z(s, u, E[k, \rho(r)]))/s$. Substituting this into (6.120) and applying the envelope theorem, we can readily obtain (6.107) and (6.108).
44. Relation (6.122) can be obtained by applying the envelope theorem to (6.120), and using the equilibrium condition, $\pi(r) = 0$ for all $r \leq r_f$. Residential land rent $R(r)$ may not always be decreasing in r. For more detailed characteristics of the land use pattern under specific conditions, see Helpman, Pines, and Borukhov (1976).
45. The same relation as (6.123) was obtained by Hochman (1982a).
46. For the study of case (a), see Hochman (1982a), Sakashita (1987a,b), and Kuroda (1988). The discussion of case (b) is based on Koide (1985, 1988).
47. It is conjectured that if $K_1 = K_2$, the optimal location of the two facilities will always be symmetric with respect to the CBD. This conjecture, however, has not yet been proved.
48. Notice again that the solution to this maximization problem is independent of Y^0.
49. Actually, given arbitrary y, this may not always be true. However, it can readily be seen that if some agricultural land is left (at the optimal allocation) within the city fringes, then $(y, -y)$ is not the optimal location of the two facilities. Therefore, for the purpose of determining the optimal location, we can safely assume as above.
50. Again, we can show that the following conditions are necessary and sufficient for the optimal.
51. Notice that in equations (6.135)–(6.138), two real unknowns are G^* and r_f. Suppose we have Assumptions 6.1–6.4. Then by using the boundary rent curve approach similar to that in Section 3.4, we can readily show that for

each set of (u, y, K, N), the values of G^* and r_f are uniquely determined; hence, there exists a unique solution to the $\text{HS}(Y^0, u, N, K; y)$ problem.

52. The envelope theorem $\partial\mathcal{S}/\partial y = \partial\mathcal{L}/\partial y$ can be obtained in the same manner as the transversality condition, (*h*), of Theorem 1 of Van Long and Vousden (1977).
53. Since

$$\int_{-r_f}^{r_f} \frac{\partial \psi}{\partial y}\, dx = \frac{\partial}{\partial y} \int_{-r_f}^{r_f} (\psi - R_A)\, dx = \frac{\partial \text{TDR}}{\partial y},$$

we can restate the above result as follows: *The benefits of a marginal change in y are entirely embodied in the change in the total differential land rent.* This result, of course, holds true only when the change in y is *marginal.*

54. For the proof of inequality (6.148), see Koide (1988).
55. This conclusion can be obtained by analyses similar to those in Koide (1985, Ch. 4). As a special case, suppose that (a) $T(x) = 0$ for all x, (b) $R_A = 0$, and (c) r_f is exogenously fixed ($r_f < \infty$). Then we can show that if $\gamma/\beta \geq (1 - e^{-(\gamma/\beta)\omega r_f})$, then $\mathcal{S}$ is maximized at $y = 0$; otherwise, $\mathcal{S}$ is maximized at some $y > 0$.
56. Suppose that the aggregate production function of the city is given by (5.33). Then considering the symmetric case of $K_1 = K_2 = K/2$, the optimal size $\hat{K}$ can be determined as follows: Setting $Y^0 = \delta$, let us define

$$\mathcal{S}(\delta, u, N, K) \equiv \max_y \mathcal{S}(\delta, u, N, K, y).$$

Then using this surplus function $\mathcal{S}(\delta, u, N, K)$, we can determine the optimal city population $\hat{N}$ and facility size $\hat{K}$ by solving the community's problem (6.46). Hence, as explained in Section 6.3, at the optimal choice of $(\hat{N}, \hat{K})$, the Henry George theorem, (6.44), holds.

57. This topic of efficient provision of local public goods with spillover effects has been largely unexplored. It is hoped that some progress on this topic will be reported in our planned second book.

CHAPTER 7

Neighborhood externalities and traffic congestion

7.1 Introduction

A city is a place where a large number of people reside in close quarters. This concentration of people causes various kinds of *technological externalities.*[1] There are both positive (beneficial) and negative (harmful) externalities. For example, externalities from local public goods, which were discussed in the preceding chapter, represent the most important types of positive externalities. In this chapter, we focus on the negative externalities that arise as the consequences of interactions among households themselves.[2] In particular, we consider three different types of such externalities: crowding externalities, racial (or ethnic) externalities, and traffic congestion associated with commuting.

As the *density of households* in a neighborhood increases, the environmental quality tends to diminish partly because of an increase in noise, littering, crimes, and so on and partly because of a decrease in the open space and green areas in a neighborhood. Such negative consequences of household concentrations, called *crowding externalities,* may occur even if the residents of a city consist of relatively homogeneous households. On the other hand, in a city with more than one racial or ethnic group, if some groups have *prejudices* against other groups, the prejudiced groups feel that they suffer from the presence of these other groups in their neighborhoods. For example, some whites may have a prejudice against living near blacks. We call such externalities caused by prejudices among different groups *racial externalities.* Both crowding externalities and racial externalities arise because of the closeness of residences; hence, together we call them *neighborhood externalities.* In contrast, *traffic congestion* represents an entirely different type of externality. Each car on a highway adds to the congestion and hence increases travel time for all others. Probably, traffic congestion represents the most important type of negative externality in cities.

These externalities are a possible cause of market failures. For example, in the presence of traffic congestion on highways, if drivers are not required to compensate others for their contribution to congestion, the commuting cost of each household does not include such externality costs. Thus, since residential land rents reflect commuting cost differentials, they are also distorted; hence, competitive equilibria of residential land markets will not be socially efficient.

Therefore, in the presence of these externalities, we must examine not only the characteristics of land markets in the absence of public interventions, but also possible policy measures that would enhance the efficiency of such land markets. In the following section, we consider each of the three types of externalities separately and investigate the "first-best" policies that would restore the efficiency of land markets. It must be noted, however, that such first-best policies may turn out to be impractical for various reasons such as high administrative costs, informational limitations, and political or moral constraints. Therefore, we also consider various "second-best" policies, which would be the best under a given set of practical constraints. In Section 7.2, we consider crowding externalities. In Section 7.3, we examine the impact of racial externalities. Finally, in Section 7.4, we study land allocations between housing and transportation in the presence of traffic congestion.

7.2 Crowding externalities and density zoning

Households generally prefer a low-density residential area to a high-density one (other factors being equal). This is partly because a household enjoys the "green" not only on its own lot, but also in the neighborhood; and areas of lower density provide more green. In addition, a high-density area is generally noisier, less clean, and less safe than a low-density area. Considering this preference for low densities, let us assume that at each distance r (from the CBD), the environmental quality level $E(r)$ is a decreasing function of the household density $\rho(r)$ there,

$$E(r) \equiv E[\rho(r)], \tag{7.1}$$

where

$$dE(\rho)/d\rho < 0. \tag{7.2}$$

Then, substituting r for x and $E[\rho(r)]$ for $E(x)$ in (6.1), we now obtain the *crowding model* of residential choice expressed as

$$\max_{r,z,s} U(z, s, E[\rho(r)]), \qquad \text{subject to} \quad z + R(r)s = Y^0 - G(r) - T(r). \tag{7.3}$$

Notice that each household chooses a residential location assuming the density $\rho(r)$ at r to be a given constant. Actually, however, the choice of a residential location, or a neighborhood, by a household causes the density in that neighborhood to increases marginally; hence, every other household in that neighborhood suffers a negative externality due to the presence of that household. Since the locational choice of each household does not take into account this negative externality to others, the resultant competitive equilibria of residential land markets would not be efficient.

7.2.1 Optimal allocation

In order to examine corrective measures for restoring the efficiency of such land markets, as usual let us first consider the *optimal residential allocation* in the framework of the Herbert–Stevens model. Fortunately, however, this task can be achieved without any new analysis. This is because the present crowding model can be considered, mathematically, to be a special case of the neighborhood-good model studied in Section 6.5. Namely, if we omit variable $k(r)$ in (6.89), we then obtain (7.1).[3] Therefore, *if we omit variable k(r) everywhere in Section 6.5, all the results there become applicable to the present problem.*

Specifically, assuming that there exist N homogeneous households in the city, we can rewrite the HS problem (6.98)–(6.100) as follows:

$$\max_{r_f, s(r), \rho(r)} \int_0^{r_f} \left(\frac{Y^0 - T(r) - Z(s(r), u, E[\rho(r)])}{s(r)} - R_A \right) L(r)\, dr, \tag{7.4}$$

$$\text{subject to} \qquad \rho(r) = 1/s(r),\ r \leq r_f: \quad \textit{density constraint,} \tag{7.5}$$

$$\int_0^{r_f} \frac{L(r)}{s(r)}\, dr = N: \quad \textit{population constraint.} \tag{7.6}$$

Namely, the problem is to choose the lot size $s(r)$ and household density $\rho(r)$ at each r and the urban fringe distance r_f so as to maximize the surplus while achieving the target utility u for all N households. The optimality conditions for this problem can be obtained from (6.102)–(6.110) [by omitting the variable $k(r)$] as follows:

$$R(r) = \begin{cases} \psi(Y^0 - g - \tau(r) - T(r), u, E[\rho(r)]) & \text{for } r \leq r_f \quad (7.7) \\ R_A - \tau(r)\rho(r) & \text{at } r = r_f: \quad \textit{boundary condition} \quad (7.8) \\ R_A & \text{for } r > r_f, \quad (7.9) \end{cases}$$

$$s(r) = s(Y^0 - g - \tau(r) - T(r), u, E[\rho(r)]) \qquad \text{for } r \leq r_f, \tag{7.10}$$

$$\rho(r) = 1/s(r) \qquad \text{for} \quad r \leq r_{\mathrm{f}}, \tag{7.11}$$

$$\tau(r) = \rho(r)\frac{\partial Z}{\partial E}\frac{\partial E}{\partial \rho} \qquad \text{for} \quad r \leq r_{\mathrm{f}}: \qquad \textit{congestion tax rule}, \tag{7.12}$$

$$n(r) = \begin{cases} L(r)/s(Y^0 - g - \tau(r) - T(r), u, E[\rho(r)]) & \text{for} \quad r \leq r_{\mathrm{f}}, \\ 0 \quad \text{for} \quad r > r_{\mathrm{f}}, \end{cases} \tag{7.13}$$

$$\int_0^{r_{\mathrm{f}}} n(r)\, dr = N. \tag{7.14}$$

Here, g, $\tau(r)$, and $R(r)$ represent, respectively, the shadow population tax, the shadow congestion tax, and the shadow land rent at each r. As usual, we can interpret these optimality conditions as representing the conditions of the compensated equilibrium in which the target utility u is achieved with the aid of population tax and congestion tax policies [for details, recall the discussion after equation (6.110)].

In the system of equations (7.7)–(7.14), if we consider that u is a fixed constant and g a variable, they represent the conditions of the *compensated equilibrium* under the target utility u. However, in the same equations, if we consider that g is a fixed constant and u a variable, they now represent the conditions of the *competitive equilibrium* under the population tax rate g. In either context, if the city government chooses the congestion tax $\tau(r)$ at each r according to the rule (7.12), the resultant equilibrium allocation becomes efficient. Notice, however, that the direct implementation of the congestion tax rule (7.12) requires the unobservable information $\partial Z/\partial E$ and $\partial E/\partial \rho$ on the part of the city government. Therefore, applying the results from Section 6.5.2, let us consider the following decentralized scheme for achieving this efficient allocation. As before, suppose that each unit of land in the city is to be developed by a developer. Unlike before, however, the only active role of each developer is to collect congestion taxes from households. That is, a developer at distance r rents a unit of raw land (i.e., agricultural land) from a landowner there at the market *raw-land rent* $R_0(r)$. The developer then rents the same land to households at the market *residential land rent* $R(r)$, while he or she is empowered to collect any congestion tax $\tau(r)$ from each household there. Then the profit of the developer (per unit of land) at r is given by

$$\begin{aligned} \pi(r) &= \text{differential rent} + \text{congestion taxes} \\ &= (R(r) - R_0(r)) + \tau(r)\rho(r). \end{aligned} \tag{7.15}$$

Since the raw-land rent $R_0(r)$ at each r is competitively determined by all developers, the value of $R_0(r)$ in equation (7.15) is beyond the control of the developer. The developer, however, can influence the values of $R(r)$ and $\rho(r)$ in equation (7.15) by appropriately choosing $\tau(r)$. Hence, the *developer's problem* at r is to choose τ so as to maximize the profit $\pi(r)$:[4]

$$\max_{\tau} \pi(r) = R(r) - R_0(r) + \tau\rho(r). \tag{7.16}$$

We can show, as before, that the first-order condition for this maximization problem is identical to the congestion tax rule, (7.12). Therefore, we can conclude that *given any population tax rate g, if each developer chooses the congestion tax rate τ(r) so as to maximize the sum of the differential land rent and congestion tax revenue, then an efficient residential allocation will be achieved in equilibrium.* Furthermore, if one appropriately changes g, all efficient allocations can be obtained.

At the equilibrium under any choice of g, each developer earns a zero profit. Hence, it holds from (7.15) that

$$R(r) = R_0(r) - \tau(r)\rho(r), \qquad r \leq r_f. \tag{7.17}$$

Namely, *at each r within the urban fringe, the residential land rent equals the raw-land rent minus the congestion tax revenue.* This implies that now, in Figure 6.10, the curve $R(r)$ should be located below the curve $R_0(r)$. This is because developers earn congestion taxes without any cost. We can also confirm that relation (6.125) still holds in any equilibrium.

7.2.2 Density zoning as a second-best policy

We have just seen that in the presence of crowding externalities, if the developer of each neighborhood were empowered to collect congestion taxes from its residents, an efficient residential allocation would be achieved in equilibrium. In practice, however, we seldom observe such a congestion tax policy. This is presumably because the developer's role as a pure-tax collector would be unpopular; or if the developers were once endowed with such power, they might abuse it. In this subsection, as an alternative policy we consider *density zoning* for remedying crowding externalities. Namely, we introduce a zoning regulation that sets a *minimum lot size* per household in residential land uses and examine the impact of such regulation.

To make the discussion concrete, let us assume that

$$\begin{aligned} E[\rho(r)] &= 1/\rho(r) \\ &\equiv s(r). \end{aligned} \tag{7.18}$$

Namely, the environmental quality at each location is measured by the reciprocal of household density, or the *average lot size*, in the neighborhood.[5] Furthermore, let us assume that the utility function of each household is given by the log-linear function of Example 6.1. Then substituting (7.18) into (6.10), the utility function of each household at r is given by

$$U(z, s, s(r)) = \alpha \log z + \beta \log s + \gamma \log s(r), \tag{7.19}$$

where $\alpha + \beta = 1$. For simplicity, we also assume that

$$T(r) = ar \qquad \text{and} \qquad L(r) = \theta \qquad \text{for all} \quad r \geq 0, \tag{7.20}$$

$$R_A = 0. \tag{7.21}$$

The assumption of $L(r) = \theta$ (i.e., a linear city) is useful because it enables us to obtain explicit solutions readily in the subsequent analyses.

Notice that in the utility function (7.19), the individual lot size s and the average lot size $s(r)$ in the neighborhood are substitutes. Moreover, since $s(r)$ is a free good, a household tends to substitute $s(r)$ for s. Since all households at r do the same, the equilibrium lot size [which equals $s(r)$] tends to be smaller than the socially optimal one. It turns out that the impact of a minimum lot size regulation depends critically on the nature of landownership. To compare systematically the results from the two models, the absentee ownership model and the public ownership model, first we treat household income Y parametrically and obtain the equilibrium land use for each Y; then we set Y equal to Y_0 for the absentee ownership model, and $Y = Y_0 + \text{TDR}/N$ for the public ownership model, where Y_0 represents the nonland income per household (which is a given constant).[6] Before studying the impact of regulations, however, it is helpful to examine the equilibrium land use patterns without any regulation.

With no regulation. Suppose that each household can freely choose its lot size s. Then given a per capita income Y, the residential choice behavior of each household can be described as

$$\max_{r,z,s} \alpha \log z + \beta \log s + \gamma \log s(r), \qquad \text{subject to} \quad z + R(r)s = Y - ar. \tag{7.22}$$

Setting I equal to $Y - ar$ and E equal to $s(r)$ in (6.11) and (6.12), we obtain the associated bid rent function and bid-max lot size function as

$$\psi(Y - ar, u, s(r)) = \alpha^{\alpha/\beta}\beta(Y - ar)^{1/\beta}s(r)^{\gamma/\beta}e^{-u/\beta}, \tag{7.23}$$

$$s(Y - ar, u, s(r)) = \alpha^{-\alpha/\beta}(Y - ar)^{-\alpha/\beta}s(r)^{-\gamma/\beta}e^{u/\beta}. \tag{7.24}$$

Notice that in equilibrium all households at the same distance r consume the same amount of land, and hence it holds that $s(Y - ar, u, s(r)) = s(r)$, or

$$s(r) = \alpha^{-\alpha/\beta}(Y - ar)^{-\alpha/\beta}s(r)^{-\gamma/\beta}e^{u/\beta}. \tag{7.25}$$

If we let $s^*(Y - ar, u)$ be the solution to equation (7.25) for $s(r)$, we then have

$$s^*(Y - ar, u) = \alpha^{-\alpha/(\beta+\gamma)}(Y - ar)^{-\alpha/(\beta+\gamma)}e^{u/(\beta+\gamma)}, \tag{7.26}$$

which is called the *equilibrium lot size function*. Setting $s(r)$ equal to $s^*(Y - ar, u)$ in (7.23), we obtain the associated *equilibrium bid rent function* as

$$\psi^*(Y - ar, u) = \alpha^{\alpha/(\beta+\gamma)}\beta(Y - ar)^{(1+\gamma)/(\beta+\gamma)}e^{-u/(\beta+\gamma)}. \tag{7.27}$$

The equilibrium conditions (3.17) and (3.18) now become as follows:

$$\int_0^{r_f} \frac{\theta}{s^*(Y - ar, u)}\, dr = N: \qquad \textit{population constraint}, \tag{7.28}$$

$$\psi^*(Y - ar_f, u) = 0: \qquad \textit{boundary condition}. \tag{7.29}$$

From (7.27) and (7.29), it follows that $r_f = Y/a$. Using this result together with (7.26), we can determine from (7.28) the equilibrium utility level u^* as a function income Y as follows:

$$u^*(Y) = \alpha \log \alpha + (\beta + \gamma) \log\left(\frac{\beta + \gamma}{1 + \gamma}\frac{\theta}{aN}\right) + (1 + \gamma) \log Y, \tag{7.30}$$

or

$$e^{u^*(Y)} = \alpha^{\alpha}\left(\frac{\beta + \gamma}{1 + \gamma}\frac{\theta}{aN}\right)^{\beta+\gamma} Y^{1+\gamma}. \tag{7.31}$$

Now, for the absentee ownership model, setting Y equal to Y_0 in (7.30) and (7.31), we can obtain the equilibrium utility level $u_a^* \equiv u^*(Y_0)$ as follows:

$$u_a^* = \alpha \log \alpha + (\beta + \gamma) \log\left(\frac{\beta + \gamma}{1 + \gamma}\frac{\theta}{aN}\right) + (1 + \gamma) \log Y_0, \tag{7.32}$$

or

$$e^{u_a^*} = \alpha^{\alpha}\left(\frac{\beta + \gamma}{1 + \gamma}\frac{\theta}{aN}\right)^{\beta+\gamma} Y_0^{1+\gamma}. \tag{7.33}$$

After substituting (7.33) into (7.26) and (7.27), if we define $s_a^*(r) \equiv s^*(Y_0 - ar, u_a^*)$ and $R_a^*(r) \equiv \psi^*(Y_0 - ar, u_a^*)$, we can obtain the *equilibrium lot size curve* $s_a^*(r)$ and *equilibrium land rent curve* $R_a^*(r)$ for the absentee ownership model, respectively, as follows: At each $r \leq Y_0/a$,

$$s_a^*(r) = \frac{\beta + \gamma}{1 + \gamma} \frac{\theta}{aN} Y_0^{(1+\gamma)/(\beta+\gamma)} (Y_0 - ar)^{-\alpha/(\beta+\gamma)}, \tag{7.34}$$

$$R_a^*(r) = \beta \left(\frac{\beta + \gamma}{1 + \gamma} \frac{\theta}{aN} \right)^{-1} Y_0^{-(1+\gamma)/(\beta+\gamma)} (Y_0 - ar)^{(1+\gamma)/(\beta+\gamma)}. \tag{7.35}$$

From (7.34), it also follows that

$$s_a^*(0) = \frac{\beta + \gamma}{1 + \gamma} \frac{\theta Y_0}{aN}. \tag{7.36}$$

Notice that both curves $s_a^*(r)$ and $R_a^*(r)$ have usual shapes; that is, $s_a^*(r)$ is increasing in r and $R_a^*(r)$ is decreasing in r. The precise nature of these curves, of course, depends on the value of γ.[7]

Next, for the public ownership model, remember that $Y = Y_0 + \mathrm{TDR}/N$. However, the value of the total differential rent TDR also depends on Y and u. Hence, we must determine the equilibrium values of Y, TDR, and u simultaneously. To do so, we first obtain from (7.21) and (7.27)

$$\begin{aligned} \mathrm{TDR} &= \int_0^{Y/a} \psi^*(Y - ar, u)\theta \, dr \\ &= \frac{\theta\beta(\beta + \gamma)}{a(1 + \beta + 2\gamma)} \alpha^{\alpha/(\beta+\gamma)} Y^{(1+\beta+2\gamma)/(\beta+\gamma)} e^{-u/(\beta+\gamma)}. \end{aligned} \tag{7.37}$$

Similarly, we can obtain from (7.26) and (7.28)

$$N = \frac{(\beta + \gamma)\theta}{(1 + \gamma)a} \alpha^{\alpha/(\beta+\gamma)} Y^{(1+\gamma)/(\beta+\gamma)} e^{-u/(\beta+\gamma)}. \tag{7.38}$$

By definition,

$$Y = Y_0 + \mathrm{TDR}/N. \tag{7.39}$$

The system of equations (7.37)–(7.39) can be solved for three unknowns, Y, TDR, and u. Denoting the solutions respectively as Y_p^*, TDR_p^*, and u_p^*, we have

$$Y_p^* = \frac{1 + \beta + 2\gamma}{1 - \beta\gamma + 2\gamma} Y_0, \tag{7.40}$$

$$\mathrm{TDR}_p^* = \frac{\beta(1 + \gamma)}{1 - \beta\gamma + 2\gamma} Y_0 N, \tag{7.41}$$

$$u_{\mathrm{p}}^{*} = \alpha \log \alpha + (\beta + \gamma) \log\left(\frac{\beta + \gamma}{1 + \gamma} \frac{\theta}{aN}\right) + (1 + \gamma) \log\left(\frac{1 + \beta + 2\gamma}{1 - \beta\gamma + 2\gamma} Y_0\right), \tag{7.42}$$

or

$$e^{u_{\mathrm{p}}^{*}} = \alpha^{\alpha}\left(\frac{\beta + \gamma}{1 + \gamma} \frac{\theta}{aN}\right)^{\beta+\gamma} \left(\frac{1 + \beta + 2\gamma}{1 - \beta\gamma + 2\gamma} Y_0\right)^{1+\gamma}. \tag{7.43}$$

Finally, after substituting (7.40) and (7.43) into (7.26) and (7.27), if we define $s_{\mathrm{p}}^{*}(r) \equiv s^{*}(Y_{\mathrm{p}}^{*} - ar, u_{\mathrm{p}}^{*})$ and $R_{\mathrm{p}}^{*}(r) \equiv \psi^{*}(Y_{\mathrm{p}}^{*} - ar, u_{\mathrm{p}}^{*})$, we can obtain the *equilibrium lot size curve* $s_{\mathrm{p}}^{*}(r)$ and *equilibrium land rent curve* $R_{\mathrm{p}}^{*}(r)$ for the public ownership model, respectively, as follows:

$$s_{\mathrm{p}}^{*}(r) = \frac{\beta + \gamma}{1 + \gamma} \frac{\theta}{aN} \left(\frac{1 + \beta + 2\gamma}{1 - \beta\gamma + 2\gamma} Y_0\right)^{(1+\gamma)/(\beta+\gamma)} \cdot \left(\frac{1 + \beta + 2\gamma}{1 - \beta\gamma + 2\gamma} Y_0 - ar\right)^{-\alpha/(\beta+\gamma)}, \tag{7.44}$$

$$R_{\mathrm{p}}^{*}(r) = \beta\left(\frac{\beta + \gamma}{1 + \gamma} \frac{\theta}{aN}\right)^{-1} \left(\frac{1 + \beta + 2\gamma}{1 - \beta\gamma + 2\gamma} Y_0\right)^{-(1+\gamma)/(\beta+\gamma)} \cdot \left(\frac{1 + \beta + 2\gamma}{1 - \beta\gamma + 2\gamma} Y_0 - ar\right)^{(1+\gamma)/(\beta+\gamma)}. \tag{7.45}$$

It also follows from (7.44) that

$$s_{\mathrm{p}}^{*}(0) = \frac{(\beta + \gamma)(1 + \beta + 2\gamma)}{(1 + \gamma)(1 - \beta\gamma + 2\gamma)} \frac{\theta Y_0}{aN}. \tag{7.46}$$

We can readily see that $Y_{\mathrm{p}}^{*} > Y_0$, $u_{\mathrm{p}}^{*} > u_{\mathrm{a}}^{*}$, and $s_{\mathrm{p}}^{*}(0) > s_{\mathrm{a}}^{*}(0)$, as expected.

With minimum lot size regulations. Suppose that we introduce a regulation that requires the lot size per household to be no less than a given constant s_{m}. We call this regulation the *minimum lot size regulation (MLS regulation) with* s_m, or simply the s_{m} *regulation*. In order to examine the impact of such a regulation, let us introduce a new bid rent function associated with the regulation. Instead of (6.5), let us now consider the following utility-maximization problem under the s_{m} regulation:

$$\max_{r,z,s} U(z, s, E), \qquad \text{subject to} \quad z + Rs = I \quad \text{and} \quad s \geq s_{\mathrm{m}}. \tag{7.47}$$

Then, as with (6.6), the associated bid rent function can be defined by

$$\psi_M(I, u, E; s_m) = \max_{s \geq s_m} \frac{I - Z(s, u, E)}{s}, \qquad (7.48)$$

which is called the *bid rent function under the s_m regulation* [as before, $Z(s, u, E)$ is the solution to $U(z, s, E) = u$ for z]. We also denote the optimal lot size for the maximization problem of (7.48) by $s_M(I, u, E; s_m)$, which is called the *bid-max lot size function under the s_m regulation.*

Now, in the present context of the log-linear utility function (7.19), the residential choice behavior of each household under the s_m regulation can be described as

$$\max_{r,z,s} \alpha \log z + \beta \log s + \gamma \log s(r),$$

$$\text{subject to} \qquad z + R(r)s = Y - ar \quad \text{and} \quad s \geq s_m, \qquad (7.49)$$

where $s(r)$ represents the average lot size at each r. In this context, setting $I = Y - ar$, $E = s(r)$, and $Z(s, u, E) = s^{-\beta/\alpha} s(r)^{-\gamma/\alpha} e^{u/\alpha}$, the bid rent function (7.48) becomes

$$\psi_M(Y - ar, u, s(r); s_m) = \max_{s \geq s_m} \frac{Y - ar - s^{-\beta/\alpha} s(r)^{-\gamma/\alpha} e^{u/\alpha}}{s}, \qquad (7.50)$$

and the associatetd bid-max lot size function can be denoted as $s_M(Y - ar, u, s(r); s_m)$.

To obtain the equilibrium land use under the s_m regulation, first observe that in equilibrium, the market land rent $R(r)$ at each distance r within the urban fringe r_f should equal the bid rent $\psi_M(Y - ar, u, s(r); s_m)$ at r: Here, Y, u, and $s(r)$ are assumed to be those values in equilibrium. Therefore, the optimal lot size of each household at r should equal the bid-max lot size $s_M(Y - ar, u, s(r); s_m)$. It also holds in equilibrium that the individual lot size equals the average lot size at each r. Therefore, the following relationships must hold in equilibrium:

$$s(r) = s_M(Y - ar, u, s(r); s_m) \qquad \text{for} \quad r \leq r_f, \qquad (7.51)$$

$$R(r) = \psi_M(Y - ar, u, s(r); s_m) \qquad \text{for} \quad r \leq r_f. \qquad (7.52)$$

Furthermore, it follows from (7.51) that if $s(r) > s_m$, then $s_M(Y - ar, u, s(r); s_m) > s_m$, which implies that the s_m regulation is not binding at r in choosing the bid-max lot size in (7.50). Hence, it must hold that $s_M(Y - ar, u, s(r); s_m)$ equals $s(Y - ar, u, s(r))$, which is the bid-max lot size at r without the s_m regulation [given by (7.24)]. This in turn implies that $\psi_M(Y - ar, u, s(r); s_m)$ equals $\psi(Y - ar, u, s(r))$ [which is given by

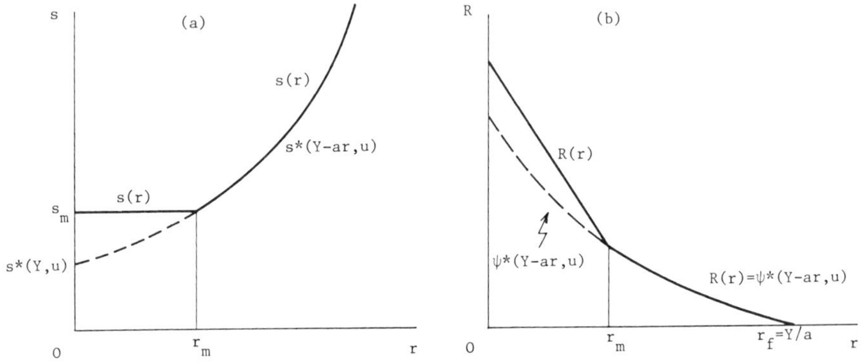

Figure 7.1. Equilibrium $s(r)$ curve and $R(r)$ curve under s_m regulation.

(7.23)]. Therefore, we can conclude as follows: At each $r \leq r_{\mathrm{f}}$,

$$s(r) > s_{\mathrm{m}} \Rightarrow s(r) = s(Y - ar, u, s(r)), \tag{7.53}$$

$$s(r) > s_{\mathrm{m}} \Rightarrow R(r) = \psi(Y - ar, u, s(r)). \tag{7.54}$$

Since $s(r) = s(Y - ar, u, s(r))$ implies that $s(r) = s^*(Y - ar, u)$, it follows that $R(r) = \psi(Y - ar, u, s^*(Y - ar, u)) \equiv \psi^*(Y - ar, u)$, where functions s^* and ψ^* are defined, respectively, by (7.26) and (7.27). Therefore, we can further conclude from (7.53) and (7.54) that at each $r \leq r_{\mathrm{f}}$,

$$s(r) > s_{\mathrm{m}} \Rightarrow s(r) = s^*(Y - ar, u), \tag{7.55}$$

$$s(r) > s_{\mathrm{m}} \Rightarrow R(r) = \psi^*(Y - ar, u). \tag{7.56}$$

Notice that (7.53) also implies that if $s(r) \neq s(Y - ar, u, s(r))$, then $s(r) \leq s_{\mathrm{m}}$. However, since it must hold in equilibrium that $s(r) \geq s_{\mathrm{m}}$, and since $s(r) \neq s(Y - ar, u, s(r))$ means $s(r) \neq s^*(Y - ar, u)$, we can conclude that

$$s(r) \neq s^*(Y - ar, u) \Rightarrow s(r) = s_{\mathrm{m}}. \tag{7.57}$$

Suppose that $s^*(Y, u) < s_{\mathrm{m}}$. Then at the residential land market equilibrium, considering (7.51)–(7.57) we can draw the average lot size curve $s(r)$ and land rent curve $R(r)$, respectively, as in Figure 7.1a and b. Let $r_{\mathrm{m}} \equiv r_{\mathrm{m}}(Y, u, s_{\mathrm{m}})$ be the *effective distance* that is determined by the intersection between the $s^*(Y - ar, u)$ curve and the horizontal s_{m} line. Since the $s^*(Y - ar, u)$ curve is increasing in r, it follows from (7.51), (7.55), and (7.57) that[8]

$$s(r) = \begin{cases} s^*(Y - ar, u) > s_{\mathrm{m}} & \text{for } r_{\mathrm{m}}(Y, u, s_{\mathrm{m}}) < r \leq r_{\mathrm{f}}, \\ s_{\mathrm{m}} & \text{for } r \leq r_{\mathrm{m}}(Y, u, s_{\mathrm{m}}), \end{cases} \tag{7.58}$$

and hence we can also derive from (7.50), (7.56), and (7.57)

$$R(r) = \begin{cases} \psi^*(Y - ar, u), & \text{for } r_{\mathrm{m}}(Y, u, s_{\mathrm{m}}) < r < r_{\mathrm{f}}, \\ \dfrac{Y - ar - s_{\mathrm{m}}^{-(\beta+\gamma)/\alpha} e^{u/\alpha}}{s_{\mathrm{m}}} & \text{for } r \leq r_{\mathrm{m}}(Y, u, s_{\mathrm{m}}). \end{cases} \tag{7.59}$$

Using (7.26), the effective distance can be obtained by solving the following equation for r_{m}:

$$s_{\mathrm{m}} = \alpha^{-\alpha/(\beta+\gamma)}(Y - ar_{\mathrm{m}})^{-\alpha/(\beta+\gamma)} e^{u/(\beta+\gamma)}, \tag{7.60}$$

which yields $r_{\mathrm{m}} \equiv r_{\mathrm{m}}(Y, u, s_{\mathrm{m}}) = (1/a)(Y - \alpha^{-1} s_{\mathrm{m}}^{-(\beta+\gamma)/\alpha} e^{u/\alpha})$. We can see from Figure 7.1a that the s_{m} regulation is effective within the distance r_{m}, provided that $s_{\mathrm{m}} > s^*(Y, u)$. However, if $s_{\mathrm{m}} \leq s^*(Y, u)$, that is, if $Y - \alpha^{-1} s_{\mathrm{m}}^{-(\beta+\gamma)/\alpha} e^{u/\alpha} \leq 0$, then the s_{m} regulation is not effective anywhere; in this case, we define $r_{\mathrm{m}}(Y, u, s_{\mathrm{m}}) = 0$. Hence, we can generally define the effective distance as follows:

$$r_{\mathrm{m}}(Y, u, s_{\mathrm{m}}) = \begin{cases} \dfrac{1}{a}(Y - \alpha^{-1} s_{\mathrm{m}}^{-(\beta+\gamma)/\alpha} e^{u/\alpha}) & \text{if it is positive,} \\ 0 & \text{otherwise.} \end{cases} \tag{7.61}$$

Notice from (7.59) that at each $r \leq r_{\mathrm{m}}$, the equilibrium land rent $R(r)$ equals the bid rent under the minimum lot size s_{m}. Hence, as is depicted in Figure 7.1b, the $R(r)$ curve is straight for $r \leq r_{\mathrm{m}}$. It is not difficult to see that this straight segment of the $R(r)$ curve is above the tangent line of the $\psi^*(Y - ar, u)$ curve at r_{m}. Therefore, *within the effective distance r_m, the equilibrium land rent curve $R(r)$ is above the $\psi^*(Y - ar, u)$ curve at least in the area close to r_m; and when the minimum lot size s_m is not too much larger than $s^*(Y, u)$, the $R(r)$ curve is above the $\psi^*(Y - ar, u)$ curve for all $r < r_m$*. (Figure 7.1b depicts the latter situation).[9] This suggests the potential benefits of MLS regulations. Namely, in the effective area of the s_{m} regulation, each household is forced to consume an amount of land s_{m} that is greater than the bid-max lot size without such regulation; however, at least in the effective area close to r_{m}, the increase in external benefits resulting from the greater average lot size s_{m} will outweigh the loss from the restriction of individual lot size choice.

Next, in order to determine the equilibrium values of u, r_{f}, and Y, let us consider the following additional equilibrium conditions:

$$\int_0^{r_f} \frac{\theta}{s(r)}\, dr = N: \qquad \textit{population constraint,} \tag{7.62}$$

$$R(r_f) = 0: \qquad \textit{boundary condition.} \tag{7.63}$$

From (7.27), (7.59), and (7.63), we have that $r_f = Y/a$. Using this relation together with (7.26), (7.58), and (7.61), we can determine from (7.62) the equilibrium utility u as a function of Y and s_m as follows:

$$u(Y, s_m) = \begin{cases} \alpha \log\left\{\left(\dfrac{\theta Y}{as_m} - N\right)\dfrac{a(1+\gamma)}{\theta}\right\} + (1+\gamma)\log s_m & \text{for } s_m \geq \tilde{s}_m, \\ u^*(Y) & \text{for } s_m \leq \tilde{s}_m, \end{cases} \tag{7.64}$$

where $u^*(Y)$ is given by (7.30), and $\tilde{s}_m$ is defined as

$$\tilde{s}_m = \frac{\beta + \gamma}{1 + \gamma}\frac{\theta Y}{aN}. \tag{7.65}$$

The *critical lot size* $\tilde{s}_m$ defined above is the unique lot size that satisfies the following conditions:

$$r_m(Y, u(Y, \tilde{s}_m), \tilde{s}_m) = 0 \qquad \text{and} \qquad \tilde{s}_m = s^*(Y, u(Y, \tilde{s}_m)). \tag{7.66}$$

Moreover, since $R_A = 0$ and $r_f = Y/a$, the total differential rent can be defined as $\text{TDR} = \int_0^{Y/a} \theta R(r)\, dr$. Substituting (7.59) into this equation and using (7.27), (7.37), (7.61), and (7.64), we can express the TDR as a function of Y and s_m as follows:

$$\begin{aligned} \text{TDR}(Y, s_m) = {} & \frac{\theta}{2as_m}\left(Y - \frac{1+\gamma}{\alpha}\left[Y - \frac{as_m}{\theta}N\right]\right) \\ & \cdot \left(Y + \frac{(\beta-\alpha)(1+\gamma)}{\alpha}\left[Y - \frac{as_m}{\theta}N\right]\right) \\ & + \frac{\theta\beta(\beta+\gamma)(1+\gamma)^2}{\alpha^2(1+\beta+2\gamma)as_m}\left(Y - \frac{as_m}{\theta}N\right)^2 \qquad \text{for } s_m \geq \tilde{s}_m, \end{aligned} \tag{7.67}$$

$$\text{TDR}(Y, s_m) = \frac{\beta(1+\gamma)}{1+\beta+2\gamma} YN \qquad \text{for } s_m \leq \tilde{s}_m. \tag{7.68}$$

Now, *for the absentee ownership model,* setting Y equal to Y_0 in (7.64), (7.67), and (7.68), we can obtain the equilibrium utility level $u_a(s_m) \equiv u(Y_0, s_m)$ and equilibrium total differential rent $\text{TDR}_a(s_m) \equiv \text{TDR}(Y_0, s_m)$ as function of s_m as follows:

$$u_a(s_m) = \begin{cases} \alpha \log\left\{\left(\dfrac{\theta Y_0}{a s_m} - N\right)\dfrac{a(1+\gamma)}{\theta}\right\} + (1+\gamma)\log s_m & \text{for} \quad s_m \geq s_a^*(0), \\ u_a^* & \text{for} \quad s_m \leq s_a^*(0), \end{cases} \tag{7.69}$$

$$\begin{aligned} \text{TDR}_a(s_m) = {} & \frac{\theta}{2as_m}\left(Y_0 - \frac{1+\gamma}{\alpha}\left[Y_0 - \frac{as_m}{\theta}N\right]\right) \\ & \cdot \left(Y_0 + \frac{(\beta-\alpha)(1+\gamma)}{\alpha}\left[Y_0 - \frac{as_m}{\theta}N\right]\right) \\ & + \frac{\theta\beta(\beta+\gamma)(1+\gamma)^2}{\alpha^2(1+\beta+2\gamma)as_m}\left(Y_0 - \frac{as_m}{\theta}N\right)^2 \quad \text{for} \quad s_m \geq s_a^*(0), \end{aligned} \tag{7.70}$$

$$\text{TDR}_a(s_m) = \frac{\beta(1+\gamma)}{1+\beta+2\gamma}Y_0 N \quad \text{for} \quad s_m \leq s_a^*(0), \tag{7.71}$$

where u_a^* and $s_a^*(0)$ are given, respectively, by (7.32) and (7.36). From (7.69)–(7.71), we can readily see that

$$\frac{du_a(s_m)}{ds_m}\begin{cases} <0 & \text{for} \quad s_m > s_a^*(0), \\ =0 & \text{for} \quad s_m \leq s_a^*(0), \end{cases} \tag{7.72}$$

$$\frac{d\text{TDR}_a(s_m)}{ds_m}\begin{cases} >0 & \text{for} \quad s_m > s_a^*(0), \\ =0 & \text{for} \quad s_m \leq s_a^*(0). \end{cases} \tag{7.73}$$

Namely, under absentee landownership, whenever the s_m regulation is effective, the equilibrium utility level decreases as s_m increases, and the total differential rent increases as s_m increases. *Therefore, effective MLS regulations benefit only absentee landowners, and households are better off without such regulations.*

This result can be explained intuitively as follows. Suppose in Figure 7.2 that the dashed curve $s_a^*(r)$ represents the equilibrium lot size curve before the introduction of an MLS regulation. Now, suppose that we introduce an effective MLS regulation, s_m. If there were no change in the equilibrium utility level u_a^*, the equilibrium lot size curve under the reg-

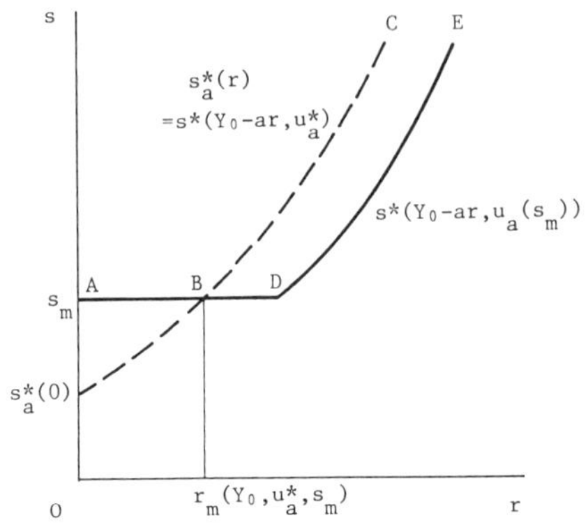

Figure 7.2. Impact of s_m regulation on the equilibrium lot size curve (the absentee ownership case).

ulation would be given by the curve *ABC* in Figure 7.2. In this situation, however, s_{m} exceeds the previous equilibrium lot size $s^*(Y_0 - ar, u_{\mathrm{a}}^*)$ everywhere for $r < r_{\mathrm{m}}(Y_0, u_{\mathrm{a}}^*, s_{\mathrm{m}})$. Since the population constraint (7.62) has been satisfied previously under the lot size curve $s(r) = s^*(Y_0 - ar, u_{\mathrm{a}}^*)$, this implies that now the left side of (7.62) is smaller than N (notice that the urban fringe $r_{\mathrm{f}} = Y_0/a$ remains the same). Therefore, since the equilibrium lot size function $s^*(Y_0 - ar, u)$ is increasing in u, in order to satisfy the population constraint (7.62) *the equilibrium utility level* $u_a(s_m)$ *under the* s_m *regulation must become lower than* u_a^*; hence, the new equilibrium lot size curve is given by the curve *ADE* in Figure 7.2.[10] Turning to the impact of the s_{m} regulation on the TDR, suppose in Figure 7.1a that Y equals Y_0 and u equals u_{a}^* (the equilibrium utility level before the regulation). If the equilibrium utility level remained the same, the associated land rent curve under the regulation would be given by the kinked curve $R(r)$ in Figure 7.1b, which exceeds the $\psi^*(Y_0 - ar, u_{\mathrm{a}}^*)$ curve for $r < r_{\mathrm{m}}$ (at least in the area close to r_{m}). However, since the equilibrium utility level under the regulation is actually lower than u_{a}^*, and since the bid rent function $\psi^*(Y_0 - ar, u)$ increases as u becomes lower, we can see that the equilibrium land rent curve under the regulation will exceed the previous rent curve $\psi^*(Y_0 - ar, u_{\mathrm{a}}^*)$ everywhere. Hence, the total differential rent will also increase with the regulation, as is indicated by (7.73).

Therefore, under the absentee landownership, the potential benefits of an MLS regulation will be absorbed entirely by an increase in the total differential rent, and households will be worse off. However, under the public landownership, the situation is entirely different. To see this, suppose now that in Figure 7.1b, $Y = Y_p^*$ and $u = u_p^*$, and hence the curve $\psi^*(Y - ar, u) \equiv \psi^*(Y_p^* - ar, u_p^*)$ represents the equilibrium land rent curve before the introduction of the s_m regulation. As was already explained, under an effective MLS regulation s_m, *if u and Y remained the same,* the equilibrium land rent curve under the regulation would be given by the kinked curve $R(r)$, which exceeds $\psi^*(Y - ar, u)$ for all $r < r_m$, provided that s_m is not too much larger than $s^*(Y, u)$. However, under the public landownership, the increased total differential rent [which equals the area between the $R(r)$ curve and the $\psi^*(Y - ar, u)$ curve for $r < r_m$ times θ] will be redistributed among households, and hence the income of each household will actually increase. This will in turn expand the urban fringe distance $r_f = Y/a$ and also increase the equilibrium utility level u. However, if s_m is too large, it may happen in a variation of Figure 7.1b that $R(r) < \psi^*(Y - ar, u)$ in the area close to $r = 0$; hence, it is also possible that the increase in the total differential rent in the area close to r_m is outweighed by the decrease in the total differential rent in the area close to $r = 0$. In this situation, the equilibrium utility level will decrease with the introduction of the s_m regulation. This suggests that there will be an *optimal MLS regulation* with some $\hat{s}_m$ under which the equilibrium utility is maximized.

To determine the optimal MLS regulation, we must first obtain the *equilibrium utility level $u_p(s_m)$ for the public ownershsip model* under each s_m regulation. To do so, let us consider an MLS regulation with some s_m. Assuming that this regulation is effective, we can obtain from (7.64) that

$$e^{u(Y,s_m)} = \left(\frac{\theta Y}{a s_m} - N\right)^{\alpha} \left(\frac{a(1+\gamma)}{\theta}\right)^{\alpha} s_m^{1+\gamma} \qquad \text{for} \quad s_m \geq \tilde{s}_m .$$

For simplicity, let us denote $u(Y, s_m)$ by u. Then the above equation can be solved for Y as follows:

$$Y = \frac{a s_m}{\theta} N + \frac{1}{1+\gamma} s_m^{-(\beta+\gamma)/\alpha} e^{u/\alpha} \qquad \text{for} \quad s_m \geq \tilde{s}_m . \tag{7.74}$$

Recall that for the public ownership model, we have $Y = Y_0 + \mathrm{TDR}/N$, or

$$\mathrm{TDR} = (Y - Y_0)N. \tag{7.75}$$

Therefore, substituting (7.75) for $\mathrm{TDR}(Y, s_m)$ in the left side of (7.67), and then substituting (7.74) into the same equation, we obtain the following relation:

$$\left(\frac{1}{1+\gamma} s_m^{-(\beta+\gamma)/\alpha} e^{u/\alpha} + \frac{as_m}{\theta} - Y^0\right) N$$

$$= \frac{\theta}{2as_m}\left(\frac{as_m}{\theta} N - \frac{\beta+\gamma}{\alpha(1+\gamma)} s_m^{-(\beta+\gamma)/\alpha} e^{u/\alpha}\right)$$

$$\cdot \left(\frac{as_m}{\theta} N + \frac{\beta-\gamma+2\beta\gamma}{\alpha(1+\gamma)} s_m^{-(\beta+\gamma)/\alpha} e^{u/\alpha}\right)$$

$$+ \frac{\theta\beta(\beta+\gamma)}{\alpha^2(1+\beta+2\gamma)as_m} (s_m^{-(\beta+\gamma)/\alpha} e^{u/\alpha})^2 \quad \text{for} \quad s_m \geq \tilde{s}_m. \tag{7.76}$$

Let us define

$$v \equiv e^{u/\alpha}. \tag{7.77}$$

Then (7.76) becomes a quadratic equation of a single unknown v. Solving the equation for v, we have[11]

$$v = \frac{1+\gamma}{A} s_m^{(\beta+\gamma)/\alpha} \left\{ (1+\gamma)\frac{as_m}{\theta} N - \left[((1+\gamma)^2 + A)\left(\frac{as_m}{\theta} N\right)^2 - 2AY_0 \frac{as_m}{\theta} N \right]^{1/2} \right\}, \tag{7.78}$$

where

$$A \equiv (1+2\gamma)(\beta+\gamma)^2 \alpha^{-1}(1+\beta+2\gamma)^{-1}. \tag{7.79}$$

From (7.77), we have that $u = \alpha \log v$. Hence, if we define $u_p(s_m) \equiv \alpha \log v$, the *equilibrium utility level* $u_p(s_m)$ under each s_m regulation can be obtained as follows:

$$u_p(s_m) = \alpha \log \frac{1+\gamma}{A} + (\beta+\gamma)\log s_m$$
$$+ \alpha \log \left\{ (1+\gamma)\frac{as_m}{\theta} N - \left[((1+\gamma)^2 + A)\left(\frac{as_m}{\theta} N\right)^2 - 2AY_0 \frac{as_m}{\theta} N \right]^{1/2} \right\} \quad \text{for} \quad s_m \geq s_p^*(0). \tag{7.80}$$

The above solution is valid, of course, only when the s_m regulation is effective, that is, $s_m \geq s_p^*(0)$, where $s_p^*(0)$ is the equilibrium lot size at $r = 0$ for the no-regulation case [given by (7.46)]. When an s_m regulation is not effective, we can define

$$u_p(s_m) = u_p^* \quad \text{for} \quad s_m \leq s_p^*(0), \tag{7.81}$$

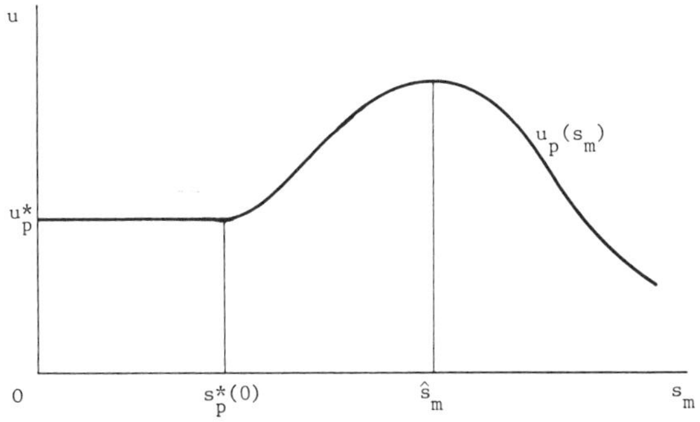

Figure 7.3. Equilibrium utility curve for the public ownership model.

where u_{p}^* is given by (7.42). Then it can be readily shown that at $s_{\mathrm{m}} = s_{\mathrm{p}}^*(0)$, equations (7.80) and (7.81) give the same value. Moreover, using (7.80) and (7.81), it is not difficult to show that there is an $\hat{s}_{\mathrm{m}}$ regulation such that

$$du_{\mathrm{p}}(s_{\mathrm{m}})/ds_{\mathrm{m}} = 0 \quad \text{for} \quad s_{\mathrm{m}} \leq s_{\mathrm{p}}^*(0) \quad \text{and for} \quad s_{\mathrm{m}} = \hat{s}_{\mathrm{m}}, \tag{7.82}$$

$$du_{\mathrm{p}}(s_{\mathrm{m}})/ds_{\mathrm{m}} > 0 \quad \text{for} \quad s_{\mathrm{p}}^*(0) < s_{\mathrm{m}} < \hat{s}_{\mathrm{m}}, \tag{7.83}$$

$$du_{\mathrm{p}}(s_{\mathrm{m}})/ds_{\mathrm{m}} < 0 \quad \text{for} \quad s_{\mathrm{m}} > \hat{s}_{\mathrm{m}}, \tag{7.84}$$

where $\hat{s}_{\mathrm{m}}$ is given by

$$\hat{s}_{\mathrm{m}} = \left(1 + \frac{2\alpha\gamma(1+\gamma)(1-\beta\gamma+2\gamma)}{\alpha(1+\gamma)^2(1+\beta+2\gamma)+(1+2\gamma)(\beta+\gamma)^2}\right) s_{\mathrm{p}}^*(0). \tag{7.85}$$

Since $\beta < 1$, it always holds that $\hat{s}_{\mathrm{m}} > s_{\mathrm{p}}^*(0)$. Therefore, the equilibrium utility curve $u_{\mathrm{p}}(s_{\mathrm{m}})$ can be depicted as in Figure 7.3. For $s_{\mathrm{m}} < s_{\mathrm{p}}^*(0)$, of course, the MLS regulation is not effective, and hence $u_{\mathrm{p}}(s_{\mathrm{m}})$ equals u_{p}^*, which is the equilibrium utility level for the no-regulation case [given by (7.42)]. After the MLS regulation starts to be effective at $s_{\mathrm{m}} = s_{\mathrm{p}}^*(0)$, the equilibrium utility level achieves the highest utility level under the MLS regulation with $\hat{s}_{\mathrm{m}}$. Hence, $\hat{s}_{\mathrm{m}}$ can be called the *optimal minimum lot size* for the public ownership model. Moreover, it is not difficult to see from (7.46) and (7.85) that $\hat{s}_{\mathrm{m}}$ becomes larger as β, γ, θ, or Y_0 increases or as α, N, or a decreases.

7.3 Racial externalities

The impact of racial externalities on residential land markets (or housing markets) has been studied most extensively in the United States, where racial problems have been a prime concern. Specifically, three types of model have been proposed to capture the effects of racial externalities. In this section, we introduce and compare them.

Before these models are introduced, however, a few notes may be useful. First, distinctions among several terms are important in the study of racial externalities. Following Yinger (1976, p. 383), we define *prejudice* as an attitude (or preference) of an individual toward a particular group of people. *Discrimination,* in contrast is a behavior that denies one group of people rights or opportunities given to others, and *segregation* is the actual physical separation of different groups of people. Although these three concepts are closely related, it is important to separate them logically. Second, it must be admitted that traditional economic theory (on which this book is based) is weak in normative analyses of racial externalities. For example, although one of the fundamental issues in the study of racial externalities is whether we approve of the preferences of individuals who are racially prejudiced, traditional economic theory provides little help in answering such a basic question. Therefore, in the following discussion, we are obliged to avoid such moral or political issues and focus instead on the economic consequences of racial externalities. Specifically, in the normative side of our analyses, we ask, If we were to accept the preferences of all individuals, what could be done to improve the welfare of the city? Third, therefore, we must be cautious about the results of such purely economic analyses. For example, even if complete segregation were economically efficient, it could foster racial tensions in the long run.

Following the literature, let us assume that the city consists of two types of residents, called *black households (B households)* and *white households (W households),* where all B households are assumed to be identical, and the same is true for all W households. Although many different combinations are conceivable in the racial attitudes of the two groups, let us consider the following standard hypothetical case in the literature: W households have an aversion to living near B households, whereas B households are indifferent to the location of W households (and other B households).[12] Then we can represent the utility function of B households by $U_B(z, s)$, which is free of racial externalities, and that of W households by $U_W(z, s, E(x))$. Here $E(x)$ denotes the environmental quality level that W households feel at location x given the spatial distribution of B households in the city. Following the convention of the externality model in Section 6.2, it is assumed that the utility level of W households increases as $E(x)$ increases:

$$\partial U_W(z, s, E(x))/\partial E(x) > 0. \tag{7.86}$$

This implies that $E(x)$ decreases as W households at x receive stronger externalities from B households.

We assume that the residential choice behavior of each B household can be described as

$$\max_{x,z,s} U_B(z, s), \qquad \text{subject to} \quad z + R(x)s = Y_B^0 - G_B(x) - T_B(x), \tag{7.87}$$

and that of W households as

$$\max_{x,z,s} U_W(z, s, E(x)), \qquad \text{subject to} \quad z + R(x)s = Y_W^0 - G_W(x) - T_W(x), \tag{7.88}$$

where the notation is the same as that of the externality model (6.1) [except, of course, that the subscript B (W) stands for B households (W households)]. The utility function U_B is assumed to satisfy Assumptions 2.1 and 2.3, and U_W Assumptions 6.1, 6.3, and 6.4. Furthermore, both transport cost functions $T_B(x)$ and $T_W(x)$ are assumed to satisfy Assumption 6.2. Then the bid rent function of B households can be defined by

$$\psi_B(Y_B^0 - G_B(x) - T_B(x), u_B) = \max_s \frac{Y_B^0 - G_B(x) - T_B(x) - Z_B(s, u_B)}{s}, \tag{7.89}$$

where $Z_B(s, u_B)$ represents the solution to the equation $U_B(z, s) = u_B$ for z. The solution of the maximization problem of the right side of (7.89) defines the bid-max lot size function $s_B(Y_B^0 - G_B(x) - T_B(x), u_B)$ of B households. Similarly, the bid rent function of W households can be defined by

$$\psi_W(Y_W^0 - G_W(x) - T_W(x), u_W, E(x)) \\ = \max_s \frac{Y_W^0 - G_W(x) - T_W(x) - Z_W(s, u_W, E(x))}{s}, \tag{7.90}$$

where $Z_W(s, u_W, E)$ represents the solution to $U_W(z, s, E) = u_W$ for z; and we denote the bid-max lot size of W households by $s_W(Y_W^0 - G_W(x) - T_W(x), u_W, E(x))$.

The three model types to be introduced below differ in the specification of the *environmental quality function* $E(x)$. The *border models* developed by Bailey (1959) and Rose-Ackerman (1975, 1977) assume that B households and W households are completely segregated, with B households (W households) occupying the inner ring (the outer ring), and that $E(x)$ increases as the distance from the black–white border increases. Models of the second type, which were proposed by both Yinger (1976) and Schnare (1976) and called *local externality models,* assume that $E(x)$ is a decreasing function of the proportion of B households at location x.[13] This implies that W households care about the racial composition of their location, but not about that of other locations. Finally, models of the third type, called *global externality models,* assume that $E(x)$ is decreasing in the total amount of externalities received by a W household at x, which is a weighted sum of externalities from all B households in the city. Examples are Yellin (1974), Papageorgiou (1978a,b), Kanemoto (1980, Ch. 6), and Ando (1981, Ch. 5). In the following subsections, we compare the economic implications of these three types of model.

7.3.1 Border models

Let us assume that the populations of B households and W households are exogenously given, respectively, by N_B and N_W and that all land in the city is owned by absentee landlords. For simplicity, the CBD is treated as a point. We consider no location-dependent tax and hence set $G_B(x) = 0 = G_W(x)$ for all x. In this context, we first examine the equilibrium spatial configuration of the city.

As noted before, we assume *a priori* that the equilibrium land use pattern of the city is symmetric with respect to the CBD, with B households (W households) residing in the inner ring (the outer ring). Hence, we can replace the location index x with the distance r from the CBD. If we let b denote the *boundary distance* (or border distance) between blacks and whites, B households will reside in the area between distance 0 and b, and W households between b and r_f. The environmental quality function $E(r)$ for W households at each distance r (beyond the boundary b) is assumed to be an increasing function of the distance $r - b$ from the boundary. That is,

$$E(r) \equiv E(r - b) \qquad \text{for} \quad r \geq b, \tag{7.91}$$

where

$$E'(r - b) \equiv dE(r - b)/d(r - b) > 0. \tag{7.92}$$

Without loss of generality, we can also assume that

$$0 < E_{\min} \equiv E(0) < \lim_{r\to\infty} E(r - b) \equiv E_{\max} = 1. \tag{7.93}$$

In order to facilitate the comparison between the equilibrium land use pattern of the *prejudiced city* (i.e., the present city) and that of the *unprejudiced city* (i.e., a city where W households are also unprejudiced), let us assume that the utility function of W households is *separable* with respect to the environmental quality function:

$$U_W(z, s, E(r-b)) = U(z, s)E(r-b), \tag{7.94}$$

where the subutility function $U(z, s)$ is assumed to satisfy Assumptions 2.1 and 2.3.[14] In this context, it is assumed that *in the unprejudiced city, the utility function of W households is given by* $U(z, s)E_{max} \equiv U(z, s)$.

For the comparison of equilibrium land use patterns of the two cities, it is convenient to introduce another bid rent function $\psi(I, v)$, which is defined as

$$\psi(I, v) = \max_s \frac{I - Z(s, v)}{s}, \tag{7.95}$$

where $Z(s, v)$ represents the solution to $U(z, s) = v$ for z; and the associated bid-max lot size function is denoted by $s(I, v)$. Then recalling (7.90) and setting $I = Y_W^0 - T_W(r)$, we can see that the following relations hold identically between functions ψ_W and ψ and between s_W and s:

$$\psi_W(Y_W^0 - T_W(r), u_W, E(r-b)) = \psi(Y_W^0 - T_W(r), u_W/E(r-b)), \tag{7.96}$$

$$s_W(Y_W^0 - T_W(r), u_W, E(r-b)) = s(Y_W^0 - T_W(R), u_W/E(r-b)). \tag{7.97}$$

For simplicity of notation, let us introduce *Alonso functions* Ψ_W and S_W defined, respectively, as

$$\Psi_W(r, v_W) \equiv \psi(Y_W^0 - T_W(r), v_W), \tag{7.98}$$

$$S_W(r, v_W) \equiv s(Y_W^0 - T_W(r), v_W). \tag{7.99}$$

Notice that if we interpret $v_W = u_W$, then Ψ_W and S_W represent, respectively, the (Alonso) bid rent function and bid-max lot size function of W households *in the unprejudiced city*. Similarly, for B households, we define *Alonso functions* Ψ_B and S_B by

$$\Psi_B(r, u_B) \equiv \psi_B(Y_B^0 - T_B(r), u_B), \tag{7.100}$$

$$S_B(r, u_B) \equiv s_B(Y_B^0 - T_B(r), u_B), \tag{7.101}$$

which are common to both cities.

To be consistent with the initial assumption that B households (W households) reside in the inner ring (in the outer ring), let us assume that *the bid rent function Ψ_B is steeper than the bid rent function Ψ_W* (recall Definition 2.2 and refer to Figure 2.9 by setting i equal to B and j equal to W).[15] In other words, we assume that *in the unprejudiced city, the bid rent curves of B households are steeper than those of W households*. Then applying the boundary rent curve approach of Section 4.3.2, the equilib-

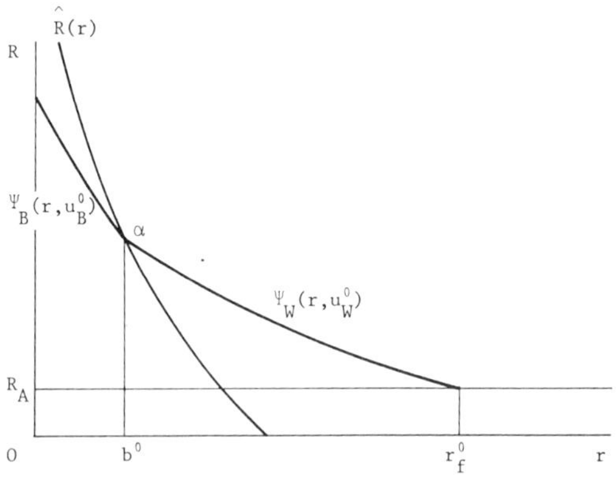

Figure 7.4. Equilibrium spatial configuration in the unprejudiced city.

rium spatial configuration of the unprejudiced city can be depicted as in Figure 7.4. Let u_{B}^0 and u_{W}^0 be, respectively, the equilibrium utility level of B households and that of W households in the unprejudiced city. Then, as is depicted in Figure 7.4, the equilibrium bid rent curve $\Psi_{\mathrm{B}}(r, u_{\mathrm{B}}^0)$ of B households must intersect the equilibrium bid rent curve $\Psi_{\mathrm{W}}(r, u_{\mathrm{W}}^0)$ at a point on the *boundary rent curve* $\hat{R}(r)$. Here the $\hat{R}(r)$ curve is obtained as follows: Given each utility level u_{B}, consider the next population constraint,

$$\int_0^b L(r)/S_{\mathrm{B}}(r, u_{\mathrm{B}})\, dr = N_{\mathrm{B}}. \tag{7.102}$$

Solving this equation for the unknown b under each u_{B}, we obtain the *boundary function* $b(u_{\mathrm{B}})$. Denoting the inverse of $r = b(u_{\mathrm{B}})$ by $u_{\mathrm{B}}(r)$, we define the boundary rent curve $\hat{R}(r)$ as follows:

$$\hat{R}(r) \equiv \Psi_{\mathrm{B}}(r, u_{\mathrm{B}}(r)) \qquad \text{for each} \quad r > 0. \tag{7.103}$$

By definition, $\hat{R}(r)$ represents the market land rent at r when the boundary between B households and W households occurs at r. The equilibrium point α on the boundary rent curve in Figure 7.4 can be determined by choosing u_{B}^0 and u_{W}^0 so that the following population constraints are satisfied:

$$\int_0^{b^0} \frac{L(r)}{S_{\mathrm{B}}(r, u_{\mathrm{B}}^0)}\, dr = N_{\mathrm{B}}, \tag{7.104}$$

$$\int_{b^0}^{r_{\mathrm{f}}^0} \frac{L(r)}{S_{\mathrm{W}}(r, u_{\mathrm{W}}^0)}\, dr = N_{\mathrm{W}}, \tag{7.105}$$

where $b^0 \equiv b(u_B^0)$ represents the equilibrium boundary distance, and the equilibrium urban fringe distance r_f^0 is determined by the intersection between the bid rent curve $\Psi_W(r, u_W^0)$ and the horizontal agricultural land rent curve R_A.[16]

Next, introducing the W households' aversion to B households, let u_B^* and u_W^* denote, respectively, the equilibrium utility level of B households and that of W households in the prejudiced city, and let b^* and r_f^* be, respectively, the associated equilibrium boundary distance and urban fringe distance. Then, if u_W^* and b^* are substituted into (7.96) and (7.97), the equilibrium bid rent curve of W households is given by $\psi(Y_W^0 - T_W(r), u_W^*/E(r - b^*))$ and the associated bid-max lot size curve by $s(Y_W^0 - T_W(r), u_W^*/E(r - b^*))$. Similarly, substituting u_B^* into (7.100) and (7.101), the equilibrium bid rent curve of B households is given by $\Psi_B(r, u_B^*)$ and the associated bid-max lot size curve by $S_B(r, u_B^*)$. The unknown parameters u_W^*, u_B^*, b^*, and r_f^* should be determined so as to satisfy the following population constraints and boundary rent conditions:[17]

$$\int_0^{b^*} \frac{L(r)}{S_B(r, u_B^*)} dr = N_B, \tag{7.106}$$

$$\int_{b^*}^{r_f^*} \frac{L(r)}{s(Y_W^0 - T_W(r), u_W^*/E(r - b^*))} dr = N_W, \tag{7.107}$$

$$\Psi_B(b^*, u_B^*) = \psi(Y_W^0 - T_W(b^*), u_W^*/E_{\min}), \tag{7.108}$$

$$\psi(Y_W^0 - T_W(r_f^*), u_W^*/E(r_f^* - b^*)) = R_A. \tag{7.109}$$

Notice that condition (7.106) implies that the point $(b^*, \Psi_B(b^*, u_B^*))$ must be on the boundary rent curve $\hat{R}(r)$ in Figure 7.4. This fact, together with condition (7.108), implies that the two equilibrium bid rent curves $\Psi_B(r, u_B^*)$ and $\psi(Y_W^0 - T_W(r), u_W^*/E(r - b^*))$, must intersect at some point, say β, on the curve $\hat{R}(r)$ in Figure 7.4. Using the population constraints (7.105) and (7.107), we can readily show that *the point β must be located below the point α on curve $\hat{R}(r)$* (see Appendix C.12). Therefore, the equilibrium spatial configurations of the two cities can be depicted as in Figure 7.5. In this figure, $\hat{R}(r)$ represents the same boundary rent curve as that in Figure 7.4; and the curve $\Psi_B(r, u_B^0) - \Psi_W(r, u_W^0)$ duplicates the equilibrium rent curve of the unprejudiced city in Figure 7.4. The equilibrium rent curve of the prejudiced city is given by the curve $\Psi_B(r, u_B^*) - \psi(Y_W^0 - T_W(r), u_W^*/E(r - b^*))$ in Figure 7.5. *With the introduction of the W households' aversion to B households, the boundary distance moves*

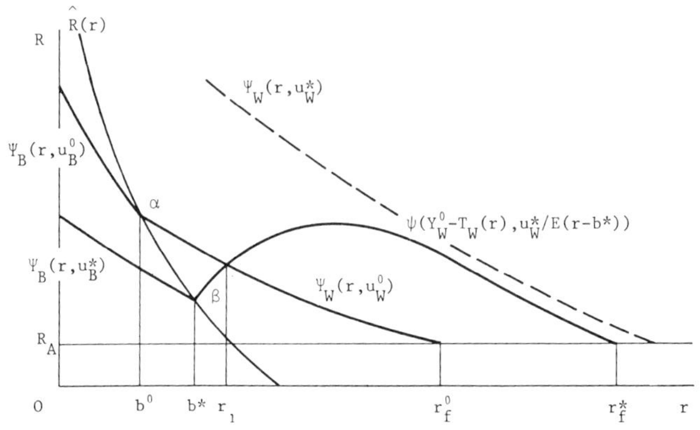

Figure 7.5. Comparison of the equilibrium spatial configurations of the two cities.

outward from b^0 to b^*, and the land rent in the area close to the boundary b^* becomes lower. This is because the suburbs now become relatively more attractive to W households, and hence the land market around the boundary b^* becomes less competitive. In the prejudiced city, the slope of the equilibrium rent curve to the right of b^* is given by

$$\frac{\partial\psi(Y_W^0 - T_W(r), u_W^*/E(r - b^*))}{\partial r}$$

$$= \frac{\partial\psi}{\partial I}\frac{\partial(Y_W^0 - T_W(r))}{\partial r} + \frac{\partial\psi}{\partial v}\frac{\partial(u_W^*/E(r - b^*))}{\partial r}$$

$$= -\frac{T_W'(r)}{s^*(r)} - \frac{\partial\psi}{\partial v}\frac{u_W^*}{E(r - b^*)^2}E'(r - b^*) \qquad \text{for} \quad r > b^*, \qquad (7.110)$$

where $s^*(r) \equiv s(Y_W^0 - T_W(r), u_W^*/E(r - b^*))$. In the last equation above, the first term is negative; however, since $\partial\psi/\partial v$ is negative [from Property 3.1(i)] and $E'(r - b^*)$ is positive by assumption, the second term is positive. Therefore, the racial prejudice of W households tends to make the equilibrium rent curve flatter. This is because the prejudiced W households pay a premium for moving away from the black–white boundary. As is depicted in Figure 7.5, the equilibrium rent curve in the prejudiced city may even rise with r over a certain range beyond the black–white boundary. However, since $E(r - b^*)$ approaches 1 ($\equiv E_{max}$) as the distance from b^* increases, the bid rent curve $\psi(Y_W^0 - T_W(r), u_W^*/E(r - b^*))$ eventually approaches another bid rent curve, $\psi(Y_W^0 - T_W(r), u_W^*) \equiv \Psi_W(r, u_W^*)$, which is always decreasing in r. Therefore, the equilibrium rent curve in the prejudiced city also falls in r in the far suburbs. It can also be shown that *the equilibrium rent curve in the prejudiced city must cross that in the unprejudiced city at some distance r_l, and the prejudiced W households pay higher rents in the far suburbs than the W households in the unprejudiced city;* otherwise, the total demand for land generated under rents that are too low cannot be accommodated inside the urban fringe distance (see Appendix C.12). This implies that *r_f^* is greater than r_f^0, and hence the area of the prejudiced city is larger than that of the unprejudiced city*. Moreover, since the bid rent function Ψ_B is decreasing in u [from Property 2.1(i)], we can immediately conclude from Figure 7.5 that $u_B^* > u_B^0$. On the other hand, if $u_W^* \geq u_W^0$, then we would have $\Psi_W(r, u_W^*) \leq \Psi_W(r, u_W^0)$ for all r [again from Property 2.1(i)]. Then the equilibrium bid rent curve $\psi(Y_W^0 - T_W(r), u_W^*/E(r - b^*))$ could never cross the curve $\Psi_W(r, u_W^0)$, which contradicts our previous result. Therefore, it must hold that $u_W^* < u_W^0$. Namely, *with the introduction of the W households' aversion to B households, the equilibrium utility level of B households becomes higher, and that of W households becomes lower.*

In the prejudiced city, W households tend to move away from B households. Therefore, as has been shown above, the residential rings of both B households and W households tend to expand outward farther than in the unprejudiced city. This suggests that the equilibrium land use pattern of the prejudiced city would not be socially efficient. Therefore, we now examine the optimal land use pattern of the prejudiced city, in particular the optimal black–white boundary distance. This task can be achieved by modifying the HS model of Section 4.4 with multiple household types. Namely, let us arbitrarily specify a pair of target utility levels u_B and u_W for B households and W households, respectively. As before, we assume *a priori* that the two household types are completely segregated. Namely, B households (W households) occupy the inner ring (the outer ring), with b being the boundary distance (which is still unknown). Let $n_B(r)$ denote the number of B households per unit distance at r ($0 \leq r \leq b$), and $n_W(r)$ that of W households at each r ($b < r \leq r_f$). Then if we modify the previous HS model, (4.30)–(4.32), for the present context, our optimization problem can be formulated as follows:

$$\max_{\substack{b, r_f, n_B(r)\\ n_W(r), s_B(r), s_W(r)}} \mathcal{S} = \int_0^b \{Y_B^0 - T_B(r) - Z_B(s_B(r), u_B) - R_A s_B(r)\} n_B(r)\, dr$$

$$+ \int_b^{r_f} \{Y_W^0 - T_W(r) - Z_W(s_W(r), u_W, E(r - b))$$

$$- R_A s_W(r)\} n_W(r)\, dr, \qquad (7.111)$$

subject to (a) land constraints

$$\begin{aligned} s_B(r)n_B(r) &\leq L(r) \qquad \text{for} \quad 0 \leq r \leq b, \\ s_W(r)n_W(r) &\leq L(r) \qquad \text{for} \quad b < r \leq r_f, \end{aligned} \tag{7.112}$$

(b) population constraints

$$\int_0^b n_B(r)\,dr = N_B\,, \qquad \int_b^{r_f} n_W(r)\,dr = N_W\,, \tag{7.113}$$

where $n_i(r) \geq 0$, $s_i(r) > 0$ for $i = B, W$, and $0 < b < r_f$.

Namely, the problem is to determine the resource/land allocation of the city so as to maximize the city's surplus while satisfying the target utilities. We call this maximization problem the *Herbert–Stevens model with racial externality (HS_R model)*. The associated Lagrangian function is given by

$$\begin{aligned} \mathcal{L} = &\int_0^b \{Y_B^0 - T_B(r) - Z_B(s_B(r), u_B) - R_A s_B(r)\} n_B(r)\,dr \\ &+ \int_b^{r_f} \{Y_W^0 - T_W(r) - Z_W(s_W(r), u_W, E(r-b)) - R_A s_W(r)\} n_W(r)\,dr \\ &- \int_0^b DR(r)\,(s_B(r)n_B(r) - L(r))\,dr - \int_b^{r_f} DR(r)\,(s_W(r)n_W(r) - L(r))\,dr \\ &- G_B\left\{\int_0^b n_B(r)\,dr - N_B\right\} - G_W\left\{\int_b^{r_f} n_W(r)\,dr - N_W\right\}. \end{aligned}$$

Here, the Lagrangian multiplier $DR(r)$ has the economic implication of the differential rent at each r, and the multiplier G_B (G_W) the shadow income tax for each B household (W household). From Assumption (7.94), $Z_W(s_W(r), u_W, E(r-b)) = Z(s_W(r), u_W/E(r-b))$. Hence, rearranging the terms of $\mathcal{L}$, it follows that

$$\begin{aligned} \mathcal{L} = &\int_0^b \left\{\frac{Y_B^0 - G_B - T_B(r) - Z_B(s_B(r), u_B)}{s_B(r)} - R(r)\right\} s_B(r)n_B(r)\,dr \\ &+ \int_b^{r_f} \left\{\frac{Y_W^0 - G_W - T_W(r) - Z(s_W(r), u_W/E(r-b))}{s_W(r)} \right. \\ &\left. - R(r)\right\} s_W(r)n_W(r)\,dr + \int_0^{r_f} DR(r)L(r)\,dr + G_B N_B + G_W N_W\,, \end{aligned} \tag{7.114}$$

where $R(r) \equiv DR(r) + R_A$, which represents the shadow land rent at each r. We must choose all unknowns so as to maximize the Lagrangian function above. Using the bid rent functions (7.89) and (7.96), and associated bid-max lot size functions, the optimality conditions for the HS_R model are given by (7.112) and (7.113) and by the following conditions:[18]

$$R(r) = \begin{cases} \psi_B(Y_B^0 - G_B - T_B(r), u_B) & \text{for } 0 \leq r \leq \hat{b}, \\ \psi(Y_W^0 - G_W - T_W(r), u_W/E(r-b)) & \text{for } \hat{b} < r \leq r_f, \\ R_A & \text{at } r = r_f, \end{cases} \tag{7.115}$$

$$s_B(r) = s_B(Y_B^0 - G_B - T_B(r), u_B), \qquad n_B(r) = L(r)/s_B(r), \qquad 0 \leq r \leq \hat{b}, \tag{7.116}$$

$$s_W(r) = s(Y_W^0 - G_W - T_W(r), u_W/E(r-b)),$$
$$n_W(r) = L(r)/s_W(r), \ \hat{b} < r \leq r_f, \tag{7.117}$$

$$\psi_B(Y_B^0 - G_B - T_B(\hat{b}), u_B)L(\hat{b}) = \psi(Y_W^0 - G_W - T_W(\hat{b}), u_W/E(0))L(\hat{b}) - \int_{\hat{b}}^{r_f} \frac{\partial\psi}{\partial v}\frac{\partial(u_W/E(r-b))}{\partial b} L(r)\, dr, \tag{7.118}$$

where $\hat{b}$ denotes the black–white boundary distance associated with the optimal allocation, and $\partial\psi/\partial v \equiv \partial\psi(Y_W^0 - G_W - T_W(r), v)/\partial v$ at $v = u_W/E(r - \hat{b})$. Except for equation (7.118), we should be familiar with these optimality conditions. Namely, if we exclude (7.118), they represent the conditions of the *compensated equilibrium under the given boundary distance* $\hat{b}$, in which the target utilities u_B and u_W are achieved through the competitive land market with the aid of (per capita) income taxes G_B and G_W. The optimal boundary distance $\hat{b}$ must be determined so as to satisfy condition (7.118). Notice that the left side (the right side) of equation (7.118) represents the land rent increase in the B households' residential area (the land rent decrease in the W households' residential area) from one unit expansion of the black–white boundary distance. Therefore, condition (7.118) means that *the optimal boundary distance* $\hat{b}$ *must be chosen in such a way that the net gain in the total land rent of the city is zero with respect to the marginal change in the boundary distance*. This indicates that the benefits (in terms of $\mathcal{S}$) of a marginal change in b are embodied entirely in the change in the total land rent. Notice also that since $\partial\psi/\partial v < 0$ and $\partial(u_W/E(r - \hat{b}))/\partial b = u_W E'(r - \hat{b})/E(r - \hat{b})^2 > 0$, the second term of the right side of (7.118) is positive. Therefore, we have that

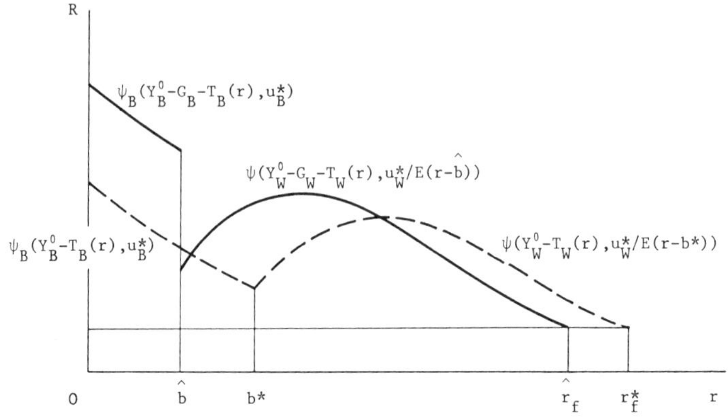

Figure 7.6. Comparison of the equilibrium and optimal spatial configurations.

$$\psi_B(Y_B^0 - G_B - T_B(\hat{b}), u_B) > \psi(Y_W^0 - G_W - T_W(\hat{b}), u_W/E(0)). \qquad (7.119)$$

Therefore, recalling (7.115), we can conclude that *at the optimal boundary $\hat{b}$, the land rent drops discontinuously from the B households' side to the W households' side.*

As an example, let us consider the case in which

$$u_B = u_B^*, \qquad u_W = u_W^*. \qquad (7.120)$$

Namely, we set the target utility levels of the two household types at their respective equilibrium utility levels (in the case with the prejudiced W households). Then we can draw the optimal spatial configuration and the equilibrium one, respectively, as in Figure 7.6. It is not difficult to show that

$$\hat{b} < b^*, \qquad \hat{r}_f < r_f^*,$$

$$G_B < 0, \qquad G_W > 0.$$

Namely, the optimal black–white boundary $\hat{b}$ is closer to the CBD than the equilibrium boundary b^*, and hence B households are confined to a smaller area. To compensate for this deduction in land consumption, each B household receives an income *subsidy*, $-G_B$, while each W household pays income *tax* G_W. Consequently, in the residential area of B households, land rent becomes higher. Notice, however, that this optimal spatial configuration can be maintained only with the aid of a zoning policy that confines B households within the optimal boundary distance $\hat{b}$. This is because in the near suburbs of the boundary, B households are willing to pay higher land rents than W households.[19] This presents a serious moral dilemma, whereby if we accept the W households' prejudice against

B households, the economic efficiency of the city can be improved only by restricting the freedom of choice of B households in land markets.

7.3.2 *Local externality models and global externality models*

As we have already seen, the border models are analytically simple and can generate realistic spatial configurations of cities with racial externalities. Courant and Yinger (1977), however, criticized the border models for two main reasons. First they *a priori* assume a completely segregated pattern with blacks in the city center; namely, segregation is not derived endogenously but simply assumed. Second, if some B households have higher incomes than some poor W households, this completely segregated pattern may not be sustainable within the context of the border models.[20] This is because these rich B households have an incentive to "hop" over the poor W households. This hopping would lead to an equilibrium land use pattern with more than one area of B households, thereby contradicting a basic assumption of the border models.

The local externality model proposed by Yinger (1976) and Schnare (1976) does not have these difficulties. The model assumes that the environmental quality function $E(x)$ for W households at each location x is a decreasing function of the proportion of B households at x. Namely, let $B(x)$ denote the proportion of B households at location x. Then it is assumed that

$$E(x) \equiv E[B(x)], \tag{7.121}$$

where

$$E'[B(x)] \equiv dE[B(x)]/dB(x) < 0,$$

with $0 < E[1] < E[0]$. In the context of the monocentric city under the case of absentee landownership, let us further assume that no location-dependent tax is imposed on households; hence, we set $G_B(x) = 0 = G_W(x)$ for all x. Then the bid rent function and bid-max lot size function of B households are given by $\psi_B(Y_B^0 - T_B(x), u_B)$ and $s_B(Y_B^0 - T_B(x), u_B)$, respectively, and those of W households by $\psi_W(Y_W^0 - T_W(x), u_W, E[B(x)])$ and $s_W(Y_W^0 - T_W(x), u_W, E[B(x)])$. For simplicity of notation, let us define Alonso functions Ψ_B, S_B, Ψ_W, and S_W, as follows:

$$\Psi_B(x, u_B) \equiv \psi_B(Y_B^0 - T_B(x), u_B),$$

$$S_B(x, u_B) \equiv s_B(Y_B^0 - T_B(x), u_B),$$

$$\Psi_W(x, u_W) \equiv \psi_W(Y_W^0 - T_W(x), u_W, E[0]),$$

$$S_W(x, u_W) \equiv s_W(Y_W^0 - T_W(x), u_W, E[0]).$$

Notice that $\Psi_W(x, u_W)$ represents the W households' bid rent at each x

under the "best" environment, that is, when $B(x) = 0$. Let us assume that *the bid rent function* Ψ_B *is steeper than the bid rent function* Ψ_W (recall again Definition 2.2); namely, the bid rent curves of B households are steeper than those of W households assuming that the $B(x)$ were equal to zero for all x.[21] Then we can show that *the only stable equilibrium land use pattern of the city is a complete segregation in which B households occupy the inner ring with a boundary radius b, and W households the outer ring between b and a fringe radius* r_f.

First let us show that such an equilibrium indeed exists. To do so, in the first stage we obtain the equilibrium land use assuming that *for all x*, the bid rent function and bid-max lot size function of W households would be given by $\Psi_W(x, u_W)$ and $S_W(x, u_W)$, respectively [those of B households are, of course, given by $\Psi_B(x, u_B)$ and $S_B(x, u_B)$]. Notice that this represents a fictitious situation because in any equilibrium land use, $B(x)$ cannot be zero for all x. Hence, in the second stage, we show that the equilibrium land use obtained under this assumption indeed represents an actual equilibrium land use. Now, to begin with the first stage, let us notice that all functions $\Psi_i(x, u_i)$ and $S_i(x, u_i)$ for i = B and W are symmetric with respect to the CBD. Hence, replacing x with r (the distance from the CBD), let us represent them respectively by $\Psi_i(r, u_i)$ and $S_i(r, u_i)$ for i = B and W. Then under the assumptions of the utility functions and transport cost functions stated at the beginning of Section 7.3, we can readily see that for each i = B and W, the pair of functions (Ψ_i, S_i) is *well behaved* in the sense of Definition 4.1. Furthermore, the function Ψ_B is assumed to be steeper than Ψ_W. Therefore, applying Proposition 4.1 to the present case, we can immediately conclude that the equilibrium land use exists uniquely, which can be depicted as in Figure 7.4. (This equilibrium solution can be obtained in much the same way as in the case of the unprejudiced city in the previous subsection.) In the figure, the u_i^0 represent the equilibrium utility level for type i households (i = B, W), and B households (W households) occupy the area between $r = 0$ and b^0 (between b^0 and r_f). Now, turning to the second stage, let us notice that under the land use pattern depicted in Figure 7.4, we have that $E[0] > E[B(r)] = E[1]$ for all $0 \leq r < b^0$ and $E[B(r)] = E[0]$ for all $b^0 < r \leq r_f^0$. Therefore, since the bid rent function $\psi_W(Y_W^0 - T_W(r), u_W, E)$ is increasing in E, and since the $\Psi_B(r, u_B^0)$ curve is steeper than the $\Psi_W(r, u_W^0)$ curve, it holds that

$$\begin{aligned}\Psi_B(r, u_B^0) > \Psi_W(r, u_W^0) &\equiv \psi_W(Y_W^0 - T_W(r), u_W^0, E[0]) \\ &> \psi_W(Y_W^0 - T_W(r), u_W^0, E[1]) \qquad \text{for } r < b^0, \\ \Psi_B(r, u_B^0) < \Psi_W(r, u_W^0) &\equiv \psi_W(Y_W^0 - T_W(r), u_W^0, E[0]) \qquad \text{for } b^0 < r \leq r_f.\end{aligned}$$

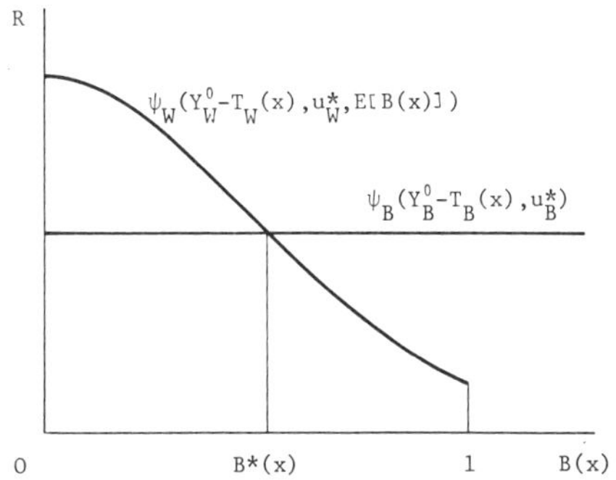

Figure 7.7. Instability of mixed equilibria.

Consequently, under the land use pattern of Figure 7.4, no household has a motivation to change its location, and hence it indeed represents an equilibrium land use.

We have seen above that in the context of the local externality model, the equilibrium land use of the unprejudiced city also represents an equilibrium land use of the prejudiced city (i.e., for the present context). This does not, of course, mean that it would be the unique equilibrium land use (of the prejudiced city). However, we can show that it represents the unique *stable* equilibrium. To show this, let us consider an (arbitrary) equilibrium land use, and let $u_B^*(u_W^*)$ represent the associated equilibrium utility level of B households (W households), and let $B^*(x)$ denote the proportion of B households at each location x. Suppose that at a location x, we have that $0 < B^*(x) < 1$; that is, households of both types reside at x. Then they should have the same bid rent at x, that is, $\psi_B(Y_B^0 - T_B(x), u_B^*) = \psi_W(Y_W^0 - T_W(x), u_W^*, E[B^*(x)])$. Therefore, as depicted in Figure 7.7, if we consider $B(x)$ to be a parameter, the downward-sloping curve $\psi_W(Y_W^0 - T_W(x), u_W^*, E[B(x)])$ must intersect the horizontal line $\psi_B(Y_B^0 - T_B(x), u_B^*)$ at $B^*(x)$. This implies that if the proportion of B households at x happens to increase (decrease) slightly from the equilibrium value $B^*(x)$, then the B households' bid rent at x becomes higher (lower) than that of the W households. This in turn implies that the proportion of B households at x will further increase (decrease). Therefore, we can conclude that $B^*(x)$ can be stable only if $B^*(x) = 0$ or $B^*(x) = 1$. Consequently, the equilibrium land use pattern depicted in Figure 7.4 represents the unique stable equilibrium one.

Recall that the equilibrium land use of the unprejudiced city is always efficient (from Proposition 4.5). This in turn implies that the stable equilibrium land use of the prejudiced city is also efficient.[22] Then since unstable equilibria would be seldom realized, we can conclude that in the context of the local externality model, racial externalities do not bring about any problem.[23]

This surprising result, however, contradicts the intensity of racial problems in many cities in the United States. This suggests that racial externalities are not so local as are assumed in the local externality model. Therefore, we now turn to a more general model, called the global externality model, in which the total externalities received by a W household are a weighted sum of externalities from all B households in the city, where weights are given by a decreasing function of distance between a W household and a B household. Namely, let

$$A(x) = \int_{\mathbf{R}^2} a(|x - y|) n_{\mathrm{B}}(y)\, dy,$$

which represents the total externalities received by a W household from all B households distributed in the city. Here, $a(|x - y|)$ is a decreasing function of distance $|x - y|$. Then the global externality model assumes that

$$E(x) \equiv E[A(x)], \tag{7.122}$$

where

$$E'[A(x)] \equiv dE[A(x)]/dA(x) < 0.$$

This global model is more general than the preceding two types of racial externality model. However, it is also analytically more complex. The systematic analysis of solution characteristics (for both equilibrium and optimal) for global externality models such as existence, uniqueness, symmetry, and stability is largely left for the future. In particular, there is no *a priori* reason to assume that the optimal land use pattern is symmetric with respect to the CBD. It is also quite possible that multiple equilibria will occur under a broad range of parameter values, which in turn will bring about discontinuous changes in the equilibrium land use pattern with respect to parameter changes.[24]

7.4 Traffic congestion and land use for transportation

Thus far, we have assumed that the city is free of traffic congestion, and hence the transport cost $T(r)$ of each household can be given as an exogenous function of commuting distance r. However, as noted before, traffic congestion is probably the most important type of negative externality in cities. In this section, we extend the basic theory of Part I to include traffic congestion in commuting. For simplicity, we assume that automobiles are the only mode of commuting and that there are so many radial roads that circumferential travel costs can be neglected.[25] Because of traffic congestion, transport costs $T(r)$ depend on the amount of land that is used for roads. Therefore, the main problem in this section is determining how to allocate land between transportation and housing. We examine this problem in the context of an extended HS model and show that a location tax (or traffic congestion tax) is necessary for an efficient allocation of land through competitive land markets.

Let r denote the distance from the center of the CBD, $N(r)$ the number of households residing *beyond* distance r, and $L_T(r)$ the amount of land devoted to transport use at distance r. Provided that one member of each household commutes to the CBD, $N(r)$ equals the number of commuters passing through radius r. We assume that the transport cost per commuter per unit distance at radius r, or the *marginal transport cost* at r, is a function of the traffic–land ratio $N(r)/L_T(r)$, and it is denoted by $c(N(r)/L_T(r))$.[26] Then the transport cost $T(r)$ at each distance r is given by

$$T(r) = \int_{r_c}^{r} c\left(\frac{N(x)}{L_T(x)}\right) dx, \tag{7.123}$$

where r_c is the radius of the CBD. We assume r_c is a given *positive* constant, but neglect the transport cost within the CBD. The marginal transport cost function $c(\omega)$ is assumed to be positive, increasing, and strictly convex for all $\omega \geq 0$:

$$c(\omega) > 0, \qquad c'(\omega) > 0, \qquad \text{and} \qquad c''(\omega) > 0 \qquad \text{for all} \quad \omega \geq 0, \tag{7.124}$$

and hence

$$\lim_{\omega \to \infty} c(\omega) = \infty, \tag{7.125}$$

where $c'(\omega) \equiv dc(\omega)/d\omega$ and $c''(\omega) \equiv dc'(\omega)/d\omega$. For simplicity, we also assume that the only cost of building roads is the opportunity cost of land, which equals R_A per unit of land.

Except for these new assumptions on transport cost, we follow the same framework presented for the optimal land use problem of Section 3.4. This implies, among other things, that all N households in the city have the same utility function, $U(z, s)$, which satisfies Assumptions 2.1 and 2.3; furthermore, the land distribution $L(r)$ is positive for all $r > 0$ (Assumption 3.1). Given an arbitrary target utility level u, the previous HS model, (3.50), now changes as follows:

$$\max_{r_f, L_T(r), n(r), s(r)} \mathcal{S} = \int_{r_c}^{r_f} \{[Y^0 - T(r) - Z(s(r), u)$$

$$- R_A s(r)]n(r) - R_A L_T(r)\} \, dr, \qquad (7.126)$$

subject to (7.123) and the following constraints:

$$n(r)s(r) + L_T(r) \leq L(r) \qquad \text{for} \quad r_c \leq r \leq r_f, \qquad (7.127)$$

$$N(r) = \int_r^{r_f} n(x)\, dx \qquad \text{for} \quad r_c \leq r \leq r_f, \qquad (7.128)$$

$$N = N(r_c) \equiv \int_{r_c}^{r_f} n(r)\, dr, \qquad (7.129)$$

where each of $L_T(r)$, $n(r)$, and $s(r)$ are nonnegative, and $Z(s(r), u)$ represents the solution to $U(z, s(r)) = u$ for z. Namely, the problem is to choose the urban fringe distance r_f, transport–land distribution $L_T(r)$, household distribution $n(r)$, and lot size distribution $s(r)$ so as to maximize the surplus (7.126) subject to the transport cost constraint (7.123), the land constraint (7.127), the commuter-number constraint (7.128), and the population constraint (7.129). Notice that in the surplus function (7.126), the last term, $R_A L_T(r)$, represents the opportunity cost of land for transportation at r. We call the above maximization problem the *Herbert–Stevens model with traffic congestion (HS_T model).*[27]

To state the optimality conditions for the HS_T model in terms of bid rent functions, let us introduce the following model of residential choice behavior by each household:

$$\max_{r,z,s} U(z, s) \qquad \text{subject to} \quad z + R(r)s = Y^0 - g - l(r) - T(r), \qquad (7.130)$$

where Y^0 denotes the pretax income of each household, g the *population tax* per household, and $l(r)$ the *location tax* per household at distance r.[28] Here g and $l(r)$ are assumed to be specified by the city government. Then setting I equal to $Y^0 - g - l(r) - T(r)$ in (3.2), we obtain the household bid rent at each distance r

$$\psi(Y^0 - g - l(r) - T(r), u) = \max_s \frac{Y^0 - g - l(r) - T(r) - Z(s, u)}{s}, \qquad (7.131)$$

and the corresponding bid-max lot size is given by $s(Y^0 - g - l(r) - T(r), u)$. Next, we define the *bid rent ψ_T of the transport sector* at each distance r as the marginal benefit of land for transport at r:

$$\psi_T\left(\frac{N(r)}{L_T(r)}\right) = -\frac{\partial c(N(r)/L_T(r))}{\partial L_T(r)} N(r)$$

$$= c'\left(\frac{N(r)}{L_T(r)}\right)\left(\frac{N(r)}{L_T(r)}\right)^2. \tag{7.132}$$

Namely, if one unit of land is added to transport use at r, the marginal transport cost at r decreases $-\partial c(N(r)/L_T(r))/\partial L_T(r)$, which is enjoyed by each of $N(r)$ commuters there. Hence, $\psi_T(N(r)/L_T(r))$ represents the sum of these benefits for all $N(r)$ commuters at r. Using these bid rent functions and bid-max lot size function, the necessary and sufficient conditions for the optimal solution for the HS_T model are given by (7.123), (7.127)–(7.129), and the following conditions:[29]

$$R(r) = \begin{cases} \max\{\psi(Y^0 - g - l(r) - T(r), u), \psi_T(N(r)/L_T(r))\}, & r_c \le r \le r_f, \\ R_A, \quad r \ge r_f, \end{cases} \tag{7.133}$$

$$R(r) = \psi(Y^0 - g - l(r) - T(r), u) \qquad \text{if} \quad n(r) > 0, \tag{7.134}$$

$$R(r) = \psi_T(N(r)/L_T(r)) \qquad \text{if} \quad L_T(r) > 0, \tag{7.135}$$

$$s(r) = s(Y^0 - g - l(r) - T(r), u), \qquad r_c \le r \le r_f, \tag{7.136}$$

$$n(r) = (L(r) - L_T(r))/s(Y^0 - g - l(r) - T(r), u), \qquad r_c \le r \le r_f, \tag{7.137}$$

$$l(r) = \int_{r_c}^{r} c'\left(\frac{(N(x)}{L_T(x)}\right)\frac{N(x)}{L_T(x)}\,dx, \qquad r_c \le r \le r_f, \tag{7.138}$$

where $R(r)$ represents the shadow land rent at each r, g the shadow population tax, and $l(r)$ the shadow location tax per household at r.

As usual, we can interpret these optimality conditions as representing the conditions of the *compensated equilibrium,* in which the target utility u is achieved through the competitive land market with the aid of population tax and location tax policies. In this market, in addition to the usual participants of households, landowners, and the city government, we have the *transport sector (t sector)* as a new participant. The role of the t sector is twofold: First the t sector is entitled to collect a location tax $l(r)$ from each household (i.e., each commuter) at each r; in determining $l(r)$, however, the t sector must follow the *location tax formula* given by (7.138), the meaning of which will be explained below. Second, the t sector must determine the amount of land to be used for transport $L_T(r)$ at each distance r so as to satisfy condition (7.135), the meaning of which will also be explained in detail below.

The role of the city government is, as usual, to choose an appropriate population tax g so that the target utility u will be attained at equilibrium. Given a population tax g and location tax $l(x)$, the residential choice behavior of each household can be expressed by (7.130). In this context, condition (7.133) implies that at each distance r within the residential area between r_c and r_f, the market land rent $R(r)$ equals the maximum of the household bid rent and t sector bid rent. Furthermore, conditions (7.133)–(7.135) together ensure that land at each distance will be occupied only by highest bidders. The meaning of the rest of the conditions, (7.123), (7.127)–(7.129), (7.136), and (7.137), is obvious. Notice also that if in considering these optimality conditions, we take g as fixed and u as a variable, they now represent the conditions of the *competitive equilibrium* under the population tax rate g. Furthermore, if we vary u or g over all possible values, we can obtain all efficient allocations.

In order to see the meaning of the location tax formula (7.138), notice that when an additional commuter residing at distance r commutes through each $x(<r)$, this person causes the additional congestion cost of $\partial c(N(x)/L_T(x))/\partial N(x) = c'(N(x)/L_T(x))/L_T(x)$ for *each* of $N(x)$ existing commuters through x; hence, the $N(x)$ commuters together suffer the additional congestion costs of

$$c'\left(\frac{N(x)}{L_T(x)}\right)\frac{N(x)}{L_T(x)}. \tag{7.139}$$

Thus, (7.138) says that *the location tax $l(r)$ equals the sum of the additional congestion cost caused by a person commuting from distance r to the CBD*. We can also interpret (7.139) as representing the *congestion toll* per commuter per unit distance at r. Then (7.138) means that $l(r)$ *equals the sum of the congestion tolls paid by a person commuting from distance r to the CBD.*[30] Next, in order to see the meaning of condition (7.135) more precisely, notice that if $L_T(r) = 0$ at some $r_c \leq r < r_f$, then we have from (7.123) and (7.125) that $T(r') = \infty$ for all $r' > r$, and hence $\mathcal{S} = -\infty$.[31] This implies that the land allocation is not optimal. Therefore, in the optimal allocation, it must hold that

$$L_T(r) > 0 \qquad \text{for all} \quad r_c \leq r < r_f, \tag{7.140}$$

and hence, using (7.132), we can restate condition (7.135) as

$$R(r) = c'\left(\frac{N(r)}{L_T(r)}\right)\left(\frac{N(r)}{L_T(r)}\right)^2 \qquad \text{for} \quad r_c \le r < r_f. \tag{7.141}$$

This represents none other than a *cost–benefit rule* for determining the optimal amount of transport land $L_T(r)$ at each r. Namely, when the t sector adds a unit of land for transport at r, it must pay the cost of the land $R(r)$. On the other hand, as explained by equation (7.132), the benefit of adding a unit of transport land at r equals the right side of (7.141). Therefore, (7.141) requires that *the optimal $L_T(r)$ shall be chosen so as to equate the marginal cost and marginal benefit of transport land at each r.*

We can see that *if the t sector follows the location tax formula (7.138) and the cost–benefit rule (7.142), its budget is balanced at the competitive (or compensated) equilibrium.* To see this, notice that (7.138) implies that $l'(r) \equiv dl(r)/dr = c'(N(r)/L_T(r))N(r)/L_T(r)$ at each $r \in (r_c, r_f)$. Hence, using (7.141), we have that

$$R(r)L_T(r) = l'(r)N(r) \qquad \text{for} \quad r_c < r < r_f. \tag{7.142}$$

From integration by parts,

$$\int_{r_c}^{r_f} l'(r)N(r)\,dr = (l(r_f)N(r_f) - l(r_c)N(r_c)) - \int_{r_c}^{r_f} l(r)N'(r)\,dr.$$

By definition, $N(r_f) = 0$ and $l(r_c) = 0$; and from (7.128), $N'(r) = -n(r)$. Therefore, integrating both sides of (7.142), we can conclude that

$$\int_{r_c}^{r_f} R(r)L_T(r)\,dr = \int_{r_c}^{r_f} l(r)n(r)\,dr. \tag{7.143}$$

Namely, *the total cost of transport land equals total location tax revenues.*[32]

Next, let us examine some additional characteristics of the competitive (or compensated) equilibrium associated with the solution to the HS_T model. First, we can readily see from (7.138) that

$$l(r) > 0 \qquad \text{for} \quad r_c < r \le r_f \tag{7.144}$$

and

$$l'(r) = c'\left(\frac{N(r)}{L_T(r)}\right)\frac{N(r)}{L_T(r)} > 0 \qquad \text{for} \quad r_c < r < r_f. \tag{7.145}$$

Namely, the location tax $l(r)$ is positive and increasing in r throughout the residential area. From (7.123) the transport cost $T(r)$ is, of course, increasing in r:

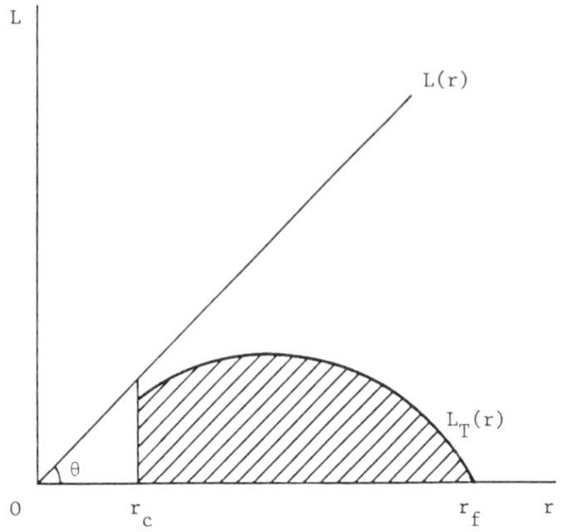

Figure 7.8. Optimal land use configuration.

$$T'(r) = c(N(r)/L_T(r)) > 0 \qquad \text{for} \quad r_c < r < r_f. \tag{7.146}$$

Therefore, applying the envelope theorem to (7.131), we can see from (7.134) that

$$R'(r) = -(l'(r) + T'(r))/s(r) < 0 \qquad \text{if} \quad n(r) > 0. \tag{7.147}$$

Namely, in the *nonsaturated area,* where all the available land is not used up for transportation, the land rent is always decreasing in r. However, in the *saturated area,* where all the land is used for transportation, the land rent can increase in r. To see this, observe from (7.141) that

$$R'(r) = \left[c''\left(\frac{N(r)}{L_T(r)}\right)\frac{N(r)}{L_T(r)} + 2c'\left(\frac{N(r)}{L_T(r)}\right)\right]\left[N'(r) - \frac{N(r)}{L_T(r)}L_T'(r)\right]\frac{N(r)}{L_T(r)^2}. \tag{7.148}$$

Since in the saturated area we have that $L_T(r) = L(r)$ and $N'(r) = 0$, it follows that $R'(r) > 0$ if $L'(r) < 0$. This can happen near the entrance of a transport-bottleneck area. Figure 7.8 depicts a possible optimal land use configuration.[33] In this example, no area is saturated with all available land used for transportation. However, when the city population N is large, all the land near the CBD fringe could be consumed by transport uses.

As noted before, in the context of either a compensated equilibrium or a competitive equilibrium, an equilibrium allocation is efficient if and only if the t sector collects location taxes based on the formula (7.138) and determines the amount of transport land following the cost–benefit rule (7.141) [i.e., (7.135)]. In practice, however, it is possible that the t sector does not have control over location taxes and/or transport land. Even under such circumstances, it is desirable to allocate the resources as efficiently as possible, although the resulting allocations are necessarily inferior to the one given by the solution to the HS_T model. In the rest of this section, we discuss briefly these *second-best problems*.

As the first case, suppose that the city has already established transport networks, and it is extremely difficult to modify them. In this situation, the t sector has no choice but to accept the existing transport land $L_T(r)$ as exogenously given. The t sector's objective is then to choose the location tax $l(r)$ at each distance so that the competitive land market allocates the households in the most efficient manner. This second-best problem with exogenous transport land leads to the same optimality conditions (with those of the HS_T model) *except* that $L_T(r)$ is now fixed at each r. Therefore, we can immediately conclude that a competitive equilibrium of the residential land market is efficient (i.e., the second best) if and only if the t sector follows the formula (7.138) in determining the location tax $l(r)$ at each distance.

As the second case, let us consider the opposite situation. Namely, suppose that no location tax is presently levied in the city and it is not possible to introduce such legislation (because of the strong opposition of the residents or because of the high administration costs of collecting location taxes). Therefore, the t sector must optimally choose the transport land $L_T(r)$ at each distance subject to the constraint that no location tax can be levied. It turns out that in achieving the second-best allocation, the t sector can no longer rely on the previous cost–benefit rule (7.141). The reason is as follows: Since commuters do not pay congestion externality costs in the form of location taxes, the market land rents now reflect only differentials of *private* transport cost $T(r)$ among locations. Thus, the market land rents are now distorted, failing to represent the social value of an additional unit of land at each distance. Therefore, in the left side of (7.141), $R(r)$ fails to represent the *social cost* of an additional unit of transport land at distance r. Furthermore, the right side of (7.141) (which equals the marginal direct saving in transport cost from an additional unit of transport land at r) also fails to represent the *social benefit* of an additional unit of transport land at r. This is because an increase in transport land at any distance also causes a change in market land rent everywhere; and in the present situation of distorted market land rents, this indirect effect must also be taken into account in calculating the social benefit of an additional unit of transport land at each r. Therefore, in achieving the second-best optimal allocation, the t sector must use a *modified cost–benefit rule* that is based on *social land rents* (instead of market land rents).[34] It must also be noted that in the second-best city, the optimal urban fringe distance must be determined at the intersection of the agricultural rent curve and the social rent curve (instead of the market rent curve). Kanemoto (1980, Ch. V) shows that the social rent curve is steeper than the market rent curve (i.e., the former is higher than the latter near the CBD, and lower near the urban fringe).[35]

7.5 Conclusion

In this chapter, we have examined the impact of negative externalities on residential land markets. Specifically, we have studied equilibrium and optimal spatial configurations of cities in the presence of crowding externalities, racial externalities, and traffic congestion. Because of space limitations, however, our discussions in this chapter have not been comprehensive. In particular, traffic congestion represents one of the most thoroughly examined topics in urban economics. For further studies on these topics, see the articles referred to in the bibliographical notes below.

Bibliographical notes

Crowding externalities have been studied by Richardson (1977b), Grieson and Murray (1981), Tauchen (1981), and Scotchmer (1982). Our model, (7.22), is a log-linear specification of the original model by Richardson (1977b). Richardson (1977b) suggested that crowding may result in a positive rent gradient. That is, if households' preference for low density is sufficiently strong, increasing average lot size may cause a rising land rent curve near the CBD. This interesting conjecture was proved unlikely, however, by Grieson and Murray (1981) and Tauchen (1981).

Border models of racial externalities have been developed by Bailey (1959) and Rose-Ackerman (1975, 1977). In our discussion of border models in Section 7.3.1, we introduced the assumption of a separable utility function, (7.94). This is because without this assumption (or a similar assumption), the comparison of equilibrium spatial configurations for prejudiced and unprejudiced cities would lead to no clear conclusion. The local externality model was proposed by Yinger (1976) and Schnare (1976) and was further developed by Kern (1981). It must be noted that although we considered in Section 7.3.2 only the case in which whites have an aversion to living near blacks while blacks are indifferent to the location of whites, these original papers considered many different combinations of the racial attitudes of the two groups. Furthermore, King (1980) developed computational algorithms for local externality models (based on the Scarf algorithm) and presented many interesting examples. Global externality models were developed by Yellin (1974), Papageorgiou (1978a,b), Kanemoto (1980, Ch. 6), and Ando (1981, Ch. 5). In particular, Kanemoto (1980, Ch. 6) examined in detail the characteristics of market equilibria in the global externality model and demonstrated a possibility of dynamic instability in racially mixed cities; for example, a small increase in the number of blacks in the neighborhood may drive away all whites, causing a sudden change in the racial composition. Phenomena of this type, called *neighborhood tippings* or *cumulative decay processes,* were further studied by Miyao (1978a,b), Schnare and MacRae (1978), and Anas (1980). For a comprehensive survey of racial externality models, see Kanemoto (1987).

Optimal urban land use with transport congestion was first studied by Strotz (1965) in the context of monocentric discrete rings. Solow and Vickrey (1971) examined the optimal allocation of land between business activity and transportation in a long, narrow city. Mills and de Ferranti (1971) were the first to study the optimal allocation of land between housing and transport in a standard, continuous monocentric city. This topic was further developed by Legey, Ripper, and Varaiya (1973), Robson (1976), Kanemoto (1977, 1980, Ch. 4), and Ando (1981, Ch. 3). Our discussion in Section 7.4 is based on their work. The second-best problems of land allocation between housing and transport were examined by Solow and Vickrey (1971), Solow (1973), Kanemoto (1980, Ch. 5), Arnott and MacKinnon (1978), Arnott (1979), Pines and Sadka (1981), Ando (1981, Ch. 4), Wilson (1983), and Sullivan (1983a,b). Henderson (1981) presented an analysis of staggered work hours with endogenous departure time. Miyao (1978c) examined land use for transportation in a square city with a grid-type transportation network. Wheaton (1978) considered a second-best transportation investment problem in a nonspatial model with more than one type of road. For a comprehensive survey of urban transportation and land use, see Kanemoto (1987).

Finally, for studies of externalities between firms and households (e.g., air pollution), see Stull (1974), Henderson (1977), Hochman and Ofek (1979), Miyao, Shapiro, and Knapp (1980), and the survey article by Kanemoto (1987).

Notes

1. For a definition of externalities, see note 4, Chapter 5.
2. For the negative externalities generated by firms and borne by households (such as air pollution and water pollution from chemical plants), see the bibliographical notes at the end of this chapter.
3. In other words, the crowding model is a special case of the neighborhood-good model, in which the capacity $k(r)$ of the neighborhood good is fixed at the same constant everywhere and the cost of $k(r)$ is neglected.

4. Since $R_0(r)$ is independent of τ, the developer's problem at r can be restated as

$$\max_{\tau} R(r) + \tau\rho(r).$$

5. To distinguish it from an individual lot size, we call $s(r)$ the *average lot size* at r. In the present context of homogeneous households, at equilibrium, of course, $s(r)$ equals the individual lot size at each r.
6. We have previously denoted Y_0 by Y^0. However, since the subsequent analyses often involve power function of Y^0, we adopt this notation.
7. It is not difficult to see that as γ increases, in the area close to the CBD the value of $s_a^*(r)$ [$R_a^*(r)$] increases (decreases); and in the suburbs, the opposite results occur.
8. It can readily be shown that if $s(r) = s_m$ at some $r > r_m$, then we have that $s_M(Y - ar, u, s(r)) > s(r)$, which violates condition (7.51). Therefore, it must hold that $s(r) > s_m$ at each $r > r_m$; hence, from (7.55), we have $s(r) = s^*(Y - ar, u)$ at each $r > r_m$. On the other hand, if $s(r) = s^*(Y - ar, u)$ at some $r < r_m$, then $s_m > s^*(Y - ar, u) = s(r)$, which violates the MLS regulation; hence, we can conclude from (7.57) that $s(r) = s_m$ at each $r < r_m$. We can also readily confirm that under (7.58) and (7.59), all conditions (7.51)–(7.57) are satisfied.
9. Let $X(r) = (Y - ar - s_m^{-(\beta+\gamma)/\alpha} e^{u/\alpha}) s_m^{-1} - \alpha^{\alpha/(\beta+\gamma)} \beta (Y - ar)^{(1+\gamma)/(\beta+\gamma)} e^{-u/(\beta+\gamma)}$. Using (7.60) and the condition that $X(r_m) = 0$, we have that $s_m X(r) = a(r_m - r) + \beta(Y - ar_m)[1 - ((Y - ar)/(Y - ar_m))^{(1+\gamma)/(\beta+\gamma)}]$. From this, we can readily see that $X(r)$ is strictly concave and $X'(r_m) = -s_m^{-1} a\alpha\gamma(\beta + \gamma)^{-1} < 0$. Then since $X(r_m) = 0$ and r_m is small when s_m is close to $s^*(Y, u)$, we can draw the same conclusion as in the text.
10. Notice that this logic can be applied under any reasonable utility functions, land distributions, and transport cost functions. Hence, this conclusion (i.e., that under absentee landownership, an effective MLS regulation always lowers the equilibrium utility level) is a very general proposition. We can also readily see that even when R_A is positive and hence r_f is decreasing in u, this conclusion holds.
11. We can see that the other solution to the quadratic equation violates the requirement that $r_m(Y, u, s_m) \geq 0$, where function r_m is given by (7.61).
12. For other variations, see the bibliographical notes.
13. The terms *local externality models* and *global externality models* are those of Kanemoto (1987). Yinger (1979) calls local externality models *amenity models*.
14. Alternatively, we can assume that $U_W(z, s, E(r - b)) = U(z, s) f(E(r - b))$ or $U_W(z, s, E(r - b)) = U(z, s) + g(E(r - b))$, where f and g are increasing functions of E. However, with appropriate choices of functions f and g, all three utility functions represent the same preferences, and hence they are equivalent. Miyao (1978a) assumed a multiplicative form, whereas Yinger (1976) used an additive form.
15. For this assumption to hold, it is sufficient to assume, for example, that $U_B(z,$

$s) = U(z, s)$ for all z and s, $T_B(r) = T_W(r)$ for all r, and $Y_B < Y_W$; namely, in the unprejudiced city, B households and W households have the same utility function and the same transport cost function, and W households' income is higher than that of B households (recall Proposition 2.1).

16. For details of this solution procedure, see Section 4.3.2. The $\hat{R}(r)$ curve here corresponds to the first boundary rent curve $R_1(r)$ there. In order to determine the equilibrium urban fringe distance r_f^0, we need to introduce the second boundary rent curve. However, since we do not use it in the following analysis, we omit any discussion of it. Notice that by applying Proposition 4.1 to the present problem, we can readily see that there exists a unique equilibrium land use for the unprejudiced city.
17. Here we are implicitly assuming that at the equilibrium of the prejudiced city, no agricultural land would be left between B households and W households (i.e., in Figure 7.5, point β is located above the agricultural rent line). Although it is theoretically possible that at the equilibrium, some amount of agricultural land is left between B households and W households, this would happen only when the W households' aversion to B households was extremely strong. Hence, we omit this case in the following discussion. As with Proposition 4.1, we can show that the equilibrium land use (for the prejudiced city) exists uniquely.
18. In deriving these optimality conditions, we are implicitly assuming as before that no agricultural land will be left between B households and W households, i.e., $s_i(r)n_i(r) = L(r)$ at each $r \in [0, r_f]$ either for i = B or for i = W. Using this implicit assumption, we obtain conditions (7.115)–(7.117) as we did (4.38)–(4.40), and condition (7.118) can be obtained from the first-order condition $\partial\mathcal{L}/\partial b = 0$.
19. Notice that since relation (7.119) holds in the optimal city under any pair of target utility levels, this conclusion holds in any optimal (i.e., efficient) city, including those optimal cities in which $u_B > u_B^*$.
20. For example, in the context of Figure 7.5, if $Y_B^0 > Y_W^0$, it may happen that the $\Psi_B(r, u_B^*)$ curve is less steep than the $\psi(Y_W^0 - T_W(r), u_W^*/E(r - b^*))$ curve at the border b^*.
21. For this assumption to hold, it is sufficient to assume, e.g., that $U_B(z, s) = U_W(z, s, E[0])$ for all z and s, $T_B(x) = T_W(x)$ for all x, and $Y_B < Y_W$.
22. Notice that the equilibria of the prejudiced city cannot be more efficient than those of the unprejudiced city.
23. It must be noted, however, that this conclusion was obtained under the assumption that B households are indifferent to the location of W households. Kern (1981) showed that if the preference for white neighbors is stronger among blacks than among whites, no segregated equilibrium is possible, but there is a stable integrated equilibrium. In this case, the stable equilibrium may not be efficient, and hence racial problems become important.
24. For pioneering work on the global externality models, see the bibliographical notes at the end of this chapter.
25. For extensions with more realistic assumptions, see the bibliographical notes.
26. Although this assumption seems intuitively reasonable, this represents a "black-

box" approach to the complex problem of traffic flow and transport cost; namely, it does not specify the behavior of traffic flow over time. One possible specification is as follows: During the morning commuting period of t_M minutes (e.g., $t_M = 90$), $1/t_M$-th of all commuters (from every residential location) arrives at the CBD in every minute. Similarly, during the evening commuting period of t_E minutes, $1/t_E$-th of all commuters (to all destinations) leaves the CBD in every minute.

27. Notice that as in all previous Herbert–Stevens models, the solution to the HS_T model is independent of the value of Y^0.
28. We can obtain (7.130) from the basic model (2.1) by replacing Y with $Y^0 - g - l(x)$. Alternatively, if we set, in the externality model (6.1), $U(z, s, E(x))$ equal to $U(z, s)$ and $G(x)$ equal to $g + l(x)$, we have (7.130).
29. For the derivation of these optimality conditions, see Appendix C.13.
30. Although this interpretation is mathematically valid, it is practically impossible to collect a toll at every distance from each commuter. Therefore, $l(r)$ must be collected at the residence of each commuter as a lump-sum tax.
31. Recall that the optimal $L_T(r)$ function is assumed to be *piecewise continuous*. Hence, $L_T(r) = 0$ implies that $T(r') = \infty$ for all $r' > r$.
32. As was explained by (7.139), we can interpret that $l'(r) \equiv c'(N(r)/L_T(r))N(r)/L_T(r)$, as representing the congestion toll per commuter per unit distance at r. In this context, (7.142) says that the land cost $R(r)L_T(r)$ and the toll revenue $l'(r)N(r)$ are balanced at *each* distance.
33. Figure 7.8 is based on the following specifications: $L(r) = \theta r$, $U(z, s) = \alpha \log z + \beta \log s$ and $c(N/L_T) = a(N/L_T)^b$, where both a and b are positive constants.
34. The modified cost–benefit rule is very complex. For this, see Kanemoto (1980, Ch. 5) and other articles referred to in the bibliographical notes.
35. For further discussions of the second-best problems, see the articles referred to in the bibliographical notes.

CHAPTER 8

External economies, product variety, and city sizes

8.1 Introduction

In Section 5.2, we discussed various causes of city formation. In this chapter, we examine in more depth the roles of *external economies* and *product variety* in city formation.

In the literature of location theory and urban economics, production scale economies are often classified into two types: *economies of scale* within a firm, and *(Marshallian) external economies* which are external to individual firms but internal to the industry.[1] In our earlier discussion (Section 5.7), this distinction of production scale economies was unnecessary because the developer or city government was assumed to control the entire production activity and hence to internalize all externalities. Indeed, in the case of economies of scale within a firm, it is natural to assume that each firm will behave as the developer of its own city and control all aspects of city formation. This model of a *factory town* or *company town,* however, cannot explain the formation of a city with more than one major firm and hence rarely corresponds to the nature of modern cities.

The concept of *external economies,* in contrast, provides a convenient framework within which to explain scale economies, due to spatial agglomeration of firms and population, and hence it has been widely used in the literature. This is because these economies are supposed to be *external* to individual firms, and thus *increasing returns to scale become compatible with perfectly competitive equilibrium* (as will be explained in Section 8.2). In particular, this concept of external economies has often been used to explain the nature of many *specialized cities* in modern economies, where each city is founded on a basic industry that consists of many similar firms producing the same traded good (or similar traded goods). For example, one may consider Silicon Valley (California), which is specialized in the computer industry.[2] Firms producing the same traded good may find it profitable to agglomerate for various reasons, such as the sharing of skilled subcontractors and specialized service firms, the formation of skilled labor pools, better access to technological and market information, and the sharing of a common infrastructure including transport facilities. These *agglomeration economies* are often called *(Marshallian) external economies* because they are a consequence of an enlargement of the total activity level of the industry in the same city and hence are beyond the control of each individual firm. In Section 8.2, we introduce the *external economy model* of cities and discuss the determination of city sizes in both positive and normative contexts.

Although this external economy model of cities provides a convenient framework, it has the disadvantage of being based on the vague concept of *external economies*. When normative or policy questions are addressed, we need to know more precisely the nature of "external" economies.[3] This suggests that one may develop an alternative framework that models agglomeration economies endogenously, explicitly showing their origins. It has been frequently noted in the literature that one of the major causes of industrial agglomeration is the availability of *specialized local producer services* such as repair and maintenance services, engineering and legal support, transportation and communication services, and financial and advertising services. On the basis of these considerations, in Section 8.3 we develop a *monopolistic competition model* of industrial agglomeration, which focuses on the availability of a variety of producer services as the origin of agglomeration economies. We consider a city with a traded-good industry and a service-good industry, where the latter provides a large variety of specialized services to the former. The central idea behind our model is that increasing returns to scale in the service industry and the desire of the traded-good industry to employ a variety of intermediate services may provide the basic forces of industrial agglomeration in a city; that is, the larger the variety of available intermediate services, the higher will be the productivity of the traded-good industry in a city. The market for intermediate services is described by a Chamberlinian monopolistic competition model à la Dixit and Stiglitz (1977). That the service industry is characterized by monopolistic competition is a direct consequence of the observation that the service industry generally faces relatively minor entry and exit barriers and hence is highly competitive; at the same time, users of services (in the present case, producers of the traded good) have highly specialized diverse demands for them, making each supplier specialized in a service differentiated from others.

It turns out that at the equilibrium of industries, the monopolistic competition model yields the same aggregate production function and wage function as those of the external economy model in Section 8.2; thus, the two models also yield the same equilibrium city size and wage rate. Therefore, for the purpose of descriptive analyses of urban aggregates, the two models are equivalent. However, it is shown in Section 8.4 that from the viewpoint of normative analyses, the two models lead to substantially different results; they give different estimates of the "true" urban production function, different optimal city sizes, and different policy recommendations. Hence, we must investigate which model describes more accurately the city in question. Finally, in Section 8.5, we briefly discuss possible extensions of our study in this chapter.

8.2 Marshallian external economies

Consider a monocentric city in which a traded good X is produced by many small firms, $j = 1, 2, \ldots, m$, located at the CBD. The price of the traded good is assumed to be determined by the international market and hence treated as a given constant; for convenience it is normalized at unity. For simplicity, let us assume that each firm produces the traded good using only labor, and the (common) production function of these firms can be described as

$$x(N_j, N) = g(N)N_j, \qquad j = 1, 2, \ldots, m, \tag{8.1}$$

where $x(N_j, N)$ represents the amount of the traded good produced by firm j when it employs labor N_j, and the total labor force (= population) of the city is given by N.[4] Function $g(N)$ represents the *(Marshallian) external economies* that are enjoyed equally by all the firms in the city. Each firm is assumed to take N as given, and hence $g(N)$ equals the *private marginal product* (PMP) of labor, which changes with the city's population N. We call $g(N)$ the *agglomeration function* and assume that

$$g(N) > 0 \qquad \text{for all} \quad N > 0. \tag{8.2}$$

It is also assumed that function $g(N)$ is initially increasing in N (reflecting the positive effects of agglomeration), but it may eventually start decreasing in N (reflecting the negative effects of agglomeration):

$$g'(N) \equiv \frac{dg(N)}{dN} \begin{cases} >0 & \text{for} \quad N < \tilde{N}, \\ <0 & \text{for} \quad N > \tilde{N}, \end{cases} \tag{8.3}$$

where $\tilde{N}$ is a given constant such that $0 < \tilde{N} \leq \infty$. Note that $\tilde{N} = \infty$ means that $g(N)$ is increasing for all N.

Given a city's population N and wage rate W, each firm will choose its labor input so as to maximize the profit:

$$\max_{N_j} x(N_j, N) - WN_j, \qquad j = 1, 2, \ldots, m. \tag{8.4}$$

Provided that the output level of each firm is positive, the following first-order condition must hold at equilibrium:

$$\frac{\partial x(N_j, N)}{\partial N_j} = W, \tag{8.5}$$

or from (8.1),

$$g(N) = W,$$

which means that the private marginal product of labor equals the wage rate. Hence, if we let $W(N)$ denote the equilibrium wage rate when the city population is N, we have

$$W(N) = g(N). \tag{8.6}$$

Now, we assume as usual that each household is endowed with one unit of labor and that full employment prevails in the city. Aggregating the outputs of all firms, we have

$$\sum_{j=1}^{m} x(N_j, N) = g(N) \sum_{j=1}^{m} N_j = g(N)N. \tag{8.7}$$

Hence, if we define

$$F(N) \equiv g(N)N, \tag{8.8}$$

then $F(N)$ represents the total output of the traded good when the city's population equals N. We call $F(N)$ the *aggregate production function* of the city.

In order to determine both the equilibrium and optimal city sizes, it is crucial to clarify the situation of landownership in the city. In the following, we consider two situations, absentee ownership and public ownership, in turn. Throughout this chapter, we adopt the following standard assumptions on households. All households in the economy are homogeneous, having the same utility function $U(z, s)$. Given a (posttax) income Y, the residential choice behavior of each household in the city can be expressed by the basic model of (2.1), with Assumptions 2.1–2.3 being met. Here, in Assumption 2.2, we also assume that $T(0) = 0$. Migration between the city and the rest of the economy is costless. Finally, we assume that the agricultural land rent is positive, that is, $R_A > 0$.

8.2.1 City sizes under absentee landownership

Let us assume that the land in the city is owned by absentee landlords; hence, the wage W is the sole income of each household in the city.[5] We

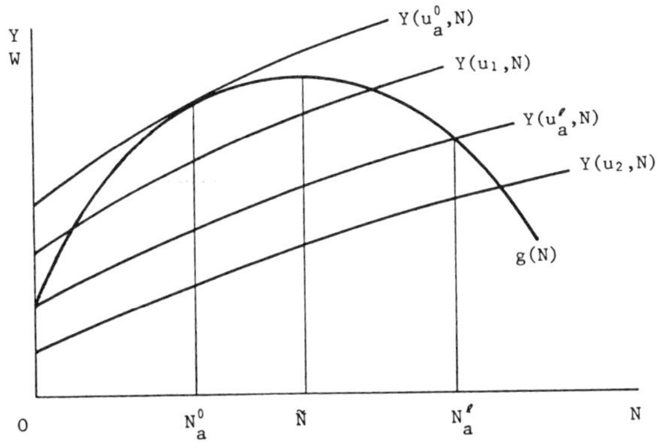

Figure 8.1. Determination of equilibrium city sizes (the absentee ownership case).

can see from (8.6) that given each population N, firms in the city are willing to pay a wage rate $g(N)$. Recall also from Section 5.4 that the *supply–income function* (i.e., *inverse population supply function*), $Y(u, N)$, represents the household income that is just necessary to ensure that N households will be supplied from the national economy to the city. Hence, given a national utility level u, the equilibrium number of households in the city, or *equilibrium city size,* can be determined by solving the following equation for N:

$$g(N) = Y(u, N). \tag{8.9}$$

Figure 8.1 explains the determination of equilibrium city sizes under various national utility levels. In this figure, the $g(N)$ curve is depicted by a bold concave curve, and a set of $Y(u, N)$ curves is depicted by upward-sloping curves. Given a national utility level u, an equilibrium city size is determined at an intersection between the $g(N)$ curve and a $Y(u, N)$ curve. For example, when $u = u_1$, there are two equilibrium city sizes; when $u = u_2$, only one exists. When $u = u_a^0$, the $Y(u_a^0, N)$ curve is tangent to the $g(N)$ curve at population N_a^0 from above. Since a supply–income curve $Y(u, N)$ shifts upward as u increases (Property 5.2), u_a^0 *represents the highest equilibrium utility level the city can attain under the situation of absentee landownership*. Notice also from Figure 8.1 that u_a^1 gives the lowest utility level under which there are two equilibrium city sizes.

Next, let $u_a(N)$ represent the national utility level when the equilibrium city size is N. From Figure 8.1 we can derive the $u_a(N)$ curve as in Figure 8.2. Formally, $u_a(N)$ can be determined by solving equation (8.9) for u under each value of N. Although it may not always be the case, for sim-

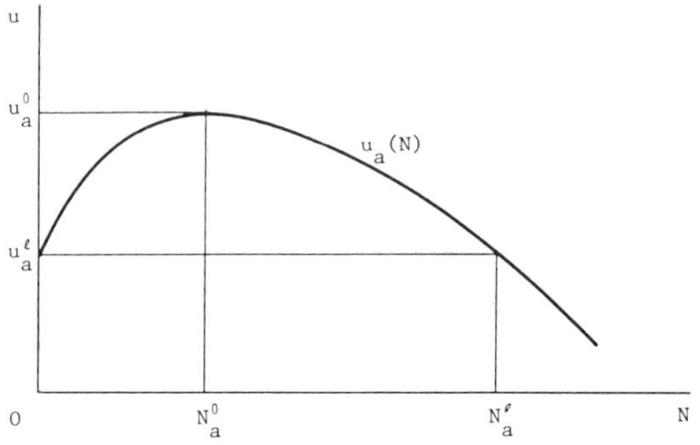

Figure 8.2. Equilibrium utility curve (the absentee ownership case).

plicity of discussion, we assume in the subsequent analyses that the $u_a(N)$ curve is *single-peaked,* as in Figure 8.2. More precisely, let the *highest utility* u_a^0 be defined as

$$u_a^0 = \max \{u \mid g(N) = Y(u, N) \text{ for some } N > 0\}, \tag{8.10}$$

and the *limiting utility* u_a^l be defined by the relation

$$g(0) = Y(u_a^l, 0). \tag{8.11}$$

Then we assume that the following four conditions are satisfied:

1. There exist the highest utility $u_a^0 < \infty$ and the limiting utility $u_a^l \geq -\infty$.
2. u_a^0 is achieved at a unique city size N_a^0, called the *critical city size,* such that $0 < N_a^0 < \infty$.
3. There exists a unique city size N_a^l, called the *limiting city size,* such that

$$g(N_a^l) = Y(u_a^l, N_a^l), \qquad 0 < N_a^l \leq \infty. \tag{8.12}$$

4. For each u such that $u_a^l < u < u_a^0$, equation (8.9) has two solutions for N.

Figure 8.1 depicts the situation in which all four conditions above are satisfied. Notice that condition 4 implies that the $u_a(N)$ curve is single-peaked, as in Figure 8.2. Since each $Y(u, N)$ curve is upward-sloped (Property 5.2), we can readily see from Figure 8.1 that $N_a^0 < \tilde{N}$, which implies that the highest utility u_a^0 is attained at the city size N_a^0 that is in the increasing phase of the agglomeration function. It is also apparent from Figure 8.1 that $N_a^0 < N_a^l$, that is, the critical city size is smaller than the limiting city size.[6]

Notice from Figure 8.2 that given each national utility level u such that $u_a^1 \leq u < u_a^0$, there are two equilibrium city sizes, one smaller than N_a^0 and the other larger than N_a^0. In this event, it turns out that *given any such utility level u, the equlibrium city size smaller than N_a^0 is (locally) unstable, and the one larger than N_a^0 is (locally) stable*. To see this, suppose, for example, that the national utility level equals u_1 in Figure 8.1, and N_1 and N_1' are the equilibrium city sizes under u_1 such that

$$g(N_1) = Y(u_1, N_1), \qquad g(N_1') = Y(u_1, N_1'), \qquad N_1 < N_a^0 < N_1'.$$

Then *at $N = N_1$, the demand–wage curve $g(N)$ is steeper than the supply–income curve $Y(u_1, N)$*; hence, given a sufficiently small ΔN, we can see that

$$g(N_1 + \Delta N) \gtrless Y(u_1, N_1 + \Delta N) \quad \text{as} \quad \Delta N \gtrless 0. \tag{8.13}$$

This implies that if ΔN households move into (or out of) the city, the wage rate of the city increases (decreases) to $g(N_1 + \Delta N)$, which is greater (less) than the supply–income $Y(u_1, N_1 + \Delta N)$; hence, the equilibrium utility level of the city becomes higher (lower) than the national utility level u_1. This will, in turn, induce more households to move into (out of) the city, and the city size will move farther away from N_1. In this sense, the original equilibrium city size N_1 is *(locally) unstable.*[7] In contrast, at $N = N_1'$, *the $g(N)$ curve is flatter than the $Y(u_1, N)$ curve*. In this situation, we will have the opposite result. Namely, for each small ΔN, it holds that

$$g(N_1' + \Delta N) \lesseqgtr Y(u_1, N_1' + \Delta N) \qquad \text{as} \quad \Delta N \gtrless 0. \tag{8.14}$$

From this, we can readily see that even if the city size happens to deviate slightly from N_1', it will move back toward the original size N_1'. In this sense, the equilibrium city size N_1' is *(locally) stable.*[8]

Next, observe that for each national utility level lower than u_a^1, there exists a unique equilibrium city size, which is greater than the limiting city size N_a^1. It turns out, however, that *if the technology of traded-good production is independent of location, any city size greater than N_a^l is also unstable;* in other words, *any national utility level lower than u_a^l* is not sustainable. To see this, suppose, for example, that the national utility level equals u_2 in Figure 8.1, and let $N_2 (> N_a^1)$ be the equilibrium city size of the city. In this situation, suppose a new firm establishes itself at a new location outside the city and produces the traded good, hiring a small number of workers ΔN. Then since the firm can hire ΔN workers at the wage rate $Y(u_2, \Delta N)$, its profit is given by

$$\pi = g(\Delta N)\,\Delta N - Y(u_2, \Delta N)\,\Delta N$$
$$\doteqdot g(0)\,\Delta N - Y(u_2, 0)\,\Delta N$$
$$= (g(0) - Y(u_2, 0))\,\Delta N.$$

Then since the supply–income $Y(u, 0)$ is increasing in u, and since $u_2 < u_a^l$ by assumption, from (8.11) we have that

$$\pi \doteqdot (g(0) - Y(u_2, 0))\,\Delta N$$
$$> (g(0) - Y(u_a^l, 0))\,\Delta N = 0.$$

This implies that every firm in the city in question will stop operating there and will start operating at a new location outside the city with positive profits. Hence, the original city cannot be sustained. This also implies that if the national utility level u were lower than u_a^l, new firms would continue to be established, and the demand for labor would eventually exceed the total population of the economy. Therefore, a national utility level lower than u_a^l cannot persist in an economy at equilibrium.

In summary, we can conclude that *only those city sizes between N_a^0 and N_a^l are stable*. Since unstable city sizes would be observed rarely, it is sufficient to focus on these stable city sizes. It should be noted, however, that the realization of a particular (stable) city size depends on the national utility level. To determine this national utility level endogenously, let us consider a simple case. Namely, suppose that all cities in the nation are the same as the one discussed above. Suppose also that the total population of the urban sector in the nation is exogenously given by M. Then, given any $N > 0$, if the population of each city equals N and there are M/N cities in the nation, each household in every city will attain the common utility $u_a(N)$; hence, such a city system is in equilibrium.[9] In particular, *given any city size N between N_a^0 and N_a^l, such a city system is (locally) stable.*[10] *Therefore, there exists potentially a continuum of stable equilibrium city systems.*

To examine which equilibrium city system is more likely to be observed, let us consider the following dynamic process: Suppose at present there exist a large number of cities having the same population N such that $N_a^0 \le N < N_a^l$. As the populations of these cities grow, all of the cities will gain the population moving toward N_a^l. However, when the populations of all the cities reach N_a^l, a further increase in population will induce the formation of a new city. Since all populations beyond N_a^l in the old cities will migrate into the new city, this new city will grow rapidly while the populations of the old cities will remain close to N_a^l. When the new city catches up to the old cities in population, another new city will soon be generated. And the process will continue. This implies that *most cities are likely to have their population close to* N_a^l.

Among all stable equilibrium city sizes, N_a^0 (N_a^1) gives the highest (lowest) equilibrium utility level. Therefore, from the viewpoint of urban households, the city system under the individual city size N_a^0 (N_a^1) is the best (worst). However, in the present context of absentee landownership, we must also consider the welfare of absentee landlords, which is represented by the total differential rent from all cities, (M/N)TDR, where TDR is the total differential rent from each city. If (M/N)TDR is decreasing for all N between N_a^0 and N_a^1, the city system with the individual city size N_a^0 is the best (among all stable city systems) for both households and landlords. If, however, (M/N)TDR is increasing for all N between N_a^0 and N_a^1, the city system with N_a^0 (N_a^1) is the best for the households (landlords). Hence, the overall welfare implications of city systems are not clear. This is in contrast to the following situation of public landownership, in which only the welfare of households matters and thus we can reach clear conclusions on the welfare implications of city sizes.

8.2.2 *City sizes under public landownership*

Let us assume that the city residents form a government, which rents the land for the city from rural landlords at agricultural rent R_A. The city government, in turn, subleases the land to city residents at a competitively determined rent. The TDR is equally divided among the city residents. Then the income of each household in the city equals its wage W plus a share of differential land rent TDR/N.

From (8.6), the per capita wage in the city equals $g(N)$ when the city population is N. Let TDR($g(N)$, N) be the total differential rent of the city when the population is N; formally, TDR($g(N)$, N) is obtained from the solution to the CCP($g(N)$, N) model of Section 3.3, in which nonland income Y^0 now equals the wage $g(N)$.[11] Then when the city population is N, the total income of each household in the city equals

$$g(N) + \mathrm{TDR}(g(N), N)/N, \tag{8.15}$$

which represents the inverse population demand function of the city. Hence, given the national utility level u, the equilibrium city size can be determined by solving the following equation for N,

$$g(N) + \mathrm{TDR}(g(N), N)/N = Y(u, N), \tag{8.16}$$

where $Y(u, N)$ represents the inverse population supply function of Section 5.4. Or solving equation (8.16) for u under each value of N, we

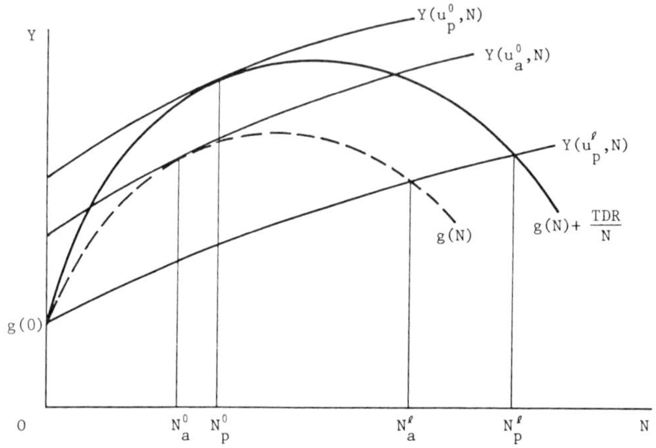

Figure 8.3. Determination of equilibrium city sizes (the public ownership case).

obtain the *equilibrium utility function* $u_p(N)$ for the case of public landownership.

Figure 8.3 explains the determination of equilibrium city sizes under various utility levels. In this figure, the bold concave curve represents function (8.15), and the dashed-curve depicts the same $g(N)$ curve as in Figure 8.1. In the present context of public landownership, let the *highest utility* u_p^0 be defined as

$$u_p^0 = \max\left\{u \mid g(N) + \frac{\mathrm{TDR}(g(N), N)}{N} = Y(u, N), N > 0\right\}, \tag{8.17}$$

and the *limiting utility* u_p^1 by the relation[12]

$$g(0) = Y(u_p^1, 0). \tag{8.18}$$

Let us assume as before that the $u_p(N)$ curve is single-peaked, as in Figure 8.4. This implies that for each u such that $u_p^1 < u < u_p^0$, in Figure 8.3 the supply curve $Y(u, N)$ intersects the demand curve $g(N) + \mathrm{TDR}/N$ twice. Let N_p^0 be the *critical city size* at which u_p^0 is achieved, and N_p^1 the *limiting city size* that corresponds to u_p^1. Here, it is assumed that $0 < N_p^0 < \infty$ and $0 < N_p^1 \leq \infty$. Suppose that each new city must start from a population close to zero. Then, as in the case of absentee landownership, we can see that *only those equilibrium city sizes between N_p^0 and N_p^1 are stable*.

Comparing Figure 8.1 with 8.3, we see

$$u_p^0 > u_a^0, \qquad N_p^1 > N_a^1, \qquad u_p^1 = u_a^1. \tag{8.19}$$

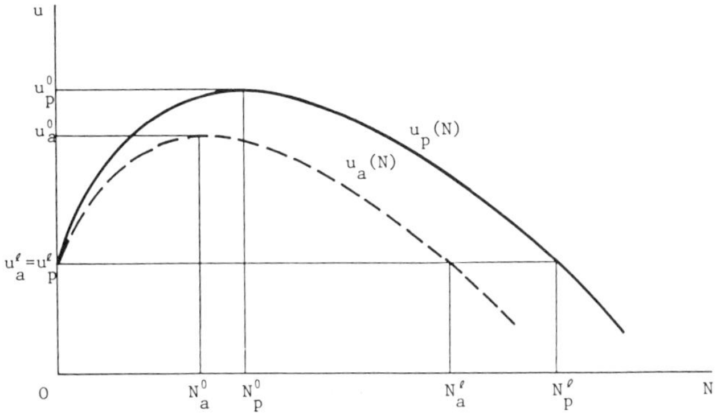

Figure 8.4. Equilibrium utility curve (the public ownership case).

These results are obvious because given any population $N > 0$, each household in the city has a higher income under public landownership. Notice that although $N_{\mathrm{p}}^0 > N_{\mathrm{a}}^0$ according to Figure 8.3, this may not always be the case (see Examples 8.1 and 8.2, in which the relationship $N_{\mathrm{p}}^0 > N_{\mathrm{a}}^0$ indeed holds).

Suppose that the total population of the urban sector in the nation is exogenously given by M. Then given any $N > 0$, if the population of each city equals N and there are M/N cities in the nation, each household in every city will attain the common utility $u_{\mathrm{p}}(N)$; hence, such a city system is in equilibrium. In particular, *it is stable if and only if* $N_p^0 \leq N < N_p^l$.

Among all equilibrium city systems, the utility level of households is highest when individual city size equals N_{p}^0. In the present situation of public landownership, the welfare of any other party is not affected by the outcomes of these city systems. Therefore, *among all the equilibrium city systems, the one that has the individual city size* N_p^0 *is socially optimal*.

In fact, we can show that this city system is socially optimal not only among all equilibrium city systems, but also *among all feasible city systems* (subject to the equal-utility constraint). To see this, let us recall the *community's problem* in Section 5.7. Namely, suppose that a certain number of households form a community (i.e., a city), the aggregate production function of which is given by (8.8). The community rents the city's land from absentee landlords at the agricultural land rent R_{A}. Then from (5.62), the community's problem can be summarized as follows:

$$\max_{N>0} u, \qquad \text{subject to} \qquad F(N) - C(u, N) \geq 0. \qquad (8.20)$$

Namely, the community chooses the optimal population so as to attain the highest common utility while satisfying the budget constraint. Next, notice that the highest utility u_{p}^0 [determined by (8.17)] can be defined equivalently as

$$u_{\mathrm{p}}^0 = \max_{N>0} u_{\mathrm{p}}(N). \tag{8.21}$$

Here, $u_{\mathrm{p}}(N)$ is obtained by solving equation (8.16) for u under each N. Notice also that, *formally, $u_p(N)$ equals the equilibrium utility of the CCP($g(N)$, N) model.*[13] Hence, setting Y^0 equal to $g(N)$ and u equal to $u_{\mathrm{p}}(N)$ in equation (5.14), we have

$$Ng(N) = C(u_{\mathrm{p}}(N), N),$$

or

$$F(N) = C(u_{\mathrm{p}}(N), N). \tag{8.22}$$

That is, in any equilibrium city under public landownership, the city's total output $F(N)$ is spent entirely on the population cost $C(u_{\mathrm{p}}(N), N)$. Furthermore, it can be readily seen that *$u_p(N)$ is the equilibrium utility of the CCP($g(N)$, N) model if and only if $u_p(N)$ equals the solution of the following equation for u:*[14]

$$F(N) = C(u, N). \tag{8.23}$$

Hence, recalling (8.21), we can see that u_{p}^0 can be obtained by solving the next problem:

$$\max_{N>0} u, \qquad \text{subject to} \qquad F(N) - C(u, N) = 0. \tag{8.24}$$

Since the population cost function $C(u, N)$ is increasing in u, this problem is equivalent to (8.20). Therefore, we can conclude that *the highest utility u_p^0 defined by (8.17) equals the utility level attained in the optimal community*. In other words, the equilibrium city system with *individual city size N_p^0 gives the highest possible utility level common to all the households in the urban sector;* in this sense, it represents the optimal city system.

Since $(u_{\mathrm{p}}^0, N_{\mathrm{p}}^0)$ coincides with the solution to the community's problem (8.20), it corresponds to $(\hat{u}, \hat{N})$ in Figure 5.12. Since in Figure 5.12 the two curves $F(N)$ and $C(\hat{u}, N)$ are tangent at $\hat{N}$ [equivalently, from the first-order condition for the problem (8.24)], it must hold that

$$F'(N) = \partial C(u, N)/\partial N \qquad \text{at} \quad (u, N) = (u_{\mathrm{p}}^0, N_{\mathrm{p}}^0). \tag{8.25}$$

Namely, in each city of the optimal city system, the *social marginal product* (SMP) of labor, $F'(N)$, equals the marginal population cost $\partial C(u,$

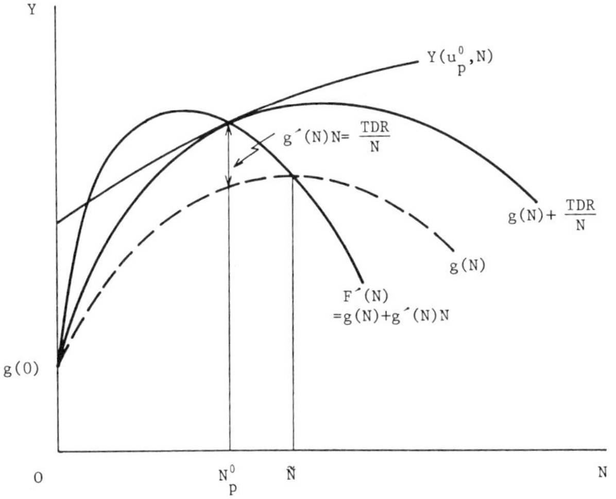

Figure 8.5. Social marginal cost curve $F'(N)$ and inverse population supply and demand curves.

$N)/\partial N$. Since $F'(N) = g(N) + g'(N)N$ and $\partial C(u, N)/\partial N = Y(u, N)$ [from (5.25)], condition (8.25) can be restated as

$$g(N) + g'(N)N = Y(u_p^0, N) \qquad \text{at} \quad N = N_p^0. \tag{8.26}$$

This means, as depicted in Figure 8.5, that the SMP curve $F'(N)$ intersects the inverse population supply curve $Y(u_p^0, N)$ at N_p^0. Recall also from Figure 8.3 that the $Y(u_p^0, N)$ curve is tangent to the inverse population demand curve $g(N) + \text{TDR}/N$ at N_p^0; this implies that

$$g(N) + \text{TDR}/N = Y(u_p^0, N) \qquad \text{at} \quad N = N_p^0. \tag{8.27}$$

From (8.26) and (8.27), it holds that

$$g'(N)N = \text{TDR}/N \qquad \text{at} \quad N = N_p^0. \tag{8.28}$$

That is, in the optimal city system, each household receives a share of total differential rent TDR/N, which equals the *marginal external economies of population* $g'(N)N$; hence, we can interpret TDR/N to represent a Pigouvian subsidy to households for achieving the optimal city system. Since TDR > 0 for each $N > 0$, (8.28) also implies that

$$g'(N) > 0 \qquad \text{at} \quad N = N_p^0, \tag{8.29}$$

and hence $N_p^0 < \tilde{N}$. Namely, *the optimal city size N_p^0 is attained in the increasing phase of the agglomeration function $g(N)$.*

Notice that although the highest common utility level can be achieved in the city system with individual city size N_{p}^{0}, this represents only one of infinitely many stable equilibrium city systems. Therefore, there is no *a priori* reason to expect that this optimal city system would be achieved in the market economy. On the contrary, in the context of city population growth, for the same reason explained in the case of absentee landownership, *the populations of most cities are likely to remain close to* N_{p}^{l}; *that is, the worst city system (among all stable city systems) is most likely to be realized.* In other words, *a market economy tends to overshoot the optimal city size.*[15] This suggests the necessity of strong public interventions for realizing the optimal city system.

For example, suppose that all existing cities have a population that exceeds the optimal size N_{p}^{0}. Then the central government may impose a population tax on the households in these cities. At the same time, the central government will organize the formation of a new city and will use the tax revenue from the existing cities to subsidize the income of each household in the new city. The central government must keep increasing the population tax rate (and hence the subsidy rate) until the new city starts growing rapidly (i.e., until the new city reaches an unstable equilibrium size); then the tax rate will be gradually reduced as the size of the new city approaches that of the existing (stable) cities. This process (of tax and subsidy for new city formation) will be repeated until the following optimality criterion is observed: The new city needs a continuing subsidy until it reaches the size of the existing cities.

8.3 Product variety and monopolistic competition

Consider a monocentric city in which a traded good X and nontraded differentiated services q_i $(i = 1, 2, \ldots)$ are produced at the CBD. As before, we assume that these production activities do not use land; hence, the CBD is treated as a point. The traded good is produced using labor and differentiated services $\{q_i\}$. Each differentiated service is produced using labor only. The price of the traded good is assumed to be determined by the international market; hence, it is treated as a given constant and normalized at unity. All households in the economy are assumed to be homogeneous, with each being endowed with a unit of labor. In Section 8.3.1 we examine the equilibrium of production sectors under a fixed city population. In Section 8.3.2, we analyze equilibrium city sizes. Finally, in Section 8.3.3, we examine effects of parameter changes on equilibrium city sizes.

8.3.1 Production sectors and demand for labor

Traded-good sector. To capture in a simple form the desire to employ a variety of intermediate services in the production process, let us assume that the production function facing each firm in the *traded-good sector (t sector)* is given as[16]

$$X = N_x^{\eta}\left\{\left(\sum_{i=1}^{n} q_i^{\rho}\right)^{1/\rho}\right\}^{\nu}, \tag{8.30}$$

where X is the amount of the traded good produced by a firm, N_x the amount of labor, and q_i the amount of each service i employed by the firm, and η, ν, and ρ are positive constants such that $\eta + \nu = 1$ and $0 < \rho < 1$. The parameter ρ can be interpreted as representing the intensity of desire to employ a variety of intermediate services. When ρ is close to 1, differentiated services $\{q_i\}$ are close to perfect substitutes; as ρ decreases toward 0, the desire to employ a greater variety of services increases. Notice that the total number n of services produced in the city is unknown, to be determined later.

Since the production function (8.30) is homogeneous of degree 1, the equilibrium output level of each individual firm in the t sector is indeterminate. Hence, in the subsequent analysis, we proceed as if the total output X in the t sector is produced by a single representative firm that behaves competitively. Then if we let p_i be the price of q_i ($i = 1, 2, \ldots$) and W the wage rate in the city, the problem of the firm is to choose inputs N_x and $\{q_i\}$ so as to maximize the profit,

$$X - WN_x - \sum_{i=1}^{n} p_i q_i, \tag{8.31}$$

subject to the production function (8.30). Provided that the equilibrium output X is positive, from the first-order conditions for this maximization problem, we can derive the demand for N_x and each q_i as[17]

$$N_x = \eta X W^{-1}, \tag{8.32}$$

$$q_i = (\nu X Q^{-\rho} p_i^{-1})^{1/(1-\rho)}, \qquad i = 1, 2, \ldots, n, \tag{8.33}$$

where

$$Q \equiv \left(\sum_{i=1}^{n} q_i^{\rho}\right)^{1/\rho}. \tag{8.34}$$

Service-good sector. All intermediate services are assumed to be produced by an identical production process, where the only input is labor. The amount of labor N_i required for production of q_i is assumed to be given as

$$N_i = f + cq_i, \tag{8.35}$$

where f is the fixed labor requirement and c the marginal labor requirement ($f > 0$, $c > 0$). Hence, the average labor requirement is decreasing in the amount of output q_i. Assuming that each firm in the *service-good sector (s sector)* can differentiate its product without cost, at equilibrium it can be seen that each service will be supplied by only one firm. Then the profit of the firm producing q_i equals $p_i q_i - WN_i$.

Following the Chamberlinian approach to monopolistic competition (Chamberlin 1933; Dixit and Stiglitz 1977), it is assumed that each firm in the s sector acts in a Cournot–Nash fashion, taking the output levels of all the other firms in the sector are given; it is also assumed that each firm takes the total output level X of the t sector as given. Then the profit-maximizing condition for each active firm is the familiar equality of marginal revenue and marginal cost:

$$p_i\left(1 - \frac{1}{E_i}\right) = Wc, \tag{8.36}$$

where E_i is the (subjective) price elasticity of demand q_i. From (8.33), $E_i = (1 - \rho)^{-1} + \rho(1 - \rho)^{-1}(p_i/Q)(\partial Q/\partial p_i)$; and since by assumption $\partial q_j/\partial p_i = 0$ for all $j \neq i$, from (8.34) $\partial Q/\partial p_i = -(Q/p_i)(q_i/Q)^{\rho}E_i$. Thus, $E_i = (1 - \rho)^{-1}(1 + \rho(1 - \rho)^{-1}(q_i/Q)^{\rho})^{-1}$. So long as the prices of the n services (being produced) are not of different orders of magnitude, $(q_i/Q)^{\rho}$ is of the order $(1/n)$. Hence, provided that n is sufficiently large, it is reasonable to assume that the firm neglects the term $(q_i/Q)^{\rho}$ and uses the following (subjective) elasticity:[18]

$$E \equiv (1 - \rho)^{-1}. \tag{8.37}$$

Then replacing E_i in (8.36) with E, we write the common equilibrium price p_q for each service as

$$p_q = Wc\rho^{-1}. \tag{8.38}$$

This indicates that each firm will charge its price at a markup over the marginal cost. Notice that the markup ratio ρ^{-1} is larger the smaller the value of ρ, that is, the larger the desire of the t sector to employ a variety of services in production. Given the common output price p_q, each firm will produce the same amount of the output q. Setting p_i equal to p_q and

q_i equal to q in (8.33) and (8.34), we can obtain the equilibrium output of each firm as

$$q = \nu X\rho(Wcn)^{-1}. \tag{8.39}$$

Substituting (8.39) into (8.35), we obtain the demand for labor N_q by each firm as

$$N_q = f + \nu X\rho(Wn)^{-1}. \tag{8.40}$$

Equilibrium in the production sectors. In the long run, firms will continue to enter the market until profit is driven to zero in the s sector, that is, $p_q q - WN_q = 0$.[19] Substituting (8.38)–(8.40) into this equilibrium condition, we have

$$n = \nu X(1 - \rho)(Wf)^{-1}. \tag{8.41}$$

Next, assuming that full employment prevails in the city, the total population N is given by

$$N = N_x + nN_q. \tag{8.42}$$

Now we can determine all unknown variables but one. It turns out that it is convenient to express first all other unknowns as functions of the number of service goods n. From (8.30), (8.32), and (8.38)–(8.42), we can readily obtain the following results:

$$N = f[\nu(1 - \rho)]^{-1}n, \tag{8.43}$$

$$X = \eta^{\eta}\nu^{-\eta}c^{-\nu}f\rho^{\nu}(1 - \rho)^{-1}n^{(\nu+\rho\eta)/\rho}, \tag{8.44}$$

$$W = \eta^{\eta}\nu^{\nu}c^{-\nu}\rho^{\nu}n^{(1-\rho)\nu/\rho}, \tag{8.45}$$

$$N_x = f\eta[\nu(1 - \rho)]^{-1}n, \tag{8.46}$$

$$q = f\rho[c(1 - \rho)]^{-1}, \tag{8.47}$$

$$N_q = f(1 - \rho)^{-1}, \tag{8.48}$$

$$p_q = Wc\rho^{-1} = \eta^{\eta}\nu^{\nu}c^{1-\nu}\rho^{\nu-1}n^{(1-\rho)\nu/\rho}. \tag{8.49}$$

Notice that all of N, X, W, N_x, and p_q are increasing functions of n, reflecting the increase in the productivity of the t sector due to the increase in the variety of intermediate services. From (8.47) and (8.48), the output q and labor input N_q of *each* active firm in the s sector is independent of the output price p_q and wage rate W. This is due to the special nature of the production function (8.35). However, the *total* labor requirement of the s sector, nN_q, is increasing proportionally in n; from (8.46) the same is true for the t sector. Therefore, as indicated by (8.43), the total labor requirement N of the city is also increasing proportionally in n.

Next, using (8.43), all other variables in the production sectors can be expressed as functions of N as follows:

$$n(N) = f^{-1}\nu(1 - \rho)N, \tag{8.50}$$

$$X(N) = \eta^{\nu}\nu^{\nu/\rho}c^{-\nu}f^{-(1-\rho)\nu/\rho}\rho^{\nu}(1 - \rho)^{(1-\rho)\nu/\rho}N^{(\nu+\rho\eta)/\rho}, \tag{8.51}$$

$$W(N) = \eta^{\eta}\nu^{\nu/\rho}c^{-\nu}f^{-(1-\rho)\nu/\rho}\rho^{\nu}(1 - \rho)^{(1-\rho)\nu/\rho}N^{(1-\rho)\nu/\rho}, \tag{8.52}$$

$$N_x(N) = \eta N, \tag{8.53}$$

$$q(N) = f\rho[c(1 - \rho)]^{-1}, \tag{8.54}$$

$$N_q(N) = f(1 - \rho)^{-1}, \tag{8.55}$$

$$p_q(N) = W(N)c\rho^{-1}, \tag{8.56}$$

and

$$n(N)N_q(N) = \nu N. \tag{8.57}$$

Or setting

$$A \equiv \eta^{\eta}\nu^{\nu/\rho}c^{-\nu}f^{-(1-\rho)\nu/\rho}\rho^{\nu}(1 - \rho)^{(1-\rho)\nu/\rho}, \tag{8.58}$$

$$b \equiv (1 - \rho)\nu/\rho, \tag{8.59}$$

we can rewrite (8.51) and (8.52), respectively, as follows:

$$X(N) = AN^{1+b}, \tag{8.60}$$

$$W(N) = AN^{b}. \tag{8.61}$$

By definition, $X(N)$ represents the *net output of the city* (which equals the output of the t sector) as a function of the total labor force of the city. We call $X(N)$ the *aggregate production function* of the city. The *wage function* $W(N)$ represents the inverse demand function of labor, or the *inverse population demand function* of the city. Notice that since $b > 0$, *the aggregate production function exhibits increasing returns to the city's population*. This is because a larger population is associated with a greater variety of intermediate service goods and hence with a higher productivity in the t sector. For the same reason, *the wage function $W(N)$ is also increasing in the city's population*. Notice, however, that since we have from (8.60) and (8.61) the following relation,

$$W(N) = \frac{X(N)}{N}, \tag{8.62}$$

the wage function $W(N)$ represents the *average* product of labor in the city, not the *marginal* product of labor. Notice, finally, from (8.53) and (8.57) that the t sector and s sector use, respectively, η and ν proportions of the total labor force in the city.

8.3.2 Equilibrium city sizes

Having described the equilibrium of production sectors as a function of city population, our next task is to determine equilibrium city sizes. Fortunately, this task can be achieved without new analyses. This is because the urban aggregates derived from the monopolistic competition model above have the same structural relationships as those from the external economy model of Section 8.2. To see this, observe that if we define in terms of (8.58) and (8.59) that

$$g(N) \equiv AN^b, \tag{8.63}$$

then it follows from (8.60) and (8.61) that

$$X(N) = g(N)N, \tag{8.64}$$

$$W(N) = g(N). \tag{8.65}$$

Comparing (8.64) and (8.65) with (8.8) and (8.6), we can conclude that *under the specification of agglomeration function (8.63), the external economy model of Section 8.2 and the monopolistic competition model of this section yield the same aggregate production function and the same wage function.*

Therefore, all the results on city sizes (and systems of cities) obtained in Section 8.2 also hold true in the present context. More specifically, first let us consider the case of absentee landownership. Then under each national utility level u, the equilibrium city size (or sizes) can be determined by solving equation (8.9) for N. Figure 8.1 explains the determination of equilibrium city sizes under various national utility levels.[20] Provided that conditions 1–4 of Section 8.2.1 also hold in the present context, we can derive from Figure 8.1 the equilibrium utility curve $u_a(N)$ as in Figure 8.2. Then we can conclude as before that an equilibrium city size N is stable if and only if $N_a^0 \leq N < N_a^1$.

Example 8.1 (the absentee landownership case). In the context of Example 5.1 (with a log-linear utility function, linear transport cost function, and linear city), substitution of (5.18) and (8.63) into (8.9) yields

$$AN^b = D(N + E)^{\beta}e^u. \tag{8.66}$$

Solving this equation for u, we can obtain the following *equilibrium utility function:*

$$u_a(N) = \log \frac{A}{D} + \beta \log \frac{N^{b/\beta}}{N+E}, \tag{8.67}$$

which yields

$$\frac{du_a(N)}{dN} = \frac{\beta}{N}\left(\frac{b}{\beta} - \frac{N}{N+E}\right). \tag{8.68}$$

Hence, the $u_a(N)$ *curve is single-peaked as in Figure 8.2 if and only if*

$$b/\beta < 1 \qquad \text{or} \qquad b < \beta. \tag{8.69}$$

In other words, conditions 1–4 of Section 8.2.1 can be satisfied if and only if condition (8.69) holds. In this situation, setting $du_a(N)/dN$ equal to 0 in (8.68), we obtain the critical city size as

$$N_a^0 = \frac{bE}{\beta - b} \equiv \frac{\theta a^{-1} R_A}{(\rho\beta/(1-\rho)\nu) - 1} > 0. \tag{8.70}$$

It follows from (8.11) and (8.12) that the limiting utility u_a^1 equals $-\infty$ and the limiting city size N_a^1 equals ∞. Notice from (8.70) that the critical city size N_a^0 becomes larger as θ, R_A, or ν increases and becomes smaller as a, ρ, or β increases. This implies, in particular, that as the desire of the t sector for a variety of intermediate services becomes stronger (i.e., ρ becomes smaller), N_a^0 becomes larger.

Next, turning to the case of public landownership, recall that the equilibrium utility function $u_p(N)$ can be obtained by solving equation (8.23) for u. In the present context, substituting $X(N)$ for $F(N)$ in (8.23), we determine function $u_p(N)$ by solving the next equation for u:

$$X(N) = C(u, N). \tag{8.71}$$

Provided that function $u_p(N)$ is single-peaked as in Figure 8.4, we can uniquely determine u_p^0 (the highest utility), u_p^1 (limiting utility), N_p^0 (critical city size), and N_p^1 (limiting city size), respectively. Then we can conclude as before that an equilibrium city size N is stable if and only if $N_p^0 \leq N < N_p^1$.

Example 8.2 (the public landownership case). In the context of Examples 5.1 and 5.2, let us now consider the case of public landownership. Substitution of (5.30) and (8.60) into (8.71) yields

$$AN^{b+1} = (1+\beta)^{-1}D\{(N+E)^{1+\beta} - E^{1+\beta}\}e^u. \tag{8.72}$$

Solving this equation for u, we can obtain the following equilibrium utility function:

$$u_p(N) = \log \frac{(1+\beta)A}{D} + \log \frac{N^{1+b}}{(N+E)^{1+\beta} - E^{1+\beta}}, \tag{8.73}$$

which gives

$$\frac{du_p(N)}{dN} = \frac{f(N)}{[(N+E)^{1+\beta} - E^{1+\beta}]N}, \tag{8.74}$$

where

$$f(N) = [(1+b)E - (\beta - b)N](N+E)^{\beta} - (1+b)E^{1+\beta}.$$

It follows that

$$f'(N) = (1+\beta)[bE - (\beta - b)N](N+E)^{\beta-1}$$

and

$$f''(N) = -\beta(1+\beta)[(1-b)E + (\beta - b)N](N+E)^{\beta-2}.$$

Suppose condition (8.69) holds. Then $b < \beta < 1$, and hence $f''(N) < 0$ for all $N \geq 0$, which means $f(N)$ is strictly concave. Furthermore, $f(0) = 0$ and $f'(0) = (1+\beta)bE^{\beta} > 0$. Hence, as depicted in Figure 8.6, $f(N)$ achieves the (positive) maximum at $N = bE/(\beta - b) > 0$, and it is negative at $N = (1+b)E/(\beta - b)$. Since the denominator of the right side of equation (8.74) is always positive, this implies that we can uniquely determine the *critical city size* N_p^0 such that

$$\frac{du_p(N)}{dN} \gtreqless 0 \quad \text{as} \quad N \lesseqgtr N_p^0,$$

which means that the *equilibrium utility function* $u_p(N)$ *achieves the unique maximum at* N_p^0 (as depicted in Figure 8.4). It is also clear from (8.70) and Figure 8.6 that

$$N_a^0 = \frac{bE}{\beta - b} < N_p^0. \tag{8.75}$$

Namely, the critical city size under public landownership is greater than that under absentee landownership. We can also see as before that the *limiting city size* N_p^1 equals ∞.

8.3.3 Comparative statics

In terms of urban aggregates (i.e., population, net output, and wage rate), the monopolistic competition model and the external economy model yield

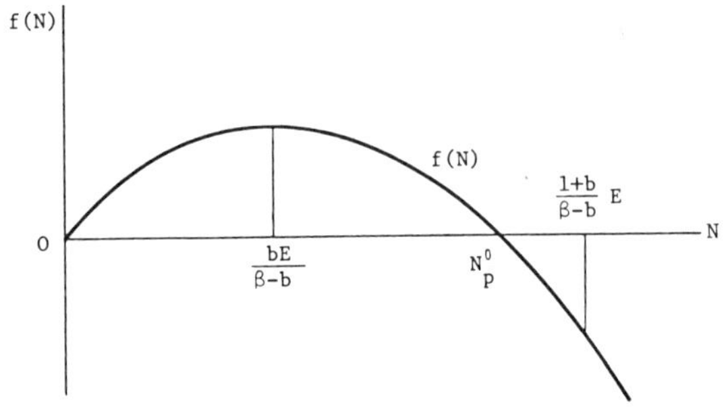

Figure 8.6. Shape of function $f(N)$.

the same structural relationships of city economy. However, since the monopolistic competition model has derived the agglomeration function (8.63) *endogenously,* it provides more information on the city economy. Such information is useful, in particular, for possible explanations of variation in city sizes in a national (or an international) economy.

To elaborate these points, let us focus on the absentee landownership case. For simplicity, let us assume that the equilibrium utility function $u_a(N)$ is single-peaked, as in Figure 8.2. Then given each national utility level u such that $u_a^1 < u < u_a^0$, a *stable* equilibrium city size is uniquely determined, which is denoted by N^*. Furthermore, substituting N^* into equations (8.50)–(8.56), we can uniquely determine the equilibrium values of the rest of the variables, which are denoted, respectively, as n^*, X^*, W^*, N_x^*, q^*, N_q^*, and p_q^*. Thus, for each $u \in (u_a^1, u_a^0)$, we can uniquely determine a stable *equilibrium configuration* (N^*, n^*, X^*, W^*, N_x^*, q^*, N_q^*, p_q^*).[21] Such an equilibrium city configuration is affected not only by u, but also by all the other parameters of the model. Table 8.1 summarizes the impact of marginal changes in parameters u, p_x, ρ, f, and c, where p_x represents the unit price of the traded good (see Appendix C.14 for calculations).[22]

For example, let us consider the impact of an increase in the national utility level u. In Figure 8.1, the $Y(u, N)$ curve shifts upward as u increases; hence, the stable equilibrium city size N^* will be reduced. From (8.50), this in turn causes the equilibrium number of the s sector's firms, n^*, to decrease. Since a decrease in n^* implies a decrease in the variety of services used in the production process of the t sector, the average productivity of the city's labor decreases. From (8.62), this in turn reduces the wage W^*, output X^*, and the service price p_q^*. From (8.54) and (8.55), while the output q^* and labor input N_q^* *per firm* in the s sector are not affected, their total values, n^*q^* and $n^*N_q^*$, are reduced.

For another example, let us consider the impact of parameter ρ. In

Table 8.1. *Comparative statics of a stable equilibrium*

	N^*	n^*	X^*	W^*	N_x^*	q^*	N_q^*	p_q^*
u	−	−	−	−	−	0	0	−
p_x	+	+	+	+	+	0	0	+
ρ	−	−	−	−	−	+	+	−
f	−	−	−	−	−	+	+	−
c	−	−	−	−	−	−	0	?

equilibrium, the output levels of all active firms in the s sector are the same. Hence, setting $q_i = q$ for all i's in equation (8.30), we obtain the following production function of the t sector:

$$X = n^{\nu/\rho} N_x^{\eta} q^{\nu}. \tag{8.76}$$

Hence, *as ρ increases, that is, as the desire to employ a variety of services decreases, the t sector becomes less productive*. This causes a reduction in the equilibrium values of N^*, n^*, X^*, W^*, N_x^*, and p_q^*, respectively. However, as ρ increases, the demand for each existing service good increases. Hence, as we can see from (8.54) and (8.55), the equilibrium values of q^* and N_q^* increase.

From Table 8.1, we can conclude as follows: *Provided that an equilibrium city configuration is stable, all values of N^*, n^*, X^*, N_x^* and W^* will increase as*

1. the national utility level u decreases,
2. the price of the traded good, p_x, increases,
3. the degree of the desire for a variety of services in the traded-good production, ρ^{-1}, increases,
4. the fixed labor input in the s sector, f, decreases, or
5. the marginal labor input in the s sector, c, decreases.

Results 2–5 suggest a possible explanation for the variation in city sizes within a national economy (under the condition of the free migration of labor). Namely, a city will be larger if its industrial structure is such that p_x and ρ^{-1} are greater while f and c are smaller. The first result provides a possible explanation for international variations in city sizes. Namely, given two cities (with the same industrial structure) in two different countries, the city in the country with a lower living standard will be larger.

8.4 Optimal production processes and first-best policies

As we have seen in the preceding section, the external economy model and the monopolistic competition model are equivalent for the purpose of descriptive analysis of urban aggregates. However, from the viewpoint of normative analysis, the two models lead to substantially different results. Namely, they bring about different estimates of the "true" urban production function, different optimal city sizes, and hence different policy recommendations. To elaborate these points, in Section 8.4.1 we examine optimal production processes; then, in Section 8.4.2 we discuss optimal policies for achieving efficient cities and city systems.

8.4.1 Optimal production processes

Let us recall the production function (8.1) of the individual firm in the external economy model. Given a city population N, this production function is assumed to represent the maximum output of each firm at each labor input N_j. Therefore, the sum of outputs by all individual firms, the aggregate production function $F(N)$ represents the *true urban production function* that describes the maximum net output technologically possible from each given total labor force N in the city. In other words, given each population N, the production process of the city is efficient. Thus, in the context of the external economy model, the only possible normative question is whether the city population itself is socially optimal.

However, in the context of the monopolistic competition model of Section 8.3 the aggregate production function $X(N)$ from (8.60) does not describe the true urban production function; it gives less than the maximum net output technologically possible from total labor force N, reflecting the inefficiency due to monopolistic competition in the service sector. To understand this, note that the true urban production function $\hat{X}(N)$ (in the context of the monopolistic competition model) can be obtained by solving the following maximization problem under each N:

$$\hat{X}(N) \equiv \max_{n, X, N_x, \{q_i\}, \{N_i\}} X, \tag{8.77}$$

$$\text{subject to} \quad X = N_x^{\eta} \left\{ \left(\sum_{i=1}^{n} q_i^{\rho} \right)^{1/\rho} \right\}^{\nu}, \tag{8.78}$$

$$N_i = f + cq_i, \qquad i = 1, 2, \ldots, n, \tag{8.79}$$

$$N_x + \sum_{i=1}^{n} N_i = N, \tag{8.80}$$

where (8.78) represents the t sector's production function, (8.79) the labor constraint in the production of each service i, and (8.80) the city's population constraint. In order to solve this maximization problem, let us introduce the following Lagrangian function:

$$\mathcal{L} = N_x^{\eta}\left\{\left(\sum_{i=1}^{n} q_i^{\rho}\right)^{1/\rho}\right\}^{\nu} + \sum_{i=1}^{n} \hat{p}_i\left(\frac{N_i - f}{c} - q_i\right)$$
$$+ \hat{W}\left(N - N_x - \sum_{i=1}^{n} N_i\right), \tag{8.81}$$

where each $\hat{p}_i$ represents the shadow price of service good i, and $\hat{W}$ the shadow price of labor in the city. For convenience, first let us fix n (at an arbitrary integer) and obtain the optimal values of other variables as functions of n and N. From the corresponding first-order conditions, we can readily obtain the following results:[23]

$$\hat{X} = \eta^{\eta}\nu^{\nu}c^{-\nu}(N - nf)n^{(1-\rho)\nu/\rho}, \tag{8.82}$$

$$\hat{W} = \eta^{\eta}\nu^{\nu}c^{-\nu}n^{(1-\rho)\nu/\rho}, \tag{8.83}$$

$$\hat{N}_x = \eta(N - nf), \tag{8.84}$$

$$\hat{q}_i = \nu c^{-1}(N - nf)n^{-1} \qquad \text{for all} \quad i = 1, \ldots, n, \tag{8.85}$$

$$\hat{N}_i = f + \nu(N - nf)n^{-1} \qquad \text{for all} \quad i = 1, \ldots, n, \tag{8.86}$$

$$\hat{p}_i = \hat{W}c = \eta^{\eta}\nu^{\nu}c^{1-\nu}n^{(1-\rho)\nu/\rho} \qquad \text{for all} \quad i = 1, \ldots, n. \tag{8.87}$$

Next, let us assume that the optimal number of service goods, n, is sufficiently large so that we can safely treat it as a continuous number. Then from the first-order condition for the maximization of the right side of (8.82) with respect to n, the optimal n can be obtained as[24]

$$\hat{n}(N) = f^{-1}\nu(1 - \rho)N\{(\nu + \rho\eta)^{-1}\}. \tag{8.88}$$

Since $\hat{q}_i$, $\hat{N}_i$, and $\hat{p}_i$ are the same for all $i = 1, \ldots, n$, let us simply represent them as $\hat{q}$, $\hat{N}_q$, and $\hat{p}_q$, respectively. Then substituting (8.88) into (8.82)–(8.87), we can express the optimal values of the other variables as functions of N as follows:

$$\hat{X}(N) = \eta^{\eta}\nu^{\nu/\rho}c^{-\nu}f^{-(1-\rho)\nu/\rho}\rho(1 - \rho)^{(1-\rho)\nu/\rho}$$
$$\times (\nu + \rho\eta)^{-(\nu+\rho\eta)/\rho}N^{(\nu+\rho\eta)/\rho}, \tag{8.89}$$

$$\hat{W}(N) = \eta^{\eta}\nu^{\nu/\rho}c^{-\nu}f^{-(1-\rho)\nu/\rho}(1 - \rho)^{(1-\rho)\nu/\rho}$$
$$\times (\nu + \rho\eta)^{-(1-\rho)\nu/\rho}N^{(1-\rho)\nu/\rho}, \tag{8.90}$$

$$\hat{N}_x(N) = \eta N\{\rho(\nu + \rho\eta)^{-1}\}, \tag{8.91}$$

$$\hat{q}(N) = f\rho[c(1 - \rho)]^{-1}, \tag{8.92}$$

$$\hat{N}_q(N) = f(1 - \rho)^{-1}, \tag{8.93}$$

$$\hat{p}_q(N) = \hat{W}(N)c, \tag{8.94}$$

and

$$\hat{n}(N)\hat{N}_q(N) = \nu N\{(\nu + \rho\eta)^{-1}\}. \tag{8.95}$$

Or using notations (8.58) and (8.59), we can rewrite (8.89) and (8.90), respectively, as

$$\hat{X}(N) = AN^{1+b}\{\rho^{\eta}(\nu + \rho\eta)^{-(1+b)}\}, \tag{8.96}$$

$$\hat{W}(N) = AN^{b}\{\rho^{-\nu}(\nu + \rho\eta)^{-b}\}. \tag{8.97}$$

Comparing (8.88)–(8.97) with (8.50)–(8.61), we can see that the optimal production process is substantially different from the market production process. By definition, $\hat{X}(N)$ represents the maximum amount of the traded good that can be produced in the city using the total labor N; in this sense, it represents the *(true) urban production function*. Since $b > 0$, this production function also exhibits increasing returns to scale in N. Notice from (8.59), (8.96) and (8.97) that

$$\hat{W}(N) = \frac{d\hat{X}(N)}{dN}, \tag{8.98}$$

which means that in the optimal process, *the shadow price of labor equals the (social) marginal product of labor*. This relation should be contrasted with (8.62), which says that in the market production process, the wage rate equals the averge product of labor in the city. Similarly, (8.94) says that in the optimal process, *the shadow price of each service equals its marginal cost* (in terms of the shadow price of labor), whereas in the market relationship of (8.56), the price of each service equals its marginal cost times the markup ratio ρ^{-1}.

Taking the ratio between each optimal variable from (8.89)–(8.95) and the corresponding market variable from (8.50)–(8.57), we have

$$\hat{n}(N)/n(N) = (\nu + \rho\eta)^{-1} > 1, \tag{8.99}$$

$$\hat{X}(N)/X(N) = \rho^{\eta}(\nu + \rho\eta)^{-(1+b)} > 1, \tag{8.100}$$

$$\hat{W}(N)/W(N) = \rho^{-\nu}(\nu + \rho\eta)^{-b} > 1, \tag{8.101}$$

$$\hat{N}_x(N)/N_x(N) = \rho(\nu + \rho\eta)^{-1} < 1, \tag{8.102}$$

$$\hat{q}(N)/q(N) = 1, \tag{8.103}$$

$$\hat{N}_q(N)/N_q(N) = 1, \tag{8.104}$$

$$\hat{p}_q(N)/p_q(N) = \hat{W}(N)/(W(N)\rho^{-1}) = \rho^{\eta}(\nu + \rho\eta)^{-b} \tag{8.105}$$

$$\hat{n}(N)\hat{N}_q(N)/n(N)N_q(N) = (\nu + \rho\eta)^{-1} > 1. \tag{8.106}$$

We can see from (8.99) that given the same amount of total labor N, the optimal production process introduces more variety of service goods than the market process. This makes the former more productive than the latter; thus, we have $\hat{X}(N) > X(N)$, as indicated by (8.100). In fact, if we set in equation (8.100)

$$h(\rho) \equiv \rho^{\eta}(\nu + \rho\eta)^{-(1+b)}, \tag{8.107}$$

then[25]

$$h(\rho) > 1 \quad \text{for all} \quad \rho < 1, \quad \text{and} \quad h(1) = 1,$$
$$h'(\rho) < 0 \quad \text{for all} \quad \rho < 1, \quad \text{and} \quad \lim_{\rho \to 0} h(\rho) = \infty. \tag{8.108}$$

Hence, $\hat{X}(N) > X(N)$ for all $\rho < 1$, and the difference becomes larger as ρ becomes smaller. In addition to this productivity difference, recall that in the optimal production process the shadow price of labor, $\hat{W}(N)$, equals its marginal product, whereas in the market process the wage rate $W(N)$ equals the average product of labor. Hence, we naturally have that $\hat{W}(N) > W(N)$. Or in equation (8.101) if we set

$$k(\rho) \equiv \rho^{-\nu}(\nu + \rho\eta)^{-b}, \tag{8.109}$$

then

$$k(\rho) > 1 \quad \text{for all} \quad \rho < 1, \quad \text{and} \quad k(1) = 1,$$
$$k'(\rho) < 0 \quad \text{for all} \quad \rho < 1, \quad \text{and} \quad \lim_{\rho \to 0} k(\rho) = \infty. \tag{8.110}$$

Hence, $\hat{W}(N) > W(N)$ for all $\rho < 1$. Next, we can see from (8.103) and (8.104) that in the two situations, the optimal and the market, each service firm produces the same amount of output using the same amount of labor.[26] This indicates that when variety is desirable, that is, when intermediate services are not perfect substitutes, it is optimal for each service firm to produce at the output level that does not exploit economies of scale beyond the extent achieved in the market equilibrium. Furthermore, notice from (8.102) and (8.106) that the s sector (t sector) as a whole consumes a larger (smaller) proportion of total labor in the optimal process than in the market process. This is because in the optimal production process, the t sector substitutes a greater amount of service goods for labor. Finally, in equation (8.105), we have $\hat{W}(N) > W(N)$ but $1 < \rho^{-1}$ (= the markup ratio). Therefore, without making further assumptions about parameters, we cannot determine the relative size between $\hat{p}_q(N)$ and $p_q(N)$.

8.4.2 *First-best policies*

Given a city population N, the optimal production process (described in the preceding subsection) can be achieved by the following simple subsidy scheme. In the context of the monopolistic competition model of Section 8.3.1, suppose that the government provides *ad valorem sales subsidies* to the s sector's firms at the rate

$$\hat{\sigma} \equiv (1 - \rho)/\rho. \tag{8.111}$$

Then under this subsidy scheme, the profit function of each firm in the s sector becomes

$$(1 + \hat{\sigma})p_i q_i - WN_i, \qquad i = 1, 2, \ldots, n.$$

Using this profit function, as with (8.38) we can now obtain the equilibrium price of each service good as

$$p_q = Wc, \tag{8.112}$$

which implies that the marginal cost pricing also prevails in the s sector. It can readily be seen that if we use (8.112) [instead of (8.38)] together with (8.30), (8.32), and (8.39)–(8.42), we obtain [instead of (8.50)–(8.57)] the new set of equilibrium conditions, which are identical to (8.88)–(8.95). Recall that (8.88)–(8.95) represent the necessary and sufficient conditions for the optimal production process for population N. Hence, we can conclude that *under the subsidy scheme (8.111), the production equilibrium for any population N is efficient.*

For each population N, let us define

$$\mathrm{TS}(N) = \hat{\sigma}\hat{p}_q(N)\hat{q}(N)\hat{n}(N), \tag{8.113}$$

$$\mathrm{FC}(N) = \hat{n}(N) f \hat{W}(N), \tag{8.114}$$

$$\pi(N) = \hat{X}(N) - N\hat{W}(N), \tag{8.115}$$

where $\mathrm{TS}(N)$, $\mathrm{FC}(N)$, and $\pi(N)$ represent, respectively, the *total subsidies* to s-sector firms, the *fixed labor cost* of s-sector firms, and the *total production profit*. Substituting (8.88)–(8.94) into (8.113)–(8.115), we can readily see that

$$\mathrm{TS}(N) = \mathrm{FC}(N) = -\pi(N). \tag{8.116}$$

That is, in the optimal production process for each N (under the subsidy scheme), both the total subsidies and the fixed labor cost equal the production loss.

Next, we examine the equilibrium and optimal city sizes under the efficient production process. To avoid repetition, we consider only the case of public landownership. Suppose that the city residents share equally TDR and TS. Then given a city population N, the total income of each household in the city is expressed by

$$\hat{W}(N) + \frac{\text{TDR} - \text{TS}(N)}{N} = \frac{\hat{X}(N)}{N} + \frac{\text{TDR}}{N} \qquad \text{[from (8.115) and (8.116)].} \tag{8.117}$$

From (8.63), (8.96), and (8.107), we have

$$\hat{X}(N)/N = g(N)h(\rho). \tag{8.118}$$

To be precise, TDR equals TDR$[g(N)h(\rho), N]$, which represents the total differential rent from the solution of the CCP$(g(N)h(\rho), N)$ model. Hence, the total income of each city household equals

$$g(N)h(\rho) + \text{TDR}[g(N)h(\rho), N]/N, \tag{8.119}$$

which represents the inverse population demand function of the city.

Thus, under the subsidy scheme (8.111), given a national utility level u, we can determine the equilibrium population of the city by solving the next equation for N:

$$g(N)h(\rho) + \text{TDR}[g(N)h(\rho), N]/N = Y(u, N). \tag{8.120}$$

Or solving equation (8.120) for u, we can obtain the *equilibrium utility function,* which is denoted by $\hat{u}_p(N)$. Notice also that substituting $\hat{X}(N)$ for $F(N)$ in (8.23), we can obtain function $\hat{u}_p(N)$ alternately by solving the next equation for u:

$$\hat{X}(N) = C(u, N). \tag{8.121}$$

Let us assume that *function $\hat{u}_p(N)$ is single-peaked;* that is, there exists a *critical city size* $\hat{N}_p^0$ such that

$$\frac{d\hat{u}_p(N)}{dN} \gtreqless 0 \qquad \text{as} \quad N \lesseqgtr \hat{N}_p^0. \tag{8.122}$$

The highest utility $\hat{u}_p(\hat{N}_p^0)$ is simply denoted by $\hat{u}_p^0$. Then for each national utility level $u < \hat{u}_p^0$, the relationship between the $\hat{X}(N)$ curve and the $C(u, N)$ curve can be depicted as in Figure 8.7. Notice that relationship (8.122) is equivalent to the following: At each $u = \hat{u}_p(N)$,

$$\frac{d\hat{X}(N)}{dN} \gtreqless \frac{\partial C(u, N)}{\partial N} \qquad \text{as} \quad N \lesseqgtr \hat{N}_p^0. \tag{8.123}$$

Since $d\hat{X}(N)/dN = \hat{W}(N)$ and $\partial C(u, N)/\partial N = Y(u, N)$, this means that at each $u = \hat{u}_p(N)$,

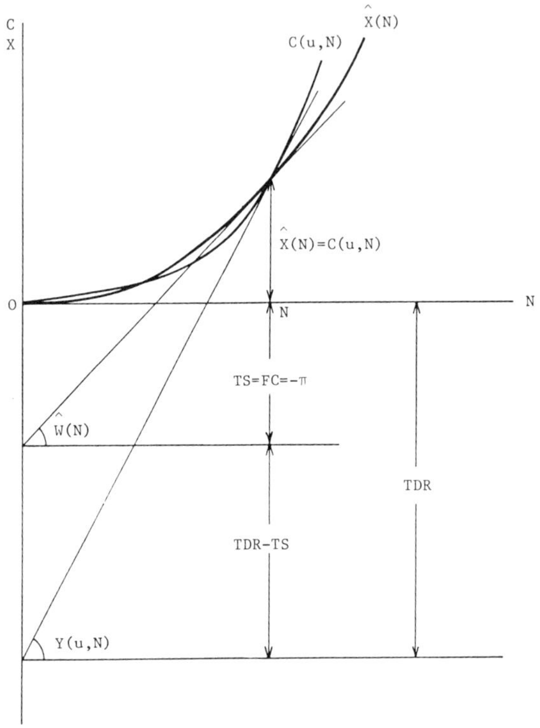

Figure 8.7. Relationship between $\hat{W}(N)$ and $Y(u, N)$ when $N > \hat{N}_p^0$.

$$\hat{W}(N) \gtreqless Y(u, N) \qquad \text{as} \quad N \lesseqgtr \hat{N}_p^0. \tag{8.124}$$

Figure 8.7 depicts the situation in which $N > \hat{N}_p^0$. From (8.117) and (8.118), the equilibrium condition (8.120) can be restated as

$$\hat{W}(N) + \frac{\text{TDR}(N) - \text{TS}(N)}{N} = Y(u, N), \tag{8.125}$$

where $\text{TDR}(N) \equiv \text{TDR}[g(N)h(\rho), N]$. Thus, we can conclude from (8.116), (8.124), and (8.125) that

$$\text{TDR}(N) \gtreqless \text{TS}(N) = \text{FC}(N) = -\pi(N) \qquad \text{as} \quad N \gtreqless \hat{N}_p^0. \tag{8.126}$$

Notice that in the present context, an equilibrium city size N is (locally) stable if and only if $N \geq \hat{N}_p^0$.[27] Thus, we can conclude that *at any stable equilibrium city, the total subsidies* TS(N) *can be financed by confiscating a part of* TDR(N). In particular, we have from (8.126) that

$$\mathrm{TDR}(N) = \mathrm{TS}(N) = \mathrm{FC}(N) = -\pi(N) \qquad \text{at} \quad N = \hat{N}_{\mathrm{p}}^{0}, \tag{8.127}$$

which represents the familiar Henry George theorem of public financing.[28]

Notice that the highest utility $\hat{u}_{\mathrm{p}}^{0}$ will be achieved when the equilibrium city size equals $\hat{N}_{\mathrm{p}}^{0}$. This implies that when the total population of the urban sector in the nation is exogenously given by M, and $M/\hat{N}_{\mathrm{p}}^{0}$ cities of size $\hat{N}_{\mathrm{p}}^{0}$ are formed, each household in every city will achieve the highest utility $\hat{u}_{\mathrm{p}}^{0}$. Since $\hat{u}_{\mathrm{p}}^{0}$ represents the highest common utility that is technologically feasible for the urban sector, $\hat{N}_{\mathrm{p}}^{0}$ represents the optimal, or *first-best,* city size.

Since $\hat{X}(N) > X(N)$ for all N, comparing (8.71) with (8.121) we can readily see that

$$\hat{u}_{\mathrm{p}}(N) > u_{\mathrm{p}}(N) \qquad \text{for all} \quad N > 0, \tag{8.128}$$

and hence, not surprisingly,

$$\hat{u}_{\mathrm{p}}^{0} > u_{\mathrm{p}}^{0}. \tag{8.129}$$

When the optimal (or any other) subsidy scheme is politically or technically infeasible, u_{p}^{0} represents the highest feasible utility level. In this sense, the critical city size N_{p}^{0} associated with u_{p}^{0} represents the *second-best* city size. Notice that without making further assumptions we cannot determine the relative size between $\hat{N}_{\mathrm{p}}^{0}$ and N_{p}^{0}; but generally they are not the same.

Example 8.3. In the context of Example 5.1, the population cost function is given by (5.30). From (8.121) and (8.123), at $(u, N) = (\hat{u}_{\mathrm{p}}^{0}, \hat{N}_{\mathrm{p}}^{0})$ it must hold that

$$\hat{X}(\hat{N}_{\mathrm{p}}^{0}) = C(\hat{u}_{\mathrm{p}}^{0}, \hat{N}_{\mathrm{p}}^{0}), \qquad d\hat{X}(\hat{N}_{\mathrm{p}}^{0})/dN = \partial C(\hat{u}_{\mathrm{p}}^{0}, \hat{N}_{\mathrm{p}}^{0})/\partial N. \tag{8.130}$$

Similarly, at $(u, N) = (u_{\mathrm{p}}^{0}, N_{\mathrm{p}}^{0})$ it must hold that

$$X(N_{\mathrm{p}}^{0}) = C(u_{\mathrm{p}}^{0}, N_{\mathrm{p}}^{0}), \qquad dX(N_{\mathrm{p}}^{0})/dN = \partial C(u_{\mathrm{p}}^{0}, N_{\mathrm{p}}^{0})/\partial N. \tag{8.131}$$

From (5.30), (8.96), and (8.130), we have

$$(1+b)^{-1}\hat{N}_{\mathrm{p}}^{0} = (1+\beta)^{-1}\{(\hat{N}_{\mathrm{p}}^{0} + E) - E^{1+\beta}(\hat{N}_{\mathrm{p}}^{0} + E)^{-\beta}\},$$

and similarly from (5.30), (8.60), and (8.131), we have

$$(1+b)^{-1}N_{\mathrm{p}}^{0} = (1+\beta)^{-1}\{(N_{\mathrm{p}}^{0} + E) - E^{1+\beta}(N_{\mathrm{p}}^{0} + E)^{-\beta}\}.$$

Hence, it follows that

$$\hat{N}_{\mathrm{p}}^{0} = N_{\mathrm{p}}^{0}, \tag{8.132}$$

which together with (5.30), (8.130), and (8.131) implies that

$$e^{\hat{u}_p^0}/e^{u_p^0} = \rho^{\eta}(\nu + \rho\eta)^{-(1+b)} > 1 \qquad \text{[from (8.100)].} \tag{8.133}$$

Therefore, in the context of Example 5.1, the first-best and second-best city sizes turn out to be the same. Notice, however, that this coincidence happened because the population cost function (5.30) is separable with respect to u and N. Otherwise, the two city sizes would not be the same.

Finally, suppose that we have obtained the relationships (8.6) and (8.8) [equivalently, (8.64) and (8.65)] from the observations of actual data on a city (or cities). Then since these aggregate relationships hold in both the external economy model and the monopolistic competition model, without further investigation we cannot determine which hypothesis, the external economy hypothesis or monopolistic competition hypothesis, represents the actual city. However, depending on which hypothesis holds in the actual city, we reach different policy recommendations. Namely, if the external economy hypothesis is valid, no subsidy (to firms or households) is required, and N_p^0 represents the optimal (i.e., first-best) city size.[29] If, however, the monopolistic competition hypothesis is valid, a subsidy scheme becomes necessary to achieve the highest utility $\hat{u}_p^0$, and $\hat{N}_p^0$ represents the optimal city size.

8.5 Conclusion

In this chapter, we have developed two related models of urban agglomeration, the external economy model and the monopolistic competition model. It has been shown that the urban aggregates derived from the two models have the same structural relationships. Thus, from the viewpoint of descriptive analysis of urban aggregates, the monopolistic competition model can be considered to be a specific example of the external economy model. However, it has also been shown that from the viewpoint of normative analysis, the two models lead to substantially different results. Thus, in the empirical implementation of these models, it is essential to identify which model represents more closely the actual city economy.

In our monopolistic competition model, we have focused on the availability of a variety of *local producer services* as the origin of agglomeration economies. In a parallel manner, we may develop a monopolistic competition model of consumer agglomeration, which focuses on *local consumer services* such as restaurants, theaters, beauty shops, and all other kinds of personal service. Imagine a city with a traded-good industry and (local consumer) service industry. The service industry provides a variety of differentiated services to consumers and has a market structure of monopolistic competition. In the presence of consumer preference for product variety, an increase in population will increase the number of consumer services available in the city, shifting household utility upward (recall the discussion in Section 5.2). This will in turn lower the real wage in the city, enabling the traded-good industry to employ more workers. In this way, consumer preference for product variety will generated a basic mainspring of urban agglomeration. See Hobson (1987), Abdel-Rahman (1988), and Fujita (1988) for some initial studies in this direction. Rivera-Batiz (1988) developed a model that examines simultaneously the effects of increased diversity in both producer services and consumer services on urban agglomeration. Finally, one may develop a similar model for examining the roles of variety in *local public goods* in urban agglomeration.

Bibliographical notes

The external economy model of Section 8.2 is based on the traditional city-size models with Marshallian externalities, which have been studied, among others, by Henderson (1974, 1977, 1987), Arnott (1979), Kanemoto (1980, Ch. 2), Upton (1981), and Abdel-Rahman (in press). Before these urban models were developed, Chipman (1970) developed a general equilibrium model with Marshallian externalities and demonstrated that increasing returns to scale (due to Marshallian externalities) are compatible with a perfectly competitive equilibrium. In developing this section, the author owes much to Henderson (1977) and Kanemoto (1980). For city-size models with multiple industries, see Henderson (1977, 1985) and Abdel-Rahman (in press).

The monopolistic competition model of Sections 8.3 and 8.4 is based on Abdel-Rahman and Fujita (1987). This work reflects a renewed interest in the modeling of product diversity in the framework of Chamberlinian monopolistic competition, which was formalized by Dixit and Stiglitz (1977) using CES-type utility functions. In international economics, this approach has been employed by Ethier (1982) and Krugman (1979). See Fujita (1988) for a spatial version of the Chamberlinian monopolistic competition model, which introduces land consumption and location choice by firms (and households).

Notes

1. In location theory, Marshallian external economies are also called *localization economies*, which represent the economies due to expansion of the total activity level of all firms in the same industry at the same location (see Isard 1956, Ch. 8). For Marshallian external economies, see Chipman (1970).

2. According to Henderson (1986, 1987), specialization in the United States seems to be pervasive among smaller and medium-sized urban areas; about half of the 243 Standard Metropolitan Statistical Areas in 1970 could be classified as being specialized in one industry.
3. If we interpret external economies in the sense of *technological external economies,* representing unintentional consequences of one agent's action on others, then most sources of agglomeration economies previously mentioned are not at all "external" economies. For example, in real cities, no service firm would "unintentionally" provide its service to others. Therefore, we must interpret most of these agglomeration economies as so-called pecuniary external economies, representing the benefits acquired through market transactions. However, the term *pecuniary external economies* is quite misleading, and economic theory might be better served without it.
4. More generally, we may assume that $x(N_j, N) = f(N_j, N)$, where given each N, function $f(\cdot, N)$ is S-shaped; i.e., $\partial^2 f(N_j, N)/\partial N_j^2 > 0$ for small N_j and $\partial^2 f(N_j, N)/\partial N_j^2 < 0$ for large N_j. In this context, assuming that the equilibrium number of firms in the city is very large, we can obtain essentially the same results with this section. For this approach, see Kanemoto (1980, Ch. 2).
5. Note that since the production function (8.1) exhibits a contant returns to scale in N_j, in equilibrium the profit of each firm is zero. Hence, we need not consider the distribution of profits.
6. Although we have in Figure 8.1 that $\tilde{N} < N_{\mathrm{a}}^1$, this does not always hold (e.g., if $\tilde{N} = \infty$, then $N_{\mathrm{a}}^1 < \tilde{N} = \infty$).
7. This definition of an unstable equilibrium city size is based on the implicit assumption that the national utility level will change (if it does) much more slowly than populations of individual cities. This assumption is valid when each city is very small compared with the national economy, and the populations of only a small number of cities will change rapidly at any time. Otherwise, to examine the stability of equilibrium city sizes, we must consider explicitly the population-adjustment process of the entire national city system. The same applies to the definition of a stable equilibrium city size below.
8. Here we are implicitly assuming that any new city must start from a population close to zero. If a large coalition between firms and households were possible, even those city sizes between N_{a}^0 and N_{a}^1 might not be stable.
9. As usual, M is assumed to be sufficiently large that the number of cities M/N can be treated as a continuous number.
10. It is stable in the following sense. When every city has the same population N such that $N_{\mathrm{a}}^0 < N < N_{\mathrm{a}}^1$, households in any city do not have any incentive to move to another city, because an increase in the population of the receiving city would lower the utility level there; similarly, no firm in any city has an incentive to move to another city or to form a new (small) city in the rural area.
11. From Proposition 3.3, the value of $\mathrm{TDR}(g(N), N)$ can be determined uniquely.

12. Originally, u_p^1 is defined by the relation

$$\lim_{N\to 0} \{g(N) + (\text{TDR}[g(N), N]/N)\} = Y(u_p^1, 0).$$

However, we can show that $\lim_{N\to 0}(\text{TDR}[g(N), N]/N) = 0$. Hence, u_p^1 can be defined from (8.18). This also implies that in Figure 8.3, both the $g(N)$ curve and the $g(N) + (\text{TDR}/N)$ curve start from the same point on the vertical axis.

13. Let $u(N)$ be the solution to (8.16) for u under each N. Then from Figure 3.4 (i.e., Proposition 3.5), we can see that the CCP($g(N)$, N) model has the same solution as the CCA[$g(N)$ + TDR($g(N)$, N)/N, N] model, which in turn has the same solution as the OCA[$g(N)$ + TDR($g(N)$, N)/N, $u_p(N)$] model, which in turn has the same solution as the OCA[$Y(u_p(N), N)$, $u_p(N)$] model. In particular, given each N, all four models have the same equilibrium utility level, $u_p(N)$.

14. *Necessity:* If $u_p(N)$ is the equilibrium utility of the CCP($g(N)$, N) model, then from (5.14) we have $Ng(N) = C(u_p(N), N)$, i.e., $F(N) = C(u_p(N), N)$. *Sufficiency:* Recall from Proposition 3.3 that the CCP($g(N)$, N) model has a unique solution for each N [because $g(N) > T(0) = 0$ for all $N > 0$ by assumption], and the solution satisfies the relation $F(N) = C(u_p(N), N)$. Therefore, since the equation $F(N) = C(u, N)$ has a unique solution for u under each N, the solution should equal $u_p(N)$, i.e., the equilibrium utility of the CCP($g(N)$, N) model.

15. This conclusion was first reached by Henderson (1974). [The same conclusion was also derived in a dynamic context by Fujita (1978, Ch. 6).] Note that this conclusion follows because of the difficulty of forming a coalition to create a large city. We know from Proposition 5.5 that the optimal city system would be attained at the equilibrium of competition among surplus-maximizing developers. However, in the present context of the external economy model, the economy of each city is supposed to be complex (i.e., many small firms operate in the environment of external economies) and any economical city size (close to N_p^0) is likely to be quite large. Hence, it will be unrealistic to assume that a developer (or a coalition of firms and households) can create a new city of an economical size (without the help of the central government). Note also, however, that this conclusion is not inconsistent with many empirical observations that larger cities are more productive and have higher (nominal) per capita incomes. To see this, suppose that $g'(N) > 0$ for all $N > 0$ (and hence $\tilde{N} = \infty$). Then in any equilibrium city system, the private marginal product of labor, $g(N)$, becomes greater as a city population N increases; hence, the per capita income $g(N) + (\text{TDR}/N)$ also tends to increase in N.

16. This production function (a combination of a Cobb–Douglas function and CES function) is a version of a utility function introduced by Dixit and Stiglitz (1977). A similar production function was introduced by Ethier (1982).

17. Again, since the production function (8.30) is homogeneous of degree 1, the

equilibrium output X cannot be determined until later, together with all other unknowns.

18. For this argument, see Dixit and Stiglitz (1977).
19. Notice that in the traded-good sector, the satisfaction of the first-order conditions for profit maximization implies that the zero-profit condition is already satisfied.
20. Notice that under the specification (8.63), $g'(N) > 0$ for all $N > 0$ [in terms of (8.3), this implies that $\tilde{N} = \infty$]; hence, in Figure 8.1, $g(N)$ should be increasing for all $N > 0$. However, this does not affect the results of Section 8.2 at all.
21. As noted before, unstable equilibrium city sizes would seldom be observed in practice. Hereafter, we consider only those equilibrium city configurations that are associated with stable equilibrium city sizes.
22. The impact of the other two parameters, η and ν, is mainly indeterminate, and hence we omit any discussion of them. Notice that when we represent the unit price of the traded good generally as p_x, the right-hand side of equations (8.45), (8.49), (8.52), and (8.58) must be multiplied by p_x.
23. These first-order conditions represent the necessary and sufficient conditions for the optimum.
24. See note 23.
25. Differentiating equation (8.107) logarithmically with respect to ρ, we have $(1/h)(dh/d\rho) = (1 - \eta)\rho^{-2} \log[1 - \eta(1 - \rho)] < 0$. Hence, $dh/d\rho < 0$ for all $\rho < 1$. It can also be readily seen that $h(1) = 1$ and $\lim_{\rho \to 0} h(\rho) = \infty$. We can similarly show the relations in (8.110).
26. A similar result was obtained by Dixit and Stiglitz (1977).
27. Notice that in the present context, the *limiting city size* $\hat{N}_{\mathrm{p}}^{1}$ equals ∞.
28. Notice that when $N = \hat{N}_{\mathrm{p}}^{0}$, Figure 8.7 becomes (essentially) the same as Figure 5.15.
29. Namely, when there are M/N_{p}^{0} cities of size N_{p}^{0}, all households can achieve the highest utility u_{p}^{0} without any subsidy (in addition to the share of total differential rent, TDR/N).

Basic mathematics and consumer theory

In this appendix, we review some of the basic mathematical concepts and results from consumer theory that have been used in the text. Statements are given here without proof. For a complete treatment of these topics, the reader is referred, for example, to Henderson and Quandt (1980), Takayama (1974), Varian (1984), and Barten and Böhm (1982).

A.1 Concave and convex functions

Let $\mathbf{R}$ represent the set of real numbers. For any positive integer n, the *n-dimensional Euclidean space* $\mathbf{R}^n = \{(x_1, x_2, \ldots, x_n) \mid x_i \in \mathbf{R}, i = 1, 2, \ldots, n\}$ represents the set of all n-tuples of real numbers.

Because convex and concave functions are defined on convex sets, we introduce the latter concept first. A *convex set* in $\mathbf{R}^n$ is a set such that the line segment joining any two points in the set is also in the set. More precisely, a subset of C of $\mathbf{R}^n$ is said to be convex if for any $\mathbf{x}, \mathbf{y} \in C$,

$$\alpha\mathbf{x} + (1 - \alpha)\mathbf{y} \in C \qquad \text{for all} \qquad \alpha, 0 \leq \alpha \leq 1.$$

Examples of convex sets are

1. a segment of a straight line in $\mathbf{R}^n$,
2. a ball in $\mathbf{R}^n$,
3. the *nonnegative orthant* $\mathbf{R}^n_+ = \{\mathbf{x} = (x_1, x_2, \ldots, x_n) \mid x_i \geq 0, i = 1, 2, \ldots, n\}$ in $\mathbf{R}^n$,
4. $\mathbf{R}^n$ itself.

Next, let f be a real-valued function defined on a convex set C in $\mathbf{R}^n$. Then, f is called a *concave function* if for any $\mathbf{x}, \mathbf{y} \in C$,

$$f(\alpha\mathbf{x} + (1 - \alpha)\mathbf{y}) \geq \alpha f(\mathbf{x}) + (1 - \alpha)f(\mathbf{y}) \qquad \text{for all} \quad \alpha, 0 \leq \alpha \leq 1.$$

Similarly, f is called a *convex function* if for any $\mathbf{x}, \mathbf{y} \in C$,

$$f(\alpha\mathbf{x} + (1 - \alpha)\mathbf{y}) \leq \alpha f(\mathbf{x}) + (1 - \alpha)f(\mathbf{y}) \qquad \text{for all} \quad \alpha, 0 \leq \alpha \leq 1.$$

Hence, f is convex if and only if $-f$ is concave. If the above inequalities

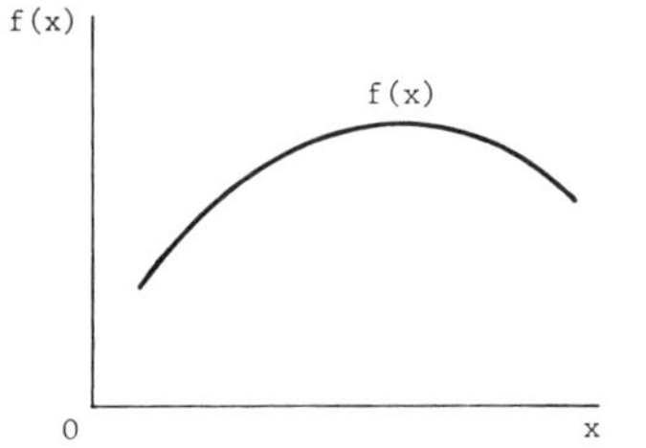

Figure A.1. A concave function.

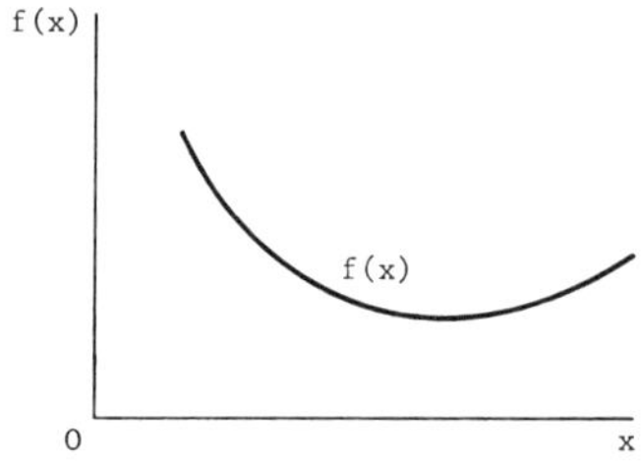

Figure A.2. A convex function.

are strict for all $x \neq y$ and $\alpha \neq 0, 1$, we say that f is *strictly concave* or *strictly convex*. Figure A.1 depicts a strictly concave function on a segment in **R**, and similarly Figure A.2 depicts a strictly convex function. Notice that a *linear function* $f(\mathbf{x}) = \Sigma_{i=1}^{n} a_i x_i + b$ is both concave and convex.

If a function is differentiable, we have the following equivalent definition of concave (or convex) functions:

Property A.1. Let f be a real-valued function defined on an open interval **I** in **R** and suppose that its second derivative $f''(x)$ exists at each point $x \in \mathbf{I}$. Then

(i) f is concave (convex) on **I** if and only if $f''(x)$ is nonpositive (nonnegative) for all $x \in \mathbf{I}$.
(ii) f is strictly concave (strictly convex) on **I** if and only if $f''(x)$ is negative (positive) for all $x \in \mathbf{I}$.

For extensions of these results to functions on $\mathbf{R}^n$, see the articles referred to at the beginning of this appendix.

Some important properties of concave and convex functions are the following:

Property A.2. Let f be a concave (or convex) function on a convex set C in $\mathbf{R}^n$. Then f is continuous at any interior point of C.

Property A.3. Let f be a real-valued function on a convex set C in $\mathbf{R}^n$. Then we have the following:

(i) If f is concave, then for any $\alpha \in \mathbf{R}$, the set $\{\mathbf{x} \mid \mathbf{x} \in C, f(\mathbf{x}) \geq \alpha\}$ is convex.
(ii) If f is convex, then for any $\alpha \in \mathbf{R}$, the set $\{\mathbf{x} \mid \mathbf{x} \in C, f(\mathbf{x}) \leq \alpha\}$ is convex.

We can readily see, however, that the converse of (i) [or (ii)] does not always hold. Namely, even if the set $\{\mathbf{x} \mid \mathbf{x} \in C, f(\mathbf{x}) \geq \alpha\}$ is convex for each $\alpha \in \mathbf{R}$, function f may not be concave. This observation leads to a broader class of functions, which are closely related to *utility functions* (to be discussed later). A real-valued function f on a convex set C in $\mathbf{R}^n$ is called a *quasi-concave function* (*quasi-convex function*) if for each $\alpha \in \mathbf{R}$, the set $\{\mathbf{x} \mid \mathbf{x} \in C, f(\mathbf{x}) \geq \alpha\}$ (resp. $\{\mathbf{x} \mid \mathbf{x} \in C, f(\mathbf{x}) \leq \alpha\}$) is convex. By definition, f is quasi-concave if and only if $-f$ is quasi-convex. It is not difficult to see the following:

Property A.4. A real-valued function f on a convex set C in $\mathbf{R}^n$ is quasi-concave (quasi-convex) if and only if for any $\mathbf{x}$, $\mathbf{y}$, $\in C$,

$$f(\alpha\mathbf{x} + (1 - \alpha)\mathbf{y}) \geq \min\{f(\mathbf{x}), f(\mathbf{y})\} \qquad \text{for all} \quad \alpha, 0 \leq \alpha \leq 1$$

$$(\text{resp. } f(\alpha\mathbf{x} + (1 - \alpha)\mathbf{y}) \leq \max\{f(\mathbf{x}), f(\mathbf{y})\} \qquad \text{for all} \quad \alpha, 0 \leq \alpha \leq 1).$$

If the above inequalities are strict for all $\mathbf{x} \neq \mathbf{y}$ and $\alpha \neq 0, 1$, we say that f is *strictly quasi-concave* or *strictly quasi-convex*.

Finally, notice that for any real-valued continuous function f on an interval $\mathbf{I}$ in $\mathbf{R}$, the locus of points $\{(x, f(x)) \mid x \in \mathbf{I}\}$ defines a continuous *curve* (or *graph*) in $\mathbf{R}^2$. We say that the curve is concave (convex) if and only if function f is concave (convex) on $\mathbf{I}$; similarly, the curve is strictly concave (strictly convex) if and only if f is strictly concave (strictly convex). Figure A.1 (Figure A.2) depicts a strictly concave curve (strictly convex curve). When the function is differentiable on $\mathbf{I}$, we say that its corresponding curve is *smooth* on $\mathbf{I}$.

A.2 Envelope theorem

When we have solved a maximization (or minimization) problem, we are next often interested in knowing how the maximum (or minimum) value of the objective function changes with a change in some parameter. For example, when the bid rent $\Psi(r, u)$ is obtained by solving the maximization problem in the right side of (2.8), we are interested in knowing how the maximum value $\Psi(r, u)$ changes as r (or u) increases. The envelope theorem provides a convenient method for answering such a question.

First, let us consider the following simple maximization problem,

$$\max_x f(x, a), \tag{A.1}$$

where x is the choice variable and a the fixed parameter. The objective function f is assumed to be a real-valued function defined on the domain $X \times A$, which is assumed to be an open subset of $\mathbf{R}^2$. Notice that the optimal value of x is assumed to be chosen from the *open subset* X in $\mathbf{R}$ (i.e., the choice set X does not include the boundary points). For example, $X = \mathbf{R}$ or $X = \{x \in \mathbf{R} \mid x > 0\}$. Suppose that for each $a \in A$, there exists a unique maximizing choice of x, which is denoted by $x(a)$. If we let

$$M(a) \equiv f(x(a), a),$$

then $M(a)$ represents the maximum value of the objective function for each parameter value a. Let us examine how $M(a)$ changes with a. Provided that f is continuously differentiable on its domain, $M(a)$ is differentiable in a. Hence, using the chain rule of differentiation, we have

$$\frac{dM(a)}{da} = \frac{\partial f(x(a), a)}{\partial x}\frac{dx(a)}{da} + \frac{\partial f(x(a), a)}{\partial a}, \tag{A.2}$$

where $\partial f(x(a), a)/\partial x$ represents the value of the partial derivative $\partial f(x, a)/\partial x$ at $(x, a) = (x(a), a)$, and $\partial f(x(a), a)/\partial a$ denotes the value of $\partial f(x, a)/\partial a$ at $(x, a) = (x(a), a)$. Notice, however, that since the optimal value $x(a)$ has been chosen from the open set X, the first-order condition for maximization requires that $\partial f(x(a), a)/\partial x = 0$. Hence, (A.2) reduces to the form

$$\frac{dM(a)}{da} = \frac{\partial f(x(a), a)}{\partial a}, \tag{A.3}$$

which is often called the *envelope theorem*. To interpret this result, observe that in expression (A.2), $dM(a)/da$ consists of the two terms. The second term, $\partial f(x(a), a)/\partial a$, represents the *direct effect* of a marginal change in parameter a on the value of the objective function f holding x fixed at $x(a)$. The first term represents the *indirect effect* (or *induced effect*) of parameter a on f through its effect on the optimal choice of x. The envelope theorem (A.3) then says that *this indirect effect is so small compared with the direct effect that we can omit it* in calculating the impact of a marginal change in the parameter a on the objective function.

We can readily extend the envelope theorem to the case of many variables and many parameters. To do so, let us now assume in the optimization problem (A.1) that $\mathbf{x} \equiv (x_1, x_2, \ldots, x_m)$ represents a vector of m choice variables and that $\mathbf{a} \equiv (a_1, a_2, \ldots, a_n)$ represents a vector of n parameters. Function f is now assumed to be a real-valued function on the domain, $X \times A$, where X is an open subset of $\mathbf{R}^m$ and A is an open subset of $\mathbf{R}^n$. Assuming that $\mathbf{x}(\mathbf{a}) = (x_1(\mathbf{a}), x_2(\mathbf{a}), \ldots, x_m(\mathbf{a}))$ represents the unique maximizing choice of $\mathbf{x}$ for each $\mathbf{a} \in A$, the maximum value of the objective function for each $\mathbf{a} \in A$ is given by $M(\mathbf{a}) \equiv f(\mathbf{x}(\mathbf{a}), \mathbf{a})$. Provided that f is continuously differentiable on the domain $X \times A$, it follows that for each $i = 1, 2, \ldots, n$,

$$\frac{\partial M(\mathbf{a})}{\partial a_i} = \sum_{j=1}^{m} \frac{\partial f(\mathbf{x}(\mathbf{a}), \mathbf{a})}{\partial x_j} \frac{\partial x_j(\mathbf{a})}{\partial a_i} + \frac{\partial f(\mathbf{x}(\mathbf{a}), \mathbf{a})}{\partial a_i},$$

where $\partial f(\mathbf{x}(\mathbf{a}), \mathbf{a})/\partial x_j$ denotes the value of $\partial f(\mathbf{x}, \mathbf{a})/\partial x_j$ at $(\mathbf{x}, \mathbf{a}) = (\mathbf{x}(\mathbf{a}), \mathbf{a})$ and $\partial f(\mathbf{x}(\mathbf{a}), \mathbf{a})/\partial a_i$ denotes the value of $\partial f(\mathbf{x}, \mathbf{a})/\partial a_i$ at $(\mathbf{x}, \mathbf{a}) = (\mathbf{x}(\mathbf{a}), \mathbf{a})$. Again, since the choice set X is assumed to be open, the first-order condition requires that $\partial f(\mathbf{x}(\mathbf{a}), \mathbf{a})/\partial x_j = 0$ for each $j = 1, 2, \ldots, m$. Therefore, we obtain the following envelope theorem:

$$\frac{\partial M(\mathbf{a})}{\partial a_i} = \frac{\partial f(\mathbf{x}(\mathbf{a}), \mathbf{a})}{\partial a_i}, \qquad i = 1, 2, \ldots, n. \tag{A.4}$$

For further extensions of the envelope theorem to the case with constraint equations, see the articles referred to at the beginning of this appendix.

A.3 Basic results from consumer theory

In this section, we summarize some of the important characteristics of demand functions and related functions from consumer theory. In the following discussion, the *positive orthant* of $\mathbf{R}^n$ is denoted by $\mathbf{P}^n \equiv \{\mathbf{x} = (x_1, x_2, \ldots, x_n) \in \mathbf{R}^n \mid x_i > 0, i = 1, 2, \ldots, n\}$. For any $\mathbf{x} = (x_1, x_2, \ldots, x_n)$ and $y = (y_1, y_2, \ldots, y_n)$ in $\mathbf{R}^n$, we write $\mathbf{x} \geqq \mathbf{y}$ if $x_i \geq y_i$ for all i and write $\mathbf{x} \gg \mathbf{y}$ if $x_i > y_i$ for all i. In addition, we define $\mathbf{x} \cdot \mathbf{y} = \Sigma_{i=1}^{n} x_i y_i$.

Let us now consider the following utility-maximization problem of a consumer:

$$\max_{\substack{x_i > 0 \\ i=1,\ldots,n}} U(x_1, x_2, \ldots, x_n), \qquad \text{subject to } \sum_{i=1}^{n} p_i x_i \leq I,$$

or, in short,

$$\max_{\mathbf{x} \in \mathbf{P}^n} U(\mathbf{x}), \qquad \text{subject to } \mathbf{p} \cdot \mathbf{x} \leq I. \tag{A.5}$$

Here U represents the consumer's utility function, $\mathbf{x} = (x_1, x_2, \ldots, x_n)$ a consumption vector, $\mathbf{p} = (p_1, p_2, \ldots, p_n)$ the given price vector, and I the income of the consumer. Notice that we have restricted the consumption set to $\mathbf{P}^n$ since optimal consumption levels are always assumed to be positive in this book. To ensure this, it is assumed that the utility function U satisfies the following conditions:

Assumption A.1. U is a real-valued function defined on $\mathbf{P}^n$ such that

(i) U is twice continuously differentiable (i.e., all its second-order partial derivates exist and are continuous),
(ii) U is strictly quasi-concave, and the marginal rate of substitution for any pair of goods (i, j) is decreasing in x_i,
(iii) the marginal utility is positive for all i, that is, $\partial U(x)/\partial x_i > 0$ for all $i = 1, 2, \ldots, n$ and $x \in \mathbf{P}^n$,
(iv) the closures of the indifference surfaces are contained in $\mathbf{P}^n$.

Conditions (ii) and (iii) together means that U is *strongly quasi-concave* (see Barten and Böhm 1982). Condition (iv) means that indifference curves do not cut axes; that is, each good is *essential*.

Notice that for the two-commodity case, that is, for $n = 2$, Assumption A.1 is equivalent to Assumption 2.1 together with conditions (2.3) and (2.5) (see Chapter 2). We adopt the rather strong conditions of Assumption A.1 because they provide sharper results in the following analyses.

Solving (A.5) for each given price vector $\mathbf{p}$ and income, I, we obtain a system of *Marshallian demand functions* (or *uncompensated demand functions*), denoted by

$$\hat{\mathbf{x}}(\mathbf{p}, I) \equiv (\hat{x}_1(\mathbf{p}, I), \hat{x}_2(\mathbf{p}, I), \ldots, \hat{x}_n(\mathbf{p}, I)). \tag{A.6}$$

These functions exhibit the following properties (given Assumption A.1):

Property A.5. For each $i = 1, 2, \ldots, n$, the Marshallian demand function $\hat{x}_i(\mathbf{p}, I)$ is well defined for all $\mathbf{p} \gg 0$ and $I > 0$, and in addition,

(i) $\hat{x}_i(\mathbf{p}, I)$ is continuously differentiable in $(\mathbf{p}, I)$,
(ii) $\hat{x}_i(\mathbf{p}, I) > 0$ for all $\mathbf{p} \gg 0$ and $I > 0$,
(iii) $\Sigma_{i=1}^n p_i \hat{x}_i(\mathbf{p}, I) = I$.

For a proof of Property A.5 (and for the proofs of the rest of the properties in this section), see Barten and Böhm (1982). Next, we define the *indirect utility function* associated with U by

$$V(\mathbf{p}, I) = \max \{U(\mathbf{x}) \mid \mathbf{p} \cdot \mathbf{x} \leq I, \mathbf{x} \in \mathbf{P}^n\}, \tag{A.7}$$

which represents the maximum utility level attainable under each price vector $\mathbf{p}$ and income I. By definition,

$$V(\mathbf{p}, I) = U(\hat{x}_1(\mathbf{p}, I), \hat{x}_2(\mathbf{p}, I), \ldots, \hat{x}_n(\mathbf{p}, I)). \tag{A.8}$$

Using Assumption A.1 and Property A.5, the following can be shown:

Property A.6. The indirect utility function $V(\mathbf{p}, I)$ is well defined for all $\mathbf{p} \gg 0$ and $I > 0$, and in addition,

(i) $V(\mathbf{p}, I)$ is twice continuously differentiable in $(\mathbf{p}, I)$,
(ii) $\partial V(\mathbf{p}, I)/\partial I > 0$, that is, V is increasing in income,
(iii) $\partial V(\mathbf{p}, I)/\partial p_i < 0$ for all i, that is, V is decreasing in each price,
(iv) $V(\mathbf{p}, I)$ is quasi-convex in $\mathbf{p}$.

Let us consider the equation $u = V(\mathbf{p}, I)$. Since V is a continuous and increasing in I, its *inverse*, $I = E(\mathbf{p}, u)$, exists for each price vector $\mathbf{p}$, which is called the *expenditure function*. By definition, $E(\mathbf{p}, u)$ represents the *minimum amount of income required to achieve utility level u under price vector* $\mathbf{p}$. From the definitions of V and E, the following relations are seen to hold identically:

$$u \equiv V(\mathbf{p}, E(\mathbf{p}, u)) \qquad \text{and} \qquad I \equiv E(\mathbf{p}, V(\mathbf{p}, I)). \tag{A.9}$$

Without loss of generality, it can be assumed that

$$\inf \{V(\mathbf{p}, I) \mid \mathbf{p} \gg 0, I > 0\} = -\infty, \ \sup \{V(\mathbf{p}, I) \mid \mathbf{p} \gg 0, I > 0\} = \infty.$$

Using Property A.6 and (A.9), we can then show the following:

Property A.7. The expenditure function $E(\mathbf{p}, u)$ is well defined for all $\mathbf{p} \gg 0$ and $u \in \mathbf{R}$, and in addition,

(i) $E(\mathbf{p}, u)$ is twice continuously differentiable in $(\mathbf{p}, u)$,
(ii) $\partial E(\mathbf{p}, u)/\partial u > 0$, that is, E is increasing in utility level,
(iii) $\partial E(\mathbf{p}, u)/\partial p_i > 0$ for all i, that is, E is increasing in each price,
(iv) $E(\mathbf{p}, u)$ is concave in $\mathbf{p}$.

An alternative definition of the expenditure function is given by

$$E(\mathbf{p}, u) = \min \{\mathbf{p} \cdot \mathbf{x} \mid U(\mathbf{x}) \geq u, \mathbf{x} \in \mathbf{P}^n\}. \tag{A.10}$$

By solving the minimization problem above for each given $(\mathbf{p}, u)$, we obtain the system of *Hicksian demand functions* (or *compensated demand functions*) denoted by

$$\tilde{\mathbf{x}}(\mathbf{p}, u) \equiv (\tilde{x}_1(\mathbf{p}, u), \tilde{x}_2(\mathbf{p}, u), \ldots, \tilde{x}_n(\mathbf{p}, u)). \tag{A.11}$$

From these definitions, we immediately obtain the following additional pair of identities, which describe the fundamental relationship between the Hicksian and the Marshallian demand functions:

$$\hat{\mathbf{x}}(\mathbf{p}, I) \equiv \tilde{\mathbf{x}}(\mathbf{p}, V(\mathbf{p}, I)) \qquad \text{and} \qquad \tilde{\mathbf{x}}(\mathbf{p}, u) \equiv \hat{\mathbf{x}}(\mathbf{p}, E(\mathbf{p}, u)). \tag{A.12}$$

These Hicksian demand functions can be shown to exhibit the following important properties (under Assumption A.1):

Property A.8. For each $i = 1, 2, \ldots, n$, the Hicksian demand function $\tilde{x}_i(\mathbf{p}, u)$ is well defined for all $\mathbf{p} \gg 0$ and $I > 0$, and in addition,

(i) $\tilde{x}_i(\mathbf{p}, u)$ is continuously differentiable in $(\mathbf{p}, u)$,
(ii) $\tilde{x}_i(\mathbf{p}, u) = \partial E(\mathbf{p}, u)/\partial p_i > 0$ for all i,
(iii) $\partial \tilde{x}_i(\mathbf{p}, u)/\partial p_i = \partial^2 E(\mathbf{p}, u)/\partial p_i^2 .< 0$ for all i, that is, the own-price effect of each good on Hicksian demand is negative.

Finally, these results lead to the following important relationship, which clarifies the effect of price changes on Marshallian demand. From the second identity in (A.12), it follows that for each i and j,

$$\frac{\partial \tilde{x}_j(\mathbf{p}, u)}{\partial p_i} = \frac{\partial \hat{x}_j(\mathbf{p}, I)}{\partial p_i} + \frac{\partial \hat{x}_j(\mathbf{p}, I)}{\partial I}\frac{\partial E(\mathbf{p}, u)}{\partial p_i}.$$

But since $\partial E(\mathbf{p}, u)/\partial p_i = \tilde{x}_i(\mathbf{p}, u)$ [from Property A.8(ii)], we must then have

$$\frac{\partial \hat{x}_j(\mathbf{p}, I)}{\partial p_i} = \frac{\partial \tilde{x}_j(\mathbf{p}, u)}{\partial p_i} - \frac{\partial \hat{x}_j(\mathbf{p}, I)}{\partial I}\tilde{x}_i(\mathbf{p}, u), \tag{A.13}$$

which is called the *Slutsky equation*. In this equation, the change in the Marshallian demand for good j induced by a marginal increase in the price of good i is decomposed into two separate effects: the *substitution effect,* $\partial \tilde{x}_j(\mathbf{p}, u)/\partial p_i$, and the *income effect,* $-(\partial \hat{x}_j(\mathbf{p}, I)/\partial I)\tilde{x}_j(\mathbf{p}, u)$. In particular, by setting i equal to j, we see that

$$\frac{\partial \hat{x}_i(\mathbf{p}, I)}{\partial p_i} = \frac{\partial \tilde{x}_i(\mathbf{p}, u)}{\partial p_i} - \frac{\partial \hat{x}_i(\mathbf{p}, I)}{\partial I}\tilde{x}_i(\mathbf{p}, u). \tag{A.14}$$

But since Property A.8(iii) implies that $\partial \tilde{x}_i(\mathbf{p}, u)/\partial p_i < 0$, it follows that if $\partial \hat{x}_i(\mathbf{p}, I)/\partial I$ is positive, then the own-price effect of good i on the Marshallian demand is negative. A good with a positive income effect [i.e., with $\partial \hat{x}_i(\mathbf{p}, I)/\partial I > 0$] is called a *normal good* (or *superior good*). If $\partial \hat{x}_i(\mathbf{p}, I)/\partial I$ is negative (i.e., good i is an *inferior good*), then $\partial \hat{x}_i(\mathbf{p}, I)/\partial p_i$ may be positive. In this case, good i is called a *Giffen good.*

Transport cost and land rent

In this appendix, we show that under a set of reasonable assumptions on transport cost function and land distribution, a simple, general relationship holds between the *total transport cost* (TTC) and *total differential rent* (TDR) of a city. As before, we consider the CBD to be a point; we assume that all households are identical and hence have the same transport cost function $T(r)$. Then, TTC and TDR can be defined respectively as follows:

$$\mathrm{TTC} = \int_0^{r_{\mathrm{f}}} T(r)n(r)\,dr, \tag{B.1}$$

$$\mathrm{TDR} = \int_0^{r_{\mathrm{f}}} (R(r) - R(r_{\mathrm{f}}))L(r)\,dr, \tag{B.2}$$

where $n(r)$, $R(r)$, $L(r)$, and r_{f} represent, respectively, the household distribution, land rent curve, land distribution, and urban fringe distance. Although we first discuss these in the context of equilibrium land use, it can readily be shown that if TDR is considered to represent the total *shadow* differential rent, the same relationship also holds for optimal land use.

First, let us take a simple case, which was examined by Mohring (1961). Tastes of households are such that every household lives on a lot of unit size (i.e., a perfectly inelastic demand for land). Then we can immediately conclude that in equilibrium, the sum of land rent and transport cost must be constant everywhere within the urban fringe:

$$R(r) + T(r) = \text{const} \qquad \text{for all} \quad r \leq r_{\mathrm{f}}. \tag{B.3}$$

Otherwise, households could save money on land and transportation by moving outward or inward and hence could enhance their utilities by spending that money on other goods. This is a contradiction of equilibrium, and hence relation (B.3) must hold. In equilibrium, the following standard relationship also holds at the urban fringe:

$$R(r_f) = R_A.$$

Since the constancy of $T(r) + R(r)$ implies $T(r) + R(r) = T(r_f) + R(r_f)$, we finally obtain

$$(R(r) - R_A) + T(r) = T(r_f) \qquad \text{for all} \quad r \leq r_f. \tag{B.4}$$

That is, everywhere within the urban fringe, the sum of the differential rent and transport cost equals the transport cost at the urban fringe. This relationship is depicted in Figure B.1.[1]

Now, suppose that the transport cost function is linear:

$$T(r) = ar.$$

Then in Figure B.1, line *AC* is straight with slope a. Assume further that there is a constant amount of land, θ, at each distance (a linear city):

$$L(r) = \theta.$$

Then in Figure B.1, TDR equals the area *ACD* times the width θ. Since the lot size of each household is unity, $N(r) = \theta$ at each $r < r_f$. Hence, TTC equals the area *ABC* times the width θ. Then since *ABC* equals *ACD*, we can conclude that TDR equals TTC.

Instead of a linear city let us assume that the city is circular or pie-shaped:

$$L(r) = \theta r.$$

Then since $R(r) - R_A = a(r_f - r)$ and $n(r) = \theta r$ at each $r \leq r_f$,

$$\text{TDR} = \int_0^{r_f} (R(r) - R_A)L(r)\,dr = \int_0^{r_f} a(r_f - r)\theta r\,dr = \left(\frac{a\theta}{6}\right) r_f^3,$$

$$\text{TTC} = \int_0^{r_f} T(r)n(r)\,dr = \int_0^{r_f} ar\theta r\,dr = \left(\frac{a\theta}{3}\right) r_f^3,$$

and hence TDR = TTC/2.[2] In summary, we can conclude that

$$\text{TDR} = \begin{cases} \text{TTC} & \text{if} \quad T(r) = ar \quad \text{and} \quad L(r) = \theta. \\ \text{TTC}/2 & \text{if} \quad T(r) = ar \quad \text{and} \quad L(r) = \theta r. \end{cases} \tag{B.5}$$

To what extent can we generalize the above result? As the reader may have noticed, the derivation of relation (B.5) is crucially based on the assumption of a fixed lot size. It may therefore be a surprise to learn that

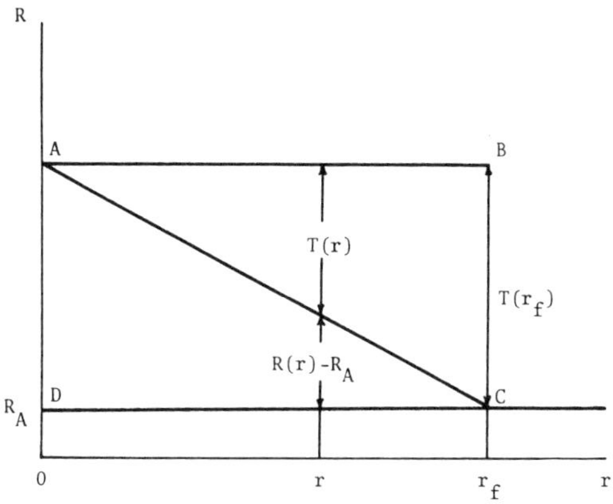

Figure B.1. Relationship between the differential land rent and transport cost.

relation (B.5) holds true even when demand for land is elastic. This can be shown by following the method introduced by Arnott (1979).

Let us assume that the residential choice behavior of each household is given by the basic model (2.1). Then $R(r) = \Psi(r, u^*)$ for all $r \leq r_f$, and from (2.27)

$$\frac{\partial \Psi(r, u^*)}{\partial r} = -\frac{T'(r)}{S(r, u^*)}, \tag{B.6}$$

where u^* is the equilibrium utility level. Therefore, we have

$$R'(r) = -\frac{T'(r)}{S(r, u^*)}. \tag{B.7}$$

Then since $n(r)S(r, u^*) = L(r)$ at each $r < r_f$,

$$T'(r)n(r) = -R'(r)S(r, u^*)n(r) = -R'(r)L(r) = -(R(r) - R(r_f))'L(r), \tag{B.8}$$

where $(R(r) - R(r_f))' \equiv d(R(r) - R(r_f))/dr$. Let us assume that the distribution of land is given as

$$L(r) = \theta r^{\lambda}, \tag{B.9}$$

for some constant $\lambda > -1$, and the transport cost function as[3]

$$T(r) = ar^{\mu}, \tag{B.10}$$

for some constant $\mu > 0$. Then,

$$\begin{aligned}
\text{TTC} &= \int_0^{r_f} T(r)n(r)\,dr \\
&= \int_0^{r_f} \frac{T'(r)n(r)T(r)}{T'(r)}\,dr \\
&= \int_0^{r_f} -\frac{(R(r) - R(r_f))'L(r)T(r)}{T'(r)}\,dr \qquad \text{from (B.8)} \\
&= \int_0^{r_f} -\frac{(R(r) - R(r_f))'\theta r^{\lambda+1}}{\mu}\,dr \qquad \text{from (B.9) and (B.10)} \\
&= \left[-(R(r) - R(r_f))\left(\frac{\theta}{\mu}\right)r^{\lambda+1}\right]_0^{r_f} + \int_0^{r_f} (R(r) \\
&\quad - R(r_f))\left(\frac{\theta}{\mu}\right)(\lambda + 1)r^{\lambda}\,dr \qquad \text{from integration by parts,} \\
&= 0 + ((\lambda + 1)/\mu)\int_0^{r_f} (R(r) - R(r_f))L(r)\,dr \\
&= ((\lambda + 1)/\mu)\text{TDR}. \qquad \text{(B.11)}
\end{aligned}$$

Therefore, it holds that

$$\text{TDR} = \frac{\mu}{\lambda + 1}\text{TTC}. \qquad \text{(B.12)}$$

Note that relation (B.12) includes (B.5) as a special case. That is, relation (B.5) holds to be true even when demand for land is elastic. It is also evident from the above derivation that relation (B.12) holds true regardless of whether the city is closed or open, or whether the city's lands are owned by absentee landlords or by the public. Note also that in the case of optimal land use, from (3.63),

$$R'(r) = \partial\psi(Y^0 - G^* - T(r), \bar{u})/\partial r = -T'(r)/s(Y^0 - G^* - T(r), \bar{u}), \qquad \text{(B.13)}$$

where $R(r)$ represents the shadow land rent curve. Therefore, replacing (B.7) with (B.13), we can derive the same result, (B.12), for an optimal city.

In summary, we can conclude as follows:

Proposition B.1. Suppose the distribution of land is given as

$$L(r) = \theta r^{\lambda}, \qquad \lambda > -1,$$

and the transport cost function of each household as

$$T(r) = ar^{\mu}, \qquad \mu > 0.$$

Then in the context of either an equilibrium city or an optimal city, it holds that

$$\mathrm{TDR} = \frac{\mu}{\lambda + 1}\,\mathrm{TTC}.$$

In particular, we have

$$\mathrm{TDR} = \begin{cases} \mathrm{TTC} & \text{if} \quad T(r) = ar \quad \text{and} \quad L(r) = \theta. \\ \mathrm{TTC}/2 & \text{if} \quad T(r) = ar \quad \text{and} \quad L(r) = \theta r. \end{cases}$$

This result is interesting because of its simplicity and generality.[4] It may also be of practical use. In cost–benefit analyses of transport investment, for example, it often becomes necessary to estimate the change in TDR. Although a direct estimation of TDR is difficult, it is relatively easy to estimate TTC.

Bibliographical notes

As noted before, relation (B.5) was first derived by Mohring in the case of a fixed lot size and by Arnott (1979) in the case of variable lot size. Arnott (1981) presents various extensions of this result.

Notes

1. Equation (B.4) can be restated as $R(r) - R(r_f) = T(r_f) - T(r)$, which means that at each location the *differential land rent equals the savings in transport cost*. In the earlier literature of rent theory before Alonso (1964), this simple result was somewhat overemphasized. Note, however, that it holds true only when the lot size of every household is fixed at a constant.
2. Mohring (1961) provided an ingenious geometric explanation of this result. Take the case of a complete circular city, $\theta = 2\pi$. In Figure B.1, if we rotate the rectangular *ABCD* around the axis *AD* for 360°, we obtain a cylinder. The volume of this cylinder is TDR plus TTC. TDR is given by the volume of a cone with the same base and height. Since the volume of a cone is one-third of a cylinder with the same base and height, TDR is one-half of TTC. This geometric interpretation, unfortunately, does not extend to our next case of variable lot size.

3. If $T(r) = T(0) + ar^{\mu}$ and $T(0) > 0$, then in the subsequent discussion we must replace TTC with TDT, where TDT represents the total differential transport cost defined as

$$\mathrm{TDT} = \int_0^{r_f} (T(r) - T(0))n(r)\,dr.$$

4. In the derivation of Proposition B.1, we have assumed that the residential choice behavior of each household is given by the basic model (2.1). It is easy to see, however, that as long as relation (B.6) holds, this proposition holds under any behavioral model of households. For example, in the context of either the time-extended model of (2.42) or the Muth model of (2.70)–(2.71), relation (B.6) holds [recall (3.106)]. Note, however, that in the case of the time-extended model, $T(r)$ includes both the pecuniary cost and the time cost. It is also not necessary to assume that all households are identical. Consider the basic model (2.1) of residential choice with m-type households, where the transport cost function of each household type i is given by $T_i(r) = a_i r^{\mu}$, $i = 1, 2, \ldots, m$. In equilibrium, from (4.9), at each r with positive $n_i(r)$ we have $R(r) = \Psi_i(r, u_i^*)$ and $R'(r) = \partial\Psi_i(r, u_i^*)/\partial r = -T_i'(r)/S_i(r, u_i^*)$. Hence,

$$\begin{aligned}
\mathrm{TTC} &= \int_0^{r_f} \sum_{i=1}^{m} T_i(r)n_i(r)\,dr \\
&= \int_0^{r_f} \sum_{i=1}^{m} \frac{T_i'(r)n_i(r)T_i(r)}{T_i'(r)}\,dr \\
&= \int_0^{r_f} \sum_{i=1}^{m} -\frac{R'(r)S_i(r, u_i^*)n_i(r)T_i(r)}{T_i'(r)}\,dr \\
&= \int_0^{r_f} -R'(r)\frac{r}{\mu}\sum_{i=1}^{m} S_i(r, u_i^*)n_i(r)\,dr \\
&= \int_0^{r_f} -R'(r)\left(\frac{r}{\mu}\right)L(r)\,dr \\
&= \int_0^{r_f} -\frac{(R(r) - R(r_f))'\theta r^{\lambda+1}}{\mu}\,dr \qquad \text{[from (B.9)]}.
\end{aligned}$$

Thus, continuing the same calculation as before, we can obtain (B.12). Actually, the same relation holds even when each transport cost function is *directionally linear* [i.e., $T_i(r) = a_i(\omega)r^{\mu}$, where ω is the angle from an arbitrary baseline from the *CBD*]. Moreover, if land rent $R(r)$ is replaced with land price $P(r)$ (i.e., asset price of land), the same relation holds between the *total differential land price* and the *total discounted value of transport costs* for dynamic city models under perfect foresight without tulip-mania expectation.

(This point will be demonstrated in our planned second book.) It would be interesting to test this relation empirically for actual cities [either relation (B.12) or its dynamic version]. For further discussion of this topic, see Arnott (1981) and Arnott, Pines, and Sadka (1986).

Mathematical notes to the text

C.1 Calculation for Example 2.1

$u = \alpha \log z + \beta \log s = \log z^{\alpha}s^{\beta}$. Hence, $e^u = z^{\alpha}s^{\beta}$ and $z = s^{-\beta/\alpha}e^{u/\alpha}$. Therefore, $Z(s, u) = s^{-\beta/\alpha}e^{u/\alpha}$. From (2.10),

$$\frac{Y - T(r) - Z(s, u)}{s} = -\frac{\partial Z(s, u)}{\partial s} = \frac{\beta}{\alpha} s^{-(\beta/\alpha)-1}e^{u/\alpha} = \frac{\beta}{\alpha}(s^{-\beta/\alpha}e^{u/\alpha})s^{-1}$$

$$= \frac{\beta}{\alpha} Z(s, u)s^{-1}.$$

Hence, $Y - T(r) = ((\beta/\alpha) + 1)Z(s, u) = \alpha^{-1}Z(s, u)$ (since $\alpha + \beta = 1$) $= \alpha^{-1}s^{-\beta/\alpha}e^{u/\alpha}$. From this, we have

$$Z(s, u) = \alpha(Y - T(r)),\ S(r, u) = \alpha^{-\alpha/\beta}(Y - T(r))^{-\alpha/\beta}e^{u/\beta},$$

which leads to

$$\Psi(r, u) = \frac{Y - T(r) - Z(s, u)}{S(r, u)} = \frac{Y - T(r) - \alpha(Y - T(r))}{S(r, u)} = \frac{(1 - \alpha)(Y - T(r))}{S(r, u)}$$

$$= \beta(Y - T(r))[\alpha^{-\alpha/\beta}(Y - T(r))^{-\alpha/\beta}e^{u/\beta}]^{-1}$$

$$= \alpha^{\alpha/\beta}\beta(Y - T(r))^{1/\beta}e^{-u/\beta}.$$

C.2 Derivation of optimality conditions for the HS model (Section 3.4)

Given a set of parameters, Y^0, $\bar{u}$, and N such that $-\infty < Y^0 < \infty$, $-\infty < \bar{u} < \infty$, and $N > 0$, we represent the associated *HS problem* of surplus maximization as follows:

$$\max_{r_f, n(r), s(r)} \int_0^{r_f} [Y^0 - T(r) - Z(s(r), \bar{u}) - R_A s(r)]n(r)\,dr, \tag{C.1}$$

$$\text{subject to} \quad n(r)s(r) \leq L(r) \quad \text{for} \quad r \leq r_f, \tag{C.2}$$

$$\int_0^{r_f} n(r)\,dr = N, \tag{C.3}$$

where $r_f \geq 0$, $n(r) \geq 0$, and $s(r) > 0$ at each $r \in [0, r_f]$. Here Assumptions 2.1, 2.2, 3.1, and 3.2 are assumed to be satisfied. This maximization problem can be considered as a special case (i.e., a degenerated case without differential equation) of the *optimal control problem of Bolza-Hestenes* (see, e.g., Hestenes 1966, Takayama 1974, or Van Long and Vousden 1977). Hence, applying the *maximum principle* of optimal control theory, we can derive the optimality conditions (necessary conditions) for the HS problem as follows (for the maximum principle used in the following analyses, see Hestenes 1966, Theorem 11.1, or, equivalently, Takayama 1974, Theorem 8.C.4, or Van Long and Vousden 1977, Theorem 1).

Suppose that (r_f, $n(r)$, $s(r)$; $0 \leq r \leq r_f$) represents a solution to the HS problem (where each of $n(r)$ and $s(r)$ is assumed to be piecewise continuous on $[0, r_f]$). Then the maximum principle requires that there exist multipliers, λ_0 and G, such that

(i) $\lambda_0 \geq 0$, $(\lambda_0, G) \neq (0, 0)$.

(ii) At each $r \in [0, r_f]$, $(n(r), s(r))$ maximizes the following *Hamiltonian function*,

$$H \equiv \lambda_0[Y^0 - T(r) - Z(s, \bar{u}) - R_A s]n - Gn,$$

subject to (C.2) and $n \geq 0$, $s > 0$.

(iii) $\hat{H} \equiv \lambda_0[Y^0 - T(r) - Z(s(r), \bar{u}) - R_A s(r)]n(r) - Gn(r)$ is continuous on $[0, r_f]$, and $\hat{H} = 0$ at r_f.

Since r_f can be chosen freely (subject to $r_f \geq 0$), it is not difficult to show that $\lambda_0 > 0$ (see Van Long and Vousden 1977, p. 16). Hence, without a loss of generality, we can set λ_0 equal to 1. Therefore, condition (ii) can now be restated as follows: At each $r \in [0, r_f]$, $(n(r), s(r))$ must be a solution to the following maximization problem:

$$\max_{n,s} H = \left[\frac{Y^0 - G - T(r) - Z(s, \bar{u})}{s} - R_A\right] ns,$$

$$\text{subject to} \quad ns \leq L(r), \quad n \geq 0, \quad \text{and} \quad s > 0.$$

Recall the bid rent function $\psi(I, u)$ defined by (3.2) and the associated bid-max lot size function $s(I, u)$. Since $\psi(Y^0 - G - T(r), \bar{u}) < R_A$ implies that the term inside the brackets of the objective function is negative for any $s > 0$, in order to maximize the objective function it must hold that $n(s)s(r) = 0$; that is, $n(r) = 0$ and $s(r)$ can be any positive number. If, however, $\psi(Y^0 - G - T(r), \bar{u}) > R_A$, then in order to maximize the objective function, we must set $n(r)s(r)$ equal to $L(r)$, and $s(r)$ equal to $s(Y^0 - G - T(r), \bar{u})$; hence, $n(r) = L(r)/s(Y^0 - G - T(r), \bar{u})$. In short, we have

$$\psi(Y^0 - G - T(r), \bar{u}) > R_A \Rightarrow \begin{cases} s(r) = s(Y^0 - G - T(r), \bar{u}), \\ n(r) = L(r)/s(Y^0 - G - T(r), \bar{u}), \end{cases} \tag{C.4}$$

$$\psi(Y^0 - G - T(r), \bar{u}) < R_A \Rightarrow n(r) = 0 \qquad \text{and} \qquad s(r) > 0. \tag{C.5}$$

Next, recall that $\psi(Y^0 - G - T(r), \bar{u})$ is continuously decreasing in r and becomes zero at some distance (Property 3.2). Therefore, if $\psi(Y^0 - G - T(0), \bar{u}) \geq R_A$, we can uniquely define a distance $\hat{r}$ such that

$$\psi(Y^0 - G - T(\hat{r}), \bar{u}) = R_A. \tag{C.6}$$

If $\psi(Y^0 - G - T(0), \bar{u}) < R_A$, we define $\hat{r} = 0$. Suppose that $r_f < \hat{r}$. Then since $\psi(Y^0 - G - T(r), \bar{u}) > R_A$ for all $r \leq r_f$, we have from (C.4) that $\hat{H} = [\psi(Y^0 - G - T(r_f), \bar{u}) - R_A]L(r_f) > 0$ [since $L(r_f) > 0$ because of Assumption 3.1], which violates the terminal condition, (iii). Therefore, the optimal urban fringe distance r_f must be sure that $r_f \geq \hat{r}$. In fact, we can readily see that for any $r_f \geq \hat{r}$, we can find $(n(r), s(r); 0 \leq r \leq r_f)$ such that all the conditions (i)–(iii) are satisfied, where we have from (C.5) that

$$n(r) = 0 \qquad \text{for} \quad \hat{r} < r < r_f. \tag{C.7}$$

However, because of (C.7), the value of the objective function (C.1) is not affected by any choice of $r_f \geq \hat{r}$. Therefore, for convenience, we can set $r_f = \hat{r}$. Notice also that if $\hat{r} = 0$, the population constraint can never be satisfied; hence, it must hold that $\hat{r} > 0$. Therefore, we can define the optimal urban fringe distance r_f by the following relation:

$$\psi(Y^0 - G - T(r_f), \bar{u}) = R_A. \tag{C.8}$$

Notice also that at $r = r_f$, the optimal value of $n(r)$ and $s(r)$ cannot be determined uniquely. Following the convention in optimal control theory, in order to make $n(r)$ and $s(r)$ be *left-continuous* in r, let us set

$$s(r_f) = s(Y^0 - G - T(r_f), \bar{u}), \; n(r_f) = L(r_f)/s(Y^0 - G - T(r_f), \bar{u}). \tag{C.9}$$

Finally, at each $r \geq 0$, let us define $R(r)$ as follows:

$$R(r) = \begin{cases} \psi(Y^0 - G - T(r), \bar{u}) & \text{for} \quad r \leq r_f, \\ R_A & \text{for} \quad r \geq r_f. \end{cases} \tag{C.10}$$

Then setting G equal to G^* in (C.4), (C.5), (C.8), (C.9), and (C.10), respectively, we can conclude that if $(r_f, n(r), s(r); 0 \leq r \leq r_f)$ represents a solution to the HS problem, then it is *necessary* that conditions (3.59)–(3.63) be satisfied.

Next, in order to show that these necessary conditions also represent the *sufficient* conditions for an allocation $(r_f, n(r), s(r); 0 \leq r \leq r_f)$ to be optimal for the HS problem, note that the problem does not include any constraint with a differential equation (and hence any *state variable*) and that (C.4) and (C.5) together represent the sufficient conditions for satisfying requirement (ii) [here if $\psi(Y^0 - G - T(r), \bar{u}) = R_A$, we choose $s(r) = s(Y^0 - G - T(r), \bar{u})$ and $n(r) = L(r)/s(Y^0 - G - T(r), \bar{u})$]. Therefore, we can conclude from Van Long and Vousden (1977, Theorem 6) that (C.2), (C.3), (C.4), and (C.5) together represent a set of sufficient conditions for an allocation $(n(r), s(r); 0 \leq r \leq r_f)$ to be optimal for the *HS problem with any fixed* $r_f > 0$. Furthermore, if we determine r_f so as to satisfy condition (C.8), we can readily see that $\hat{H} \geq 0$ for $r \leq r_f$ and $\hat{H} = 0$ for all $r \geq r_f$. Therefore, from Seierstad (1984a,b), we can conclude that these necessary conditions, (3.59)–(3.63), also represent the sufficient conditions of optimality for the HS problem.

C.3 Proof of Property 3.3

Recall that the surplus function, $\mathcal{S}(Y^0, u, N)$, is defined by

$$\mathcal{S}(Y^0, u, N) \equiv \max_{r_f, n(r), s(r)} \int_0^{r_f} [Y^0 - T(r) - Z(s(r), u) - R_A s(r)] n(r)\, dr,$$

$$\text{subject to (3.46) and (3.47),} \qquad \text{(C.11)}$$

and the population cost function $C(u, N)$ is defined by

$$C(u, N) \equiv \min_{r_f, n(r), s(r)} \int_0^{r_f} [T(r) + Z(s(r), u) + R_A s(r)] n(r)\, dr,$$

$$\text{subject to (3.46) and (3.47).} \qquad \text{(C.12)}$$

Hence, it holds identically that

$$\mathcal{S}(Y^0, u, N) = NY^0 - C(u, N). \qquad \text{(C.13)}$$

In order to prove Property 3.3, let us first obtain some preliminary results.

Lemma C.1. $\mathcal{S}(Y^0, u, N)$ is continuously decreasing in u.

Proof. From (C.13), $\partial \mathcal{S}(Y^0, u, N)/\partial u = -\partial C(u, N)/\partial u = -\int_0^{r_f} (\partial Z(s(r), u)/\partial u) n(r) dr < 0$ [from (5.27)]. ■

Lemma C.2. $\lim_{u\to-\infty} \mathcal{S}(Y^0, u, N) = N(Y^0 - T(0))$.

Proof. In the positive quadrant of z–s space, let us arbitrarily choose a ray starting from the origin, and let $(z(u), s(u))$ denote the intersection between the ray and the indifference curve for each utility level u. Then

$$z(u)/s(u) = Z(s(u), u)/s(u) = k \quad \text{(a positive constant)}.$$

Define $r(u)$ by the relation, $\int_0^{r(u)} L(r)/s(u)\, dr = N$. Then by definition of function $C(u, N)$,

$$\begin{aligned} C(u, N) &\leq \int_0^{r(u)} \frac{[T(r) + Z(s(u), u) + R_A s(u)]L(r)}{s(u)} dr \\ &= \int_0^{r(u)} \frac{T(r)L(r)}{s(u)} dr + \int_0^{r(u)} kL(r)\, dr \\ &\quad + \int_0^{r(u)} R_A L(r)\, dr \\ &< NT(r(u)) + \int_0^{r(u)} kL(r)\, dr + \int_0^{r(u)} R_A L(r)\, dr. \end{aligned}$$

From Assumption 2.1, $s(u) \to 0$ as $u \to -\infty$. Hence, $r(u) \to 0$ as $u \to -\infty$. By definition, $NT(0) < C(u, N)$. Therefore, we can conclude that

$$C(u, N) \to NT(0) \qquad \text{as} \quad u \to -\infty. \tag{C.14}$$

This implies that

$$\mathcal{S}(Y^0, u, N) \to N(Y^0 - T(0)) \qquad \text{as} \quad u \to -\infty,$$

as was to be shown. ■

Lemma C.3. $\lim_{u\to\infty} \mathcal{S}(Y^0, u, N) = -\infty$.

Proof. For each $u \in (-\infty, \infty)$, let $(r_f(u), n(r, u), s(r, u); 0 \leq r \leq r_f(u))$ be the solution to the maximization problem in (C.11) [equivalently, the solution to the minimization problem in (C.12)]. Recall that the unique existence of such solution is ensured by Proposition 3.8. Then we have by definition

$$C(u, N) = \int_0^{r_f(u)} [T(r) + Z(s(r, u), u) + R_A s(r, u)]n(r, u)\, dr. \tag{C.15}$$

Since $C(u, N)$ is increasing in u (recall the proof of Lemma C.3.1), $\lim_{u\to\infty} C(u, N) \equiv \tilde{C}$ exists. Suppose that $\tilde{C} < \infty$. Then

$$\int_0^{r_f(u)} Z(s(r, u), u)n(r, u)\, dr < \tilde{C} < \infty \qquad \text{for any} \quad u \in (-\infty, \infty),$$

which implies that

$$\bar{z}(u) \equiv \int_0^{r_f(u)} \frac{Z(s(r, u), u)n(r, u)}{N}\, dr < \tilde{C}/N$$

$$\text{for any} \quad u \in (-\infty, \infty). \tag{C.16}$$

Let $S(z, u)$ be the solution to $U(z, s) = u$ for s. Since $U(z, s)$ is quasi-concave and increasing in z and s, $S(z, u)$ is convex and decreasing in z. By definition, $\int_0^{r_f(u)} n(r, u)/N\, dr = 1$. Therefore, using *Jensen's inequality* (see Feller 1971, p. 153), we have

$$\begin{aligned} \bar{s}(u) &\equiv \int_0^{r_f(u)} \frac{s(r, u)n(r, u)}{N}\, dr \\ &= \int_0^{r_f(u)} \frac{S(Z(s(r, u), u), u)n(r, u)}{N}\, dr \qquad \text{(identically)} \\ &\geq S(\bar{z}(u), u) \qquad \text{(from Jensen's inequality)} \\ &> S(\tilde{C}/N, u) \qquad \text{[from (C.16)]} \end{aligned}$$

Since $S(\tilde{C}/N, u) \to \infty$ as $u \to \infty$, this implies that $\bar{s}(u) \to \infty$ as $u \to \infty$. Hence, since $R_A > 0$ by assumption, we have from (C.15) that

$$\tilde{C} \geq \lim_{u\to\infty} \int_0^{r_f(u)} R_A s(r, u)n(r, u)\, dr \equiv \lim_{u\to\infty} R_A N \bar{s}(u) = \infty,$$

which contradicts the initial assumption that $\tilde{C} < \infty$. Therefore, it must be true that $\tilde{C} = \infty$, that is,

$$\lim_{u\to\infty} C(u, N) = \infty, \tag{C.17}$$

and hence $\lim_{u\to\infty} \mathcal{S}(Y^0, u, N) = -\infty$. ■

Lemma C.4. $G(Y^0, u, N)$ is continuously decreasing in u.

Proof. We can prove this by using the results obtained in Chapter 5. Namely, if we let $G(Y^0, u, N) \equiv G$ and $\text{TDR}(Y^0, u, N) \equiv \text{TDR}$, we can obtain the following identity from (5.10):

$$N(Y^0 - G) = C(u, N) + \text{TDR}. \tag{C.18}$$

Starting from this equation, if we repeat the same procedure from (5.21) to (5.25), we can obtain the following result:

$$Y^0 - G = \partial C(u, N)/\partial N. \tag{C.19}$$

From (C.19) and (5.25), it follows that $Y^0 - G = Y(u, N)$, or

$$G = Y^0 - Y(u, N). \tag{C.20}$$

Since $Y(u, N)$ is continuously increasing in u [Property 5.2(ii)], G is continuously decreasing in u. ■

Lemma C.5. $\lim_{u\to-\infty} G(Y^0, u, N) = Y^0 - T(0)$ and $\lim_{u\to\infty} G(Y^0, u, N) = -\infty$.

Proof. From (C.20) and Property 5.2(iii), we have that

$$\lim_{u\to-\infty} G = Y^0 - \lim_{u\to-\infty} Y(u, N) = Y^0 - T(0),$$

$$\lim_{u\to\infty} G = Y^0 - \lim_{u\to\infty} Y(u, N) = Y^0 - \infty = -\infty.$$ ■

Now we can prove Property 3.3. Namely, Lemmas C.3.1–C.3.3 together demonstrate Property 3.3(i), and Lemmas C.3.4 and C.3.5 together show Property 3.3(ii).

C.4 Proof of relation (3.83)

Suppose, now, that $u_a^* \geq u_b^*$. Then from identity (2.20), we have

$$V(\Psi_a(0, u_a^*), I_a(0)) = u_a^* \geq u_b^* = V(\Psi_b(0, u_b^*), I_b(0)).$$

Since V is increasing in I and decreasing in R, and since $I_a(0) \leq I_b(0)$ by assumption, the above inequality implies that $\Psi_a(0, u_a^*) \leq \Psi_b(0, u_b^*)$. Then since Ψ_a is steeper than Ψ_b, we have that $\Psi_a(r, u_a^*) < \Psi_b(r, u_b^*)$ for all $0 < r \leq r_f^a$. Since the compensated demand function $\tilde{s}(R, u)$ is decreasing in R and increasing in u (from the normality of land), this in turn implies that

$$S_a(r, u_a^*) = \tilde{s}(\Psi_a(r, u_a^*), u_a^*) > \tilde{s}(\Psi_b(r, u_b^*), u_b^*) = S_b(r, u_b^*),\ 0 < r \leq r_f^a.$$

Since r_f^a (r_f^b) is the urban fringe before (after) parameter changes,

$$\int_0^{r_f^a} \frac{L(r)}{S_a(r, u_a^*)}\, dr = N = \int_0^{r_f^b} \frac{L(r)}{S_b(r, u_b^*)}\, dr.$$

The above two relations imply that $r_f^a > r_f^b$, which contradicts (3.82). Therefore, relation (3.83) must hold to be true.

C.5 Proof of Property 3.4

First, we obtain some preliminary results. Let u^* be the equilibrium utility, and $I(r) \equiv Y - T(r)$. From application of the envelope theorem to (2.8), we have

$$\Psi_r(r) \equiv \frac{\partial \Psi(r, u^*)}{\partial r} = -\frac{T'(r)}{S(r, u^*)}, \tag{C.21}$$

$$\Psi_I(r) \equiv \frac{\partial \psi(I(r), u^*)}{\partial I} = \frac{1}{S(r, u^*)}, \tag{C.22}$$

$$\Psi_u(r) \equiv \frac{\partial \Psi(r, u^*)}{\partial u} = -\frac{Z_u(r)}{S(r, u^*)}, \tag{C.23}$$

where $\psi(I, u)$ is defined by (3.2) and $Z_u(r) \equiv \partial Z(s, u)/\partial u$ at $(s, u) = (S(r, u^*), u^*)$. From (C.21) and (C.22),

$$\Psi_I(r) = -\Psi_r(r)/T'(r). \tag{C.24}$$

Next, in equilibrium we have

$$R(0) = \Psi(0, u^*) = \psi(I(0), u^*), \tag{C.25}$$

$$R_A = \Psi(r_f, u^*) = \psi(I(r_f), u^*). \tag{C.26}$$

Furthermore, since $N = \int_0^{r_f} L(r)/S(r, u^*)\, dr$ and $1/S(r, u^*) = -\Psi_r/T'(r)$ [from (C.21)], it follows that

$$N = \int_0^{r_f} \frac{-L(r)\Psi_r}{T'(r)}\, dr. \tag{C.27}$$

Since R_A and N are assumed to be constant, from the total differentiation of (C.25), (C.26), and (C.27), respectively, with respect to Y we have

$$\frac{dR(0)}{dY} = \Psi_I(0) + \Psi_u(0)\frac{du^*}{dY}, \tag{C.28}$$

$$0 = \Psi_I(r_f)\left(1 - T'(r_f)\frac{dr_f}{dY}\right) + \Psi_u(r_f)\frac{du^*}{dY}, \tag{C.29}$$

$$0 = \int_0^{r_f} \frac{L(r)}{T'(r)}\left(\Psi_{rI} + \Psi_{ru}\frac{du^*}{dY}\right) dr - \frac{L(r_f)}{T'(r_f)}\Psi_r(r_f)\frac{dr_f}{dY}. \tag{C.30}$$

Let us define

$$l(r) = \frac{L(r)}{T'(r)} \bigg/ \frac{L(r_f)}{T'(r_f)}. \tag{C.31}$$

Then, from (C.30) we have that

$$0 = \int_0^{r_f} l(r)\left(\Psi_{rI} + \Psi_{ru}\frac{du^*}{dY}\right) dr + \Psi_r(r_f)\frac{dr_f}{dY}. \tag{C.32}$$

Solving equations (C.29) and (C.32) for du^*/dY, and using (C.24), we have

$$\frac{du^*}{dY} = \frac{-\int_0^{r_f} l(r)\Psi_{rI}\,dr + \Psi_I(r_f)}{\int_0^{r_f} l(r)\Psi_{ru}\,dr - \Psi_u(r_f)},$$

which, upon integration by parts, yields

$$\frac{du^*}{dY} = -\frac{l(0)\Psi_I(0) + \int_0^{r_f} l'\Psi_I\,dr}{l(0)\Psi_u(0) + \int_0^{r_f} l'\Psi_u\,dr} \qquad [\text{since } l(r_f) \equiv 1], \tag{C.33}$$

where $l' \equiv dl(r)/dr$. Substituting (C.33) into (C.28), we have

$$\frac{dR(0)}{dY} = \Psi_I(0)\frac{\int_0^{r_f} l'[(\Psi_u/\Psi_u(0)) - (\Psi_I/\Psi_I(0))]\,dr}{l(0) + \int_0^{r_f} l'\Psi_u/\Psi_u(0)\,dr},$$

which together with (C.22) and (C.23) yields

$$\frac{dR(0)}{dY} = \Psi_I(0)\frac{\int_0^{r_f} l'(Z_u(r) - Z_u(0))/S(r, u^*)\,dr}{l(0)Z_u(0)/S(0, u^*) + \int_0^{r_f} l'Z_u/S(r, u^*)\,dr}. \tag{C.34}$$

Now, if $L(r)/T'(r)$ is constant and hence $l'(r) = 0$ for all r, then from (C.34), we know that $dR(0)/dY = 0$, which means that case (ii) would hold. If l' is not zero for all r, we further observe that

$$Z_u(r) - Z_u(0) - \int_0^r Z_{ur}(r)\,dr$$
$$= \int_0^r Z_{us}(S(r, u^*), u^*)\frac{\partial S(r, u^*)}{\partial r}\,dr < 0, \tag{C.35}$$

which is negative since $\partial S(r, u^*)/\partial r > 0$ [from (2.28)] and $Z_{us} = Z_{su} < 0$ (from the normality of s). From (C.22), $\Psi_I(0) > 0$, and from (2.4) $Z_u > 0$. Therefore, if $l' > 0$ for all r, from (C.34) and (C.35) we have that $dR(0)/dY < 0$, which means case (i). Finally, since $S(r, u^*)$ is increasing in r, from (C.35) $Z_u/S(r, u^*) < Z_u(0)/S(0, u^*)$ for all $r > 0$. Therefore, if $l' < 0$ for all r,

$$l(0)\frac{Z_u(0)}{S(0, u^*)} + \int_0^{r_f} l' \frac{Z_u}{S(r, u^*)} dr > l(0)\frac{Z_u(0)}{S(0, u^*)}$$

$$+ \int_0^{r_f} l' \frac{Z_u(0)}{S(0, u^*)} dr = \frac{Z_u(0)}{S(0, u^*)} > 0, \tag{C.36}$$

and hence the denominator of (C.34) is positive. Therefore, if $l' < 0$ for all r, we can conclude from (C.34) and (C.35) that $dR(0)/dY > 0$, which means that case (iii) would hold.

C.6 Proofs of Properties 4.10 and 4.11

The proofs of these two properties are based on the existence and uniqueness of a set of functions ($a_i(u)$, $b_i(u)$, $R_i(r)$; $i = 1, 2, \ldots, m$) with certain characteristics. First, we need several preliminary analyses. Proofs of properties P.2 and P.3 are omitted since they are standard and purely technical (see Fujita 1984 for the proofs). Concerning Definition 4.1, we obtain the following result:

P.1. In the context of Definition 4.1, the effective domain D^0 can be expressed as follows:

$$D^0 = \{(r, u) \mid 0 \le r < \bar{r}(u),\ -\infty < u < \infty\}, \tag{C.37}$$

where $\bar{r}(u)$ is a nonincreasing function of u such that $0 \le \bar{r}(u) \le \bar{r}$ for all u and $\bar{r}(u) > 0$ for some u. Hence,

$$(r, u) \in D^0 \Rightarrow (x, v) \in D^0 \qquad \text{for all} \quad 0 \le x \le r,\ -\infty < v \le u. \tag{C.38}$$

Proof. Conditions (i) and (ii) of Definition 4.1 require that D^0 be an open set in the topological subspace D and that D^0 not be null. From (iv), $r < \bar{r}$ for all $(r, u) \in D^0$. From (iii), any such set D^0 can be expressed in the form (C.37) with a boundary curve $\bar{r}(u)$ that is nonincreasing, not identically zero, and $0 \le \bar{r}(u) < \bar{r}$ for all u. This implies (C.38). ■

We next introduce the following definition:

Definition C.1. Let Ψ be a well-behaved bid rent function from Definition 4.1. We call a function $a(u)$ a *well-behaved inner boundary function* associated with Ψ if and only if the following three conditions are satisfied:

(i) a: $(-\infty, \tilde{u}) \rightarrow [0, \tilde{a}]$, where $\tilde{u}$ and $\tilde{a}$ are some constants such that $\tilde{u} \in (-\infty, \infty]$, $\tilde{a} \in [0, \infty)$.

(ii) On $(-\infty, \tilde{u})$, $a(u)$ is continuous and nondecreasing in u, and increasing before it reaches $\tilde{a}$, where $\lim_{u\to-\infty} a(u) = 0$, $\lim_{u\to\tilde{u}} a(u) = \tilde{a}$.

(iii) $\Psi(a(u), u) > 0$ for all $u \in (-\infty, \tilde{u})$, and $\lim_{u\to\tilde{u}} \Psi(a(u), u) = 0$.

Given a well-behaved function $a(u)$, define

$$X = \{(r, u) \mid 0 \le r < \infty,\ -\infty < u < \tilde{u}\},$$

$$X^0 = \{(r, u) \mid a(u) < r,\ -\infty < u < \tilde{u}\}.$$

Let S be the well-behaved lot size function from Definition 4.1. For each $(r, u) \in D$, define

$$f(r, u) = L(r)/S(r, u),$$

where $L(r)$ is assumed to satisfy Assumption 4.1. And define function F on domain X by

$$F(b, u; a(\cdot)) = \int_{a(u)}^{b} f(r, u)\, dr. \tag{C.39}$$

Then using the conditions of Definition 4.1, we can show that

P.2

(i) F is continuous on X;

(ii) $F(b, u; a(\cdot)) \le 0$ on $X - X_0$;

(iii) $X^0 \cap D^0 = \{(r, u) \mid a(u) < r < \bar{r}(u),\ -\infty < u < \tilde{u}\} \ne \emptyset$, where $\bar{r}(u)$ is the function defined in P.1.

(iv) on $X^0 \cap D^0$, $F(b, u; a(\cdot))$ is positive, increasing in b, and decreasing in u;

(v) for any $b > 0$, $\lim_{u\to-\infty} F(b, u; a(\cdot)) = \infty$;

(vi) on $X - D^0$, $F(b, u; a(\cdot))$ is constant in b.

Next, given a positive number N, consider the equation

$$F(b, u; a(\cdot)) = N, \tag{C.40}$$

where $a(\cdot)$ is the well-behaved inner boundary function given previously. Define the *solution set* of the above equation by

$$\mathbf{S} = \{(b, u) \mid F(b, u; a(\cdot)) = N,\ (b, u) \in X\}. \tag{C.41}$$

Then by using P.2, we can conclude the following:

P.3. There are constants $\hat{u} \equiv \hat{u}(a(\cdot), N) \in (-\infty, \tilde{u}]$ and $\hat{b} \equiv \hat{b}(a(\cdot), N) \in [\tilde{a}, \infty)$ such that

(i) the set $\mathbf{S} \cap D^0$ can be uniquely expressed by a (single-valued) function $b(u) \equiv b(u; a(\cdot), N)$: $(-\infty, \hat{u}) \to (0, \hat{b})$;
(ii) on $(-\infty, \hat{u})$, $b(u)$ is continuous and increasing in u, where $\lim_{u\to-\infty} b(u) = 0$, $\lim_{u\to\hat{u}} b(u) = \hat{b}$;
(iii) on $(-\infty, \hat{u})$, $\Psi(b(u), u)$ is positive, continuous, and decreasing in u, where $\lim_{u\to-\infty} \Psi(b(u), u) = \infty$, $\lim_{u\to\hat{u}} \Psi(b(u), u) = 0$.

Let $U(r) \equiv U(r; a(\cdot), N)$ be the inverse function of $r = b(u)$ on $(-\infty, \hat{u})$. Then from P.3 we can immediately conclude as follows:

P.4

(i) U: $(0, \hat{b}) \to (-\infty, \hat{u})$.
(ii) On $(0, \hat{b})$, $U(r)$ is continuous and increasing in r, where $\lim_{r\to 0} U(r) = -\infty$, $\lim_{r\to\hat{b}} U(r) = \hat{u}$.

Furthermore, on $(0, \hat{b})$, we define the function $\hat{R}(r) \equiv \hat{R}(r; a(\cdot), N)$ by

$$\hat{R}(r) = \Psi(r, U(r)) \equiv \Psi(r, U(r; a(\cdot), N)). \tag{C.42}$$

Then from P.4 we can conclude that

P.5

(i) $\hat{R}$: $(0, \hat{b}) \to (0, \infty)$;
(ii) on $(0, \hat{b})$, $\hat{R}(r)$ is continuous and decreasing in r, where $\lim_{r\to 0} \hat{R}(r) = \infty$, $\lim_{r\to\hat{b}} \hat{R}(r) = 0$;
(iii) $\hat{R}(\cdot)$ is *steeper* than Ψ. That is, whenever $\hat{R}(r) = \Psi(r, u)$,

$$\begin{aligned} \hat{R}(x) &> \Psi(x, u) \qquad \text{for all} \quad x < r, \\ \hat{R}(x) &< \Psi(x, u) \qquad \text{for all} \quad r < x < \hat{b}. \end{aligned} \tag{C.43}$$

Proof. (i) and (ii) immediately follow from P.4. In order to show (iii), suppose that $\hat{R}(r) = \Psi(r, u)$. Take $r' \in (0, \hat{b})$, where $r' \neq r$. By definition, $\hat{R}(r) = \Psi(r, u) = \Psi(r, U(r))$ and $\hat{R}(r') = \Psi(r', U(r'))$, where $U(\cdot)$ is the inverse of $b(\cdot)$. If $r' < r$, then $U(r') < U(r)$ from P.4(ii). Thus, since Ψ is well behaved, $\Psi(x, U(r')) > \Psi(x, U(r))$ for all x such that $\Psi(x, U(r')) > 0$. Hence, since $\hat{R}(r') = \Psi(r', U(r')) > 0$, $\hat{R}(r') > \Psi(r', U(r))$. If $r' > r$, then $U(r') > U(r)$ from P.4(ii). Hence, $\Psi(x, U(r')) < \Psi(x, U(r))$ for all $x \in (0, \hat{b})$, and thus $R(r') = \Psi(r', U(r')) < \Psi(r', U(r))$. Therefore, we have (C.43). ■

Next, suppose that the set of well-behaved bid rent functions Ψ_i ($i = 1, 2, \ldots, m$) can be ordered by relative steepness, as indicated in Assumption 4.3. Then we have the following:

P.6. Take a pair of bid rent functions Ψ_i and Ψ_j, where $i < j$. Take any $u_i \in (-\infty, \infty)$, and suppose that $\Psi_i(0, u_i) > 0$. Then for each point on the bid rent curve $\Psi_i(\cdot, u_i)$ with a positive height, there exists a unique bid rent curve $\Psi_j(\cdot, u_j)$ that passes that point.

Proof. Let A be a point on the curve $\Psi_i(\cdot, u_i)$ with a positive height, and let B be the intersection between curve $\Psi_i(\cdot, u_i)$ and the R axis (which exists because of the continuity of Ψ_i on D). From Property 4.2, there exists a unique bid rent curve $\Psi_j(\cdot, u_j')$, which starts from intersection B. Since Ψ_i is steeper than Ψ_j, $\Psi_i(r, u_i) < \Psi_j(r, u_j')$ at each r such that $\Psi_i(r, u_i) > 0$ and $r \neq 0$. Thus, from Properties 4.1 and 4.4, there exists a unique bid rent curve $\Psi_j(r, u)$, which passes point A. ∎

Next, on the basis of the bid rent functions Ψ_i $(i = 1, 2, \ldots, m)$ from Assumptions 4.2 and 4.3, we introduce the following definitions:

Definition C.2. We call a function $b_i(u)$ $(i = 1, 2, \ldots, m)$ a *well-behaved outer boundary function* associated with Ψ_i if and only if

(i) $b_i(u)$: $(-\infty, \hat{u}_i) \to (0, \hat{b}_i)$, where $\hat{u}_i$ and $\hat{b}_i$ are some constants such that $\hat{u}_i \in (-\infty, \infty)$, $\hat{b}_i \in (0, \infty)$;

(ii) on $(-\infty, \hat{u}_i)$, $b_i(u)$ is continuous and increasing in u, where $\lim_{u\to-\infty} b_i(u) = 0$, $\lim_{u\to\hat{u}_i} b_i(u) = \hat{b}_i$;

(iii) on $(-\infty, \hat{u}_i)$, $\Psi_i(b_i(u), u)$ is positive, continuous, and decreasing in u, where $\lim_{u\to-\infty} \Psi_i(b_i(u), u) = \infty$, $\lim_{u\to\hat{u}_i} \Psi_i(b_i(u), u) = 0$.

Definition C.3. We say that a boundary rent curve $R_i(r)$ $(i = 1, 2, \ldots, m)$ is well behaved if and only if

(i) $R_i(r)$: $(0, \hat{b}_i) \to (0, \infty)$, where $\hat{b}_i$ is the positive constant from Definition C.2(i);

(ii) on $(0, \hat{b}_i)$, $R_i(r)$ is continuous and decreasing in r, where $\lim_{r\to 0} R_i(r) = \infty$, $\lim_{r\to\hat{b}_i} R_i(r) = 0$;

(iii) $R_i(r)$ is steeper than all Ψ_j, $j = i, i + 1, \ldots, m$. That is, whenever $R_i(r) = \Psi_j(r, u)$ for some r and u, then $R_i(x) > \Psi_j(x, u)$ for all $x < r$, and $R_i(x) < \Psi_j(x, u)$ for $r < x < \hat{b}_i$.

Now we are ready to prove the main results. Assumptions 4.1–4.3 are assumed to hold throughout.

P.7. The solution set of equation (4.18) on effective domain D_1^0 can be uniquely expressed by a well-behaved outer boundary function $b_1(u)$: $(-\infty,$

$\hat{u}_1) \to (0, \hat{b}_1)$, where $\hat{u}$ and $\hat{b}_1$ are constants such that $\hat{u}_1 \in (-\infty, \infty)$, $\hat{b}_1 \in (0, \infty)$.

Proof. In P.3, set $a(u) \equiv 0$ and $\Psi = \Psi_1$. Then P.3 implies P.7. ■

P.8. Let $U_1(r)$ be the inverse of the well-behaved outer boundary function $r = b_1(u)$ from P.7. Define function $R_1(r)$ by equation (4.19). Then $R_1(r)$: $(0, \hat{b}_1) \to (0, \infty)$, and it is well behaved.

Proof. In P.5, set $\hat{R}(r) = R_1(r)$ and $\Psi(r, u) = \Psi_1(r, u)$. Then since Ψ_1 is steeper than any Ψ_j ($j = 2, 3, \ldots, m$), P.5 implies P.8. ■

P.9. Suppose that the boundary rent function $R_{i-1}(r)$: $(0, \hat{b}_{i-1}) \to (0, \infty)$ is well behaved ($i = 2, 3, \ldots$, or m). Then the solution set of equation (4.20) on domain D_i^0 can be uniquely expressed by a well-behaved inner boundary function $a_i(u)$: $(-\infty, \tilde{u}_i) \to (0, \hat{b}_{i-1})$, where $\tilde{u}_i \in (-\infty, \infty]$ and $\lim_{u \to \tilde{u}_i} a_i(u) = \hat{b}_{i-1}$.

Proof. From definition (4.22), for each $a \in (0, \hat{b}_{i-1})$, $R_{i-1}(a) = \Psi_{i-1}(a, U_{i-1}(a))$. Hence, from P.6, there exists a unique utility level $V_i(a) \in (-\infty, \infty)$ such that $R_{i-1}(a) = \Psi_{i-1}(a, U_{i-1}(a)) = \Psi_i(a, V_i(a))$. Since $R_{i-1}(a)$ is decreasing in a on $(0, \hat{b}_{i-1})$, for any $0 < a_1 < a_2 < \hat{b}_{i-1}$, $R_{i-1}(a_1) = \Psi_i(a_1, V_i(a_1)) > R_{i-1}(a_2) = \Psi_i(a_2, V_i(a_2))$. Then since $R_{i-1}(r)$ is steeper than Ψ_i, point $(a_2, R_{i-1}(a_2))$ will be located below the curve $\Psi_i(r, V_i(a_1))$. Hence, from Property 4.4, $V_i(a_2) > V_i(a_1)$. That is, $V_i(a)$ is increasing on $(0, \hat{b}_{i-1})$. Continuity of $V_i(a)$ on $(0, \hat{b}_{i-1})$ immediately follows from the continuity of R_{i-1} on $(0, \hat{b}_{i-1})$ and the continuity of Ψ_i on D_i^0. Next, for each $a \in (0, \hat{b}_{i-1})$, $\Psi_i(a, V_i(a)) = R_{i-1}(a) < \infty$, and $\lim_{a \to 0} \Psi_i(a, V_i(a)) = \lim_{a \to 0} R_{i-1}(a) = \infty$. Hence, since $V_i(a)$ is increasing in a, $\lim_{a \to 0} V_i(a) = -\infty$. Furthermore, since $V_i(a)$ is increasing on $(0, \hat{b}_{i-1})$, $\lim_{a \to \hat{b}_{i-1}} V_i(a)$ exists uniquely (possibly equals ∞). Set $\tilde{u}_i \equiv \lim_{a \to \hat{b}_{i-1}} V_i(a)$. Then $\tilde{u}_i \in (-\infty, \infty]$. Now let $a_i(u)$: $(-\infty, \tilde{u}_i) \to (0, \hat{b}_{i-1})$ be the inverse of $V_i(a)$: $(0, \hat{b}_{i-1}) \to (-\infty, \tilde{u}_i)$. Then all conditions of Definition C.1 are satisfied by $a_i(u)$, and hence we can conclude as P.9. ■

P.10. Suppose that the inner boundary function $a_i(u)$: $(-\infty, \tilde{u}_i) \to (0, \hat{b}_{i-1})$ is well behaved ($i = 2, 3, \ldots$, or m). Then the solution set of equation (4.21) on domain D_i^0 can be uniquely expressed by a well-behaved outer boundary function $b_i(u)$: $(-\infty, \hat{u}_i) \to (0, \hat{b}_i)$, where $\hat{u}_i \in (-\infty, \tilde{u}_i)$, $\hat{b}_i \in [b_{i-1}, \infty)$.

Proof. In P.3, set $a(u) = a_i(u)$ and $\Psi = \Psi_i$ ($i = 2, 3, \ldots,$ or m). Then P.3 implies P.10. ■

P.11. Let $U_i(r)$ be the inverse of the well-behaved outer boundary function $b_i(u)$ from P.10 ($i = 2, 3, \ldots,$ or m). Define function $R_i(r)$ by equation (4.22). Then $R_i(r)$: $(0, \hat{b}_i) \rightarrow (0, \infty)$, and it is well behaved.

Proof. By reasoning similar to that followed in P.8, P.5 implies P.11. ■

From P.7 to P.11, we can immediately conclude that

> ***Theorem C.1.*** Under Assumptions 4.1–4.3, a set of functions $(a_i(u), b_i(u), R_i(u); i = 1, 2, \ldots, m)$ can be uniquely defined, and each function is well behaved.

Finally, let us prove Properties 4.10 and 4.11.

Proof of Property 4.10. (i), (ii), and (iv) of Property 4.10 immediately follow from Theorem C.1 and Definition C.3. From P.10, $0 < \hat{b}_1 \leq \hat{b}_2 \leq \cdots \leq \hat{b}_m$. It is also clear from the construction that no pair of boundary rent curves intersect each other. Hence, (iii) also holds. ■

Proof of Property 4.11

(i) First, from Theorem C.1, each of $a_i(u)$, $b_i(u)$, and $R_i(r)$ can be defined uniquely, and each is well behaved. Next, since R_m is well behaved, (4.23) determines r_m^* uniquely. (Note 12 of Chapter 4 applies here.) Then since $R_A = R_m(r_m^*) \equiv \Psi_m(r_m^*, U_m(r_m^*))$, where U_m is the inverse of function b_m, u_m^* equals $U_m(r_m^*)$. Next, $\Psi_m(r, u_m^*)$ is continuous and positive on $[0, r_m^*]$; and R_{m-1} is well behaved. Hence, relation (4.25) uniquely defines r_{m-1}^*. Then in (4.26), u_{m-1}^* is uniquely given by $U_{m-1}(r_{m-1}^*)$, where U_{m-1} is the inverse of b_{i-1}. Similarly, each pair (r_i^*, u_i^*) can be uniquely determined for $i = m - 2, \ldots, 1$.

(ii) By construction, it is obvious that the set of pairs (r_i^*, u_i^*) ($i = 1, 2, \ldots, m$) together with the market rent curve $R(r)$ defined by (4.16) constitute an equilibrium land use.

(iii) Suppose that the set of pairs (r_i', u_i') ($i = 1, 2, \ldots, m$) and $R(r)$ defined by (4.16) constitute an equilibrium land use. Suppose first that $u_1' < u_1^*$. Then curve $\Psi_1(r, u_1')$ lies above the curve $\Psi_1(r, u_1^*)$. By the definition of curve $R_1(r)$, $(r_1', \Psi_1(r_1', u_1'))$ must be a point on the curve $R_1(r)$, which is located on the upper half of curve $R_1(r)$ with respect to point $(r_1^*, \Psi_1(r_1^*, u_1^*))$. That is, $r_1' < r_1^*$ and $\Psi_1(r_1', u_1') > \Psi_1(r_1^*, u_1^*)$. Recursively, we can conclude that $r'_i < r^*_i$ and $\Psi_i(r'_i, u'_i) > \Psi_i(r^*_i, u^*_i)$ for $i = 2, 3, \ldots, m$. Hence, $\Psi_m(r'_m, u'_m) > \Psi_m(r^*_m, u^*_m) = R_A$, which contradicts the equilibrium condition (4.15). Similarly, we can show that it cannot be true that $u'_1 > u^*_1$. Thus, $u'_1 = u^*_1$, and hence $r'_1 = r^*_1$. Recursively, we can conclude that $u'_i = u^*_i$ and $r'_i = r^*_i$ for all $i = 2, 3, \ldots, m$. Therefore, there exists only one equilibrium. ■

C.7 Derivation of optimality conditions for the HS model (Section 4.4)

The optimality conditions OC($\bar{\mathbf{u}}$) can be derived in a manner quite similar to C.2. Suppose that $(r_f, n_i(r), s_i(r);\ i = 1, 2, \ldots, m,\ 0 \leq r \leq r_f)$ is a solution to the HS($\bar{\mathbf{u}}$) problem (where each of $n_i(r)$ and $s_i(r)$, $i = 1, 2, \ldots, m$, is assumed to be piecewise continuous on $[0, r_f]$). Then the maximum principle (see Hestenes 1966, Theorem 11.1; Takayama 1974, Theorem 8.C.4; or Van Long and Vousden 1977, Theorem 1) requires that there exist a set of multipliers, λ_0, G_i, $i = 1, 2, \ldots, m$, such that

(i) $\lambda_0 \geq 0$ $(\lambda_0, G_1, G_2, \ldots, G_m) \neq (0, 0, 0, \ldots, 0)$.

(ii) At each $r \in [0, r_f]$, $(n_i(r), s_i(r);\ i = 1, 2, \ldots, m)$ maximizes the following *Hamiltonian function,*

$$H \equiv \lambda_0 \sum_{i=1}^{m} [Y_i^0 - T_i(r) - Z_i(s_i, \bar{u}_i) - R_A s_i] n_i - \sum_{i=1}^{m} G_i n_i,$$

$$\text{subject to} \quad \sum_{i=1}^{m} s_i n_i \leq L(r),$$

$$n_i \geq 0,\ s_i > 0, \qquad i = 1, 2, \ldots, m.$$

(iii) $\hat{H} \equiv \lambda_0 \sum_{i=1}^{m} [Y_i^0 - T_i(r) - Z_i(s_i(r), \bar{u}_i) - R_A s_i(r)] n_i(r) - \sum_{i=1}^{m} G_i n_i(r)$ is continuous on $[0, r_f]$ and $\hat{H} = 0$ at r_f.

Since r_f can be chosen freely, it is not difficult to show that $\lambda_0 > 0$ (see Van Long and Vousden 1977, p. 16). Hence, without loss of generality, we can set λ_0 equal to 1. Therefore, condition (ii) can be restated as follows: At each $r \in [0, r_f]$, $(n_i(r), s_i(r);\ i = 1, 2, \ldots, m)$ must be a solution of the following maximization problem:

$$\max_{n_i, s_i} H = \sum_{i=1}^{m} \left[\frac{Y_i^0 - G_i - T_i(r) - Z_i(s_i, \bar{u}_i)}{s_i} - R_A \right] n_i s_i, \qquad \text{(C.44)}$$

subject to

$$\sum_{i=1}^{m} n_i s_i \leq L(r), \qquad n_i \geq 0, \qquad s_i > 0, \qquad i = 1, 2, \ldots, m. \qquad \text{(C.45)}$$

Recalling the bid rent functions $\psi_i(I, u)$ and associated bid-max lot size functions $s_i(I, u)$, $i = 1, 2, \ldots, m$, let us define $R(r)$ at each $r \geq 0$ such that

$$R(r) \equiv \max\{\max_i \psi_i(Y_i^0 - G_i - T_i(r), \bar{u}_i), R_A\}.$$

Then we can readily see that if $(s_i(r), n_i(r); i = 1, 2, \ldots, m)$ maximizes H subject to the constraints (C.45), it must hold that

$$\psi_i(Y_i^0 - G_i - T_i(r), \bar{u}_i) < R(r) \Rightarrow n_i(r) = 0,$$

$$n_i(r) > 0 \Rightarrow \begin{cases} \psi_i(Y_i^0 - G_i - T_i(r), \bar{u}_i) = R(r) \\ s_i(r) = s_i(Y_i^0 - G_i - T_i(r), \bar{u}_i). \end{cases}$$

Using these relations and recalling that each of $\psi_i(Y_i^0 - G_i - T_i(r), \bar{u}_i)$, $i = 1, 2, \ldots, m$, is decreasing in r, we can readily obtain the optimality conditions (4.38)–(4.42). In a manner quite similar to that used in C.2, we can readily show that these necessary conditions also represent the sufficient conditions of optimality for the HS($\bar{\mathbf{u}}$) problem.

C.8 Proof of relation (4.59)

Suppose, now, that

$$u_2^a \geq u_2^b. \tag{C.46}$$

Then from identity (2.20), at each r we would have

$$V(\Psi_2^a(r, u_2^a), Y_2^a - T(r)) = u_2^a \geq u_2^b = V(\Psi_2^b(r, u_2^b), Y_2^b - T(r)).$$

Since V is decreasing in R and increasing in I, and since $Y_2^a - T(r) < Y_2^b - T(r)$ for all r, the above inequality implies that

$$\Psi_2^a(r, u_2^a) < \Psi_2^b(r, u_2^b) \qquad \text{for all} \quad r. \tag{C.47}$$

Then since $R_1(r)$ is decreasing in r, from Figure 4.10 we must have that

$$r_1^a > r_1^b. \tag{C.48}$$

Next, since the compensated demand function $\tilde{s}(R, u)$ is decreasing in R and increasing in u (from the normality of land), from identity (2.25) and from (C.46) and (C.47), we have

$$S_2^a(r, u_2^a) = \tilde{s}(\Psi_2^a(r, u_2^a), u_2^a) > \tilde{s}(\Psi_2^b(r, u_2^b), u_2^b) = S_2^b(r, u_2^b). \tag{C.49}$$

However, from the population constraint, it must hold that

$$\int_{r_1^a}^{r_2^a} \frac{L(r)}{S_2^a(r, u_2^a)}\, dr = N_2 = \int_{r_1^b}^{r_2^b} \frac{L(r)}{S_2^b(r, u_2^b)}\, dr.$$

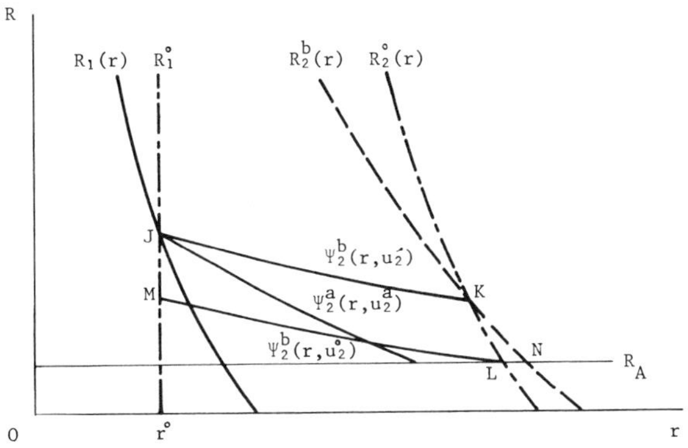

Figure C.1. For the proof of Property 4.13(i).

Then from (C.48) and (C.49), it must hold that $r_2^a > r_2^b$. This, however, contradicts (4.58). Therefore, we can conclude that relation (4.59) must be true.

C.9 Proof of Property 4.13

Using Property 3.4, we can prove Property 4.13 in a geometric way. In Figure C.1, let curves $R_1(r)$ and $R_2^b(r)$ be copies of the same boundary rent curves in Figure 4.10. Similarly, in Figure C.1, let lines $\Psi_2^a(r, u_2^a)$ and R_A be copies of the same lines in Figure 4.10. Recall that $R_2^b(r)$ is the second boundary rent curve (under income Y_2^b), with the first boundary rent curve given by $R_1(r)$. Now in Figure C.1, let point J be the intersection between curves $R_1(r)$ and $\Psi_2^a(r, u_2^a)$, and let us imagine that [instead of $R_1(r)$] the first boundary rent curve is given by the vertical line R_1^0, which passes through point J. Then by using this first boundary rent curve, we can obtain a fictitious second boundary curve (under income Y_2^b), which is depicted by curve $R_2^0(r)$ in Figure C.1. We can readily see that curve $R_2^0(r)$ is also decreasing in r and intersects the r axis at a finite distance. Let point L be the intersection between curve $R_2^0(r)$ and the agricultural rent line R_A. Let $\Psi_2^b(r, u_2^0)$ be the bid rent curve (for class 2 under income Y_2^b) that passes through point L. Suppose, for example, that $L(r)/T'(r)$ is increasing at all r [situation (i)]. Then from Property 3.4(i), we can conclude that *the intersection M between curve $\Psi_2^b(r, u_2^0)$ and line R_1^0 must be below point J*. (Note that Property 3.4 holds true when the R axis is moved parallel to any distance from 0; in the present case, it is at distance r^0 in Figure C.1.) From this, we can conclude that if $\Psi_2^b(r, u_2')$ is the bid rent curve (for class 2 under income Y_2^b) that passes through point J, *the intersection K between this bid rent curve and the boundary rent curve $R_2^0(r)$ must be above the agricultural rent line R_A* (because point L is the intersection between curve $R_2^0(r)$ and line R_A). Since point J is the intersection between curve $R_1(r)$ and line R_1^0, *the real second boundary rent curve $R_2^b(r)$ must also pass through point K*. Therefore, the intersection N between curve $R_2^b(r)$ and line R_A lies below point K. Then the equilibrium bid rent $\Psi_2^b(r, u_2^b)$, which by definition passes through point N, lies below the curve $\Psi_2^b(r, u_2')$. Therefore, we can conclude that the intersection between curves $\Psi_2^b(r, u_2^b)$ and $R_1(r)$ must lie below point J, and hence we can conclude as in Property 4.13(i). In a similar manner, we can also prove (ii) and (iii) of Property 4.13.

C.10 Proofs of Properties 5.5 and 5.6

C.10.1 Property 5.5

(i) From (5.27), $\partial C(u, N)/\partial u > 0$. From (C.14), $\lim_{u\to-\infty} C(u, N) = NT(0)$. From (C.17), $\lim_{u\to\infty} C(u, N) = \infty$.

(ii) From Property 5.2(i) and (5.25), $\partial C(u, N)/\partial N = Y(u, N) > 0$. In order to show that $\lim_{N\to 0} C(u, N) = 0$, let us arbitrarily choose a lot size $s > 0$. Then by definition,

$$C(u, N) \leq N[T(r_f^N) + Z(s, u) + R_A s],$$

where r_f^N is defined by the relation

$$\int_0^{r_f^N} L(r)\, dr = Ns.$$

Therefore, since r_f^N is decreasing in N toward zero, we can immediately conclude that $\lim_{N\to 0} C(u, N) = 0$. Next, since $C(u, N)$ is strictly convex in N (as is shown immediately below) and $\partial C(u, N)/\partial N > 0$, $\lim_{N\to\infty} C(u, N) = \infty$.

(iii) From (5.25) and Property 5.2(ii), $\partial^2 C(u, N)/\partial N^2 = \partial Y(u, N)/\partial N > 0$. Similarly, from (5.25) and Property 5.2(iii), $\lim_{N\to\infty} \partial C(u, N)/\partial N = \lim_{N\to\infty} Y(u, N) = \infty$.

(iv) From (5.25) and Property 5.2(ii), $\partial^2 C(u, N)/\partial N\, \partial u = \partial Y(u, N)/\partial u > 0$.

C.10.2 Property 5.6

From (5.25) and Property 5.2(i), $\lim_{N\to 0} \partial C(u, N)/\partial N = \lim_{N\to 0} Y(u, N) > 0$. Using (5.25) and Property 5.2, we can similarly show (ii)–(iv) of Property 5.6.

C.11 Proof of Property 5.8

Necessity. Suppose $(\hat{u}, \hat{N})$ is a solution to problem (5.62). Then $\hat{N} > 0$ by definition. Since $C(u, N)$ is increasing in u, it must hold that $F(N) \leq C(\hat{u}, N)$ for all $N > 0$ and $F(\hat{N}) = C(\hat{u}, \hat{N})$. Hence, condition (5.67) is satisfied by setting (u', N') equal to $(\hat{u}, \hat{N})$.

Sufficiency. Suppose there exist u' and N' such that condition (5.67) is satisfied. Then,

$$F(N')/N' = C(u', N')/N'.$$

Condition (5.67) also implies that

$$F'(N') \geq C_N(u', N'),$$

where $C_N(u, N) = \partial C(u, N)/\partial N$. Furthermore, since $C(u', N)$ is strictly convex in N,

$$C(u', N')/N' < C_N(u', N').$$

The above three conditions together imply that $F(N')/N' < F'(N')$, and hence

$$0 < N' < N^{\mathrm{a}}. \tag{C.50}$$

In addition, (5.67) and Property 5.6(ii) and (iii) together imply that there uniquely exist u'' such that

$$C_N(u'', 0) = F(N^{\mathrm{a}})/N^{\mathrm{a}}.$$

Then since $C(u'', N)$ is strictly convex in N, it follows that

$$F(N) < C(u'', N) \qquad \text{for all} \quad N > 0. \tag{C.51}$$

Therefore, if $(\hat{u}, \hat{N})$ is a solution to problem (5.62), conditions (5.67) and (C.51) together imply that

$$u' \leq \hat{u} < u''. \tag{C.52}$$

Condition (5.67) also implies that $N' \leq \hat{N}$. Hence, recalling (5.66), it follows that

$$N' \leq \hat{N} < N^{\mathrm{a}}. \tag{C.53}$$

Let

$$X = \{(u, N) \mid u' \leq \hat{u} \leq u'', N' \leq \hat{N} \leq N^{\mathrm{a}}, F(N) - C(u, N) \geq 0\}.$$

Then from (C.52) and (C.53), $(\hat{u}, \hat{N})$ is a solution to problem (5.62) if and only if it is a solution to the next problem:

$$\max u, \qquad \text{subject to} \quad (u, N) \in X. \tag{C.54}$$

Since functions $F(N)$ and $C(u, N)$ are continuous on $\mathbf{R}^2$, the relation $F(N) - C(u, N) \geq 0$ defines a closed set in $\mathbf{R}^2$. Hence, X is a compact set in $\mathbf{R}^2$. Then since problem (C.54) represents a maximization of a continuous function on a compact set, it has a solution. Therefore, we can conclude that problem (5.67) also has a solution.

C.12 Comparison of equilibrium rent curves (Section 7.3.1)

First, let us show that in Figure 7.5 (and Figure 7.4), point β must be located below point α on the curve $\hat{R}(r)$. Since the bid rent function ψ is decreasing in v, and since $E(r - b^*) = E_{\min}$ at $r = b^*$, it follows that

$$\begin{aligned} \psi(Y_W^0 - T_W(r), u_W^*/E(r - b^*)) &> \psi(Y_W^0 - T_W(r), u_W^*/E_{\min}) && \text{for} \quad b^* < r < r_f^* \\ &\equiv \Psi_W(r, u_W^*/E_{\min}) && \text{for} \quad b^* < r < r_f^*. \end{aligned} \tag{C.55}$$

Suppose, now, that the following *assumption x* holds: On the curve $\hat{R}(r)$, point β is not located below point α. Since $\hat{R}(r)$ is decreasing in r, this assumption implies that

$$b^* \leq b_0. \tag{C.56}$$

Since curve $\hat{R}(r)$ is steeper than curve $\Psi_W(r, u_W^0)$ and since $\psi(Y_W^0 - T_W(r), u_W^*/E(r - b^*)) = \Psi_W(r, u_W^*/E_{\min})$ at $r = b^*$, assumption x also implies that

$$\Psi_W(r, u_W^*/E_{\min}) \geq \Psi_W(r, u_W^0) \qquad \text{for} \quad b^0 \leq r \leq r_f^0, \tag{C.57}$$

which in turn implies (because Ψ_W is decreasing in u) that

$$u_W^*/E_{\min} \leq u_W^0. \tag{C.58}$$

Notice that (C.55), (C.56), and (C.57) together imply that

$$b^* \leq b^0 < r_f^0 < r_f^*. \tag{C.59}$$

Notice also that since the bid-max lot size functions s and S_W are increasing in u and $E(r - b^*) > E_{\min}$ for all $r > b^*$, we have that

$$\begin{aligned} s(Y_W^0 - T_W(r), u_W^*/E(r - b^*)) &< s(Y_W^0 - T_W(r), u_W^*/E_{\min}) && \text{for} \quad b^* < r < r_f^* \\ &\equiv S_W(r, u_W^*/E_{\min}) && \text{for} \quad b^* < r < r_f^* \\ &\leq S_W(r, u_W^0) && \text{for} \quad b^* < r < r_f^*, \end{aligned} \tag{C.60}$$

because of (C.58). We can readily see, however, that if relations (C.59) and (C.60) hold, the two population constraints (7.105) and (7.107) cannot hold simultaneously. Therefore, we must conclude that assumption x cannot be true, and hence point β must be located below point α on the curve $\hat{R}(r)$.

Next, let us show that in Figure 7.5, the curve $\psi(Y_W^0 - T_W(r), u_W^*/E(r - b^*))$ must cross the curve $\Psi_W(r, u_W^0)$ at some distance. Suppose, now, that

$$\psi(Y_W^0 - T_W(r), u_W^*/E(r - b^*)) < \Psi_W(r, u_W^0) \qquad \text{for all} \quad b^* < r < r_f^*. \tag{C.61}$$

Then since $S_W(r, u_W^0) \equiv s(Y_W^0 - T_W(r), u_W^0) = \hat{s}(\Psi_W(r, u_W^0), Y_W^0 - T_W(r))$ and $s(Y_W^0 - T_W(r), u_W^*/E(r - b^*)) = \hat{s}(\psi(Y_W^0 - T_W(r), u_W^*/E(r - b^*)), Y_W^0 - T_W(r))$ because of identity (3.5), and since the Marshallian demand function $\hat{s}(R, I)$ is decreasing in R, it follows that

$$s(Y_W^0 - T_W(r), u_W^*/E(r - b^*)) > S_W(r, u_W^0) \qquad \text{for} \quad b^* < r < r_f^*. \tag{C.62}$$

However, since (C.61) also implies that $b^0 < b^* < r_f^* < r_f^0$, if (C.62) holds, then the two population constraints (7.105) and (7.107) cannot hold simultaneously. Therefore, we can conclude that in Figure 7.5, the curve $\psi(Y_W^0 - T_W(r), u_W^*/E(r - b^*))$ must cross the curve $\Psi_W(r, u_W^0)$ at some distance.

C.13 Derivation of the optimality conditions for the HS_T model

To facilitate the derivation of the optimality conditions for the HS_T model, let us first make a few observations. Notice that the constraint (7.128) can be equivalently expressed in the following differential form:

$$\dot{N}(r) = -n(r) \qquad \text{for} \quad 0 \le r \le r_f \qquad \text{and} \quad N(r_c) = N, N(r_f) = 0, \tag{C.63}$$

where $\dot{N}(r) \equiv dN(r)/dr$. Notice also from (7.123) that $T(r_c) = 0$. Therefore, by integration by parts, we have that

$$\int_{r_c}^{r_f} T(r)n(r)\, dr = -\int_{r_c}^{r_f} T(r)\dot{N}(r)\, dr = -[T(r)N(r)]_{r_c}^{r_f} + \int_{r_c}^{r_f} T'(r)N(r)\, dr$$

$$= \int_{r_c}^{r_f} T'(r)N(r)\, dr = \int_{r_c}^{r_f} c\left(\frac{N(r)}{L_T(r)}\right)N(r)\, dr, \tag{C.64}$$

because $T'(r) \equiv dT(r)/dr = c(N(r)/L_T(r))$ from (7.123). Using (C.63) and (C.64), the original HS_T problem, (7.126)–(7.129), can be reformulated as follows:

$$\max_{r_f, n(r), s(r), L_T(r)} \mathcal{S} = \int_{r_c}^{r_f} \{[Y^0 - Z(s(r), u) - R_A s(r)]n(r) - c(N(r)/L_T(r))N(r) - R_A L_T(r)\}\, dr, \tag{C.65}$$

subject to

$$\dot{N}(r) = -n(r), \tag{C.66}$$

$$n(r)s(r) + L_T(r) \le L(r), \tag{C.67}$$

$$n(r) \ge 0, \qquad s(r) > 0, \qquad L_T(r) > 0, \tag{C.68}$$

$$N(r_c) = N, \qquad N(r_f) = 0. \tag{C.69}$$

Suppose that $(r_f, n(r), s(r), L_T(r); r_c \le r \le r_f)$ represents a solution to the HS problem above (where each of $n(r)$, $s(r)$, $L_T(r)$ is assumed to be piecewise continuous on $[r_c, r_f]$). Then the maximum principle (see Hestenes 1966, Theorem 11.1; Takayama 1974, Theorem 8.C.4; or Van Long and Vousden 1977, Theorem 1) requires that there exist a set of multipliers, λ_0 and $\lambda(r)$, $r_c \le r \le r_f$, such that

(i) $\lambda_0 \ge 0$, $(\lambda_0, \lambda(r)) \ne (0, 0)$ for any $r \in [r_c, r_f]$;

(ii) at each $r \in [r_c, r_f]$, $(n(r), s(r), L_T(r))$ maximizes the following Hamiltonian function,

$$H \equiv \lambda_0[Y^0 - Z(s, u) - R_A s]n - c(N(r)/L_T)N(r) - R_A L_T - \lambda(r)n, \tag{C.70}$$

subject to (C.67) and (6.68);

(iii) At each $r \in (r_c, r_f)$,

$$\dot{\lambda}(r) = -\partial H/\partial N \quad \text{at} \quad (n, s, L_T) = (n(r), s(r), L_T(r)), \tag{C.71}$$

where $\dot{\lambda}(r) \equiv d\lambda(r)/dr$.

(iv) $\hat{H} \equiv \lambda_0[Y^0 - Z(s(r), u) - R_A s(r)]n(r) - c(N(r)/L_T(r))N(r) - R_A L_T(r) - \lambda(r)n(r)$ is continuous on $[r_c, r_f]$, and $\hat{H} = 0$ at r_f.

Since r_f can be chosen freely, it is not difficult to show that $\lambda_0 > 0$ (see Van Long and Vousden 1977, p. 16). Hence, without loss of generality, we can set λ_0 equal to 1. Therefore, if we define $L_H \equiv ns$, conditions (ii) can be restated as follows: At each $r \in [r_c, r_f]$, $(n(r), s(r), L_H(r), L_T(r))$ must be the solution to the following maximization problem:

$$\max_{n, s, L_H, L_T} H = \left[\frac{Y^0 - \lambda(r) - Z(s, u)}{s} - R_A\right] L_H - c\left(\frac{N(r)}{L_T}\right) N(r) - R_A L_T, \tag{C.72}$$

$$\text{subject to} \quad L_H + L_T \le L(r), \qquad L_H \ge 0, \qquad L_T \ge 0, \tag{C.73}$$

$$sn = L_H, \qquad n \ge 0, \qquad s > 0. \tag{C.74}$$

Notice that this maximization problem can be solved in two steps. First, given any $L_H > 0$, in order to maximize H, we must choose s so as to maximize the first term inside the brackets in (C.72). Therefore, using the bid rent function $\psi(I, u)$ and bid-max lot size function $s(I, u)$ [defined from (3.2)], we can conclude that if $L_H(r) > 0$, then it must hold that

$$s(r) = s(Y^0 - \lambda(r), u), \qquad n(r) = L_H(r)/s(Y^0 - \lambda(r), u), \tag{C.75}$$

$$\frac{Y^0 - \lambda(r) - Z(s(r), u)}{s(r)} = \psi(Y^0 - \lambda(r), u) = \max_s \frac{Y^0 - \lambda(r) - Z(s, u)}{s}. \tag{C.76}$$

When $L_H(r) = 0$, of course, $n(r) = 0$ and $s(r)$ can be any positive number. Hence, we can require that conditions (C.75) and (C.76) always hold. Therefore, the maximization problem (C.72)–(C.74) is now reduced to the following problem:

$$\max_{L_H, L_T} [\psi(Y^0 - \lambda(r), u) - R_A]L_H - c(N(r)/L_T)N(r) - R_A L_T, \tag{C.77}$$

$$\text{subject to} \qquad L_H + L_T \le L(r), \qquad L_H \ge 0, L_T \ge 0. \tag{C.78}$$

Introducing a multiplier $DR(r)$, we define the associated Lagrangian function as

$$\mathcal{L} = [\psi(Y^0 - \lambda(r), u) - R_A]L_H - c(N(r)/L_T)N(r) - R_A L_T$$
$$+ DR(r)[L(r) - L_H - L_T].$$

Then since function $c(\omega)$ is strictly convex in ω (by assumption), the following *Kuhn–Tucker conditions* represent the set of necessary and sufficient conditions of optimality for the above maximization problem:

$$\frac{\partial \mathcal{L}}{\partial L_H} = \psi(Y^0 - \lambda(r), u) - (R_A + DR(r)) \le 0, \tag{C.79}$$

$$[\psi(Y^0 - \lambda(r), u) - (R_A + DR(r))]L_H(r) = 0, \tag{C.80}$$

$$\frac{\partial \mathcal{L}}{\partial L_T} = c'\left(\frac{N(r)}{L_T(r)}\right)\left(\frac{N(r)}{L_T(r)}\right)^2 - (R_A + DR(r)) \le 0, \tag{C.81}$$

$$\left[c'\left(\frac{N(r)}{L_T(r)}\right)\left(\frac{N(r)}{L_T(r)}\right)^2 - (R_A + DR(r))\right]L_T(r) = 0, \tag{C.82}$$

$$DR(r)[L(r) - L_H(r) - L_T(r)] = 0, \tag{C.83}$$

$$L_H(r) + L_T(r) \le L(r), \qquad L_H(r) \ge 0, \qquad L_T(r) \ge 0, \qquad DR(r) \ge 0. \tag{C.84}$$

Next, condition (C.71) means that

$$\dot{\lambda}(r) = c(N(r)/L_T(r)) + c'(N(r)/L_T(r))N(r)/L_T(r),$$

which implies that

$$\lambda(r) = \int_{r_c}^{r} c\left(\frac{N(x)}{L_T(x)}\right) dx + \int_{r_c}^{r} c'\left(\frac{N(x)}{L_T(x)}\right) \frac{N(x)}{L_T(x)} dx + g,$$

where g is some constant. Therefore, if we define

$$l(r) \equiv \int_{r_c}^{r} c'(N(x)/L_T(x))(N(x)/L_T(x))\, dx, \tag{C.85}$$

then we have

$$\lambda(r) = T(r) + l(r) + g. \tag{C.86}$$

Furthermore, let us define

$$R(r) \equiv R_A + DR(r), \tag{C.87}$$

$$\psi_T(N(r)/L_T(r)) \equiv c'(N(r)/L_T(r))(N(r)/L_T(r))^2. \tag{C.88}$$

Then, since $DR(r) \ge 0$ and hence $R(r) \ge R_A$, from (C.75) and (C.79)–(C.88) we can obtain the following relations: At each $r \in [r_c, r_f]$,

$$R(r) = \max\{\psi(Y^0 - g - l(r) - T(r), u), \psi_T(N(r)/L_T(r)), R_A\}, \tag{C.89}$$

$$R(r) = \psi(Y^0 - g - l(r) - T(r), u) \quad \text{if} \quad n(r) > 0 \quad [\text{i.e., } L_H(r) > 0], \tag{C.90}$$

$$R(r) = \psi_T(N(r)/L_T(r)) \quad \text{if} \quad L_T(r) > 0, \tag{C.91}$$

$$s(r) = s(Y^0 - g - l(r) - T(r), u), \tag{C.92}$$

$$n(r) = L_H(r)/s(Y^0 - g - l(r) - T(r), u), \tag{C.93}$$

$$l(r) = \int_{r_c}^{r} c'\left(\frac{N(x)}{L_T(x)}\right)\left(\frac{N(x)}{L_T(x)}\right) dx. \tag{C.94}$$

Finally, in order to obtain the condition for determining the optimal fringe distance r_f, recall that $N(r_f) = 0$ by definition. Hence, using (C.82), (C.88), and the terminal condition (iv), and recalling (C.76), we can obtain

$$[R_A + DR(r_f)]L_T(r_f) = 0, \tag{C.95}$$

$$\psi_T(N(r_f)/L_T(r_f)) = 0, \tag{C.96}$$

$$[\psi(Y^0 - g - l(r_f) - T(r_f), u) - R_A]L_H(r_f) - R_A L_T(r_f) = 0. \tag{C.97}$$

Suppose $R(r_f) > R_A$, that is, $DR(r_f) > 0$. Then from (C.95) $L_T(r_f) = 0$. Furthermore, from (C.83), $DR(r_f) > 0$ and $L_T(r_f) = 0$ together imply that $L_H(r_f) = L(r_f) > 0$ (by assumption). Hence, from (C.97), it must hold that

$$\psi(Y^0 - g - l(r_f) - T(r_f), u) = R_A. \tag{C.98}$$

However, since (C.89), (C.96), and (C.98) together imply that $R(r_f) = R_A$, we have a contradiction. Therefore, it must hold that

$$R(r_f) = R_A. \tag{C.99}$$

Let the distance $\hat{r}$ be defined by the relation,

$$\psi(Y^0 - g - l(\hat{r}) - T(\hat{r}), u) = R_A. \tag{C.100}$$

Since $l'(r) \geq 0$ for $r \leq r_f$, $\partial\psi(Y^0 - g - l(r) - T(r), u)/\partial r = -[l'(r) + T'(r)]/s(Y^0 - g - l(r) - T(r), u) < 0$. That is, the household bid rent curve is always decreasing in r. Using this result, in a manner similar to the case of Appendix C.2, we can readily show that the optimal r_f can be any distance such that $r_f \geq \hat{r}$. Hence, for convenience, we can always require that relation (C.98) holds at r_f. We can now readily see that conditions (C.89)–(C.94) and (C.98) can be restated as (7.133)–(7.138).

In order to show that these necessary conditions also represent a set of sufficient conditions for optimality, notice that since function $c(\omega)$ is assumed to be convex, function $c(N)N$ is also convex in N. This implies that the function $c(N/L_T)N \equiv L_T c(N/L_T)(N/L_T)$ is convex in (N, L_T) (see Rockafellar 1970, p. 35). Therefore, the Lagrangian function $\mathcal{L}$ [introduced immediately after (C.78)] is concave in (L_H, L_T, N). Hence, from Van Long and Vousden (1977, Theorem 6), we can conclude that for any *fixed* r_f, conditions (C.89)–(C.94) represent the necessary and sufficient conditions for optimality. We can also readily confirm that $\hat{H} \geq 0$ for all $r \leq r_f$ and $\hat{H} \leq 0$ for all $r \geq r_f$. Therefore, we can conclude from Seierstad (1984a,b) that (7.123), (7.127)–(7.129), and (7.133)–(7.138) represent the necessary and sufficient conditions of optimality for the HS_T problem.

C.14 Calculations for comparative statics of Table 8.1

C.14.1 Impact of a change in u

To examine the impact of a change in u, let us rewrite function $g(N) \equiv W(N)$ as $W(N, u)$. Since $\partial W/\partial u = 0$, from the total differential of the equation $W(N, u) = Y(N, u)$, we have

$$\frac{dN}{du} = \left(\frac{\partial W}{\partial N} - \frac{\partial Y}{\partial N}\right)^{-1} \frac{\partial Y}{\partial u}.$$

From the assumption of the normality of land, $\partial s(Y - T(r), u)/\partial u > 0$. Hence, from Property 5.2 $\partial Y(N, u)/\partial u > 0$. At a stable equilibrium, $\partial W/\partial N < \partial Y/\partial N$. Hence, $dN/du < 0$. This means that if an equilibrium city size N^* is stable, it is decreasing in u. The rest of the results in the u row of Table 8.1 follow immediately from (8.50)–(8.56).

C.14.2 Impact of a change in p_x

The manner of obtaining the results of the p_x row is similar to that of obtaining those for the u row.

C.14.3 Impact of a change in ρ

Similarly, from the total differentiation of the equation $W(N, \rho) = Y(N, \rho)$, we have

$$\frac{dN}{d\rho} = -\left(\frac{\partial W}{\partial N} - \frac{\partial Y}{\partial N}\right)^{-1} \frac{\partial W}{\partial \rho}.$$

Differentiating equation (8.52) logarithmically with respect to ρ and substituting (8.50), we have

$$\partial W/\partial \rho = -(\nu W/\rho^2) \log n.$$

By assumption, $n > 1$, and hence $\partial W/\partial \rho < 0$. Therefore, at a stable equilibrium, we can conclude that $dN/d\rho < 0$. Hence, at a stable equilibrium, N^* is decreasing in ρ. Furthermore, differentiating $W(N(\rho), \rho)$ with respect to ρ, we have

$$\frac{dW}{d\rho} = \frac{\partial W}{\partial N}\frac{dN(\rho)}{d\rho} + \frac{\partial W}{\partial \rho},$$

which is negative since $\partial W/\partial N > 0$, $dN(\rho)/d\rho < 0$, and $\partial W/\partial \rho < 0$. Next, differentiating equation (8.51) logarithmically with respect to ρ, we have

$$\frac{1}{X}\frac{dX}{d\rho} = -\frac{\nu}{\rho^2} \log n + \left(\frac{\nu}{\rho} + \alpha\right)\frac{1}{N}\frac{dN}{d\rho}.$$

Provided that $n > 1$, $\log n > 0$. As shown above, $dN/d\rho < 0$. Hence, $dX/d\rho < 0$. The rest of the results in the ρ row follow similarly.

C.14.4 Impact of a change in f and c

We can similarly obtain the results of the f row and c row in Table 8.1, respectively. In particular, from (8.38) we have $(1/p_q)(dp_q/dc) = 1/c + (1/W)(dW/dc)$, and hence

$$\frac{dp_q}{dc} \gtreqless 0 \qquad \text{as} \qquad \frac{dW}{dc}\frac{c}{W} \gtreqless -1.$$

We can readily see that $dW/dc < 0$. Thus, dp_q/dc is positive or negative as the elasticity $(dW/dc)(c/W)$ is greater or less than -1.

References

Abdel-Rahman, H. M. (in press). Agglomeration economies, types and sizes of cities. *Journal of Urban Economics*.

(1988). Product differentiation, monopolistic competition and city size. *Regional Science and Urban Economics*, *18*, 69–86.

Abdel-Rahman, H. M., and Fujita, M. (1987). Product variety, Marshallian externalities and city sizes. *Working Papers in Regional Science and Transportation*, No. 114. University of Pennsylvania, Philadelphia.

Alonso, W. (1964). *Location and Land Use*. Cambridge, MA: Harvard University Press.

Altmann, J. L., and DeSalvo, J. S. (1981). Tests and extensions of the Mills–Muth simulation model of urban residential land use. *Journal of Regional Science*, *21*, 1–21.

Anas, A. (1980). A model of residential change and neighborhood tipping. *Journal of Urban Economics*, *7*, 358–70.

(1987). *Modeling in Urban and Regional Economics*. Chur, Switzerland: Harwood.

Anas, A., and Dendrinos, D. S. (1976). The new urban economics: A brief survey. In G. J. Papageorgiou, ed., *Mathematical Land Use Theory*, pp. 23–51. Lexington, MA: Lexington Books.

Anas, A., and Moses, L. M. (1979). Mode choice, transport structure and urban land use. *Journal of Urban Economics*, *6*, 228–46.

Ando, A. (1981). *Development of a Unified Theory of Urban Land Use*, Ph.D. dissertation. University of Pennsylvania, Philadelphia.

Arnott, R. J. (1979). Optimal city size in a spatial economy. *Journal of Urban Economics*, *6*, 65–89.

(1981). Aggregate land rents and aggregate transport costs. *Economic Journal*, *91*, 331–47.

Arnott, R., and MacKinnon, J. (1978). Market and shadow land rents with congestion. *American Economic Review*, *68*, 588–600.

Arnott, R. J., MacKinnon, J. G., and Wheaton, W. C. (1978). The welfare implications of spatial interdependence. *Journal of Urban Economics*, *5*, 131–6.

Arnott, R. J., Pines, D., and Sadka, E. (1986). The effects of an equiproportional transport improvement in a fully-closed monocentric city. *Regional Science and Urban Economics*, *16*, 387–406.

Arnott, R. J., and Riley, J. G. (1977). Asymmetrical production possibilities, the social gains from inequality and the optimum town. *Scandinavian Journal of Economics*, *79*, 301–11.

Arrow, K. J., and Hahn, F. H. (1971). *General Competitive Analysis*. San Francisco: Holden-Day.

Asami, Y., Fujita, M., and Smith, T. E., (1987). On the foundations of land use theory. *Working Papers in Regional Science and Transportation*, No. 112. University of Pennsylvania, Philadelphia.

Bailey, M. J. (1959). Note on the economics of residential zoning and urban renewal. *Land Economics*, *35*, 288–92.

Barten, A. P., and Böhm, V. (1982). Consumer theory. In K. J. Arrow and M. D. Intriligator, eds., *Handbook of Mathematical Economics*, Vol. 2, pp. 381–429. Amsterdam: North-Holland.

Baumol, W. J., and Oates, W. E. (1975). *The Theory of Environmental Policy*. Englewood Cliffs, NJ: Prentice-Hall.

Beckmann, M. J. (1957). On the distribution of rent and residential density in cities. Paper presented at the Inter-Departmental Seminar on Mathematical Applications in the Social Sciences, Yale University.

(1973). Equilibrium models of residential land use. *Regional and Urban Economics*, *3*, 361–8.

(1974). Spatial equilibrium in the housing market. *Journal of Urban Economics*, *1*, 99–107.

Bellman, R. (1957). *Dynamic Programming*. Princeton, NJ: Princeton University Press.

Berglas, E., and Pines, D. (1981). Clubs, local public goods, and transportation models: A synthesis. *Journal of Public Economics*, *15*, 141–62.

Berliant, M. (1984). A characterization of the demand for land. *Journal of Economic Theory*, *33*, 289–300.

(1985a). Equilibrium models with land: A criticism and an alternative. *Regional Science and Urban Economics*, *15*, 325–40.

(1985b). An equilibrium existence result for an economy with land. *Journal of Mathematical Economics*, *14*, 53–6.

Berliant, M., and Dunz, K. (1987). The welfare theories and economies with land and a finite number of traders. Mimeograph, Department of Economics, University of Rochester, Rochester, N.Y.

Berliant, M., and ten Raa, T. (1987). On the continuum approach of spatial and some local public goods or product differentiation models. *Working Paper 72*, Rochester Center for Economic Research, Rochester, N.Y.

Brueckner, J. K. (1979). Spatial majority voting equilibria and the provision of public goods. *Journal of Urban Economics*, *6*, 338–51.

(1981). A dynamic model of housing production. *Journal of Urban Economics*, *10*, 1–14.

(1982). A test for allocative efficiency in the local public sector. *Journal of Public Economics*, *19*, 311–31.

Carliner, G. (1973). Income elasticity of housing demand. *Review of Economics and Statistics*, *55*, 528–32.

Casetti, E. (1971). Equilibrium land values and population density in an urban setting. *Economic Geography*, *47*, 16–20.

Chamberlin, E. H. (1933). *The theory of monopolistic competition*. Cambridge, MA: Harvard University Press.

Chipman, J. S. (1970). External economies of scale and competitive equilibrium, *Quarterly Journal of Economics*, *86*, 347–85.

Cornes, R., and Sandler, T. (1986). *The theory of externalities, public goods, and club goods*. Cambridge University Press.

Courant, P. N., and Yinger, J. (1977). On models of racial prejudice and urban residential structure. *Journal of Urban Economics*, *4*, 272–91.

Debreu, G. (1959). *Theory of Value*. New York: Wiley.

DeSalvo, J. S. (1985). A Model of urban household behavior with leisure choice. *Journal of Regional Science*, *25*, 159–74.

Dixit, A. K. (1973). The optimum factory town. *Bell Journal of Economics and Management Science*, *4*, 637–51.

Dixit, A. K., and Stiglitz, J. E. (1977). Monopolistic competition and optimum product diversity, *American Economic Review*, *67*(3), 297–308.

Ethier, W. (1982). National and International Returns to Scale in the Modern Theory of International Trade. *American Economic Review*, *72*, 389–405.

Feller, W. (1971). *An Introduction to Probability Theory and Its Applications*, 2nd ed., Vol. 2. New York: Wiley.

Fisch, O. (1976). Spatial equilibrium with local public goods: Urban land rent, optimal city size and the Tiebout hypothesis. In G. J. Papageorgiou, ed., *Mathematical Land Use Theory*, pp. 177–97. Lexington, MA: Lexington Books.

Flatters, F., Henderson, J. V., and Mieszkowski, P. (1974). Public goods, efficiency and regional fiscal equalization. *Journal of Public Economics*, *3*, 99–112.

Fujita, M. (1978). *Spatial Development Planning: A Dynamic Convex Programming Approach*. Amsterdam: North-Holland.

(1984). Existence and uniqueness of equilibrium and optimal land use: Boundary rent curve approach. *Working Papers in Regional Science and Transportation*, No. 89. University of Pennsylvania, Philadelphia.

(1985). Existence and uniqueness of equilibrium and optimal land use: Boundary rent curve approach. *Regional Science and Urban Economics*, *15*, 295–324.

(1986a). Urban land use theory. In J. J. Gabszewicz, Thisse J.-F., Fujita, M., and Schweizer, U. *Location Theory*, pp. 73–149. Chur, Switzerland: Harwood.

(1986b). Optimal location of public facilities: Area dominance approach. *Regional Science and Urban Economics*, *16*, 241–68.

(1988). A monopolistic competition model of spatial agglomeration: Differentiated product approach. *Regional Science and Urban Economics*, *18*, 87–124.

Fujita, M., and Kashiwadani, M. (1976). A study on theoretical relations between market and optimum urban residential theories. *Annals of Regional Science*, *5*, 107–34 (in Japanese).

Fujita, M., and Smith, T. E. (1985). Existence of continuous residential land use equilibria. *Working Papers in Regional Science and Transportation*, No. 98. University of Pennsylvania, Philadelphia.

(1987). Existence of continuous residential land-use equilibria. *Regional Science and Urban Economics*, *17*, 549–94.

Goldstein, G. S., and Gronberg, T. J. (1984). Economies of scope and economies of agglomeration. *Journal of Urban Economics*, *16*, 91–104.

Grieson, R. E., and Murray, M. P. (1981). On the possibility and optimality of positive rent gradients. *Journal of Urban Economics*, *9*, 275–85.

Hartwick, P. G., and Hartwick, J. M. (1974). Efficient resource allocation in a multinucleated city with intermediate goods. *Quarterly Journal of Economics*, *88*, 340–52.

Hartwick, J. M., Schweizer U., and Varaiya, P. (1976). Comparative statics of a residential economy with several classes. *Journal of Economic Theory*, *13*, 396–413.

Helpman, E., and Pines, D. (1980). Optimal public investment and dispersion policy in a system of open cities. *American Economic Review*, *70*, 507–14.

Helpman, E., Pines, D., and Borukhov, E. (1976). The interaction between local government and urban residential location: Comment. *American Economic Review*, *66*, 961–7.

Henderson, J. M., and Quandt, R. E. (1980). *Microeconomic Theory*, 3rd ed. New York: McGraw-Hill.

Henderson, J. V. (1974). The sizes and types of cities. *American Economic Review*, *64*, 640–56.

(1977). *Economic Theory and the Cities*. New York: Academic Press.

(1981). The economics of staggered work hours. *Journal of Urban Economics*, *9*, 349–64.

(1982). Systems of cities in closed and open economies. *Regional Science and Urban Economics*, *12*, 280–303.

(1985). *Economic Theory and the Cities*, 2nd ed. New York: Academic Press.

(1986). Efficiency of resource usage and city size. *Journal of Urban Economics*, *19*, 47–70.

(1987). Systems of Cities and Inter-City Trade. In P. Hansen et al., *Systems of Cities and Facility Location*, pp. 71–119. Chur, Switzerland: Harwood.

Herbert, J. D., and Stevens, B. H. (1960). A model of the distribution of residential activity in urban areas. *Journal of Regional Science*, *2*, 21–36.

Hestenes, M. R. (1966). *Calculus of Variations and Optimal Control Theory*. New York: Wiley.

Hicks, J. R. (1946). *Value and Capital*, 2nd ed. Oxford: Clarendon Press.

Hildenbrand, W. (1974). *Core and Equilibria of a Large Economy*. Princeton, NJ: Princeton University Press.

Hobson, P. A. R. (1987). Optimum product variety in urban areas. *Journal of Urban Economics*, *22*, 190–7.

Hochman, O. (1982a). Congestible local public goods in an urban setting. *Journal of Urban Economics*, *11*, 290–310.

(1982b). Clubs in an urban setting. *Journal of Urban Economics*, *12*, 85–101.

Hochman, O., and Ofek, H. (1977). The value of time in consumption and residential location in an urban setting. *American Economic Review*, *67*, 996–1003.

(1979). A theory of the behavior of municipal governments: The case of internalizing pollution externalities. *Journal of Urban Economics*, *6*, 416–31.

Isard, W. (1956). *Location and Space Economy*. Cambridge, MA: MIT Press.

Kain, J. F. (1987). Computer simulation models of urban location. In E. S. Mills, ed., *Handbook of Regional and Urban Economics*, Vol. 2, pp. 847–75. Amsterdam: North-Holland.

Kanemoto, Y. (1977). Cost–benefit analysis and the second best land use for transportation. *Journal of Urban Economics*, *4*, 483–503.

(1980). *Theories of Urban Externalities*. Amsterdam: North-Holland.

(1987). Externalities in space. In T. Miyao and Y. Kanemoto, *Urban Dynamics and Urban Externalities*, pp. 43–103. Chur, Switzerland: Harwood.

Karmann, A. (1982). Spatial barter economies under locational choice. *Journal of Mathematical Economics*, *9*, 259–74.

Kern, C. R. (1981). Racial prejudice and residential segregation: The Yinger model revisited. *Journal of Urban Economics*, *10*, 164–72.

King, A. T. (1980). General equilibrium with externalities: A computational method and urban applications. *Journal of Urban Economics*, *7*, 84–101.

Koide, H. (1985). *Studies in the Spatial Structure of Urban Concentration*. Ph.D. dissertation, University of Pennsylvania, Philadelphia.

(1988). Spatial provision of local public goods with spillover effects. *Regional Science and Urban Economics*, *18*, 283–305.

Koopmans, T. C. (1957). *Three Essays on the State of Economic Science*. New York: McGraw-Hill.

Krugman, P. (1979). Increasing returns, monopolistic competition and international trade. *Journal of International Economics*, *9*, 469–79.

Kuroda, T. (1988). Location of public facilities under the spill-over effect. *Working Papers in Regional Science and Transportation*, No. 122. University of Pennsylvania,, Philadelphia.

Legey, L., Ripper M., and Varaiya, P. (1973). Effect of congestion on the shape of a city. *Journal of Economic Theory*, *6*, 162–79.

LeRoy, S. F., and Sonstelie, J. (1983). Paradise lost and regained: Transportation innovation, income, and residential location. *Journal of Urban Economics*, *13*, 67–89.

Levhari, D., Oron Y., and Pines, D. (1978). A note on unequal treatment of equals in an urban setting. *Journal of Urban Economics*, *5*, 278–84.

Lösch, A. (1954). *The Economics of Location*. New Haven, CT: Yale University Press.

MacKinnon, J. G. (1974). Urban general equilibrium models and simplical search algorithms. *Journal of Urban Economics*, *1*, 161–83.

Malinvaud, E. (1972). *Lectures on Microeconomic Theory*. Amsterdam: North-Holland.

Mills, E. S. (1972a). *Studies in the Structure of the Urban Economy*. Baltimore, MD: Johns Hopkins University Press.

(1972b). *Urban Economics*. Glenview, IL: Scott, Foresman.

Mills, E. S., ed. (1987). *Handbook of Regional and Urban Economics*. Amsterdam: North-Holland.

Mills, E. S., and de Ferranti, D. M. (1971). Market choices and optimum city size. *American Economic Review, Papers and Proceedings*, *61*, 340–5.

Mills, E. S., and Hamilton, B. W. (1984). *Urban Economics*, 3rd ed., Glenview, IL: Scott, Foresman.

Mirrlees, J. A. (1972). The optimum town. *Swedish Journal of Economics*, *74*, 114–35.

Miyao, T. (1978a). Dynamic instability of a mixed city in the presence of neighborhood externalities. *American Economic Review*, *68*, 454–63.

(1978b). A probabilistic model of location choice with neighborhood effects. *Journal of Economic Theory*, *19*, 357–68.

(1978c). A note on land use in a square city. *Regional Science and Urban Economics*, *8*, 371–9.

(1981). *Dynamic Analysis of the Urban Economy*. New York: Academic Press.

Miyao, T., and Kanemoto, Y. (1987). *Urban Dynamics and Urban Externalities*. Chur, Switzerland: Harwood.

Miyao, T., Shapiro, P., and Knapp, D. (1980). On the existence, uniqueness, and stability of spatial equilibrium in an open city with externalities. *Journal of Urban Economics*, *8*, 139–49.

Mohring, H. (1961). Land values and the measurement of highway benefits. *Journal of Political Economy*, *69*, 236–49.

Moses, L. N. (1962). Towards a theory of intra-urban wage differentials and their influence on travel patterns. *Papers and Proceedings of the Regional Science Association*, *9*, 53–63.

Muth, R. F. (1969). *Cities and Housing*. University of Chicago Press.

(1971). The derived demand for urban residential land. *Urban Studies*, *8*, 243–54.

Niedercorn, J. H. (1971). A negative exponential model of urban land use densities and its implications for metropolitan development. *Journal of Regional Science*, *11*, 317–26.

Odland, J. (1976). The spatial arrangement of urban activities: A simultaneous location model. *Environment and Planning A*, *8*, 779–91.

Oron, Y., Pines D., and Sheshinski, E. (1973). Optimum vs. equilibrium land use pattern and congestion toll. *Bell Journal of Economics and Management Science*, *4*, 619–36.

Papageorgiou, G. J. (1978a). Spatial externalities. I: theory. *Annals of the Association of American Geographers*, *68*, 465–76.

(1978b). Spatial externalities. II: Applications. *Annals of the Association of American Geographers*, *68*, 477–92.

Papageorgiou, G. J., and Casetti, E. (1971). Spatial equilibrium residential land values in a multicentre setting. *Journal of Regional Science*, *11*, 385–9.

Papageorgiou, Y. Y., and Pines, D. (1987). The logical foundations of urban economics are consistent. Paper presented at the 34th North American Meeting of Regional Science Association, Baltimore, MD.

Pines, D., and Sadka, E. (1981). Optimum, second-best, and market allocations of resources within an urban area. *Journal of Urban Economics*, *9*, 173–89.

(1986). Comparative statics analysis of a fully closed city. *Journal of Urban Economics*, *20*, 1–20.

Polinsky, A. M. (1977). The demand for housing: A study in specification and grouping. *Econometrica*, *45*, 447–61.

Ricardo, D. (1817). *The Principles of Political Economy and Taxation* (republished 1886, London: John Murray).

Richardson, H. W. (1977a). The new urban economics: and alternatives. London: Pion.

(1977b). On the possibility of positive rent gradients. *Journal of Urban Economics*, *4*, 60–8.

Richter, D. K. (1980). A computational approach to resource allocation in spatial urban models. *Regional Science and Urban Economics*, *10*, 17–42.

Riley, J. G. (1973). Gammaville: An optimal town. *Journal of Economic Theory*, *6*, 471–82.

(1974). Optimal residential density and road transportation. *Journal of Urban Economics*, *1*, 230–49.

Rivera-Batiz, F. (1988). Increasing returns, monopolistic competition, and agglomeration economies in consumption and production. *Regional Science and Urban Economics*, *18*, 125–53.

Robson, A. J. (1976). Cost–benefit analysis and the use of urban land for transportation. *Journal of Urban Economics*, *3*, 180–91.

Rockafellar, R. T. (1970). *Convex analysis*. Princeton NJ: Princeton University Press.

Romanos, M. C. (1977). Household location in a linear multi-center metropolitan area. *Regional Science and Urban Economics*, *7*, 233–50.

Rose-Ackerman, S. (1975). Racism and urban structure. *Journal of Urban Economics*, *2*, 85–103.

(1977). The political economy of a racist housing market. *Journal of Urban Economics*, *4*, 150–69.

Sakashita, N. (1987a). Optimum location of public facilities under the influence of the land market. *Journal of Regional Science*, *27*, 1–12.

(1987b). Optimum design of public facilities under alternative rent redistribution schemes. Paper presented at the 34th North American Meeting of Regional Science Association, Baltimore, MD.

Samuelson, P. A. (1954). The pure theory of public expenditure. *Review of Economics and Statistics*, *36*, 387–9.

(1983). Thünen at two hundred. *Journal of Economic Literature*, *21*, 1468–88.

Sasaki, K. (1987). A comparative static analysis of urban structure in the setting of endogenous income. *Journal of Urban Economics*, *22*, 53–72.

Schnare, A. B. (1976). Racial and ethnic price differentials in an urban housing market. *Urban Studies*, *13*, 107–20.

Schnare, A. B., and MacRae, C. D. (1978). The dynamics of neighborhood change. *Urban Studies*, *15*, 327–31.

Schuler, R. E. (1974). The interaction between local government and urban residential location. *American Economic Review*, *64*, 682–96.

(1976). The interaction between local government and urban residential location: Reply and further analysis. *American Economic Review*, *66*, 968–75.

Schweizer, U. (1983). Efficient exchange with a variable number of consumers. *Econometrica*, *51*, 575–84.

(1985). Theory of city system structure. *Regional Science and Urban Economics*, *15*, 159–80.

(1986). General equilibrium in space and agglomeration. In J. J. Gabszewicz et al., *Location Theory*, pp. 151–85. Chur, Switzerland: Harwood.

Schweizer, U., Varaiya, P., and Hartwick, J. (1976). General equilibrium and location theory. *Journal of Urban Economics*, *3*, 285–303.

Scotchmer, S. (1982). Hedonic prices, crowding and optimal dispersion of population. Paper presented at the Table Ronde Modeles Economiques de la Localisation et des Transports, Paris.

(1985). Hedonic prices and cost/benefit analysis. *Journal of Economic Theory*, *37*, 55–75.

(1986). Local public goods in an equilibrium: How pecuniary externalities matter. *Regional Science and Urban Economics*, *16*, 463–81.

Seierstad, A. (1984a). Sufficient conditions in free final time optimal control problems: A comment. *Journal of Economic Theory*, *32*, 367–70.

(1984b). Sufficient conditions in free final time optimal control problems. Mimeograph, Department of Economics, University of Oslo.

Solow, R. M. (1973). On equilibrium models of urban locations. In J. M. Parkin, ed., *Essays in Modern Economics*, pp. 2–16. London: Longman.

Solow, R. M., and Vickrey, W. S. (1971). Land use in a long narrow city. *Journal of Economic Theory*, *3*, 430–47.

Stahl, K. (1983). A note on the microeconomics of migration. *Journal of Urban Economics*, *14*, 318–26.

Stiglitz, J. E. (1977). The theory of local public goods. In M. Feldstein and R. P. Inman, eds., *The Economics of Public Services*, 274–333. New York: Macmillan.

Strotz, R. H. (1965). Urban transportation parables. In J. Margolis, ed., *The Public Economy of the Urban Communities*, pp. 127–69. Baltimore, MD: Johns Hopkins University Press.

Stull W. J. (1974). Land use and zoning in an urban economy. *American Economic Review*, *64*, 337–47.

Sullivan, A. M. (1983a). The general equilibrium effects of congestion externalities. *Journal of Urban Economics*, *14*, 8–104.

(1983b). Second-best policies for congestion externalities. *Journal of Urban Economics*, *14*, 105–23.

(1986). A general equilibrium model with agglomerative economies and decentralized employment. *Journal of Urban Economics*, *20*, 55–74.

Takayama, A. (1972). *International Trade*. New York: Hold, Rinehart & Winston.

(1974). *Mathematical Economics*. Hinsdale, IL: Dryden Press.

Tauchen, H. (1981). The possibility of positive rent gradients reconsidered. *Journal of Urban Economics*, *9*, 165–72.

Tiebout, C. M. (1956). A pure theory of local expenditures. *Journal of Political Economy*, *64*, 416–24.

Upton, C. (1981). An equilibrium model of city size. *Journal of Urban Economics*, *10*, 15–36.

Van Long, N., and Vousden, N. (1977). Optimal control theorems. In J. D. Pitchford and S. J. Turnovsky, eds., *Application of Control Theory to Economic Analysis*, pp. 9–34. Amsterdam: North-Holland.

Varian, H. R. (1984). *Microeconomic Analysis*, 2nd ed. New York: Norton.

von Thünen, J. H. (1826). *Der Isolierte Staat in Beziehung auf Landwirtschaft und Nationalekonomie*. Hamburg.

Wheaton, W. C. (1974a). A comparative static analysis of urban spatial structure. *Journal of Economic Theory*, *9*, 223–37.

(1974b). Linear programming and locational equilibrium: The Herbert–Stevens model revisited. *Journal of Urban Economics*, *1*, 278–88.

(1976). On the optimal distribution of income among cities. *Journal of Urban Economics*, *3*, 31–44.

(1977). Income and urban residence: An analysis of consumer demand for location. *American Economic Review*, *67*, 620–31.

(1978). Price induced distortion in American highway investment. *Bell Journal of Economics*, *9*, 622–32.

(1979). Monocentric models of urban land use: Contributions and criticism. In P. Mieszkowski and M. Straszheim, eds., *Current Issues in Urban Economics*, pp. 105–29. Baltimore, MD: Johns Hopkins University Press.

White, M. J. (1976). Firm suburbanization and urban subcenters. *Journal of Urban Economics*, *3*, 323–43.

Wildasin, D. E. (1985). Income taxes and urban spatial structure. *Journal of Urban Economics*, *18*, 313–33.

(1986a). Spatial variation of the marginal utility of income and unequal treatment of equals. *Journal of Urban Economics*, *19*, 125–9.

(1986b). *Urban Public Finance*. Chur, Switzerland: Harwood.

Wilson, J. D. (1983). Optimal road capacity in the presence of unpriced congestion. *Journal of Urban Economics*, *13*, 337–57.

Wingo, L., Jr. (1961). *Transportation and Urban Land.* Washington, DC: Resources for the Future.

Witchard, L. (1984). A comparative static analysis of the optimum town. *Journal of Urban Economics, 15*, 259–69.

Yamada, H. (1972). On the theory of residential location: Accessibility, space, leisure and environmental quality. *Papers of the Regional Science Association, 29*, 125–35.

Yang, C. H. (1980). *Urban Spatial Structure with Local Public Goods: Optimum and Equilibrium.* Ph.D. dissertation, University of Pennsylvania, Philadelphia.

Yang, C. H., and Fujita M. (1983). Urban spatial structure with open space. *Environment and Planning A, 15*, 67–84.

Yellin, J. (1974). Urban population distribution, family income, and social prejudice. *Journal of Urban Economics, 1*, 21–47.

Yinger, J. (1976). Racial prejudice and racial residential segregation in an urban model. *Journal of Urban Economics, 3*, 383–96.

(1979). Prejudice and discrimination in the urban housing market. In P. Mieszkowski and M. Straszheim, eds., *Current Issues in Urban Economics*, 430–68. Baltimore, MD: Johns Hopkins University Press.

Zodrow, G. R. (1983). The Tiebout model after twenty-five years: An overview. In G. R. Zodrow, ed., *Local Provision of Public Services: The Tiebout Model After Twenty-five Years*, 1–16. New York: Academic Press.

Author index

Subject index